My World of
ASTROLOGY

by Sydney Omarr

Astrology probably has more followers, admirers, devotees, maligners and defenders —and has been more controversial—than any other subject in the world today. It is called a "pseudo-science" by scientists and scoffers—yet, according to Sydney Omarr, it is an older science than astronomy (is, indeed, the parent of astronomy), and was practiced by five of the greatest scientists in history: Nicolaus Copernicus, Galileo Galilei, Tycho Brahe, Johanne Kepler, and Sir Isaac Newton.

In *My World of Astrology*, Sydney Omarr leads you down his familiar paths so that you, too, may have a better understanding of how astrology influences the lives of Man. He actually gives you detailed instructions for casting and interpreting your own horoscope, and delightfully penetrating interpretations of every sign, the planets, the transits and cusps.

But, even more interesting and dramatic, Sydney Omarr gives you a history of how astrology has affected his own life. How, when he was a young lad a grade school teacher said the magic words that sent him seeking the great unknown in a quest that led him to indignation and defeat, pride and ultimate triumph. His love for astrology provoked him to defend it in history-making debates with leading scientists, and in this book he chronicles the most famous: a spur-of-the-moment intellectual sparring match with Dr. Roy K. Marshall, former director of Philadelphia's Fels Planetarium, when the telephone switchboard of a radio station was jammed with calls for three hours! His search for truth and knowledge led him to quiet talks and friendships with Henry Miller, the late Aldous Huxley, the great scientist Dr. Gustaf Stromberg, all "silent" exponents of astrology. He reveals, via correspondence and talks with Carl Gustav Jung's disciples, that the famous psychiatrist *used astrology to achieve a better understanding of his patients in order to create a better rapport for healing.*

And in *My World of Astrology* is the complete and warmly human story of Evangeline Adams, a young Boston girl of high lineage, who arrived in New York for the express purpose of "practicing astrology," something a young lady of good family simply did not do in the 1890's. Rejected by one hotel, accepted by another, she immediately proved her worthiness by casting the horoscope of the hotel manager, predicting a great tragedy for him in the immediate future. The next day a hotel fire took the lives of some of his close family. Even then, all was not easy for Miss Adams. Later, brought to trial on a charge of fortune-telling" she chose to be a test case and in a dramatic climax cast the horoscope of the judge's son, *which proved so accurate that all charges were dismissed.* It was this precedent-setting trial that established astrology a legal profession in the state of New York.

My World of Astrology, written from the heart by one of the best-known astrologers of our time, will convince even skeptics that astrology, practiced correctly, will prove an exciting and worthy addition to your own life. Your destiny and future may be within this one book—read it, study it, walk the interesting paths with Sydney Omarr and discover the truth in predictions by the stars.

MY WORLD
OF
ASTROLOGY

BY

SYDNEY OMARR

Melvin Powers
Wilshire Book Company

12015 Sherman Road, No. Hollywood, CA 91605

CONTENTS

ASTROLOGY

"Lexicographers call it a pseudoscience.

"I would like to argue with Webster's about the wording: '. . . the supposed influence of the relative position of the moon, sun and stars on human affairs.' It is the phrase 'human affairs' I argue with. 'Human beings' would be more correct.

"Agreed, one can debate the type of influences, but how one can deny the influence is beyond me. The arrogance which causes such denial is gigantic.

"The human being is not made of such different matter that it can remain untouched, uninfluenced by those same forces that exercise their power day and night on bodies far stronger than the human being. Nobody argues with the fact that the moon attracts the waters of the earth—the timing of the tides being related to the individual quarters of the moon. Nobody argues either with the farmer and the gardener who know when the moon is 'right' to sow or plant. Nobody argues with the effect the full moon has on certain human beings: sleep-walking. Nobody can argue with the fact—not widely known—that the police department increases the staff on nights of the full moon. (Human emotions fly high on those nights. Experience is the best teacher.) In short: What conceit to think that we human beings are immune to influences of which we have acknowledged the power. The fact that we cannot put our mental finger on the exact form these influences take cannot give us the audacity to deny them."

From MARLENE DIETRICH'S ABC
by Marlene Dietrich. Copyright
© 1961, 1962 by Marlene
Dietrich. Reprinted by
permission of Doubleday &
Company, Inc.

ACKNOWLEDGMENTS

There are many I want to thank, not only for their help and cooperation with this book, but also for their friendship and support in the past: the past starting from the days my articles first began appearing in *Horoscope* Magazine, *Current Astrology, American Astrology,* etc., to the time, in 1950 and 1951, when I published *Astrology News, The Trade Journal of Astrology,* to the times of the "great debates" with Dr. Roy K. Marshall and other astronomers and psychologists; and I want, very much, to thank the thousands of persons who, over the years, were kind enough to write and tell me they had been helped by my astrological analyses of their problems.

Specifically, I owe much, and thus this book owes much, to Edward A. Wagner, editor of Dell Publishing Company's *Horoscope* Magazine for his faith in my work, demonstrated by the publishing of my findings. I want to thank Carl Payne Tobey, not only for his faith in me, but for his great over-all contribution to astrology; I know that S. George Little, president of General Features Corporation, which syndicates my column, is already aware of my gratitude—not so much for publishing me—but for his frank, open-minded, creative view toward the subject which has become my profession by choice ("love" might be a better word!): astrology.

And a special word of gratitude belongs, also, to the American Federation of Astrologers and, in particular, to Paul R. Grell and Ernest A. Grant.

I want also to pay my respects to all persons who, in the past and in the future, have looked or will into this subject we call "astrology," and from which has sprung so much of our knowledge, indeed our very concept of time and civilization and learning.

Last, but certainly not least, a word of sincere gratitude to Camille Bourgeois for her help, encouragement and faith in me and in astrology.

—SYDNEY OMARR

PROLOGUE

Astrology, among other things, is concerned with *time*. Not only universal time, measured by the earth's movement around the Sun, but personal time. Your time, my time: a time to sow, a time to reap. Astrology starts at our beginnings, historically and personally. Astrology encompasses all of time: the past, present and the future.

Man can measure the movements of the planets, their past positions and future patterns. Out of this ability, created by man's insatiable desire to know, to be aware, grew astronomy and much of our other knowledge. Astronomy, the child, repeatedly has attempted to take over as the "parent," decrying the fact that it sprang from astrology, grew and prospered as a side effect, a concentration on sizes, distances, physical facts concerning the Solar system. Astronomy basked in the comfortable aura of acceptance. The astronomer was the astrologer's apprentice, reporting to him on where the planets were, where they had been and were going to be; and leaving it to the "parent" to evaluate, to make judgments, to correlate heavenly patterns and world and individual activities.

Astrology continues to use astronomy, but the "child," now grown, rejects the parent, asks him to get in a closet and stay there and please not to rattle. But astrology, perhaps like the mythical phoenix, refuses to die a quiet death. Instead, it revitalizes, as if drawing energy from some mysterious source. It thrives under attack, grows, enlarges its scope, embraces to it giant intellects of the ages.

Again astrology is experiencing a renaissance. Modern science, instead of moving away, comes closer. Men of letters, as often they do, stand in the vanguard, feeding upon the very symbols of the ancient scientific art, nourishing their own creative spirits on the remarkable fountainhead represented by astrology. From the most erudite to the proverbial man-in-the-street, attraction to astrology continues, warms. The heat which emanates distresses some, who are influenced mainly by hacks trying to light up the camp of the offspring. Despite the child's shouts of disapproval, astrology, in a trait common to many parents, goes about its business, never turning away the child, even proud of the youngster, continuing to hope faithfully for a reconciliation so the larger "family" might benefit.

But although astrology itself may be patient, enduring, endowed with powers of angelic forbearance, astrologers themselves, being human, have felt the need to take up cudgels, accept the challenge, go forth with weapons of defense so that, after all, the child does not succeed in forcing the parent into that closet. Already the child has succeeded in altering historical facts, rewriting biographies, dictionaries, encyclopedias. The child, though he hasn't been able to turn the lock on that closet door, has come close and certainly has made a display of taking over and running the house. Throughout, despite good intentions, astrologers have, with rare exceptions, offered only token resistance, come forth with ineffectual retaliation or have stood staunch under a shower of ridicule with remarkable determination.

But surely, now that we have entered the Space-Nuclear Age, the spectacle of watching lazily as the whirl of academic prejudice bites, chops, churns and defaces, must come to an end, because the show may affect not only those of us concerned specifically with astrology, but all of us, for academic prejudice is a blood relation to other kinds. It can no longer be afforded, let alone tolerated. Once again, the facts of the matter must take the stage; ignorance must be made to blink and shudder in the light of truth, rather than being permitted to obliterate that light. The time is past due.

That's why, with faith and hope, maybe outrageous presumption, I present this work. If, during its course, I appear bitter or arrogant, humble or bombastic—if, during this offering you marvel or shout defiance—if you observe a kaleidoscope of moods, emotions, a chameleon-like change from the personal to the purely objective—it is because the sum of my experience with astrology—the practice of it and the explanation of it and the defense of it—has made me all of these things.

I regard my role in astrology as a trust. I don't necessarily ask the same of others. I do not pass judgment on those who continue to *take* from astrology, with never a thought of giving in return. To each his own. I do not claim to have had any special kind of call from astrology. But, nevertheless, I went. I am here. I am what I am. I must, as much as I can, be true to myself.

Astrology, as I say, deals with time. So let us start at the beginning.

MY WORLD
OF
ASTROLOGY

I

KISS OR KILL

In beginning, I start with the Moon in the zodiacal sign of Leo the Lion. That's astrological talk. Or, as *Time* Magazine, which referred to me as a "highbrow astrologer," might say, "astrological lingo." I start with the Moon in Leo because I am a Leo—born August 5, 1926, in Philadelphia, with Libra on the Ascendant of my horoscope; with the Sun, Mercury and Neptune in Leo. My colleague, Carl Payne Tobey, of Tucson, Arizona, who is a brilliant mathematician and astrological researcher, has found that an individual's cycle is at a peak, each month, when the Moon transits his own sign. Conversely, the cycle is down and judgment and intuition are apt to be "off," when the Moon is in one's opposite sign. In my case, that would be Aquarius, opposite Leo.

But right now, today, the Moon is in Leo and my cycle is up and so I am beginning. This is not mystical—merely an observance of what I believe to be a tested cycle, something which "works." More and more, I feel, this kind of "lingo" will become familiar, for astrology is a universal language, just as music is, just as mathematics is—and now is the time to put some vital factors about astrology on the record, and in so doing, to make some facts known about myself. For, rightly or otherwise, I have come to be a spokesman for this unique, controversial, exciting, at times heartbreaking, but enduring subject. To paraphrase William Faulkner's comments on man, astrology *endures*. Man's history is the history of astrology. The history of astrology is the history of man. The very beginnings of astrology are rooted in those ancient times when man looked to the heavens, began to record his doings, and at the same time correlated his activities with planetary patterns.

Astrology! I respond to the word. For me, it lives and breathes. And I know it must sometimes writhe in embarrassment at the things said in its name. Like Gertrude Stein, I do have faith in words. Like the prophets of the Old Testament, I revere the word in the broadest sense. Astrology is that kind of word. It has become part of my life. The first time I heard it I was in grammar school in Philadelphia. I no longer remember the name of the teacher who mentioned the word. She was thin, pleasant enough, teaching science to youngsters—and her subject that day, so many years ago, was astronomy.

My mind was wandering. It usually did. With the Moon, Venus and Pluto in Cancer, in the Ninth House of my horoscope, it was not always easy for me to remain down-to-earth. Ninth House emphasis tends to make one live in the future; it makes for writers, publishers, poets—those who want to communicate, travel, express themselves. In the best sense, the Ninth House provides vision. But the visions often are future ones and the negative reaction is daydreaming. Sometimes those daydreams turn to realities.

I suppose I was gazing out of that school window while Miss Whatever-Her-Name-Was continued to talk and explain. I remember she made notes on the blackboard. Her writing was almost like printing. Years later, I was to learn from a book on graphology that people who "write like printing" are interested in scientific subjects, often write about them or teach science classes. So, whatever her name, she must have been suited for her profession, and probably had some Ninth House planets herself, with Virgo emphasis. She paid much attention to details and probably had some planets in the Third sector of her chart, too. I couldn't know at the time. She didn't think much of astrology. She said so. It was in the course of her discussion on astronomy, that I heard—I think for the first time—the word, *astrology*.

Miss Writes-Like-Printing rushed over the word. Dismissed it. But I couldn't dismiss it from my mind. Merely a *pseudo science,* she insisted. She did so without rancor, without knowledge, for she was a kindly woman. The classrooms were crowded. And there were many, like myself, who would rather have been out in the yard, sparring or tossing a baseball around—many with planets in the Ninth, restless, feeling the need for expression, recognition. Miss Science Teacher had said the word and had gone on, discussing planets, the Sun and Moon, their distances from earth; their sizes and orbits. All part of the story of astronomy.

She probably had forgotten she even mentioned that sidelight, that "foolish sister" of astronomy—astrology. She had called it that—foolish. But my curiosity had been aroused. With Uranus in the Fifth House of my horoscope, my need for expression was to find unusual, perhaps foolish outlets. I became interested in magic, the occult—I performed in night clubs, on stages. I looked into the mystical arts—palmistry, numerology, psychic phenomena. I visited fortune-tellers and I did mental mind reading tricks.

But astrology was something else again. The word swam in my head. And the dedicated teacher was really innocent; she had no idea what she was starting when she said the word and quickly dismissed the subject.

But I think I could perceive, even then, that astrology was to become a very familiar word. It was to change the direction of my life, to embark me on many trails—some happy and marked by reward, while others were full of ridicule, frustration, a desperate quest for knowledge, for more and more of it, until I was convinced the answer was up there, in the sky, in the heavenly patterns made by the planets as they journeyed around the Sun.

Miss Writes-Like-Printing could have no idea that, sitting in front of her, was a youngster who would become so wedded to a word she had hardly uttered that for years to come he would call upon much of his energy to prove she was mistaken. The youngster, staring toward the window, was to fight the idea she had presented—that astrology was long gone as far as serious thinking was concerned, and probably best forgotten. That youngster who loved to box, to pitch baseball and experiment with magic tricks, was to debate others who made similar statements—was to write and fight for ideas which had engrossed some of the greatest minds of all times, but which were—in his time—to be subject to attacks which could only be described as bordering on the paranoiac.

The more I heard astrology ridiculed, the more my curiosity was fed. With a passion, I probed, investigated, wanted to know upon what basis astrology was being dismissed so cavalierly. And the more I asked, the more I realized that those doing the dismissing really did not know what they were dismissing. It was good training for the journalism, the reporting, the writing which was to follow. I began early to develop an edge of skepticism, but the skepticism was directed toward the orthodox, toward authority. For, I began to reason, if authority could dismiss a subject without real knowledge, then what was to prevent the same authority from conveniently tossing aside other subjects which failed to fit in with a convenient, preconceived pattern?

It was a question born of experience, which I was to continue to ask—and it was to evolve into a part of my own pattern, my own personality and being.

Of course I don't think it was merely the mention of a word which led and continued to lead across such strange, exotic paths. I have five planets in Water signs, so knowing something "deep inside" or possessing instinctive or intuitive knowledge is not foreign to me. I know it was not just the mention of the word—but that word did trigger something; it did kindle a spark. Perhaps it was an accident of fate. And that, too, is a word: fate. A word which astrologers encounter many times. Do you believe in fate? That's usually the way the question is phrased. But the querent actually is asking, "Why don't you believe in free will?"

The answer is that modern astrologers do accept the concept of free will, but with modifications. The word *believe* is itself irritating, at least to me, when the subject of astrology is up for discussion. Do you believe? Do you really believe in it? That one, with the *really,* is reserved usually for cocktail parties. Under the influence of a few very dry, cold martinis, some persons, employing their best conspiratorial tone, take delight in asking—rather imploring, "But do you really *believe* in astrology?"

Like fate, the belief part of the question can take one spiraling along the path of semantics. Certainly I believe in free will. But I also know there are some things we do not control. We don't choose the families we are born into; we don't choose our sex. And there are other circumstances which appear, as far as individual choice or action is concerned, to be accidents, or fatalistic, not dependent upon our freedom of choice. Thus, I believe in free will after we view the equipment with which we are to work, to live.

The "equipment," from an astrologer's point of view, is the time and place of birth: the horoscope. That's our starting point. Astrology enables us to choose the right time to begin or end projects, to choose harmonious associations, places, occupations, marriages, and right on down the line of actual choices. It takes a disciplined, wise individual to follow his chart always. Astrology *is* a discipline; it is a scientific art. I don't always follow my own chart. Being an impulsive Leo, with the Sun up there in the Tenth House, in the top part of my horoscope, I sometimes want to "bend" events to my own use. I don't always know what's good for me—or when I'm well off, as some people put it. Astrology is there, to be used for the good—or the evil (Hitler!). It's easier to tell the native (the person whose horoscope is under consideration) what's good for *him,* easier to expect others to live up to the best in their own charts, easier to ignore the dictum: Physician, heal thyself.

That's the kind of free will versus fate I believe in. I believe there are certain tendencies in the horoscope. And if one chooses to work against those indications, there is bound to be trouble. That's the kind of fate in which I believe. One may as well go with the tide instead of against it—the tide in this case being the individual flow of the life path—as shown so clearly in the nativity (horoscope). To ignore the horoscope, to ignore astrology, is to ignore one of the elements of man's existence: the element of time. We observe the solar system for our time: our calendars and clocks are based on the Earth's movement around the Sun. And we each, to an extent, have our individual times: these are determined by the current movements of the planets (transits) and the angles and positions they form *in relation to the planets as they were at our birth times.*

As for *really* believing, I think the late Grant Lewi was right. He gave up his English Literature post at Dartmouth College to practice astrology as a professional. He became the editor of *Horoscope,* which has the largest circulation of any astrology magazine in the world. Grant Lewi said, "Astrology is 'believed in' by a lot of people who know practically nothing about it; and it is 'disbelieved in' by even more who know *absolutely* nothing about it."

As for me, I "believe" in astrology because it works. Just as I believe that two and two equal four. This proposition may seem very basic, but once one accepts this relatively simple proposition, one is likely to set himself off in a world apart. It could be a world of adventure: plenty of bumps, a road lit with mediocrity, glory and genius. Astrology covers the spectrum. But as a young man, I started down that road not even perceiving what lay ahead.

The paths along which astrology led me include close contacts with as diversified a group as one might imagine, including Henry Miller, Aldous Huxley and other writers, psychologists, psychiatrists, astronomers, astrologers, mystics, psychics, mediums; a wide variety, from Jayne Mansfield to Marjorie Main (Ma Kettle of motion-picture fame), to newsmen and writers such as that sensitive, powerful creator, Kenneth Patchen, to detective story-writer Craig Rice, to debates not only with psychologists and astronomers, but with the colorful, controversial Mexican artist, Diego Rivera. Included, too, are the brilliantly sensitive authoress, Anais Nin, and that chronicler of the "little magazines," a fine writer himself, James Boyer May.

The paths have led to writing and publishing, radio and television, a newspaper column published around the world. The sharp-tongued comedian, Henry Morgan, tried to utilize his wit to demolish astrology, but in front of his television audience, ended up banging his fist on the table before me, asking if I didn't know he was the "best-informed man in the industry." One of the major paths was problem consultation. Letters poured in, from housewives and laborers, from sophisticated men-about-town and the wives of the great and near-great, from sports figures and scientists, from actors and producers, directors, writers.

Madam Bricktop, that internationally known entertainer-hostess, was one of my friends and clients; and in Mexico City she brought additional ones, until (for a time) the more affluent vacationers, visitors and residents were bidding for "readings." All very heady stuff for a young man. The path was filled with pitfalls, some of which were pleasant enough, others a little too deep for the young man from Philadelphia—and, not following his own planets as he should, he made his mistakes. But the path soon turned the young man into a young-older man, if not always a wise one.

After awhile, I didn't know whether I wanted to kiss or kill Miss Whatever-Her-Name-Was.

II

THERE WAS A WOMAN INVOLVED

I said astrology "works" and I know people have been arguing that point for hundreds of years. Popular opinion has it that those who believe are the superstitious, are in the lower economic brackets and are groping for a panacea. Actually, very nearly the opposite is true.

As a newsman, I have taken some trouble to cover, over the years, what I call the borderline sciences. These include not only astrology, but psychic phenomena, extrasensory perception and the whole range of the so-called supernormal experiences of man. In fashionable scientific circles, this supernormal activity is termed parapsychology. It was a favorite word of the late Aldous Huxley. It covers the wide range of activity which does not fit into any known category. It is thus beyond psychology, beyond any known scientific explanation.

Astrology, let me make it clear, does not belong to this group. But, in a manner of speaking, it is a first cousin to the borderline subjects: those which, over the ages, have intrigued man, piqued his curiosity, made him wonder and argue. Just as astronomy is considered on the right side of the tracks in relation to astrology, it could be said that psychology and psychiatry are on the respectable side where the borderline subjects enter the picture.

Hypnotism used to be "borderline." Now it is embraced, somewhat blushingly, by the "ins." Medical men, many who formerly scorned hypnotism, would now like to claim it as their own; they want only "properly qualified" persons to practice hypnosis. The "qualified" are the medical men themselves, the same men who, for years, relegated hypnotism to the scientific doghouse.

I foresee the day, without too much of a strain on my prophetic powers, when the same will be true of the majority of borderline studies.

I have already had indications of this, not only where astrology is concerned, but in connection with other "far out" subjects. Dr. Margaret Mead, recognized as one of the world's outstanding anthropologists, stated flatly to me that, in her opinion, science should not waste another day in investigating thoroughly the phenomenon known as dowsing: man's apparent ability to locate water with the aid of a dowsing rod or forked stick. Geologists, for the most part, say it's impossible. But the record shows it is not only possible, but in some cases very practical because it "works." The late historical novelist, Kenneth Roberts, devoted two books to one New England dowser, Henry Gross. Dr. Mead feels that many persons exhibit an extraordinary ability to "find things out," things they have no "normal" way of knowing. These are psychics, or sensitives, or persons who possess extrasensory perception.

Most of us are familiar with the work of Dr. Joseph B. Rhine in this connection: his laboratory at Duke University has become internationally known, although it has not been exactly easy for Rhine to carry on his investigations because the orthodox element, both at the university and in academic circles elsewhere, has been quick to cast aspersions, if not literal stones. Jess Stearn, a former associate editor of *Newsweek,* points up numerous cases which have astounded the orthodox, doing so in his book, *The Door to the Future.* These reports no longer are unusual. Something is there and the way to find out *what* certainly is not to be found in ridicule, outright dismissal or through the technique of ignoring and hoping "it" will go away.

I raise these points because I believe that part of being an astrologer is an enthusiastic willingness to recognize that science is not only *not* a sacred cow, but should, every once in a while, be prodded with a well-aimed kick.

The first time I did any real kicking has become an historic occasion. It certainly wasn't planned. I wasn't prepared in the sense that a fighter trains for a boxing match, or in the manner in which one readies himself for a formal debate. But it happened and when it did, the "kick" was a resounding one.

It was part of the adventure that astrology has been for me and firmly convinced me that "official" science, like astrology itself, often has spokesmen who are ill-qualified, pompous and filled with overheated air.

It was not an occasion I could celebrate when it did occur, because the "results" were not immediately known. And the night I landed the "kick" was one which found me lonely and disillusioned; I had the feeling of being browbeaten, even slightly martyred. But as it turned out, it was worth it. For as events were to prove, the ordeal I went through in the process of battling orthodox science was, in turn, to affect the opinions of literally thousands of persons, and was to enable me to help disclose one of the major scientific developments of our time.

It is part of the story of astrology in the world today. And as it turned out, part of my story, too.

I have Jupiter in the Fifth House of my horoscope, so on this occasion there was a woman involved. Jupiter in that section of the chart paints a clear picture of much experience in connection with members of the opposite sex—dealings with women, attention from women—ability, in my case, to communicate with women, since Jupiter is the ruler of my Third House, which has Sagittarius on the cusp. You will learn to understand this kind of technical talk these references to signs, houses, planets. The Fifth House is sex, romance, chance, change, creative activity, children, theater, amusement. I think it is the starting point of any delineation. I believe psychologists, just as did the late Dr. Carl Jung, would find the study of a patient's horoscope generally of great aid, and a close look at the Fifth House of specific help in assessing the motives, drives and makeup of the patient.

Leo is the natural fifth sign of the zodiac, counting from and including Aries, which is the first zodiacal sign. I have the Sun, Mercury and Neptune in the fifth sign; my Fifth House is occupied by Jupiter. I also have Moon-Venus-Pluto positions in Cancer, a sign generally related to women.

I would estimate, roughly, that nearly eighty per cent of the thousands of persons who have written to me about astrology have been women.

The fact that a "woman was involved," therefore, would hardly be surprising to one knowledgeable about astrology.

This woman was a Gemini. I have written about Gemini women: "If you are not careful, she is liable to grow on you—you acquire a taste for her, just as some people do for lima beans or buttermilk or spinach or grits and eggs . . . she can be charming, seductive and on occasion, even reasonable."

This woman was that kind of Gemini. Gemini and Scorpio are probably the two most misunderstood signs of the zodiac. Many astrologers don't know what to make of them. The ordinary text-books carry trite descriptions. Scorpio, they say, has domain over the "secrets." By "secrets," they mean the sex organs, the "hidden" parts of the body. Scorpio can be violent, passionate, demanding and practical enough to want to know whether there is money set aside for the proverbial rainy day. This combination of emotion and practicality makes Scorpio a puzzling sign. If there is prejudice against any one zodiacal sign, in the sense that there exists religious prejudice, Scorpio is that maligned sign.

Gemini is next, mainly because of the women born when the Sun was in Gemini. As for the men, they are shrewd, but love to take a chance. When they go "wrong," they commit *mental* crimes—counterfeiting and the like—not crimes of violence. I've never seen any statistics, but each time I lecture on the twelve signs of the zodiac I ask all the Gemini people in the audience to raise their hands. Very few do. I then point out it's been said there are more Geminis in jail than any other sign. Some people naturally assume that's where the other Gemini persons must be—since apparently there are so few present. It always gets a laugh, one of the few times the laugh is *on* Gemini.

People *whisper* about Scorpio. They *tell anecdotes* about their experiences with Gemini.

When I was a youngster my family followed the pleasant custom of spending the summer at a New Jersey seashore resort. The cottage at which we usually stayed was owned by Miss Gemini's parents. I used to look on from afar (Ninth House emphasis) and dream.

But when enough summer seasons went by, there was a war and when I was seventeen I enlisted, went on active duty when I was eighteen, and was assigned to the Air Force. In the service, toward the end of nearly three years, I became the only American soldier ever assigned fulltime duty as an astrologer for Armed Forces Radio Service on Okinawa, conducting an astrology program, answering the questions of officers, enlisted men and civilian personnel within the wide listening range of the Okinawa-based station.

The British used astrology in more of an official manner: Captain Louis De Wohl, a fine novelist and astrologer, was assigned by British Intelligence to tell the British what Hitler's astrologers were telling him. It worked. De Wohl, after the war, was decorated for his services in this field. I have heard that our State Department, knowing full well that Hitler followed astrological advice (when it suited him), thought of finding their own Louis De Wohl. But there was enough pressure from *astronomers* (officialdom, official science) so that the project was dropped. World War II marked the first time since the Thirty Years War that astrology was so conspicious by its presence.

When I got out of the Army Air Force, a sergeant whose last official duty was *astrology,* I was nearly twenty-one, and I looked up that tantalizing Gemini girl of the seaside summer resort. She was a teacher (Gemini is the natural Third House, "ruled" by Mercury—sign and planet of teaching, communication). And she was with me the night and during the early morning hours when the "great debate" took place.

III

PUT 'EM UP, "JOE LOUIS"

The Gemini took notes. Those notes, along with a tape recording, enabled me to do a five-part series for *Horoscope* Magazine.

There must have been some inner core of "hard wisdom" on that night, June 29, 1951, when the Gemini accompanied me up the steps of the studios of radio station WPEN in Philadelphia.

I had been a civilian for about four years. I had attained a degree of fame through articles, "readings," and events in Mexico City (including studies at Mexico City College), through lectures, successful predictions and headline-making debates with that wonderfully talented Mexican artist, Diego Rivera. But where astrology was concerned, there was one man I did not want to tangle with—*Dr. Roy K. Marshall*. He was the director of the Fels Planetarium in Philadelphia, and the science editor of the largest evening newspaper in the country, the *Philadelphia Evening Bulletin*. Through his nationwide television commercials and appearances in connection with scientific subjects, he was regarded as astronomy's public spokesman. His special love, it seemed, was attacking astrology. He lectured against it. He debated with astrologers on radio and wrote vitriolic articles pertaining to the subject. I had never seen the man, but the image was there and it was fearsome. He was one of those confident, urbane, "authorities." He gave the impression of knowledge. I had heard about him and had read about him and I had, of course, read his own statements about science and about astrology. To me, he was the equal of Joe Louis as far as his particular brand of fighting was concerned. Dr. Roy K. Marshall enjoyed enormous popularity: he was successful commercially and respected professionally.

He had only recently made a "big hit" by giving a verbal spanking to a famous New York astrologer. He did this on radio and television. I had read reports of the debate, though they were not detailed. I had been invited to appear as a guest that night, June 29, 1951, over WPEN. I was not told that a debate was to take place. I was prepared simply to answer some questions on the subject of astrology and to do all I could to clear the air for a better understanding of the subject. The announcer, or moderator, however, had communicated, in the meantime, with the man whose enmity against astrology was widely known. The plan was simple. It was to have the astronomer squash the astrologer and the claims of astrology once and for all. It was thought the "squashing" process would require 10, perhaps 15 minutes.

As I entered the studio with my Gemini in tow, the program called "Open Forum" was in progress. On this program, the moderator received telephone calls from listeners while he was on the air. His manner was informal. The program was tremendously popular. As I entered the studio, the moderator spoke to me as part of the broadcast—and to the radio audience at the same time. His name was Frank Ford and he was a veteran in the radio business. He was big, broad-shouldered and looked like a Taurus; his voice carried a ring of authority. He said, "Here comes our guest, right on time, and we have a little surprise for him."

The surprise was the man who was, in my eyes, equal to Joe Louis (a Taurus, incidentally). The surprise was Dr. Roy K. Marshall. There he sat, next to Frank Ford. Try as I do, I cannot remember exactly how this famed astronomer, educator and writer looked. All I can think of is being suddenly told to put on the gloves and go in and spar with Joe Louis. Dr. Marshall didn't smile. He seemed to look through me. But I looked steadily at him, and then sat down next to him. Gemini sat toward the side of the studio, notebook in hand.

Moderator Frank Ford sat next to Dr. Marshall, chattering to his radio audience, explaining the situation. The "astrology killer," Dr. Marshall, was here—and beside him sat a young upstart by the name of Sydney Omarr, who had written articles, been consulted by persons around the world and had also earned himself somewhat of a reputation as editor and publisher of *Astrology News, The Trade Journal of Astrology.*

"Listen closely," said Frank Ford, "for you might hear a figurative bomb explode."

The engineer stared through his glass enclosure. He had his tape machine going. This was going to be too good to miss. I looked through the window at him. He didn't smile; he smirked. Dr. Marshall was clearing his throat. Frank Ford was finishing the introductions. . . . "Dr. Marshall this" and "Dr. Marshall that," and also, incidentally, Sydney Omarr was along. A shame, in this modern day and age, to have to deal with that ancient, "exploded" superstition of astrology. Anyway, here it was, to be exploded again. One could count on the good doctor to do the job.

To tell the truth, even though Dr. Marshall was "Joe Louis," I was in pretty good shape, too. And I sincerely believed there was one difference that was going to tell the story. I believed then, as I do today, that astronomers who attack astrology usually do not know what they're attacking. They don't know what they're talking about. I knew, if I kept on the subject with which I was familiar, "Joe Louis" would have himself a hell of a time that night.

But despite the talk to myself about being ready to hold my own, my mouth was dry and I was scared. I had suspected all was not as it was presented when invited on the program. But I had not expected Dr. Marshall. I had a few notes, not many. I knew Dr. Marshall was not going to pull his punches. I could tell from the way he looked—a polite nod in my direction, but no look that would recognize me as a guy on a spot. The look I received was cool, calculating.

IV

I WANTED TO KISS HER ON JULY 11, 1951

Astrologers are human and those who get into this field have a right to know what they're getting into—they will have a better chance of so doing as a result of this book. That's why I include the history, the personal references.

We want to provide a taste of what it's like to be an astrologer. In the future, those who want to have this knowledge can look into this particular book and find some of the answers. Evangeline Adams did it in *The Bowl of Heaven.* Cheiro (Count Louis Hamon) succeeded in *Fate In The Making.* To an extent, Grant Lewi did it in *Astrology For The Millions.* So did Louis De Wohl in *I Follow My Stars.*

During the very month I write these words, one of the biggest, mass-circulation news magazines, *Time,* has quoted me on the subject. In characteristic fashion, it is a misquote. Two days from now, I will address a mass audience over a major television network on the subject of astrology. Thus, for the good or otherwise, astrology and I are "related." As in the case of many close relatives, we sometimes ponder, I suppose, why providence hasn't arranged it so we can choose our relatives as we purportedly are able to choose our friends. But when an outsider attempts to step in and malign either one of us—me or astrology—then he is probably going to draw the wrath of *both:* astrology and me.

Dr. Marshall found this out. And what transpired resulted in a historic written statement from a Pulitzer Prize–winner and ultimately enabled me to report, for an astrological journal, that the largest communications organization in the world was utilizing the ancient scientific art of astrology to forecast radio weather (magnetic storms).

So it began, with moderator Frank Ford's: "Here comes our guest . . . right on time . . . and we have a little surprise for him."

The "surprise," as we know, was Dr. Marshall. After the introduction, I surprised myself by starting to talk, calmly and with assurance. I caught a glimpse of Gemini. She was smiling, listening, taking notes. The engineer furrowed his brow attentively. I spoke into the microphone, saying I would attempt to clear up some misconceptions about astrology and astrologers and that I would be glad to answer questions on the subject. Frank Ford was pleased. He apparently thought my assurance would add spice to the final kayo, the knockout, when Dr. Marshall was turned loose.

What followed caused listeners to swamp the studio's telephone wires with calls, to send a pile of telegrams and to write letters both pro and con for days afterward.

From approximately 11:30 P.M. until 2:30 A.M., Dr. Marshall and Frank Ford resorted to every means at their command to ridicule astrology, to try to prove it was a bunch of "mumbo jumbo." Fortunately, that skeptical engineer had his tape recorder going and Gemini was taking her notes. It was "on the record."

By the following week, it became evident that the public would not permit issues raised by the debate to die a quiet death. Telephone calls continued to pour in; mail was read. Violent opinions were aired—on both sides—for and against astrology.

A dominant note, however, in the majority of calls, letters and telegrams, was one of protest against the rude manner of Dr. Marshall, of protest against the unfair way in which the debate was handled. The moderator was not a moderator: he frankly stated that he shared the views of Dr. Marshall. He didn't hesitate to pitch in and assist him.

The debate raged. If Dr. Marshall was Joe Louis—then I must have become a Rocky Marciano that night. There were no punches pulled. I was calm; I gained strength when the realization hit home that Dr. Marshall was talking about a subject with which he had little or no familiarity. He was woefully ignorant of what astrology is or claims to be or has been and can be. But, like most astronomers who attack the subject, he posed as an authority. Perhaps, like many astronomers, he really believed he knew something about astrology.

By now the sparks were flying. It was a hot, fascinating debate, so much so that the Motorola Company of Philadelphia, sponsors of the program, called in the midst of the proceedings to ask that commercial announcements be deleted. The station, for its part, halted all newscasts. The "discussion" was to continue uninterrupted. It did and for three hours thousands of persons in the then third-largest city in the United States listened. Dr. Marshall wasn't looking *through* me any longer. He was looking at me; his eyes flashed with anger and disbelief. Frank Ford made us move our chairs so that he was sitting between us.

The engineer's smile was now one of gratitude. He was a man with a job to do and, on many nights, it was probably a tiring one. He was grateful to me because the time was passing so quickly. And he was grateful, I suppose, in the way one is grateful when he has attended an event in which the "favorite" is expected to put a quick end to the "underdog." He was witnessing a reversal of form. Gemini, for all of her note-taking, was being Gemini, smiling at me *and* at Dr. Marshall. Every so often he would look toward her after lashing out at me, and he would receive a nod. He interpreted it as a nod of approval, thinking, perhaps, that Gemini was a studio secretary. I interpreted the nod as one of saying, "Yes, I got what you said—I'm putting it down and everything you say can be used against you."

Out of the maze of charges, countercharges, questions, answers, assertions, denials, yelling, table-pounding, confusion and clarity, emerged a few major points. Here was one of the most important ones—for it was to pave the way for greater advancement and understanding of astrology in our time:

DR. MARSHALL: Let's denounce all astrology and start from scratch.
OMARR: No, certainly not. There is a lot of good work that has been

done in astrology, as John J. O'Neill, science editor of the *New York Herald Tribune,* has stated.

DR. MARSHALL: I don't think a man of O'Neill's standing ever said anything like that. I happen to know him very well, so be careful. He is a member of my lodge and a fellow member of an association of scientific writers. O'Neill never said astrology or astrologers ever did good for anything.

OMARR: The fact is that he did. O'Neill has spoken before astrological groups. He has stated, before one of those organizations, that while not all astrology is scientific and worthwhile, there is a certain amount of good work being done, and it is this which makes him want to do something to help astrologers.

DR. MARSHALL: If he said anything that might have sounded like that, you are probably quoting him out of context.

OMARR: I am not quoting him out of context.

DR. MARSHALL: He probably said what so many other people say about astrology. It's that people who lack guidance and consolation can be approached by way of astrology. Scientists will admit that astrology has done some good in this perverted manner.

OMARR: Mr. O'Neill did not make that kind of reference. We won't go any further. I happen to have the facts.

DR. MARSHALL: If John O'Neill said what you attributed to him, he should be unseated from the important position he holds as a science editor for a responsible newspaper. He is a dangerous man if he believes that. People who believe there is anything constructive in astrology are as dangerous as those guys who peddle dope.

OMARR: Now you're going far afield. I said Mr. O'Neill made a certain statement about astrology. He most certainly did make that statement.

DR. MARSHALL: I would like to see the complete text.

OMARR: I don't have it with me, but O'Neill is in New York and can easily be contacted. He will, I'm sure, verify what I have said.

FRANK FORD: Let me resolve this current argument. If you, Dr. Marshall, will write to your colleague, Mr. O'Neill, and ask him for the exact quotation, and if you will send it to me, I will read it. I will let you know what night it is on so that we may read the whole thing—and not out of context. I'll tell you, Mr. Omarr, so that we don't load the question to Mr. O'Neill, if you will write to him on your stationery, and if you will send me your answer, I will read them the same night. I don't want to be unfair; so I'll read both of them the same night and see whether there is any difference.

I said this was a major point in the debate. There were others. But this was the "big one," perhaps the vital one. I want to get back to the debate as a whole and go into some other details covering other areas. But for the sake of thoroughness here, let me quote the letter I *did,* the next afternoon, dispatch to John J. O'Neill, the science editor of the *New York Herald Tribune,* who had been honored with the Clement Cleveland Medal and the Pulitzer Prize:

Dear Mr. O'Neill:

During a radio debate with Dr. Roy K. Marshall, over station WPEN, in Philadelphia, from 11:30 P.M., June 29, to 2:30 A.M., June 30, I made a statement about you and astrology which Dr. Marshall hotly disputed.

It was agreed that Dr. Marshall would write you a letter and that I would also write you one—and that your answers would be read over station WPEN by Frank Ford, who conducted the debate.

Quoting from your talk before the Astrologer's Guild of America, Inc., in New York, in September or October of 1942, I said: "John J. O'Neill stated: 'While I do not believe all astrology is scientific and worthwhile, there is a certain amount of good work done; and it is that which makes me try to do something to help the astrologers.' "

Dr. Marshall insisted that he knew you well and that you never made any such statement, or any statement to the effect that astrology or astrologers ever did anything that was good.

I am taking the opportunity, in this letter, of quoting further from your talk before the Guild:

"Well, I must confess, I feel stark naked before you. What you say about difficulties due to overwork is correct. When I called on Mrs. Fleischer to discuss this evening's program, she told me very definitely about this problem of mine and where I could expect a solution. She was quite right about the problem; and quite unexpectedly, I found a solution in my *house of partnerships,* just as Mrs. Fleischer predicted.

"The last time I came to the Guild, I told you how Miss Laura Wilson had written me to the effect that I would receive some honor in connection with my work a few months hence, and another about fifteen months later. I had received the first honor, the Pulitzer Prize, just at the time she predicted—and another, a medal, at a later date."

I didn't, Mr. O'Neill, use the above quote on the program, for my point was simply that you believed some good work had been done by astrologers—and Dr. Marshall called me on it—and that's why I'm writing. I would appreciate an answer on this as soon as possible so Frank Ford can inform his listeners on this matter.

I also want to take this opportunity to invite you to hear a tape recording of the debate between Dr. Marshall and me. Frank Ford informed me that station WPEN would be glad to run off the tape, since the program made radio history and since the Motorola people were generous enough to dispense with commercials so that the listening audience could hear the facts on both sides. Please let me know when you can be in Philadelphia for the tape run-off.

Sincerely,

SYDNEY OMARR

It turned out that Dr. Marshall did not keep his end of the bargain. He did not write to O'Neill. It also turned out that station WPEN did not keep its word. The answer from O'Neill was never read, which was a betrayal of its listeners.

But O'Neill's letter since has been translated into numerous languages; I have given permission to many, including the American Federation of Astrologers, for its publication. And it undoubtedly will be used as a guide by scientists desiring to investigate astrology. I received the answer on July 11.

Dr. Marshall had been definite—he had spoken about O'Neill with a tone of authority—and his manner was calculated to assure listeners that this "astrologer fellow" was nothing but a damned liar talking about his colleague, his lodge brother, his fellow member of an association for scientific writers, in such a manner as to imply he would have anything good to say about astrology. To tell the truth, for a while during those three tension-packed hours, he almost had me convinced I was a good-for-nothing who wasn't even good at making up stories about his fine friend and lodge member.

Dr. Marshall had taken to pounding the table, almost knocking the microphone from the table. The engineer shook his head, not in disbelief, but gleefully. Frank Ford's manner was one which clearly indicated he felt Joe Louis would *yet* land that right hand. And the O'Neill business, he indicated, would eventually prove that the good doctor had the facts at hand.

July 11, 1951: that's the date O'Neill's answer reached me. I don't necessarily agree with everything in it. But the courage, the intelligence contained in that document is superb.

July 11, 1951, was one of the days on which I definitely wanted to *kiss* Miss Whatever-Her-Name-Was.

V

THE JOHN J. O'NEILL LETTER

The letter from O'Neill was dated July 8, 1951, but I received it three days later. Here it is:

Dear Mr. Omarr:

I received your letter asking me to verify a quotation from one of my lectures, which you used in a debate with Dr. Roy K. Marshall, Director of the Fels Planetarium, over Station WPEN.

The quotation you cite is: "While I do not believe all astrology is scientific and worthwhile there is a certain amount of good work being done in that field and it is that which makes me try to do something to help the astrologers."

The quotation is substantially correct.

I have no hesitancy in verifying the quotation. If I were making the statement today I would make it much stronger on the basis of developments in the meantime.

It may be asked what experience I have had that would give value to my opinions on the subject of the debate.

I am not an astrologer.

I am fundamentally an astronomer. More of my time is spent at the eyepiece of my telescope, in making astronomical gadgets, and in working on astronomical problems, than in any other of my activities. I have had, over a long period of years, extensive contact with all of the sciences from anthropology to zoology. I have a good background in history, the history of science and in philosophy.

With this useful background available, I have made numerous contacts with astrology. For years I condemned it as unscientific and totally irrational. This was the usual formula of the astronomers. Just as they have done for a long time, I condemned without making an adequate investigation of what I was condemning. Such a procedure is the utter negation of the scientific attitude, but I was quite blind to the fact at the time and mistakenly assumed I was rendering a useful service to science.

With repeated contacts yielding increasing knowledge of what astrology is, and what it stands for, I have learned that astrology is something vastly different from what I thought it was, and what most astrologers think it is. I have, undoubtedly, had greater contact with astrology than any other scientist and am, therefore, competent to express an opinion concerning it. Most of the critics have lacked the competence that comes from adequate investigation. The converse is equally true of the most outspoken and aggressive propagandists for astrology—they are less competent for the task than many who remain discreetly silent.

I speak as a scientist who does not deviate to the slightest degree from the most rigorous adherence to the highest standards of demonstrated evidence in support of truth. I do deviate from the average attitude of scientists in that I place more reliance on direct observation of nature than I place on textbooks and human authorities. Since I am not associated with any academic institution, I probably enjoy a much greater freedom to speak and write than the average run of scientists. It is only through the freedom of such individuals as myself that science can progress to new domains, and I do not intend to pull any punches in discussing what I believe to be either a truth or falsehood.

Astrology is one of the most important fields for scientific research today, and one of the most neglected. Astrology, properly defined, is the accumulated and organized knowledge of the effect on man of the forces reaching the earth from surrounding space.

The study of this subject has been under way for at least five thousand years and a vast amount of knowledge has been accumulated. Practically all of our sciences have stemmed from it and are actually specialties within the larger field of astrology. Today astrology, *per se,* occupies a more restricted and more sharply defined field. Its center of gravity lies more in the field of the biological than the physical sciences, but its borders extend into both realms. It is still a virile intellectual mother lode out of which a continuing succession of new sciences and new knowledge will be born.

There is absolutely nothing unscientific about engaging in research in this field, and no stigma of any kind should be associated with it in the mind of any scientist or layman.

The human race should not tolerate further delay in bringing the full cooperative resources of science to extended researches in this field. We know very little about the array of forces that are impinging on the earth but that little demonstrates a great urgency for further researches, and the fascinating possibilities that await discovery.

The hypothesis of the astrologers that forces are transmitted to the earth without attenuation with increasing distance, and do not vary with respect to the differences in masses of the Sun, Moon and planets on which they originate, was totally inconsistent with the old-style Newtonian mechanics, but today it is in complete accord with the much more recent Einstein photoelectric theory, which demonstrates that the effect of a photon does not diminish with distance, and which has been universally adopted by scientists to supplant the Newtonian mechanics in that field.

The hypothesis of the astrologers that different effects will be produced by different configurations of the heavenly bodies is entirely consistent with the modern developments in the field of chemistry in which the properties of substances are stated in terms of the architectural configurations of the atoms within the molecules, and with the theories of the atom physicists that the properties of the atoms are associated with the orbital architecture of the electrons.

It is well to keep in mind that the same wave length of radio transmission can carry to the listeners the "Suicide Sonata" or a lively military march with vastly different psychological effects on the audience but no indication of these effects would be detected by a wave meter.

Modern mechanistic and materialistic astronomy which makes organic man a stranger in an inorganic universe is antiquated, in this concept, by at least a century. A vitalistic cosmogony will recognize a complete and most intimate harmonic relationship, in a single pattern, between every entity from the fundamental particles, through the atoms, through man, through the planetary system, through the galaxies, the cosmos, to the Godhead itself. The hypotheses of astrology are consistent with such a vitalistic cosmogony. In this respect, the astrological concept is much more modern than the astronomical.

Scientists today cannot look down on astrology; instead they must raise their eyes to take in the higher horizons that astrologers have preserved for them.

In presenting this objective view of astrology I do not want to be misunderstood as recommending that scientists take lessons in the technique of casting and interpreting horoscopes, or that I am giving sanction to the varied misconceptions and unsupported claims in which many of the astrologers indulge. Astrology has about the same kind and magnitude of a lunatic fringe as astronomy, biology, psychology or economics. Almost all novel developments in any science pass through the lunatic fringe before being incorporated in the orthodox nucleus, but of course the mortality in making the transition is very high.

I do urge an extensive statistical investigation of every claim for specific and configurational effects attributed to the planets by the astrologers. Until this is done, no scientist can provide justification for making a statement for or against the existence of such effects.

Attacks on astrology, without previous extensive investigations by competent individuals must, from now on, be regarded as a very anti-quated, unscientific practice, closely related to witch-hunting, and must be correctly diagnosed as a symptom of professional paranoia on the part of the individual doing the attacking.

This, of course, does not include criticism of a constructive nature that is designed with good intentions to arouse an interest in a more scientific approach to the investigation of the very interesting problems which astrology presents. I am assuming that the present debate be-longs in this category for I am sure Dr. Marshall would not dissipate his valuable efforts and energy in other than constructive activities.

May I suggest to Dr. Marshall that he stage a special solar system show at the Planetarium? He could extend a special invitation to astrologers to attend. He could share the platform with an astrologer and let each have equal time to present his story about each of the heavenly bodies. It may be desirable to arrange a series of such meet-ings. The experiment would be an interesting one and I don't think the box office would suffer.

Scientists are not going to rush into this field to take up research problems. The task must rest largely on the astrologers themselves. The experimental sessions suggested could lead to a cooperative effort in which the astrologers would learn more about the astronomical prob-lems they will have to solve.

It has been my experience that when two sincere men disagree, both are right to a great extent, and that a more fully resolved statement of their differences would lead to further agreement.

Sincerely yours,

JOHN J. O'NEILL

VI

AWFUL BUT TRUE

Those were ringing, beautiful words, when they finally did arrive. And how I wished, as I read them, that they could, through some miracle of communication, have been transmitted *during* the program, while Dr. Marshall was glibly assuring the audience that his "lodge brother," the distinguished, Pulitzer Prize–winning science editor, would have nothing but contempt for astrology. I wished and wished, but it did no good. The station never kept its word; it did not permit the letter to be read over the air. Dr. Marshall, Frank Ford and the station management put their collective heads in the sand. Dr. Marshall said, "Poor O'Neill, something must be wrong. Maybe he was senile. Maybe he never should have received those awards, those honors, never should have been thought of as brilliant, perceptive, a trained observer, seeking after the truth." Dr. Marshall was a man who did not want to be disturbed by the facts; he had made up his mind and that was all there was to it. But he was shaken, much as most astronomers are disturbed and shaken when they attack astrology, and astrology is given the chance to answer. Of course, while the debate raged, the suave Dr. Marshall and the enthusiastic Frank Ford had no way of knowing of events to come, of the O'Neill answer and yet other developments which were to arise.

The calls poured in—telegrams began arriving during the program. I remained calm, although this was more "combat" than I had experienced on Okinawa. Dr. Marshall pounded his fist on the table for emphasis, causing the sound-conscious engineer to cringe. Miss Gemini, for her part, continued taking notes.

Dr. Marshall, the scientist, turned from science to religion. He was pulling out all stops. Astrology had to be put in its place. He lowered his voice. His tone was reverential; he was now "confiding" to the audience. He said that the great religions, after all, condemned astrology. I denied it. He said I was as wrong as I was about O'Neill.

Duly, communications were dispatched to Rabbi Mortimer J. Cohen of Beth Sholom Congregation in Philadelphia; to Raymon Kister, a minister of the Protestant faith and president of Beaver College, just outside Philadelphia; and to Cletus J. Benjamin, Chancellor of the Archdiocese of Philadelphia.

It turned out that the astronomer, once more, simply didn't know what he was talking about, despite the fact that he was posing as an authority and had lectured before thousands of persons over the years, with this same kind of misinformation about a subject from which sprang his own beloved *astronomy*. Rabbi Cohen made it plain that Judaism allows full freedom to Jewish scholars and thinkers and there is no official ban or condemnation where astrology is concerned, that the history of Judaism indeed was steeped in astrological lore.

Kister said he knew of no official ban by his faith, Protestantism, where astrology was concerned.

The Chancellor of the Archdiocese of Philadelphia failed to say, as Dr. Marshall predicted he would, that the Catholic faith condemned astrology.

Again, we did not know what these answers would be while the debate was in progress. So Dr. Marshall was in the position of hurling charges and accusations—and it was my word against the respected doctor's.

Dr. Marshall attempted to give the impression that astrology was fortune-telling and that it advocated a belief in fatalism. To contradict this implication, I read a letter which I had written, and which was published in the September, 1947 issue of *American Astrology* magazine. The letter stated:

"This is to congratulate Cedric W. Lemont on his article, 'The Astrologer.' If astrological practitioners would come forward and make known their claims as Mr. Lemont did, then a great deal of the confusion and suspicion surrounding astrology would be cleared.

"Whether we like to admit it or not, the public in general regards astrology as some mysterious, fatalistic force and astrologers as 'psychics' or mystics who gaze at the stars and come up with startling predictions of the future. Only when recognized astrologers endeavor to educate the public will we be rid of charlatans who abuse the public by claiming to be astrologers.

"We are working with probabilities, trends and cycles which can be measured by movements and aspects of the Sun, Moon and the planets—nothing more. A horoscope, which is based on mathematical and astronomical principles, is a scientific chart. It is merely a photograph of the heavens for a certain time and place. From this chart, we use knowledge based on our own experience and on centuries of observation which has been recorded in textbooks.

"Let us stress this point and clear away 'mystery clouds' so that the public can see through the pretenders. Let us take legal action to prevent the turban-wearing fraud from claiming to be an astrologer. Let's clear the mud from our profession."

I read this letter to prove to listeners—and to Dr. Marshall—that responsible persons in the field were concerned with protecting the public from "quacks" through *information* and *education,* not through the invective which astronomers so enthusiastically resort to when it comes to the subject of astrology. *American Astrology* had editorially commented on the letter with just two words: "We agree."

Nevertheless, Dr. Marshall and "moderator" Frank Ford continued to assert that astrology was fortune-telling and that no real astrologer or astrological publication had ever come out against fortune-telling. They simply refused to be confused by the facts.

But I was a confused young man. Like most people, I was under the impression that sincere men, in an honest exchange of opinion, would surely concede at least some points—especially a man of science, which Dr. Marshall was. But, as I was to learn, not all astronomers are scientific when they leave the narrow confines of their own field.

I was depressed, sad, inwardly tearful, as the panorama of the scientist speaking out of ignorance instead of knowledge, continued to unfold. I wanted to believe Dr. Marshall. I didn't want the apple cart upset anymore than anyone else does. I wanted the comfortable feeling that comes from believing in authorities. I wanted a sane, sensible, charming, humorous, persuasive doctor; one who would draw the line between the astrology I was advocating and the misinformation which often parades under the name of astrology. I was, as a result, as shaken up as the doctor was—I was disillusioned, bitter—and damned angry. This was an out-and-out masquerade. Frank Ford, as a professional announcer with little other background (certainly none in astrology or astronomy) could, if one wanted to be lenient, be excused.

But Dr. Marshall was another story. He was representing what all of us have come to believe is the scientific attitude. But, in reality, he was Cotton Mather howling for witches to burn. The audience could not be sure of this, but enough suspected something was wrong. Because there were so many listener-witnesses, because the program was taped as it occurred, because notes were taken, because the tape was transcribed, I was able to write about what happened, just as freely as I write about it today. What happened transcends astrology. What was being so forcibly demonstrated was the danger attached to *academic prejudice*. It is a prejudice as wretched as any other kind.

The dictionary's definition of astrology as a "pseudo-science" was introduced into the debate. I quoted from *The New International Encyclopedia* as follows:

"The natural tendency of the ignorant and credulous to seek for insight into the future has allowed a multitude of quacks to trade upon the name of astrology and to give the impression that it is beneath contempt. It is well to point out, however, that the predictions of the better class of astrologers are not mere haphazard guesses, as is frequently supposed, but are based upon rigidly scientific determination from observed phenomena, according to definite rules of interpretation. Astrology lays no claim to absolute prediction of future events, undertaking merely to point out the direction which affairs are likely to take, other things being equal."

That quotation, incidentally, was first brought to my attention by a professor who heads a department in a leading university and who is a firm "believer" in astrology. But the academic prejudice against the subject made it impossible for him to admit his interest openly. In the meantime, other men of science have confided their belief, their interest in astrology—and have done so in confidence, once more because of fear. There are economic pressures along with other, more subtle kinds of pressure which make it very inconvenient to be "friendly" toward subjects like astrology, ESP, and other "borderline" areas of intellectual inquiry.

Much happened during those three hours: much was symbolized. It was a long-short, exciting, dynamic, excruciating, painful-joyous three hours. Dr. Marshall wasn't "just anybody." He stood for science as it was understood in America. Or at least he had successfully portrayed himself in that role. Astrology was on trial.

Dr. Marshall stated that doctors and other men of science never seriously consider astrology or its principles. I pointed out that I had received a very fair reception when I lectured before a group of Philadelphia doctors in 1950. I quoted from Laurence J. Bendit, M.D., of Cambridge University, whose book, *This World and That,* was published in 1950 by Faber and Faber. Dr. Bendit said:

Astrology is worked out on a basis of pure mathematics in connection with the position of the planets and stars at the time of birth. Here we are faced either with the fact that the extraordinarily accurate readings of astrological maps, without the astrologer ever having seen the person, are purely psychic or intuitive or else with a mystery which goes deep into the question of the relationship of man with the seemingly objective world, whether as shown in the heavens or in the more mundane sphere of everyday contacts.

The fact, nevertheless, remains that even orthodox psychologists, some with a prejudice against such seemingly fantastic notions, have found themselves forced to realize that an expert astrologer can be of very real value in assessing the type and capabilities of a person whose horoscope he has made.

He can, for instance, predict such things as whether two people are likely to find marriage easy or difficult, creative or frustrating, whether there is a critical phase of life pending, and how the person concerned can best deal with it.

After I read the above quotation Dr. Marshall once more implied I was a liar. He said it wasn't true. But it *was*.

The engineer's smile now was one of respect. Miss Gemini was smiling, too. Dr. Marshall was scowling. And Frank Ford was looking around, as if seeking an explanation from out of the air. Something had gone awry. But the debate was far from over. And I still suspected this "Joe Louis" must be concealing a dynamite-packed right hand.

VII

THE BIG PUSH

Too seldom have the arguments about astrology been presented in a fair, impartial, readable manner. The argument with Dr. Marshall stands as a symbol for many such debates. References have been made to it throughout the world. There have been reports, quotes and stories in India, Great Britain, Japan, Germany, France and other nations. But never—until now—the *complete story*.

I think it is important to put the full story on record so those going into the subject of astrology may have a greater feeling of confidence—the confidence that comes when one knows he is not going into a "pseudo-science," but is putting his time and study into a long-established scientific art.

Astrology is many-dimensional; one gets from it what one puts into it. In this book I am going to tell you how to cast a horoscope and how to interpret it. I am going to tell you about the planets and the Houses and the signs. But I also want you to know more than merely the technical aspects of this tremendous subject.

For many years, without ever seeing my clients, I worked from their horoscopes, advising them through the mail: some of the cases were dramatic. For astrology does make it possible to dig deep, to develop a technique of interpretation—so much so that one of the great psychiatrists of the time utilized the technique to augment his own work with patients. This part of our adventure is also part of the Marshall debate.

The listeners soon became accustomed to Dr. Marshall's biased attitude. The telegrams were beginning to mount in one gigantic protest against the odds—2 to 1 against—Dr. Marshall and Frank

Ford versus the astrologer. Frank Ford, as the record shows, felt moved to defend himself. He said, ". . . they don't think I was fair in bringing Dr. Marshall on an unsuspecting Mr. Omarr—it was not in the spirit of sportsmanship. I think it was. Mr. Omarr, being the editor of *Astrology News, The Trade Journal of Astrology,* since he was an expert, I thought I had better bring an expert in another field."

That *sounds* reasonable. But wouldn't it have been a bit more fair to inform me there was going to be a debate—that I should come prepared rather than arrive under the impression that I was merely to be the subject of one of those "polite" interviews? Dr. Marshall was prepared. Frank Ford was prepared. Gemini and I were prepared in the manner that a cunning, wild animal is alert for trouble when he is enticed to enter certain unfamiliar areas. But not even the "prepared" team of Ford and Marshall could have known what was going to take place. It was astounding, as this excerpt from the transcribed recording of the program reveals:

FORD: I just got a call from the Motorola people; the advertising manager told me, "I don't care whether you do the commercials or not. This program is so fascinating! I want you to continue. It is informative; it is interesting. We think the listeners are as interested in this debate as we are."

The calls and telegrams continued. Frank Ford answered some of them on the air:

FORD: Hello. Yes, this is Ford. You've been trying to call us for an hour? The phones have been ringing. We have been very busy with the discussions. We want to see if we can get a public reaction to what has been said and maybe answer some questions the public might like to ask Dr. Marshall or Mr. Omarr. You say so far you think the program has been unbalanced? Dr. Marshall and I have been against the whole business of astrology, the whole scientific art of astrology—a term I learned this evening from Mr. Omarr—and Mr. Omarr has been defending his position alone?

FORD (continuing): I have a telegram to read which I think needs consideration. We have received a number of them, pro and con. This telegram reads: "I dislike your method of inviting Omarr to discuss astrology without telling him Dr. Marshall would be there. Have no brief for astrology. But your method is extremely low." That is the telegram. Let me say in answer, that I had a premonition. I knew Omarr by reputation, as a gentleman who had done a good deal of research in the field. The mere fact that Mr. Omarr came loaded down with quotations from Ptolemy on up and out is proof enough that he meant business.

Ford certainly was right on that point. I did mean business. But my "meaning business" came upon me when I saw Dr. Marshall and heard him introduced as my "little surprise." I didn't come "loaded down" with quotations. I came with a few notes and a knowledge of what I was talking about—which would not have been too much to ask of either Frank Ford or Dr. Marshall.

The Adelphia Reporting Bureau's transcription, taken from the engineer's tape recordings of the program, reveals the following exchange:

OMARR: I said I would come here and help inform the listeners.

FORD: That's right.

OMARR: Well, I hope I have, at least to some extent.

FORD: We have given you the opportunity, I think. I knew that I, myself, could not refute many of the things that you would say because I didn't have any scientific background to do so. So I felt since I didn't know what you were going to bring . . .

OMARR: Last night you seemed so sure of yourself.

FORD: That is true. Last night I was sure, and tonight I am even surer than I was last night. The entire field of astrology, to me—I am expressing an humble opinion—has no basis in scientific fact. I am in complete agreement with Dr. Marshall and other scientists who have said you cannot take a group of physical facts—when the Moon is in a certain place and when a planet is in a certain place—you cannot take those things and say because you were born when this natural phenomenon occurred in the heavens, therefore, you are the type of person you are. You have not succeeded in proving. You have only succeeded in inferring that on the basis of these physical facts, you can then judge. The mere fact, Mr. Omarr, that you will not state specifically, after looking over all the facts, that on such and such a date this will happen, or did happen; it happened again on such and such a date, therefore, it will happen again. But the mere fact that you will not state specifically that something will happen on such and such a date proves my point.

Of course I would say that Frank Ford *disproved* his point: he and Dr. Marshall had insisted astrology was fatalistic fortune-telling. He condemned it for being so. Now, when I would not fall into the trap of being fatalistic, Ford condemned astrology for that, too!

Throughout the ages, learned men have debated the merits of astrology. This is proper. For when man first began to record his own doings, man looked upward and correlated his activities with the heavenly patterns of the planets. The first astronomers were *astrologers*. This is a part of history which has, time and again, been distorted by astronomers. It is no joking matter. Astronomers, in the seat of power, have displayed a kind of psychological paranoia where astrology is concerned. They have attempted to twist the very facts of history. And because they have been getting away with it for many years, they have attempted to continue to do so. Dr. Marshall was no better, no worse than his contemporaries.

In truth, *five of the greatest scientists of all history were astrologers*. Here are their names: Nicolaus Copernicus, Galileo Galilei, Tycho Brahe, Johanne Kepler and Sir Isaac Newton.

The subject of RCA—the Radio Corporation of America—came up in the debate. I claimed that RCA, the largest communications organization in the world, was utilizing the principles of astrology to forecast magnetic storms successfully and, as a result, bettering its services and saving thousands of dollars a year. This was almost too much for Dr. Marshall. The radio audience could not see his smile, which was a combination of scorn and ridicule. I persisted. I knew that John Henry Nelson, of the RCA staff in New York, was the man responsible for the research and the program then and now in progress, a program of research and application which was astrological in nature.

Naturally, the engineer perked up even more at hearing this revelation. I could tell from a side glance at Miss Gemini that I had tossed a bombshell. Either I was "off my rocker" or I was making news in a tremendous way. As a writer and reporter, I had made a practice of thoroughly checking activities in the field of astrology, or activities in other fields in which astrology might be directly or indirectly involved. I was, after all, not only practicing astrology professionally, but publishing and editing a journal I had created, which was subscribed to and praised by leading astrologers throughout the nation. I did know what I was talking about—and, supposedly, so did Dr. Marshall. As a scientist, he was supposed to know. He sounded as though he knew. He said it was impossible for RCA to utilize the positions of the planets to aid in their communications work.

He seemed, now, to have earned his reputation knocking over members of what the sportswriting fraternity had dubbed "Bum of the Month" club. I mentioned the name, "John Henry Nelson." I told of his research, his reports, the fact that RCA currently was working with the Nelson findings. I said those findings were pure and simple astrology, probably first written about in the Second Century by Ptolemy. Dr. Marshall shot back that the years of research by Nelson were not enough to prove that the aspects (astrological aspects!) between the planets actually had any relation to magnetic storms which produce disturbances in short-wave radio reception. He said he knew of other astronomers who had spent more time in this research: that their findings disagreed with Nelson's report.

More than 10 years have passed since Dr. Marshall made his assertion. RCA and John Henry Nelson *continue* to successfully utilize their astrological technique to forecast disturbances of the earth's ionosphere: disturbances which create those magnetic storms.

Now I am going to once more leave the continuity of the debate, for the purpose of greater overall rhythm. Dr. Marshall had made it imperative for me to back up my claims of RCA and astrology. He had, in effect, pushed me on to one of the most significant stories of our time. It was related to astrology. Therefore, it was related to me.

VIII

RCA ASTROLOGY

We'll get back to the debate, just as we did after we digressed to present John J. O'Neill's historic letter, which came about as a result of Dr. Marshall's statements. "Statements" is a mild word. They were not, in actuality, mere statements. They were dogmatic, pompous claims. I'm sure listeners were inclined to believe him, specifically where O'Neill was concerned and where RCA entered the picture.

But in both cases—Dr. Marshall unknowingly provided the "big push." I realized the implications of the RCA reports which I had first written about in *Astrology News*. But now I wanted to follow through, and I did.

In order to track down one of the most exciting stories in this field, I arranged an interview with John Henry Nelson—an interview which turned out to be one of the most significant I ever conducted in connection with astrological investigation. It also turned out to be one of the most gratifying, because of the facts which were revealed during the course of the talk. John Henry Nelson had been sent a copy of the O'Neill letter. He was aware of things said about his work with RCA during the Marshall debate. He knew I was going after direct answers. He could have waived the interview, but he did not. He knew, because I told him, that I would write about our talk at RCA for astrological publications. Having read about the Marshall debate, the reader—if he wasn't aware before—must certainly now be sensitive to the fact that a connection with astrology, by a man in a "comfortable" position, is not something necessarily to be desired. John Henry Nelson was not and is not a fool. He knew.

But, being a Sagittarian (December 10, 1903), his view was far reaching. He was a natural scrapper. His attitude was, "Come on ahead." And, being a Leo, I came on.

In March of 1951, in a technical journal, Nelson had revealed the results of five years of research. The report appeared in the *RCA Review,* a scientific quarterly. His report was titled, "Short Wave Radio Propagation Correlation with Planetary Positions." It aroused controversy almost from the day of its publication.

In his report, Nelson claimed that magnetic storms coincide with periods of time when the planets are together or conjunct (0°), square (90° apart) and in opposition (180° apart). In turn, magnetic storms adversely affect shortwave radio reception. In his report Nelson also said that periods of time which would be free of magnetic disturbances could be predicted. This, he made clear, was possible also by the method of noting the aspects of the planets. (Later, we're going to go into the subject of aspects, for they make up an important factor in the delineation of a horoscope. One predicts not only magnetic storms and short-wave radio disturbances, but disturbances where human beings are concerned. One can also predict periods of harmony by checking the aspects and noting the positions of the planets.) Nelson's report stated that periods of time likely to be free of magnetic disturbances corresponded to the sextile (60°) and trine (120°) aspects. These times, he said, are most likely to be when Saturn, Jupiter and Mars are equally spaced about the Sun or in sextile or trine aspect to each other.

His research also showed that when Saturn and Jupiter, the Solar system's two largest planets, are conjunct, square or in opposition, radio disturbances are severe. When, in addition, the four minor planets are also in critical alignment during the Saturn-Jupiter critical period, the disturbances are most severe.

As we stated during the debate, these are astrological aspects, discussed in the Second Century by astrologer-astronomer Ptolemy. Prior to publication of the Nelson research, those in the field of radio weather forecasting had concentrated mainly on sunspots. Although work with sunspots had provided some significant correlations with magnetic storms, the results were not reliable enough to be practical. In turning to the planets, Nelson was able to establish an accuracy score of 85 per cent in his forecasts when he combined planetary research with signal analysis and sunspot observations.

The man I saw when I entered his office at the RCA building in New York must have done some soul-searching to grant me the interview. I know he didn't have an easy time of it where the public relations department of RCA was concerned *after* my article was written. But he displayed typical Sagittarian frankness, courage, conviction. He spoke the truth, and later insisted that the article be cleared by the public relations people. I had promised I would submit it for such clearance. I kept my bargain. Nelson was true to his convictions.

He was fully aware that his research would cause significant changes in many fields, especially where knowledge about the planets and their correlation with mundane affairs, particularly with radio weather, is concerned.

Today, his work is proving of immense value to RCA because it enables that organization to know in advance when serious magnetic disturbances are to occur. With this foreknowledge, based on the positions of the planets, RCA is able to notify Tangier, Morocco, and traffic messages through that station, which is relatively free of disturbances caused by magnetic storms.

Nelson's aim was to make RCA better able to transmit messages and thus perform a greater public service. He has succeeded in doing this. Delays in sending and receiving messages are avoided by consulting Nelson. In turn, he consults an ephemeris. An ephemeris gives the positions of the planets; it is used to cast a horoscope.

Nelson told me he was led to a consideration of the effects of planetary positions (or a correspondence with those positions) because a study of sunspots indicated that forces other than those created on the Sun were at work. His findings, it turns out, may eventually reveal that the planets themselves affect the occurrence of sunspots.

Nelson, in talking to me, was typically Sagittarian: to the point, honest, throwing pretensions and formality out of the window. We both talked, exchanged views, made suggestions. He had heard about the Dr. Marshall debate, had read O'Neill's remarkable letter. He had revealed his respect by granting the interview in the first place. He said to me: "I do not know anything about the subject. I am neutral toward astrology and would be willing to accept it if astrologers can prove their claims to me."

Let me emphasize that Nelson, prior to the time I interviewed him, had no intention of even "dabbling" in the ancient, scientific art of astrology. Nor did he realize that his findings in any way paralleled those of earlier astrologers. He simply did not know and he said so. But he had an open mind and displayed intellectual curiosity; he was not infected by academic prejudice.

I showed Nelson a copy of Ptolemy's major work, the *Tetrabiblos,* written in the Second Century. Nelson was able to see the aspects of significance contained in the book. Ptolemy talked of the aspects corresponding to periods of harmony and dissension in human activity. Nelson had used the same aspects between the planets to forecast periods of radio storms, or periods free from such disturbances. Finally, Nelson said that he now realized his research, to a great extent, did indeed verify ancient astrological concepts. He told me, "I am working with radio; radio has no brain and no conscience. Astrologers have a much more difficult task in proving planetary influence or correspondence where human beings are concerned, because of factors involving free will and a thinking apparatus."

Nelson, by this statement, showed he had an intuitive understanding of the problems faced by researchers in the field of astrology. Free will, indeed, does exist.

But let us, for a moment, talk about aspects. The aspects, specifically, are geometrical relationships between the planets. Ptolemy recognized the major aspects—the opposition, trine, square and sextile—as being significant. He did not class the conjunction as an actual aspect, although he treated it as such throughout the *Tetrabiblos.* These are the same aspects which Nelson continues to find so important in radio weather forecasting.

On the whole, astronomers claim the aspects are merely geometrical relationships holding no significance one way or an-

other—no significance where humans are concerned, no signifi-cance where radio weather is concerned.

In astrology, the square and opposition are considered "disturb-ance" aspects. The sextile and trine are considered "harmonious." Nelson's RCA research proves that disturbance aspects coincide with poor radio reception and that harmonious aspects correspond to those times when reception is relatively free of disturbance. The tie up is so obvious that the impartial observer must conclude that this type of research is at least astrological in nature.

I asked Nelson, "Do you think the aspects the planets make to each other will eventually be of aid to those interested in long-range weather forecasting?"

"Frequently," he answered, "sharp temperature drops coincide with magnetic storms."

The inference was that since magnetic storms now can be pre-dicted by observing the planets—so might, in the future, tempera-ture drops and other weather conditions. This, of course, may be a key which can open the door to a new field of research. Already, those interested in astrometeorology (predicting the weather by astrology) have made advances with this type of forecasting.

In explaining what a magnetic storm is, Nelson said the best way to do so was to describe what happens during such a storm. The earth's ionosphere becomes unstable, varies in density and height. The ionosphere belongs at 20 kilometers, but during a storm varies from 100 to 500 kilometers in height. Communica-tions are adversely affected because the ionosphere will not con-sistently reflect the same frequency with the same strength.

Storms of a magnetic nature are most severe over the great-circle paths of the North Atlantic, but are noticed only slightly on low-latitude paths. By knowing in advance when to expect a mag-netic storm, RCA is able to traffic messages over the low latitude paths, thus avoiding the destructive aspects of the storm.

It is not practical to traffic messages over low-latitude paths constantly. The process simply would cost too much money. But by knowing just when to arrange this kind of message traffic, RCA is able to save money simply by notifying stations when they actu-ally expect to have a lot of relaying to do. The stations prepare;

time is saved; the public receives a greater degree of service—all made possible by observing the positions of the planets in relationship to each other.

Reception is adversely affected during a magnetic storm because of great fluctuations in magnetic areas of the earth, which induce voltages in telegraphic lines. Before the Nelson research, RCA had to rely upon South American stations during emergencies. After the Nelson findings were verified, RCA expanded facilities at its station in Tangier.

Two disclosures were being made during this interview. I was disclosing, to Nelson, that his work was closely connected with claims made by astrological researchers throughout the centuries. Nelson was disclosing to me that he was ready to admit such was the case. He thus threw out Dr. Marshall's claim that astrology could not be involved, and that his own work, at any rate, had no value if it did utilize planetary positions. Nelson showed no sympathy for Dr. Marshall's dogmatic attitude. "I've done the work," he said. "I know what I'm talking about. Marshall doesn't know and shouldn't be so willing to make assertions about a subject of which he is ignorant."

I asked Nelson: "Do you have any idea why the planets—when in conjunction, square or opposition—should affect radio reception as they do?"

He replied: "This is just a hunch, but I think the Solar system simulates a generator. The Sun is the armature; the planets are the magnets. But the magnets are moving, which is the difference between a regular generator and the Solar system generator. Of course, with moving magnets, you have a variable output. In a generator, poles are 180° apart. When three planets are lined up, in opposition and two squares, you have a three-pole generator. A four-pole generator, for example, would be Venus and Mars in opposition. Venus and Jupiter 270° apart, Venus and Saturn at 90° angles. Mars and Saturn at 270° distance, with Mars also 90° from Jupiter at the same time."

Nelson added, "As I say, this is just a hunch; but I understand that someone is setting up an electrical replica of the Solar system to work out this theory." He also pointed out that when Jupiter and Saturn are at distances which are multiples of 60°, disturbances fall off.

Once more on the subject of Dr. Marshall, Nelson said, "It was to be expected that I would obtain results that other astronomers had not because I was using a much more *sensitive instrument*—that instrument was variations in radio signal qualities or the qualities of radio signals."

Nelson said he felt sure many people would be forced to change their views as research by others verified the RCA findings. To date, his work has received wide publicity and recognition, following my 1951 interview. But many astronomers to this day continue to insist, "It just ain't possible!"

Now, twelve years later, as this is being written (1963), Nelson and RCA know well it is possible, for the work has successfully continued. Meantime, J. H. Clark, of Press Wireless, Inc., has adopted Nelson's methods of checking planetary aspects to predict "clear" and "disturbance" periods for purposes of work in the field of communication. Clark has extended the Nelson work to include Uranus, Neptune and Pluto.

Nelson today is intensely interested in Pluto's role. He looked into the heaviest cosmic-ray shower in history, which occurred on February 2, 1956, just five days after Jupiter had moved to a 90° (square) relationship with Saturn and three days before Pluto had come into a 0 configuration (conjunction) with Jupiter. It turned out that the ionosphere was not disturbed enough to affect radio signals until 23 days later, February 25, 1956, when Mercury came into conjunction with Saturn and into square aspect with Jupiter and Pluto.

Nelson told a 1961 NATO ionospheric research conference in Naples that he is able to predict magnetic disturbances—and thereby choose radio frequencies likely to escape interruption—with progressively greater accuracy, as he studies the system of checking planetary positions.

We are now in the Space Age. We have no time for foolish prejudice, including the academic kind, maybe especially the academic variety. Let me give you one concrete example. Nelson, utilizing the principle that Dr. Marshall and other astronomers say is merely a "foolish notion," forecast the great sunstorm of November 12, 1960, more than a year in advance. America's first cosmonaut would have been trapped in that storm had our lunar exploration been on schedule!

FIND THE SAFECRACKER!

Astrology is as diverse as are people. There is the astrology of the masses; the Sun-sign readings which appear in popular astrological publications and in daily newspapers. My own column is printed across the country and throughout the world by more newspapers than any other astrology feature. That is popular astrology. And astrology is popular because the odds are that 10 out of 10 persons could tell you under which zodiacal sign they were born. There is the world of the professional astrologer: he, in effect, is the problem analyst, just as the psychologist is, as the psychiatrist is; and in many instances his work is augmented by the psychological sciences. The reverse also is true. Astrology supplies a missing element to the orthodox endeavors: astrology is concerned with the element of time. Dr. Carl Jung, the late, great psychiatrist had the moral courage to admit his use of astrology. Dr. Jung was an unusual man. Many scientists today, who not only are interested in astrology but utilize it in their work are not so outspoken. They "hide" from any association with astrology.

Astrology is a hobby and a profession; it is a field of interest which encompasses literature and knowledge of medicine, history, astronomy; it is a scientific art dealing with man and the world in which he lives. Astrology places the spotlight on cycles, moods, character; our watches, clocks and calendars are based on the earth's movement around the Sun—in a way, astrology thus is synonymous with time. For we measure time by observing the Solar system. Astrology is rich in lore, legend, history; predictions can be made by astrology, much in the way a doctor predicts a crisis period in the condition of a patient. Astrology "predicts" in the manner that a meteorologist forecasts probable weather conditions—in the manner in which John Henry Nelson "predicts" for the Radio Corporation of America.

Knowledge of astrology thus requires knowledge in various fields. The ideal astrologer is a scholar, a humanist; he is a historian and he is aware of current events. He is as curious as a journalist, as aware as a creative writer, as sensitive to trends as a poet and as scientific as a mathematician. Many astrologers don't have this kind of vision, foresight, ambition, this set of principles, nor do they realize the tremendous "karmic" load they carry when they label themselves "Astrologer."

This "ethical" question, concerning astrology, came up during the debate with Dr. Marshall. Dr. Marshall said astrologers preyed upon the public's credulity, had no ethics. I stressed the point that responsible astrologers realize that many persons abuse astrology. Organizations like the American Federation of Astrologers, with headquarters in Washington, D.C., make efforts to correct those abuses. I cited its code of ethics, which must be subscribed to by those joining the organization. I volunteered to read that code, so listeners could judge for themselves, so moderator Ford could form an opinion, and so Dr. Marshall could be enlightened. I never did get to read the code of ethics of the American Federation of Astrologers. Here's what happened:

OMARR: I would also like to point out that the American Federation of Astrologers has a code of ethics to which responsible practitioners attempt to adhere.

FORD: Listen, that doesn't mean a thing. Safecrackers have a code of ethics, even pickpockets.

OMARR: I don't like your analogy.

FORD: You cited a code of ethics for dealing with the public. It's the same thing.

OMARR: You're being absolutely ridiculous. If, in a serious discussion of astrology, we wish to arrive at facts, those analogies can best be done away with.

DR. MARSHALL: You are using the code of ethics. You must show some proof that it is okay. If you are going to set up a different kind of astrology from that which everyone in the country has believed or disbelieved so far, we have to start from scratch.

OMARR: I am here to clear up misconceptions. I am not going to permit you to set up straw men and knock them down. If that's what you expected, I am sorry to disappoint you.

DR. MARSHALL: I know this American Federation of Astrologers, or whatever that new title is. In 1941, their president was Lewis, or somebody. He said astrologers, of course, cannot make predictions. That was one part of their code of ethics at that time—that astrologers should not attempt to make predictions. You can talk all you want about tendencies and cycles and stay clear of the law. But as soon as you make a prediction you are in awful hot water in several states of the Union. You are expressly forbidden to do so in the state of Pennsylvania; the law is clear that if you pretend, for gain or loot, to foretell the future by the motion of the heavenly bodies, you are subject to fine of one thousand dollars or imprisonment. That law was revised in 1939. It is a pretty modern law, and the same kind of law exists in many places throughout the United States. Every astrologer who makes predictions is going against the law. If his victim complains, he will be convicted. If astrology doesn't make predictions, it loses all of its value for the people who believe it.

OMARR: If I might mention RCA again—I suppose they had better not attempt to carry on their research in Pennsylvania and the weather forecasters making predictions, and the news commentators. Everyone will be in jail! But now that you've strayed away from the subject, let's get back to what we were talking about: the code of ethics of the American Federation of Astrologers.

FORD: We refuse to accept the code of ethics.

OMARR: I don't see how you can refuse to accept it when you haven't heard it. Every time I attempt to read it, you interrupt. Yet you say you refuse to accept when you don't know what it contains. That is a good example of the kind of prejudice I was talking about . . . and a good example of a closed mind.

ADELPHIA REPORTING BUREAU: All participants speaking at once—impossible to report.

As the reporter states, Dr. Marshall, Ford and I began talking at once. Shouting would be a more accurate description. Dr. Marshall and the "moderator" insisted on passing judgment on something they hadn't heard and wouldn't permit me to read. Finally both said even if the code were read, they would not accept it, anyway. They implied they knew what the code would say even before they heard it. In the face of this dogmatic attitude, I shook my head in disbelief. Gemini, on the sidelines, bit her lower lip in anger. The engineer gaped through the window. Dr. Marshall and his ally, Frank Ford, sat smugly, while the telephones continued to jangle and the telegrams piled up. This was, if nothing else, one of the liveliest broadcasts ever heard in the normally staid City of Brotherly Love.

OMARR: I back down. If you know all about this code of ethics, without hearing or reading it, and you say it means nothing, I back down. I do this in respect to your greater knowledge!

DR. MARSHALL: You missed the point. Let's open up *your* mind. The astrologers say, "We are so right that we even have a code of ethics." That is making it ridiculous.

OMARR: They didn't say that.

DR. MARSHALL: Just because they have the code of ethics, it doesn't make astrology a different thing from what I said it was. Frank Ford said the code doesn't mean anything. Even a safecracker has that; it doesn't make the safecracker right, righteous or true.

OMARR: The stand you have taken here is just too fantastic! If I might repeat once again, I said that psychics and clairvoyants have nothing to do with astrology, and no legitimate astrologer ever claimed they did. The fields are disassociated. I said that in answer to remarks that many clairvoyants were fakes. That was a simple answer to a careless statement made by someone who called. Furthermore, I said there is a strict code of ethics which I think most astrologers try to adhere to.

Repeating—I never did get to read the code of ethics! Let me reproduce it now, for the reader will want to have knowledge of it as part of his general education regarding modern astrology. The following is the code of ethics of the American Federation of Astrologers, Inc.:

I, the undersigned, subscribe to the following Code of Ethics:

I recognize that a precise astrological opinion cannot honestly be rendered with reference to the life of an individual unless it is based upon a horoscope case for the year, month, day and time of day plus correct geographical location of the place of birth of that individual, and I agree not to render such an opinion without this detailed information, unless the horoscope of the individual has been rectified by accepted astrological methods, or unless I positively state to the interested party that such conclusions are reached by alternative methods.

I agree not to interpolate or introduce any astrological deduction, verbally or otherwise, any interpretation which my conclusions appear to warrant, that are irrelevant to the Science of Astrology without first stating definitely that such deductions are neither based upon the life chart nor identified with the science.

I agree to honor and respect all confidences which may be reposed in me by consultation and to hold such confidences inviolable excepting wherein they may involve an act of felony or treason.

I agree not to use my identification with the American Federation of Astrologers, Inc., as a signature of publicity in any unethical manner. I agree to assist in any way I can in the elimination of the charlatan who may be masquerading under any form of title that can be construed to mean a connection with Astrology designed to mislead the public or trade upon their credulity in any way; and I hereby subscribe to this Code of Ethics as a condition of my membership in the American Federation of Astrologers, Inc.

It's not such an unusual document—a straightforward, sincere declaration of intentions, an effort to embody the principle of ethical practice. But Dr. Marshall and Ford had created the aura of "safecrackers" and they had no intention of permitting the code to be read.

And since our astronomer insisted on talking about the legal aspects of astrology, I tried to tell him about one of the greatest of modern-day astrologers, the late Evangeline Adams—and of her successful effort to "legalize" astrology in the state of New York, where she practiced and was consulted by captains of industry and leading lights in the political, art, literary and theatrical worlds. That effort, too, was beaten down in much the same manner.

But, as we say, the listeners had their "antenna" up; they now, with good reason, begin to swing their doubts away from me and toward Dr. Marshall.

X

EVANGELINE ADAMS

Evangeline Adams tells her story brilliantly in *The Bowl of Heaven* and so I do not intend to go into details. But I do want to present some highlights, leading up to the "legal aspects" hammered at so insistently by Dr. Marshall. The legal area should be familiar to those who are entering these waters: it is part of the story of astrology in the world today; as such, it belongs here, in a treatise on the subject.

Evangeline Adams was the most famous of all American astrologers. She was a direct descendant of President John Quincy Adams. She was a woman of great integrity, an artist when it came to interpreting horoscopes. Her skill was so great that celebrities made a practice of consulting her. Never, to my knowledge, did she abuse astrology: she made money, lots of it, but she did not exploit the subject. Although she received reams of publicity, she lived a quiet life, devoted to astrology, to her work, to her clients. She was to astrology what Houdini was to magic. She was a giant in her time (1868–1932). Evangeline Adams made astrology respectable and she helped make America astrology-conscious. She was responsible for astrology being "legalized" in the state of New York.

To her studios at New York's Carnegie Hall came the great and near-great: men who guided political affairs; men like J. P. Morgan, who manipulated the financial strings; artists; writers; everyday people with troubles; the curious; thrillseekers (who were disappointed); and students and future astrologers. Thousands of people consulted her in person or wrote to her from every corner of the earth. She stole time from eating and sleeping to read the horoscope of every person who interested her. As she once said, "There is no more enthusiastic believer in the stars than Evangeline Adams of Carnegie Hall."

Her first instructor in astrology was Dr. J. Heber Smith, professor of *materia medica* at Boston University, and at the time, New England's leading diagnostician. He was not a professional astrologer, but he did use astrology in connection with his medical work. He was a student of Sanskrit and of the Eastern religions, and had thus acquired a deep understanding of astrology. When he died, he left his manuscripts to Evangeline Adams, whom he predicted would be a renowned practitioner of the art.

The Boston friends of the Adams family, like most persons, did not hold astrology in high regard. That was in the 1890's. But finally, after years of study, Evangeline Adams put her shingle outside a studio at the Hotel Copley in Boston, where she remained until she made the move to New York in 1899. She consulted her own chart and found that the middle of March, 1899, would be the best time for the change.

But when she arrived in the Big City, a Boston girl of high lineage, breaking all precedent by announcing, "I'm going to devote my life to astrology!" everything seemed to go wrong. Lugging her suitcase, with that determined look on her face which was to become so familiar to so many, she must have presented an unusual picture. She went to the Fifth Avenue Hotel, where a family friend, a Mr. Vinal, was the proprietor. He received Miss Adams with enthusiasm. He was about to give her one of his best rooms, overlooking Madison Square. Then the bombshell. "I am," she told him, "very much interested in astrology and will practice here, receiving clients." His reply: "Miss Adams, I shall always be glad to receive you as a guest. But I can't stand for your astrology!"

Evangeline was a believer in the philosophy of nonresistance, and a woman who practiced what she preached. She didn't resist. She thanked Vinal and went on her way. In later years, the same man—after the name Evangeline Adams was ranked with the celebrities of the world—was to plead with her to come back to the Fifth Avenue Hotel and set up her practice. That wasn't to be, however, although the two remained friends.

She described what happened in this way: "The dignity of my beloved science had been insulted. I had been insulted. I was what my ancestors would have described as righteously indignant. In short, I was mad clear through."

Evangeline Adams' pride was punctured; she was confused, alone in New York, but she remembered those "good aspects," and doggedly continued her quest, which she described in *The Bowl of Heaven.*

I must have made a neat picture of youthful determination as I staggered along under the weight of my carefully over-packed portmanteau. Of course, I didn't know that I was committing a social error by carrying my own bag in so fashionable a neighborhood; but I should have experienced a certain wicked pleasure if I *had* known it. I was in a mood to defy assistance—and the world. So I put off up the Avenue with my dignity in one hand and my luggage in the other, and the proverbial New England umbrella slapped under one arm.

She finally reached the Windsor Hotel and proprietor Warren Leland. He proved a good host; he took a liking to the tired, overwrought young lady who still managed to smile. Soon, they were talking—astrology! Leland confessed ignorance of the subject, but he was fascinated with it. He saw nothing wrong with Evangeline Adams practicing the art at the Windsor. That was Thursday, March 16, 1899. Miss Adams settled in a suite on the first floor, for $12 a day—much money in those days. But the "aspects" were good and, besides, she had done enough walking for one day.

Finally, when she was settled, Leland told her, "Tomorrow is Friday, my bad luck day! You'd better give me a reading now."

Evangeline Adams was not superstitious, so she laughed. But she drew up Warren Leland's horoscope. By this time he was laughing, too. It seemed like a game. It's always fun to hear about one's own birth date, one's own chart or horoscope. And Evangeline Adams was charming, not bad to look at—and her youthful-serious manner made it that much easier to listen.

But Evangeline Adams had stopped smiling. She later explained, "The man was under one of the worst possible combinations of planets—conditions terrifying in their unfriendliness."

The young astrologer told him that danger was so imminent it might overtake him the next day. The next day was St. Patrick's Day and Leland made a joke of it. He talked about the next day being a holiday—"nothing could happen." But Evangeline Adams persisted. She said the unfavorable conditions affected not only him, but his entire family. Leland dismissed the warning, but was so impressed by the general accuracy of the entire reading that, in actuality, he launched Evangeline Adams on her career in New York. He sent guests to her suite for horoscope interpretations that evening until long after midnight.

The next afternoon, while hundreds of New Yorkers marched in the St. Patrick's Day parade, the great Windsor Hotel went up in flames. Leland watched scores of his friends and guests jump from his windows to their death—he saw his hotel burn to the ground. It was the worst fire disaster, to that time, in New York history. And Warren Leland also lost several members of his family, among them his favorite daughter. The next morning, printed in big type on the front pages of New York newspapers, was Leland's statement that the disaster had been predicted by Evangeline Adams of Boston. It was, as Evangeline Adams said, a grim success story—one she would have given anything to change.

This was the start of her celebrity, which had its early beginnings in Boston: now it spread from Boston to New York and, as we know, around the world. By 1914, she was being "sniped at" by the Dr. Marshalls of her day. The procedure was to send an undercover agent for an analysis of his chart; then charge Miss Adams with "fortune-telling." In each instance, the charges were dropped. But in 1914, she became involved in a suit which was to elevate astrology in the state of New York to the status she sought so fervently. In 1914 an archaic law in New York state classed astrology with "acrobatic performers, circus riders, men who desert their wives, and people who pretend to tell fortunes." All in this category, according to the statute, were termed "disorderly persons."

Miss Adams explained, "I had but one ambition: to legalize astrology in the state of New York. So when another enemy of the science came to me anonymously, secured a reading which she claimed was 'fortune-telling,' and hailed me again to court, I went with a willing and determined heart."

She instructed her attorney, Clark L. Jordan of New York, against having the case thrown out of court. She wanted it tried.

Judge Freschi sat on the bench in the case of the People versus Adams. For her part, Evangeline Adams talked about astrology, illustrating her points with modern and ancient texts. She went into the courtroom with a pile of reference books reaching nearly to the ceiling and "a mass of evidence that reached as far back as the Babylonian seers."

Finally, she asked permission to demonstrate her science. She asked Judge Freschi to allow her to cast a horoscope, to give a reading in the presence of the court. The request was granted. Judge Freschi provided her with the month, day, year, hour and place of birth of a person he identified only as "Mr. X." Miss Adams consulted her ephemerides and Table of Houses, and drew the horoscope. Standing straight, speaking in a clear, confident voice, she gave her findings. The judge leaned forward. So did attorneys and spectators and newspapermen. What she said was interesting; no doubt about it. But did it apply? One couldn't tell from the expression on Judge Freschi's immobile face. And just who was this mysterious "Mister X"? The reporters were having a delightful time, for now the famous Evangeline Adams was really on a spot. She could have had the case thrown out. She had the influence and no one really believed she was a lawbreaking "fortune-teller." But she had insisted on the trial. If that was not enough, she had also asked for this test, this challenge not only to her ability, but also to the accuracy of her beloved astrology.

Finally the reading was over. Judge Freschi was ready to hand down his decision. Evangeline Adams sat down and waited. So did opposing attorneys and newsmen. The judge took a long look at the defendant. It was hard to try to "read" his look. Unsmilingly he announced his findings:

The defendant raises astrology to the dignity of an exact science.

She has given ample proof that she is a woman of learning and culture, and one who is very well versed in *astronomy* and other sciences. Her chart here, as made out, may be verified, as she stated, in the books and records of astronomers for years.

In the reading of the horoscope the defendant went through an absolutely mechanical, mathematical process to get at her conclusions. She claims that astrology never makes a mistake, though astrologers do, and if the figures are correct, the information given is correct.

The sincerity of the defendant's determination from her own perceptions and a study of authorities cannot be questioned. She certainly does seem to have a thorough knowledge of the subject. And in this, she claims no faculty of foretelling by supernatural or magical means that which is future, or of discovering that which is hidden and obscure; but she does claim that nature is to be interpreted by the influences that surround it.

When the defendant prepared her horoscope of the complainant and calculated the relative positions of the planets at the time of her birth, basing this horoscope on the well-known and fixed science of astronomy, she violated no law.

As for the horoscope of "Mr. X," Judge Freschi said the reading gave him a new insight into the person's mentality and character. It turned out that "Mr. X" was his own son!

Today, as a result of that trial, astrology in the state of New York stands excepted from the law which prohibits "fortune-telling."

XI

"IF A LUNATIC COMES TO YOU . . ."

Thus, the Dr. Marshalls do serve a purpose, other than that of lecturing to junior high school students at their planetariums on Saturdays. But they go about it in a peculiar manner, with malice their stated intent. The malice is directed toward their "parent," astrology. Why this should be so, after these many years, is perhaps a question better answered by a Freudian psychiatrist. The astronomers, I am sure, would have no truck with a Jungian doctor. Which brings us to the next point in that 1951 debate, which continues to reverberate, not only in the pages of this work, but wherever students and researchers study the role of astrology in the world today.

For the issues raised, the charges hurled, the heated controversy which erupted, did not die. The printed word began where the spoken word, over Station WPEN in Philadelphia, stopped. Although the participants might have thought it was over, that was to prove far from the case. I certainly was anxious, during the debate, for it to end—while I was still in one piece! It was no pleasure to watch the crumbling of the opposition, not when one considers that the opposition should have been informed, capable of pungent statements instead of watery, phoney accusations and dogmatic assertions. You see, I wanted to respect Dr. Marshall because, despite his reputation as an opponent of astrology, he did represent the "man of learning." And I revered knowledge, just as most people who undertake a study of astrology eventually come to respect scholars. The scholars have preserved astrological findings for us, have unearthed astrological tablets dating back to the dawn of history: real scholars have written our books and have practiced our art and have stood by, sometimes quietly, in our corners, ready to offer aid, comfort, encouragement.

I had, until this night, only heard about Dr. Marshall and his previous attacks. To now personally be involved, and to witness the fact that his knowledge of astrology was practically nil, had the effect of making me shake my head to make sure I wasn't dreaming. I wasn't, although, after nearly three continuous hours of vociferous argument heard by thousands of persons in the then third largest city in the United States, I was tired enough to be in a dreamlike state.

The late psychiatrist and writer Dr. Carl Jung was alive in 1951. His name came up during the debate. And once more Dr. Marshall was to be in for a surprise. Dr. Jung, too, belongs in this work, for he was perhaps the outstanding man of learning *outside* the field of astrology to show tremendous interest in the subject and make contributions to it.

I knew this to be a fact and so stated it. Dr. Marshall had the faculty of recovering from surprises quickly. He recovered fast enough to state, in effect, that Dr. Jung either was not interested in astrology or he was a highly overrated scientist. Here is the transcribed report of how Jung's name entered the discussion:

FORD: I am merely trying to say that since astrology calls itself—I just learned the term from you—a scientific art, it should be scientific in nature. I think any scientist agrees it is not. You cannot say the Moon in one sign of the zodiac will correspond to different results in planting seeds than when the Moon is in another sign of the zodiac. And I would like to ask you some questions about the personal services offered by astrology.

OMARR: Yes. But no questions concerning *my* personal services because that would constitute free advertising, and I don't want to be accused of that.

FORD: I will limit my questions to astrology. I won't ask you whether these are *your* personal services. I will ask whether this comes within the realm of astrology.

OMARR: Go ahead.

FORD: From what I have been able to read, an astrologer, a professional astrologer, can set up charts for people if they send in birth data.

OMARR: Birth data are all that is necessary, along with place of birth.

FORD: All right. They can set up charts so that characteristics of each individual can be discussed and marriage relationship prospects emphasized?

OMARR: Yes. But what is your question?

FORD: My question is if two people will send the legitimate information about their times and places of birth, that an astrologer can give them a scientific answer, "Yes," that they should get married or, "No," because of when they were born?

OMARR: Let me answer that question this way. If two persons have their maps cast and they are thinking of entering any relationship, legal partnership or marriage, I think that by analayzing the characteristics of both persons . . .

FORD: What do you mean by "analyzing characteristics"? You are discussing psychological characteristics.

OMARR: Analyzing and comparing the characteristics of the individuals . . . one might be a Martian type, the other also extremely impulsive. The characteristics of the individuals might indicate success when combined in partnership or might indicate otherwise.

FORD: What you are using, then, is nothing more than practical psychology.

OMARR: Astrology makes use of psychology and mathematics and astronomy; it does not deny it and why should it?

DR. MARSHALL: Yet you say the astrologer doesn't see these two people?

OMARR: It would be helpful if the astrologer interviewed the two persons. He would be able to give a more complete analysis. However, because of the attitude many persons have toward astrology, the astrologer often works without ever seeing his clients . . .

DR. MARSHALL: Psychological factors have nothing to do with horoscopes or astrologers!

OMARR: Carl Jung is an example of a well-known psychologist who makes use of astrology or the astrological technique in his work. He has devoted thirty years of research to the subject and says that the horoscope is extremely helpful in analyzing difficult problems of the patient.

At this point, the question arose as to who Carl Jung was and whether or not his opinion was worth listening to, whether he "amounted to anything in this world." Dr. Marshall attempted to palm off Jung as "one of those Viennese doctors." Frank Ford apparently knew well who Carl Jung was: anyone who had read anything about psychiatry knew that Jung was a pioneer in the field and had been chosen by Freud to be his successor, although the two eventually were to part company and their teachings were to be divided into two schools. Dr. Marshall switched gears. No longer was Jung "one of those Viennese doctors." Now, according to Dr. Marshall, Jung was a great man. I was "embarrassing" Jung by associating his name with astrology. If he ever was associated with astrology, he should be ashamed of himself, said the astronomer.

OMARR: I am not going to defend Carl Jung! He most certainly does not need defending.

DR. MARSHALL: You're putting him in a terribly embarrassing position.

OMARR: He won't be embarrassed.

Dr. Marshall turned away from me, after giving me a final, scathing look. He directed his remarks to the listeners, looking up now and then at the engineer, and over his shoulder at Gemini, who smiled back politely. His tone was persuasive. He tried to persuade listeners that after all he knew about Jung and his connection with astrology all the time. Only it wasn't the kind of connection this Omarr fellow here is trying to put over on us. Look, he said, Jung used astrology only on patients who were "bugs on the subject." He didn't really use astrology, but only deluded patients who believed in astrology into thinking that he, Jung, was going to utilize the horoscopic technique.

DR. MARSHALL: If a man comes to you and is a lunatic on some subject and you flatter him, you are able to give him some kind of relief. That is why we call it "psychiatry." The psychiatrist can give some kind of relief by playing on that "bug."

I replied that this might make interesting listening but it simply was not true. Jung's patients, those who were helped by the astrological technique of analysis, did not necessarily have to be aware that Jung, in fact, *was* using astrology.

Once more, the listeners were left in a quandary. Who to believe? I repeatedly insisted that Jung had made his views on astrology public. That, after 30 years of study and experimentation, he believed firmly in the principles of astrology and found those principles of great aid in his work. Frank Ford laughed and Dr. Marshall encouraged him by stating this was simply another misrepresentation of the facts—the same thing I had attempted to do in the cases of RCA and O'Neill.

XII

CARL GUSTAV JUNG

Jung (1875–1961), along with Freud, Adler, Rank, Reich and others in the field of mental health, pioneered the most controversial of modern sciences: psychiatry. While the space scientists take us outside ourselves, even outside the earth's atmosphere, the psychiatrist attempts to give us a look *inside* and, like the astrologer, attempts to show us why we are what we are, why we react the way we do—and how best to mature and live a life free from needless fear and inner opposition. No matter how far man goes in outer space, he must finally face himself.

I know that astrologers must become more familiar with psychological methods and techniques. And I am just as convinced that psychologists must learn more about astrology, for astrology provides a missing psychological element: the element of time. Without added psychological knowledge, on the other hand, the skilled astrologer loses much in his effort to help people. There is much psychology involved in interpreting a horoscope. It is not enough to parrot textbook generalities. The astrologer must, if he is to aid others, be *aware*. He cannot merely "show off" by reeling off characteristics of the native, by pinpointing periods of difficulty and times of success. He must help the native to grow, to know what to do about the indications and trends reflected in his birth chart.

Let us again utilize the Dr. Marshall debate as a springboard for added knowledge. Let us elaborate on a point which could not, during the debate, be given full play—simply because we did not have the material on hand to quote verbatim—and also because both Dr. Marshall and Frank Ford insisted to listeners that it was foolish, even dishonest on my part, to associate the name of Jung with astrology in any favorable manner.

It is important for one to have this background: it serves as a kind of emotional strength to realize that the astrological technique is one to be respected, not merely as a diversion, but as a solidly based scientific art. Surely, the reader will hear and read enough against astrology. But, with a full picture, he is better able to decide for himself. My purpose is to provide that kind of picture. Then he may know the valuable tool he has; he may study, work and experiment: then he may become a sound astrologer. He soon will find that once he is identified as being conversant on the subject, many friends, associates, sometimes perfect strangers, will flock to him—to ask questions on astrology in general and about their own horoscopes and problems in particular. How far one goes in this subject is, of course, up to the individual. But the purpose here is to provide the material for those with inquiring minds; to provide a text enabling them to get at the facts: to learn; contribute their own findings; to become, if not expert, at least skilled and knowledgeable.

The role of the Swiss psychiatrist Jung in astrology is part of the knowledge to be provided.

The listeners, as we say, were not able to learn that it was Dr. Marshall who was wrong about Jung and astrology. This was because each of us—Dr. Marshall and myself—made different claims. Ford indicated he was certainly going along with Dr. Marshall: that a man of Jung's standing had no truck with astrology. Or if he did, it was merely as a "kidding" device, to placate difficult patients who might require an unusual approach.

B. V. Raman is one of the outstanding astrologers of India and is the editor of *The Astrological Magazine,* published in that country. In 1947, he received the following letter from Jung:

Dear Prof. Raman:

I haven't yet received *The Astrological Magazine,* but I will answer your letter nevertheless.

Since you want to know my opinion about astrology I can tell you that I've been interested in this particular activity of the human mind since more than 30 years. As a psychologist I am chiefly interested in the particular light the horoscope sheds on certain complications in the character. In cases of difficult psychological diagnosis I usually get a horoscope in order to have a further point of view from an entirely different angle. *I must say that I very often found that the astrological data elucidated certain points which I otherwise would have been unable to understand.** From such experiences I formed the opinion that astrology is of particular interest to the psychologist, since it contains a sort of psychological experience which we call "projected" —this means that we find the psychological facts as it were in the constellations. This originally gave rise to the idea that these factors derive from the stars, whereas they are merely in a relation of synchronicity with them. I admit that this is a very curious fact which throws a peculiar light on the structure of the human mind.

What I miss in astrological literature is chiefly the statistical method by which certain fundamental facts could be scientifically established.

I remain,
Yours sincerely,
C. G. JUNG

In his letter, Jung uses the term "synchronicity." It is a word we often use in modern astrology. No longer must we fall into the trap of insisting that the planets cause events to occur, or cause people to respond the way they do: what we do claim is that there is a correspondence, a coincidence between the planetary patterns and mundane actions, reactions, events. There is a synchronicity. As above, so below. We don't, as Jung indicates, know why this should be. But it happens so often that it is a reliable indicator.

The Solar system, in other words, can be regarded as a giant clock. Human activity corresponds to certain "times," which are available to us to see by consulting the "clock." An earth clock, for instance, might toll noon. At that time, many people begin their lunch hour. This does not mean the clock caused the people to go to lunch. We needn't be stymied because we can't explain why people go to lunch (many of them) at noon. All we need be concerned with is that this correspondence works. There is syn-

* Italics mine.

chronicity: the hands of the clock point to certain numerals and specific things happen, or correspond to those combinations of numerals. Noon and lunch, five in the evening and time to leave work, seven in the morning and many people arise to go to work. On a more individual level, we have our own personal schedules and we consult our calendars and our clocks. The Solar system, in fact, regulates the calendar and the clock. Human activities, radio weather and other "times" express a correspondence to the positions of the planets. We need not look for causal answers. Jung has given us the word: synchronicity.

Of course the Jung letter reveals, once more, that I was relating the facts despite Dr. Marshall's claims to the contrary.

Two years after the debate, in 1953, I was in Los Angeles as a senior editor with KNX-CBS News. I had the opportunity to talk by telephone with Dr. Yolandi Jacobi, a top-row disciple of Dr. Jung. At this time, many persons—as they did with Freud—thought it their duty to "protect" him from being associated with astrology and other "borderline" subjects. So Dr. Jacobi was not exactly happy to talk about Jung in connection with astrology. She was visiting Los Angeles as part of a world lecture tour. She was a member of the staff of the Institute of Analytical Psychology at Zurich, Switzerland, and the author of *The Psychology of C. G. Jung.* She sits on the board at the famous Jung Institute in Zurich. When she *did* talk, she told me that Jung believed that even the symbolism of astrology offered food for scientific thought; she said that the eminent doctor enjoyed almost nightly discussions with one of his leading students on the subject of astrology. She concluded by admitting, though not too willingly, that Dr. Jung regarded astrology with great respect and was personally conducting experiments. I will be telling you about one of his best-known experiments, wherein he probed into human relationships in connection with planetary patterns by investigating the charts of married couples to determine, once and for all, whether there was a link, a pattern, a "connecting principle" between the planets and the people.

First, let me tell you some other opinions on astrology expressed by Jung during his lifetime. In his introduction to *The Hands of Children,* by Julius Spier, he says:

The ancient physician never hesitated to make use of such auxiliary systems as chiromancy (palmistry) and astrology for diagnostic and prognostic purposes as is shown, for instance, by the book of Dr. Goclenius who lived at the end of the 16th Century in Wurzburg.

The rise of the Natural Sciences and with it of rationalism in the 18th Century were responsible for the contemptible treatment and defamation of these ancient arts which could pride themselves on a thousand years of history, and this led to the rejection of everything which on the one hand defied a reasonable explanation and verification by experiment or, on the other, made too exclusive a claim on intuition.

In the 20th Century, however, after 200 years of intensive scientific progress, we can risk resurrecting these almost forgotten Arts which have dragged on a despised existence in semiobscurity; and we can risk testing them in the light of modern knowledge for possible truths.

In Munich in 1930 Jung delivered a memorial address on Richard Wilhelm, reprinted as part of the appendix in Wilhelm's *The Secret of the Golden Flower,* in which he had some things to say about astrology. He was speaking about the synchronistic principle. He said, "My occupation with the psychology of unconscious processes long ago necessitated my looking about for another principle of explanation, because the causality principle seemed to me inadequate to explain certain remarkable phenomena of the psychology of the unconscious." He explained that he had, in his studies, his experiments, and in his practice, come across certain parallelisms, coincidences, events which could not be related to each other causally, but which, he said, must be connected through another sequence of events. This was relative simultaneity: therefore the expression synchronistic. This is another way of explaining, as I did earlier, that I "believe" in astrology because it "works."

There is a correspondence, a parallel, a "connection" between the positions or patterns of the planets and individual, group or international activity. It is, according to Jung, not unscientific thus to observe and believe as a result of that observation without knowing the why, or cause, of such correspondences. Maybe we will never know. Maybe we will. But, in the meantime, it is perfectly valid to label the phenomena as synchronicity.

We now are at the crux of a major problem in astrology: *the why of it.* In the past, some well-meaning practitioners have attempted to explain the "why" with a mixture of reasons, from magnetism to electrical force to atoms and gravity, etc. And reasonably open-minded scientists have been stymied at the very beginning of their probes into the field by these explanations, by their own feeling of a need to know why or how. The need, actually, is to know that the correspondence does exist, between the planets and mundane matters, between planetary positions and human and other earthly actions or reactions. If, in modern astrology, we can get home this point, a huge barrier to investigation by competent scientists will have been removed.

Jung declared: "Astrology would be a large scale example of synchronism, if it had at its disposal thoroughly tested findings. But at least there are some facts adequately tested and fortified by a wealth of statistics which make the astrological problem seem worthy of philosophical investigation."

You may recall the words of Dr. Marshall, who said "Jung would be embarrassed" by my remarks which indicated he had taken a serious interest in astrology!

Jung, in that 1930 Munich address, went on to say:

Astrology is assured of recognition from psychology, without further restrictions, because astrology represents the summation of all the psychological knowledge of antiquity.

The fact that it is possible to construct, in adequate fashion, a person's character from the data of his nativity, shows the relative validity of astrology.

*Whatever is born or done this moment of time, has the qualities of this moment of time.**

What we do, in astrology, is to "freeze" the moment of time by capturing a picture of the heavens at that moment—a picture of the planetary positions as they revolve around the Sun.

* Italics mine.

Later, Jung was to publish *The Interpretation of Nature and the Psyche,* which contained the results of one of his own specific experiments in astrology. He did so by stating, "In writing this paper I have, so to speak, made good a promise which for many years I lacked the courage to fulfill."

Entering these waters does require a hardy temperament. I tell you that and Jung has told you. Yet, I want you to come further with me. For those who do come along, Jung said these words: "Not only is he expected to plunge into regions of human experience which are dark, dubious and hedged about with prejudice, but the intellectual difficulties are such as the treatment and elucidation of so abstract a subject must inevitably entail."*

Jung, explaining his approach, points out that French scientist Paul Flambart compiled a volume on the scientific basis of astrology, including a graph of statistics. Flambart noted the horoscopes of 123 outstandingly intelligent persons, checking their Ascendants—the sign rising at the time they were born. In our section on casting horoscopes, you will learn how to find the Ascendant, which is one of the most important points of the chart. The time of birth is required for discovery of the rising sign, or Ascendant. Definite accumulations were found to occur in the Air signs for the "intelligent persons." The Air signs are Gemini, Libra, Aquarius. The result, Jung explains, was confirmed by 300 additional cases. The research by Flambart was undertaken in 1921 and intrigued Jung. His own astrological experiment was involved with statistics, with chance and probability. He wanted to find out whether the astrological tradition "held up." He used, for the basis of the experiment explained in *The Interpretation of Nature and the Psyche,* the horoscopes of 966 married people—483 "pairs."

To test the astrological technique, to discover whether astrology "worked," he looked for an "absolutely certain and indubitable fact." Once this was found, he would place the "fact" up against the classical claims of astrology. He finally decided that "marriage" was such a fact.

Other obvious facts, he pointed out, would be murder and sui-

---

* In his foreword to *The Interpretation of Nature and the Psyche.*

cide. But Jung chose marriage because data (horoscopes) were more easily available. Jung pointed out that since antiquity, the main traditional astrological correspondence to marriage has been the conjunction of the Sun and Moon, the conjunction of the Moon and Moon, and the conjunction of the Moon with the Ascendant.

This view dates back to Ptolemy, who spoke of three degrees of harmony: the first, when the Sun in the man's horoscope and the Sun or Moon in the woman's chart, or the Moon in both, are trined or sextiled; the second, when the Moon in a man's horoscope and the Sun in a woman's are conjunct; the third, when the one is receptive to the other. Ptolemy said: "Generally speaking, their life together will be long and constant when in the horoscopes of both partners the luminaries (Sun and Moon) are harmoniously constellated." He regarded the conjunction of a masculine Moon with a feminine Sun as particularly favorable for marriage. Thus, according to Ptolemy, men born with the Moon in Aries would do well to seriously consider marriage to a woman born with the Sun in that sign.

Regarding the conjunction and opposition of Mars and Venus, students and astrologers have long known of the physical attraction depicted by these planetary aspects. And Jung was aware of this fact, too. To quote him: "I may say here that these are related to marriage only because the conjunction or opposition of these two planets points to a love relationship, and this may or may not produce a marriage."

With this in mind, Jung confined his astrological experiment in marriage to aspects between the Sun and Moon, the Moon and Moon and the Moon and Ascendant between the horoscopes.

The material (horoscopes) for Jung's research on marriage and astrology was obtained from donors in Zurich, London, Rome and Vienna. He was aided by, and gives credit to Dr. Liliane Frey-Rohn, "for her help with the astrological material."

In all, Jung investigated 483 marriages or 966 horoscopes. He counted all the conjunctions and oppositions between the Sun, Moon, Mars, Venus, the Ascendant and Descendant.

His graphs confirmed the traditional astrological correspondence between marriage and the Moon-Sun aspects. There was little emphasis on the Venus-Mars aspects.

Following the Sun-Moon aspects came the conjunctions (in horoscopes of married persons) between the wife's Ascendant and the man's Venus, and the woman's Moon and the man's Ascendant.

For students, this should provide inspiration for further research. Favorable Sun and Moon aspects between the charts of a man and woman link them strongly and indicate a tendency (other things being equal) for them to marry. On the other hand, Mars-Venus aspects might bring about physical attraction but do not necessarily point to legal marriage.

A man's Ascendant conjunct the Moon in a woman's horoscope, according to Jung's figures, points to marriage, as does a woman's Ascendant conjunct a man's natal Venus position.

Jung's findings bore out classical astrological claims in relation to marriage. The strongest links were the Moon conjunct Moon and the Moon conjunct the Sun in horoscopes of mated persons. His highest percentage showed the Ascendant conjunct the Moon, which is traditionally characteristic of marriage. He points out, too, that this is strange indeed (for those skeptical of astrology's worth) since the Ascendant, together with the Sun and Moon, forms the trinity that determines fate and character.

To quote Jung: " Had one wanted to falsify the statistical findings so as to bring them into line with tradition one could not have done it more successfully."

In attempting to explain "why" astrology works, Jung made note of the fact that magnetic storms occur during the squares and oppositions of the planets. By the same token, clear radio weather is evident when the planets are harmonious: trined and in sextile aspect.

We covered this in the chapter on John Henry Nelson and his work at RCA. Jung concluded that:

The statistical material shows that a practical as well as theoretically improbable chance combination occurred which coincides in the most remarkable way with traditional astrological expectations. That such a coincidence should occur at all is so improbable and so incredible that nobody could have dared to predict anything like it. It really does look as if the statistical material had been manipulated and arranged so as to give the appearance of a positive result.

In fairness to astrologers it should also be pointed out that although these traditional indicators are considered important, they are only a few of the many variables which could point to marriage. The trained astrologer always looks to the gestalt or overall design rather than merely adding up the total of auspicious or inauspicious signs.

Despite Dr. Marshall's claims, it should now be evident that Jung was intensely concerned with astrology. He even had subjects select horoscopes at random and reported some seemingly fantastic results. For example, an emotionally disturbed patient selected charts with Mars aspects dominant. That is the planet which would be expected to coincide with the flush of unchecked emotion, creating impulsive, irresponsible actions. Another patient chose aspects (at random and knowing nothing about astrology) emphasizing the Ascendant and Descendant. Her main problem was to realize and assert her personality in the face of self-suppressive tendencies. The Ascendant and Descendant traditionally are associated with personality, the public, "facing the world."

Yet another patient, whose problem centered about her broken marriage, chose horoscopes at random which, when placed side by side, showed a statistical frequency of Sun-Moon (marriage) aspects!

Of his basic marriage-aspect experiment, Jung declared: "One may be fooled by coincidence, but one has to have a very thick skin not to be impressed by the fact that, out of 50 possibilities, three times precisely those turned up as maxima which are regarded by tradition as typical."

Dr. Marshall, one might be forced to conclude, did possess such a "thick skin" if he was aware of the Jung work. In any case, he certainly wasn't going to be impressed by facts.

XIII

DO NOT CHALLENGE!

Just as Dr. Marshall had assured listeners that Jung had nothing to do with astrology, that RCA made no forecasts of radio weather based on the positions of the planets, that O'Neill had nothing favorable to say about astrology—he also presented us with other assurances, the assurances of the great majority of astronomers. His assurances had found their way into our textbooks, into history classrooms; his "assurances" had behind them the weight of respectability, of the "ins," of those with research grants, those who were in control of the communications media. Such "assurances" were and are dangerous if they are based on false information or no information or plain and fancy academic prejudice.

I dwell on the debate because it is a sum of many debates on the subject: it is symbolic. Since that time, I have discussed, argued and debated astrology with other astronomers and with psychologists—"on the air," in private and in print. I can tell you that the Dr. Marshalls, for the most part, have not changed. Each one compounds the original error. The air hungers to be cleared, and I want it to be clean as you travel farther into astrology. I want the air fresh when you begin interpreting planetary positions, patterns and aspects. This, of course, has nothing to do with criticism of a constructive nature. Admittedly, we need plenty of that—but we can hardly expect it from certain quarters!

One of the other "assurances" was Dr. Marshall's statement that Copernicus never practiced or sanctioned astrology. Yet, here is a quotation from the introduction to the English translation of Ptolemy's *Tetrabiblos,* made by Dr. F. E. Robbins of the University of Michigan and published by Harvard University:

"Regiomontanus, Copernicus, Tycho Brahe, Galileo, Kepler and Leibnitz all either practiced astrology themselves or countenanced its practice."

In trying to arrive at the truth, it is assumed that a scientist will be objective. His mind should be open to facts, no matter where they might lead, toward or away from astrology. One can decide how objective Dr. Marshall was about astrology from the following transcription of his answer to a telephone query from a listener:

LISTENER: Is there any relationship between the attitude of astronomers toward astrology and the attitude of doctors toward psychiatry in its earlier stage?

DR. MARSHALL: I am afraid it is much more deep-seated than that. We do not admit the possibility that astrology will ever amount to anything.

To another question, Dr. Marshall responded: "As long as astrology is legalized anywhere, we are in the childhood of civilization . . . believers in astrology are worshipers at the shrine of seven Babylonian gods."

I pointed out that Don Cameron Allen, in his book *Star Crossed Renaissance,* published by Duke University, reveals that during the Renaissance, evidence shows that the supporters of astrology were the most erudite and thoughtful men of the age. The real quarrel, his scholarly work reveals, centered about the *abuses* of astrology.

Today, it has been made so uncomfortable for men in academic positions to associate themselves in any favorable way with astrology, that the subject usually is covered or hidden under various names. Each year, a greater number of educators in our public school system are including, as a part of the regular instruction in courses in biology and general science, discussions of planetary influences on human and plant life, as well as physical, demonstrable effects on inanimate objects. These discussions are never referred to as having anything to do with astrology.

Many instructors, who matter-of-factly tell of physical phenomena which correspond to the movements of the planets or planetary positions, will vehemently deny the validity of astrology itself. Nevertheless, whatever they choose to call the facts they teach, it is evident that the claims of astrology are being verified daily in classrooms throughout the world.

The most common facts taught are the relationship between the Moon and the tides of the ocean; expansion and contraction of pipes during various phases of the Moon; effects of the Full Moon on mentally deranged persons; the Moon's effect on cats, dogs and other animals; the necessity of the Sun for the continuance of life; and the effect of the planets on electromagnetically controlled forces in the earth.

Astrology is also discussed in history and English classrooms. Shakespeare's works contain many references; and, of course, the history of the ancients is filled with astrology.

Despite those who would prefer to stifle knowledge, rather than admit they could have been mistaken, the subject of planetary correspondences to mundane affairs is kept alive in classrooms.

It is also true that many advances made in astronomy were for the original purpose of making astrological calculations easier, more accurate. I stated this during the debate, but Dr. Marshall again contradicted me.

XIV

HOW IT ENDED

Dr. Marshall was recognized as an astronomer who spoke and wrote with the authority which supposedly came from knowledge. That's why it was important that I did challenge his statements about astrology. Because he was so highly regarded, I use the debate with him as a symbol for numerous exciting and revealing clashes of opinion. Perhaps never before has this kind of clash been presented in a book on astrology.

The debate, as it gathered steam, exploded and ran over into many areas. It had a hypnotic effect on listeners. People began arriving at the WPEN studio. Students, lawyers, physicians, astrologers, astronomers, psychologists—people from all walks of life— came in person, telephoned, sent wires or wrote letters. Frank Ford was now trying to be as objective as it was possible for him to be: he was astounded. He had expected Dr. Marshall to demolish the astrological argument inside of 15 minutes, a half hour at the most. Miss Gemini was delighted, for she could observe the look on the face of the engineer: fascination, admiration, sheer joy from listening instead of merely "putting in his time." And Miss Gemini also noted that Dr. Marshall, once again, had loosened his tie. This had become a psychological tip-off. He wasn't happy with the way things were going. Later, he was to indicate, to press the point that, "I wasn't, I'm sure, attacking 'your kind' of astrology." But for now, he was attacking, shouting, emphasizing that he was an authority in his field and that I dare not contradict him, especially where the historical facts concerning astronomy were concerned.

I stated that an astronomer, Joseph Dalton, had created the

famed *Dalton Table of Houses,* specifically for the purpose of helping astrologers to cast horoscopes accurately. Dr. Marshall quickly interrupted, saying he had never heard of an astronomer by that name. His tone indicated that no astronomer by the name of Joseph Dalton had existed.

Here are the facts, however. Most book stores which sell astrological texts and supplies carry the *Dalton Table of Houses.* Furthermore, Joseph Dalton *was* an astronomer. At one time he was associated with the U.S. Naval Observatory. He made an extensive study of astrology, creating the Table of Houses which bears his name, so that horoscopes could be set up more easily.

Dr. Marshall denied that such great astronomers as Ptolemy, Flamstead, Galileo, Kepler, Brahe and Copernicus were favorably inclined toward astrology. Later, he contradicted himself by admitting that Tycho Brahe was an astrologer as well as an astronomer. This is the way he put it: "Astrology was almost banished from the ranks of astronomy except for a guy named Tycho Brahe up in Denmark."

Actually, the "guy" Dr. Marshall referred to was one of the most brilliant astronomers of the 16th Century. He is considered never to have been equaled as a practical astronomer. As an astrologer, he foretold that in the North, in Finland, there would be born a prince who would lay waste to Germany and vanish in 1632. Gustavus Adolphus, king of Sweden, was born in Finland and overcame Germany; when he was killed, in 1632, in the battle of Leutzen, his body was never found. Brahe was a professor of both astrology and astronomy at the time of his death.

Now we were certainly, if not before, clashing on Dr. Marshall's own territory: talking about astronomers. Like many of his colleagues, Dr. Marshall seemed actually to believe the distortions in some of our current textbooks on the history of science—distortions originally encouraged by astronomers to cover up the fact that their most illustrious predecessors were astrologers and that their interest in astronomy, in the first place, was inspired by a desire to gain greater knowledge about astrology.

Dr. Marshall *must* have known better. Yet he laughed off the possibility that I might be stating the truth in declaring that Johannes Kepler, discoverer of "Kepler's Laws" of motion in orbits, believed in astrology. He used the astronomer's standby, saying that Kepler called astrology the "silly sister of astronomy." But Kepler wrote many astrological works, and he said: "An unfailing experience of mundane events in harmony with the changes occurring in the heavens has instructed and compelled my unwilling belief." He corresponded for two years with Tycho Brahe. In 1600, he went to Prague to continue his work. He completed the "Rudolphine Tables," which Brahe had begun and had named in honor of the Emperor Rudolf, tables primarily for the use of astrologers. He made predictions based on the horoscope of Wallenstein. The original manuscript of his work on Wallenstein's chart has been preserved in the University of St. Petersburg and shows that his forecasts on the life and death of that general were fulfilled with a great degree of accuracy.

Dr. Marshall denied that Sir Isaac Newton was predisposed toward astrology. He also denied that Pythagoras had anything to do with astrology. Pythagoras' interest, not only in astrology, but in the possibility of utilizing numbers for divinatory purposes, is too well known to even argue about—but apparently Dr. Marshall didn't know, or didn't think it was convenient to admit this fact. As for Newton, when entering Cambridge, he said he wanted to study mathematics "because I wish to test Judicial Astrology." Eventually Newton became, as writer Joseph Goodavage pointed out in his brilliant article, "The First Science,"* primarily an astrologer.

John Flamstead, who was the first astronomer-royal, erected a horoscope for the "birth" of Greenwich Observatory, choosing the moment, the "birth," the time for the laying of the foundation stone. His horoscope of the observatory remains there on display.

Galileo, at the birth of each of his children, cast their horoscopes. And a study of his life will reveal that he was consulted by many of his colleagues, friends, and relatives, for interpretations of their charts. Galileo wrote much on the subject of astrology under a pen-name. As Goodavage has stated, astrology was the life work

* *Analog Magazine,* September 1962 issue, The Condé Nast Publications, New York.

of Kepler. He worked on his astronomical laws in order to sharpen the accuracy of his astrological predictions. Newton's tremendous devotion to astrology and the question of planetary "influences" sparked his investigation of light and gravity. These things are so, despite the efforts of those who would tell us that Benjamin Franklin's library books were on astronomy, when actually he was basically interested in astrology; despite "authoritative" texts which tell us only that Copernicus, Galileo, Brahe, Kepler, Newton, Flamstead, Pythagoras were astronomers, when primarily they were concerned with astrology—they are so despite the efforts of the "child," astronomy, to deny the "father," astrology. These are facts: RCA and astrology, Jung and astrology, O'Neill (the only science writer ever to receive a Pulitzer Prize) and astrology—facts they are, much to the discomfort of those who have, through these many years, successfully confined astrology to the scientific doghouse.

Be prepared for this type of experience as you progress, as your interest deepens, as you become an astrologer. That is why we have presented the debate with Dr. Marshall—not only as a springboard, enabling us to cover more fully the subjects argued about, but so that you will be better prepared when astrology—which I hope you come to love—is attacked by those who know so very little about it.

If you are interested in astrology, you certainly are not alone. Your interest in this controversial, fascinating, enduring subject is shared by hundreds of thousands of persons the world over. Astrology does represent a universal language, just as do music and mathematics. The symbols are universal: ancient alphabets were derived from those symbols—our current language is filled with astrological terms: disaster, ill-starred, saturnine, mercurial, moon-faced, Saturday, Sunday, Monday; the list can be extended and has been in numerous works. Most of us have at least some idea of the universally recognized characteristics of the zodiacal signs, from Aries the Ram to Pisces the Fish. Fewer, perhaps, have knowledge of the planets and their symbolic meanings. But many do, and almost everyone would like to know more about his own birthdate, his own horoscope.

The debate finally drew to a close—while the telephones jangled and the telegrams continued to arrive—and while Frank Ford graciously thanked Dr. Marshall for appearing, and also, changing his tone, marveled at my ability to so defend astrology. He closed the debate in this way:

FRANK FORD: Ladies and gentlemen, I'm sorry we don't have another three hours to go into this subject more fully. I want to express my sincere and deep thanks to both Dr. Roy K. Marshall and Sydney Omarr. Both gentlemen are sincere in their beliefs, and both have given us a great deal of their valuable time—from 11:30, when we started this discussion, until now. That's three long hours, and they've not received any fee. They have done this out of a feeling of public service and to straighten out this matter in the minds of many people. We are very grateful to both of them.

But, as we know, Ford wasn't "grateful" enough to live up to his agreement: that of having the O'Neill reply—whether favorable to Dr. Marshall or to my arguments—read over the air. Thus, listeners never had the opportunity of discovering just what O'Neill did have to say.

Nevertheless, I want to be fair. I am going to present Dr. Marshall's reply to O'Neill's letter. He denied receiving a copy and finally I had to show him the original. I hoped that Dr. Marshall might use his influence, which was considerable, to get the O'Neill letter read, even though it was not favorable to his cause. You see, being a Leo, I tend to be idealistic. Perhaps I should have known better! I was a man about to be vindicated. I was bursting with it. I wanted the letter read, heard, studied, responded to; I wanted a promise, apparently made in good faith before thousands of listeners, kept. It wasn't. But, as we know, the O'Neill letter has, with and without my permission, been printed around the world. Never before, however, has the actual debate been reported in this detail—I venture to predict, with publication of this book, that the details also will find their way to many quarters, both friendly and otherwise.

O'Neill stated clearly he was sending a copy of his letter to Dr. Marshall. Days passed, with no response from the doctor. The station said "nothing doing" on having it read. On August 10, I called Dr. Marshall. To my amazement, he claimed that he had not been sent a copy. I said I would immediately send him my personal copy, which he promised to return. He kept that promise! During our telephone conversation, Dr. Marshall appeared to be a different man. He was friendly. He said I did a good job. He said the kind of astrology I talked about was not the astrology he was attacking. I told him that maybe, with more study on his part and a better idea of what astrology really was, he would become one of our champions. I expected a laugh. There was silence until he said, "I'll be waiting for the letter."

That night I delivered it to the television studios of WPTZ, where the doctor was filming a commercial on the scientific wonders of some product or other. I left the letter and, finally, in a letter dated August 24, 1951, Dr. Marshall replied. I had informed him that I wanted his letter to be "on the record," just as the O'Neill letter was written with the understanding that I would be free to reprint it, to broadcast it. I want you to decide for yourself about Dr. Marshall's reply. In my opinion, it is well written to serve his purpose. Here it is:

Dear Mr. Omarr:

I'm sorry that I have not been able earlier to write this letter. Wednesday night I had to drive to Princeton, and from there on up to New York. . . . I hope this morning to write this and this afternoon to deliver it to your home, if complications of several hours of paper work and two television shows do not prevent it.

I have read J. J. O'Neill's letter with considerable interest and, I must confess, with some amazement. The latter response is provoked by the information in the letter that there is an American astronomer who is unsung as such. By this time I should have become inured to claims to the designation "astronomer" by anyone who has read a book, but somehow I never thought that a science writer would call himself an astronomer, and speak casually of spending time with his telescope. Particularly, it is startling when he then takes off into a defense or even a furthering of belief in astrology. It is undoubtedly a case of "a little knowledge." So it has been with civilizations; the beginnings have been saddled with all manner of superstitious beliefs;

as they become older, they have put away childish things. With decadence of established religion and with established moral concepts, beliefs in superstitions have increased. The growth of civilization in any land has been accompanied by, if not the result of, an abandonment of beliefs in mysterious forces; name the backward countries of the world, and you have named those where belief in witchcraft, astrology and other esoteric philosophies are most strongly entrenched. Need I cite India, China and Africa?

It appears, from your remarks and those of O'Neill, that astronomers once more must seek a new name for their science. They abandoned the name astrology, which is etymologically the correct one, to divorce themselves from any notion of the stuff of which astrology is made. Now, you wish to take over cosmic rays, corpuscular and energy radiation in general, and the law of gravitation. You're crowding us! I don't want to be misinterpreted in what I say here, but this is it: I can't help being reminded of the way in which Communists have moved into labor unions and some genuinely liberal movements, and have given them the kiss of death.

It poses the very important matter of the responsibility of astrologers to the people of the world. There should be a clear-cut statement from your kind of astrologer to the effect that the prognosticators and the weekly-horoscope vendors are charlatans. If astrology no longer includes this kind of stuff, it is the very strong responsibility of the astrologers to denounce it, because this is the vicious stuff that astronomers wish to get out of our civilization.

Frankly, O'Neill's letter contains nothing very concrete except the notion that he apparently wants to lump a lot of what is known as astronomy into what is generally known as astrology. He falls into the fallacy of saying and hoping that others will believe him, when he says tests are not made. Many have been made, that have utterly denied the statements of astrologers, when it has been possible to arrive at any statements upon which two or more astrologers can be found to agree. The American Association of Scientific Workers, as recently as 1941, gave up further investigation when they found that every test that could be applied to some of the generalities of astrologers showed nothing that would support such generalizations. I recall in particular the finding that fewest musicians are born under the sign of Libra, contrary to the beliefs of a considerable body of astrologers, which were to the effect that Libra produces most musicians. To disprove such statements, when they are made with absolutely no evidence and no reason, becomes a task in which more people than all the astronomers and all the astrologers combined would be needed. One does not disprove statements; if he is honest, he does not make them unless he has some reason for doing so, and no astrologer can advance proof of any of his statements. He uses always isolated examples, and proof by example alone has never been accepted as scientific proof. The challenge that is made to the astronomer, to disprove astrology, makes as much sense as the original advancement of astrological generalities. This is, of course, the kind of astrology which (I believe) you deplore. Then denounce it in some real organ of information, so it will be read from coast to coast by the people who don't know that even the astrologers now denounce what has been called astrology.

You can win on your point that John J. O'Neill made the statement attributed to him. After reading his letter, and after speaking with some astronomers who talked with him at the recent meeting of the American Astronomical Society, which he attended as a science writer, I can say only that it is a good thing that he has not peddled the stuff in his column, or the *Herald-Tribune* would have had a new science writer long since! There appears to be considerable confusion about what constitutes astrology. That confusion is not the making of the astronomer, but I am beginning to wonder if it is not a studied action on the part of astrologers, not to purify themselves, but to get admissions that part of what they talk about is fact, therefore all of what they talk about is fact. It is a well-known device, particularly in modern times. It still does not prove anything, but rather perpetuates misbegotten and best forgotten traces of childhood of the human race.

Thank whatever there is in man that makes him say, in the vast majority, "I am the Master of my Fate, I am the Captain of my Soul." I personally am very happy to make or break my own career; I would dislike very much having the planets telling me what I should do. In my stubborn ignorance, you see, I could never restrain my desires to nudge the planets back a little, and that is quite impossible. But I can tell the planets what they are going to do, and they will do it. Should I then say that I control the planets? That's the basis for a new psuedo-science, but I hope that civilization is too far advanced for me or anyone else to put the idea across.

Yours very truly,
ROY K. MARSHALL

Well, from the foregoing letter, it is obvious that Dr. Marshall changed his tone, if not his opinion. If only, when the debate was raging, he had stated it was his opinion he was putting forth, not facts derived from study and knowledge. When O'Neill's name came up during the debate, he was Dr. Marshall's dear friend and lodge brother—a very eminent man whose opinion deserved respect. When O'Neill does not back up the doctor's opinion, he is no longer eminent and the doctor casts black clouds of suspicion upon his standing, his ability to think and understand. Astrologers, of course, never claimed that the majority of Librans would be musicians: what they do state is that Venus, the planet associated with Libra, is often found to be prominent in the horoscopes of musicians.

The report of the American Association of Scientific Workers, to which Dr. Marshall refers, was not scientific at all and was, as a matter of fact, so ridiculous that the late Paul G. Clancy, editor and publisher of *American Astrology* magazine, gleefully answered it point by point and sent out free copies of it to all who made a request for one.

We know, despite Dr. Marshall's plea of ignorance on the matter, that tests have been conducted, with the results favorable to astrology: we talked about Jung and one such test. There are others and we will go into some of them, including a major experiment which should finally disprove Dr. Marshall's statement that astrologers do not agree on principles of interpretation. Read his letter; compare it to the O'Neill letter. Check his letter again and again, for his statements are not based on fact.

The debate was over. Gemini had filled her tablets with notes. Frank Ford and Dr. Marshall remained in the studio, while Gemini and I left, joined by many who had crowded the studio to watch and listen. We finally walked over to the Pen and Pencil Club—later Frank Ford showed up, without Dr. Marshall, and sat at another table, away from us. I recalled that many years ago, after the eighth-grade science teacher had unwittingly sparked my interest and I had used every spare dime to buy books on astrology, I had called the Fels Planetarium one evening. Dr. Marshall, the truth being stranger than fiction, had answered. I asked, as an eager student, what astronomers thought of astrology. Need I say he was very discouraging? I protested, "But I have so many books—I'm so interested . . ."

"For your own good," he had replied, "throw out the books—they're filled with nonsense."

And I sat in my room for a long time after that, looking not only at the books, but at the astrological magazines, the articles which I had read. I considered, for a moment, the proposal which had been made: to get rid of the whole lot. But the moment passed. When one is sixteen, and is told by "authority" that he is studying "junk," one is bound to be depressed. I took a closer look, turning pages, seeing familiar names: Grant Lewi, Evangeline Adams, Dr. Sidney K. Bennett (Wynn), Carl Payne Tobey, Paul G. Clancy—and I knew that "authority," this night, like that eighth-grade science teacher, had not spoken the truth.

I knew it, too, as I sat nursing a drink at the Pen and Pencil. I had not remembered, until then, that long-ago telephone conversation. It didn't last long—five minutes at the most. He was as sure of himself then as he had sounded only an hour or so ago.

At this moment I read the pages of the introduction to the newest edition of *Heaven Knows What,* remembering how wide-eyed I was when I first made the purchase so many years ago, in Atlantic City, where I also was to meet Miss Gemini, who became so great a friend of astrology, who was to utilize its principles in her public school classrooms, and who, eventually, perhaps ironically, was to marry an *astronomer,* whom she laughingly described as "nothing like most of them."

XV

A STRANGE CASE:
THE DR. BOK AFFAIR

There are points raised in Dr. Marshall's letter which require answering. The report of the American Association of Scientific Workers was issued by Harvard University astronomer Dr. Bart J. Bok. It might be well, at this point, to recall that in the 1890's another report was issued by Harvard College Observatory. It stated flatly that no heavier-than-air machine would ever fly. I insert the note here, not in the form of ridicule, but to show that scientists, like all of us, do make mistakes. Those in "authority" can be and have been wrong. Not only about astrology, but about numerous subjects, including "flying machines." Of course it would be ridiculous for Harvard scientists now to refuse to admit their original error. We know that heavier-than-air machines can fly from the ground and from continent to continent. Scientists, in this case, admit they were mistaken. But, narrowing our focus to astrology, we do not find such ready admissions. Scientists stated there was nothing to astrology. The majority, even today in the light of Jung's work and the work at RCA, have not publicly admitted even the possibility of error.

Those who would like to wash their hands of this kind of stubborn clinging to ignorance are afraid to do so. One of the major fears is economic loss. They could lose their jobs, be laughed out of the academic community, ridiculed to the extent that opportunity for promotion and advancement would be drastically limited.

Dr. Bok was used by his colleagues for the purpose of making speeches against astrology. In preparing his report, he interviewed those with obvious prejudice against astrology. In his report, he sounded like one who knew his subject—at least he sounded or "read" that way to those who were completely dependent upon the report for their information on the subject. His "report" was a case of knocking down a straw man. He couldn't be expected to draw a favorable conclusion. That wasn't what he started out to do. And, as it turned out, he completed his mission in the manner in which it was supposed to be completed.

But something happened after that Bok report was published. It is a rather pathetic story. But it is a true one, which needs the light of public knowledge.

On November 22, 1941, Dr. Bok addressed a meeting of Junior Astronomers at Roosevelt Memorial Hall in New York City. As was his custom in those days, he was going to talk about the fallacy of astrology.

It was a startled Dr. Bok, that evening, who faced not only Junior Astronomers, but numerous astrologers. They included Ernest A. Grant, then executive secretary of the American Federation of Scientific Astrologers (now known by the shorter title, American Federation of Astrologers); Edward A. Wagner, current editor of *Horoscope* Magazine; Carl Payne Tobey and other leading astrologers and publishers of astrological literature, along with the president and vice–president of the Astrologers' Guild of America.

Dr. Bok did not, to his credit, try to hide the fact that he was not only surprised, but unprepared to attack the subject according to his original plan. The astrologers had a stenographer present. The proceedings were recorded.

In effect, Dr. Bok threw away his prepared talk. What followed was an exciting, stimulating exchange of ideas—of promises of co-operation in the future. The audience seemed to sense this as a dramatic time, an historic occasion—when two forces, long opposed, were finally getting together for the benefit of both sides, and for the greater benefit of the public in general.

The tone of the meeting was underlined by Dr. Bok's closing remark, in which he said: "I would like to call on all of you to take an intelligent interest in astrology, not discard it, but to go further, try to study it and encourage further examination."

A special bulletin, issued by the American Federation of Scientific Astrologers on December 1, 1941, headed the Dr. Bok talk, with the Junior Astronomers and astrologers present, "A Milestone in the Modern History of Astrology and Astronomy."

Dr. Bok, in the beginning of his talk, said this:

. . . Ever since the days I was in high school in Holland I have always had a kind of guilty conscience about astrology; so early in the game, looking through the books of astrology, studying through the books—I found out how the astrological theory worked. I tried to examine it carefully and have kept it up quite awhile—and with never anything in mind to do anything special about it. As time marched on and I have come to Harvard, I have developed what I might call a guilty social conscience. As a scientist, you are much better off if you live in the well-known ivory tower and don't bother about anything at all. As you know, the attitude of astronomers has always been to ignore astrology completely. For awhile, it was so that you weren't supposed to mention it and if you did, they put you rather as an outcast in the scene.

As you know, astronomers have generally disapproved of it but the disapproval has not been in all cases. There are a number of astronomers—I would say about 15 to 20 per cent—who are pretty well acquainted with the premises of astrology, who have studied it, and have given their considered opinion. The rest of them have vague feelings about it but perhaps no really exact information.

The Harvard astronomer continued along these lines, saying he was pleased that astrologers were present. He said he was not only familiar with the fine statistical work in astrology performed by Tobey, but had actually brought along two of Tobey's reports. He told his audience, in effect, that it was foolish to carry on this endless battle between astrologers and astronomers. The astrologers were delighted. Dr. Bok, despite his "Bok Report" on astrology, sounded like a reasonable man. He said:

If we could get together a committee of six or seven people, half of them astrologers and half of them scientists; presumably take an astronomer or so, perhaps a physicist, perhaps a psychologist—that type of setup—I think you ought to have more than one astronomer because physicists and psychologists are notoriously dumb when it comes to the motion of the planets—could that kind of committee be gotten together? If that committee could agree on a program for research, that would be the program for the "Astrological Research Foundation."

The astrologers, presumably, could suggest along which lines to do it. If they would meet, with good faith, with the astronomers, I am quite sure that a group like that could come to a sensible, direct, straight-forward program of testing. I think a program could be probably best carried out along the lines Mr. Tobey is suggesting and is working upon in his present Bureau of Astrological Statistics. If that type of thing could be done, I would say that it would be up to the astrologers to do the work on it, to see to it that the analysis gets done, for it is definitely their function.

Dr. Bok, with a happy expression on his face, said this day could well mark the beginning of co-operation between astrologers and astronomers.

The Harvard astronomer, facing leading astrologers, was really letting loose. He had talked about having a "guilty conscience" concerning astrology. Now he added:

I think that it has been fortunate that, as an astronomer, we have finally got around to doing something about astrology, even though we have perhaps stuck our neck out and, in part, made errors of judgment. I think the atmosphere is beginning to clear and from the letters I have already received from several of the astrologers—it is quite clear that also from the astrological side we may come to something constructive and something that will be for the good of all concerned.

I can tell you that whatever we do, we ought to do it from both sides in one spirit and that is what we are all after and searching for—Truth. I believe that several of the people who believe in astrology are on the wrong track. But they believe I am just as much on the wrong track. Mr. Grant told me that a moment ago. That is all right. We may believe that, but the important thing is we don't let it go at that but go further. . . .

I would like to call on all of you to take an intelligent interest in astrology, not discard it, but to go further, try to study it and encourage further examination.

But this, as we shall see, was not to be. It is true Bok went "further." He went all the way back to Australia after his colleagues received word of his "dangerous" words. We'll come to that part of this rather amazing story, which is documented, the documents being not only in my personal library but also on file at the headquarters of the American Federation of Astrologers in Washington.

The meeting was then thrown open to questions. A Junior Astronomer put forth this one:

Dr. Bok, I think concerning astrology that you would have to take into consideration that everybody has been born into the world and naturally has a fortune—not quite a fortune—to show for them by astrology. And that you would also have to consider, I should think— the fortune. Is it accepted by the astrologers that all living things have a fortune, should I say; I don't know any other word for it, but is that so?

Dr. Bok: As far as I have been able to understand it, I think the astrologers could better answer that. I would rather like to, if possible, have Mr. Grant have an opportunity to speak briefly at this time and he could very easily answer that for us.

Ernest Grant: I am the executive secretary of the American Federation of Scientific Astrologers. The president, Mr. George J. McCormack, is also here. I told Dr. Bok, before this meeting, that we were "friendly enemies." Of course, anything that I may say, Dr. Bok, please do not consider it in the personal sense. An astrologer, in dealing with a horoscope, learns to deal impersonally with it, if he is a sincere astrologer.

Answering this lad's question: No sincere astrologer that I have ever met is a fatalist and believes that your life is predetermined or your fortune is set. You are the master of your own destiny, but you are a part of the Solar system; just as truly as the earth is a part of the Solar system. As a consequence, you are subject to the laws of the Solar system; and the true astrologer attempts to determine what those laws are and adjust himself to be in harmony with those laws.

I am very glad to note, Dr. Bok, that you have changed many of your opinions, apparently, since the publication of your report, because aside from many of the platitudes which you have uttered, some of the views you have expressed seem to contradict those that were in the report, unless I am mistaken.

I just jotted down a few notes and I want to refer to them, if I may, in a sort of a questioning way, friendly. You said: "No astronomer, no recognized astronomer in the world today takes stock of the predictions of astrology." Well, of course I don't know just what you mean by the word "predictions." You, yourself, make predictions as an astronomer. You predict the time of an eclipse, for example. The weatherman predicts the weather for tomorrow. Now, the astrologer predicts the nature of an influence that may be operating at a given time, predicated upon experience of similar configurations of the [celestial] bodies, particularly in the Solar system.

The American Federation of Scientific Astrologers includes in its membership a recognized astronomer who was a teacher of physics and mathematics in one of the highest institutions of learning in the world: Dr. Kuno Foelsch. So there is at least one astronomer whose name I can mention to you who accepts astrology—[he] has written on the subject and is a member of our organization today.

I might also say that I personally know of other astronomers whose names you are familiar with, who accept astrology. Please understand, I do not *believe* in astrology. I know it is a fact because I have tested it. I have proven it and had I known when I came here this evening that you would have known the time of your own birth as accurately as you did, it would have given me a great deal of pleasure to have cast your chart and to have interpreted it here.

(Laughter)

ERNEST GRANT (continuing): Now, you referred to the decadence of astrology in Greece. Hippocrates, the father of medicine, is reported to have said that the man who attempts to practice medicine without a knowledge of astrology is a fool. Well, I think you make a mistake as a scientist if you always look to the works of astrologers to find astrological truths. If you will read Dr. Peterson's massive works—seven large volumes, I believe—the head of the School of Pathology of the University of Illinois, on the influence of weather upon health, I think you will be utterly amazed at the amount of astrology that you will find; and his attempt to direct modern medicine back to Hippocrates and astrology, although he doesn't use the word "astrology" throughout his entire works.

Then, too, I think you will agree with me that Dr. Harlan Stetson is a recognized scientist. Do you accept him as such?

DR. BOK: Yes.

GRANT: Now, several years ago, *Time* Magazine carried an article in which it quoted a definition that Dr. Stetson gave to what he calls "Cosmecology." And I think if you will check that with the definition of astrology as laid down by your predecessor, Ptolemy, you will be amazed at the similarity in the definition that Ptolemy, in the *Tetrabiblos,* gives to astrology and that which *Time* Magazine records as Dr. Stetson's definition of Cosmecology.

Now, you have made mention and laid much emphasis upon the differences between astrologers. My, what an emphasis I could lay upon the differences between astronomers! Yet, I do not decry astronomy as not being scientific because there are differences of opinion. Differences of opinion are the very essence of progress in thought.

Then you decry that there are no workable causes; there is an unknown mechanism. What is the mechanism of gravity? Who knows? Yet you accept it as a fact; at least, I presume you do. What is the mechanism of cancer in the human system—the disease? We know it is a fact but medical science strived for ages to find the mechanism that causes it. Now, if I wanted to be philosophical, if I wanted to add the philosophical tinge which isn't strictly scientific from the materialistic viewpoint, I might say that the whole heavens is the omniscience and omnipotence of the creative force of the universe in effect. I don't personally claim that any planet has one iota of influence upon you, any more than the clock on the wall has any influence on the time of day, but it is the indicator of an influence, and I can demonstrate in the life of any person, if I have the required data.

And so the meeting continued. With questions and answers, discussion and debate—with the general tone, set by Dr. Bok, being one of "let's co-operate in the future."

But word soon reached Harvard and there was hell to pay! Had Dr. Bok taken leave of his senses? Had the astrologers threatened him, maybe even drugged him—and in front of all those Junior Astronomers, too? Maybe the good doctor had been brainwashed?

Something now had to be done. But, what? *What!* That was the moaning, beseeching question. Why were the astronomers so upset? That, of course, is part of the over-all question, perhaps a psychological one. Dr. Bok had simply put forth an attitude of co-operation. Yet, this could not be. It wasn't supposed to be this way. This could not be allowed to get out. It would be just simply awful if those nasty astrologers printed Dr. Bok's talk. What would people think? It was bad enough when, every so often, people listening to an astronomer lecturing in a planetarium, came up, after the lecture, to question him about the zodiacal signs, to ask him under which signs they were born. But, now, to have this happen! Unthinkable! Why couldn't astrology, keeping a stiff upper lip, simply lie down and allow itself to be buried? Wouldn't that be the gentlemanly thing to do? To the devil with the facts!

But it didn't take long for cooler heads to dominate. The first thing was to make sure Dr. Bok's talk was not distributed. A representative was sent to call on all of the astrology magazine editors. The editors were told that if they published Dr. Bok's speech, they would be sued. But the talk was published by the American Federation of Scientific Astrologers. No suit resulted. Tobey privately published the speech and distributed it to his many students in various states and overseas—and dared Harvard to sue. He wasn't sued. *Sky Magazine,* a publication for astronomers, also published Dr. Bok's speech. Only there was something wrong. The magazine published the talk Dr. Bok was *scheduled* to give, the one he threw away. *Sky Magazine* published an attack on astrology, originally intended by Dr. Bok, but said not one single word about the actual speech he delivered.

Dr. Bok, in the report referred to by Dr. Marshall in his letter, made specific reference to a survey made by Paul R. Farnsworth on the sign Libra. Farnsworth stated, "Books on astrology are none too clearly written. Authors do not come out squarely in saying just which is the most musical sign. Yet, they do agree fairly well in classifying Libra as the sign under which prospective musicians are most apt to be born." Then, as we know, Farnsworth said he found fewer musicians born under that sign than under any other zodiacal group. But Ralph Schaffer, an astrological researcher, decided to check. He found that of all textbooks extant at the time the experiment was undertaken, Libra was *not* mentioned by any author as the sign under which musicians are most likely to be born! As we stated, the indications are that Venus (the planet associated with Libra) is prominent in the horoscopes of musicians. It would seem, as editor Paul Clancy stated at the time, that the Bok report was anything but scientific, and merely another example of the straw man which astronomers delight in knocking down.

As Marcia Moore states in her study, *Astrology Today,* "Ideally a test of astrology should take into consideration all the many factors involved in a single horoscope. But that is to say it must also be a test of astrologers, since only the human mind can effect such a synthesis." She then spotlights an experiment which did fulfill those conditions. It was carried out by Vernon Clark, a practicing psychologist, who asked twenty astrologers, in different parts of the country and world, to match ten horoscopes (five male and five female) with ten brief case histories, describing the subject's marriage, health and children. The astrologers were asked to arrange each set of five charts in order from the most likely to correspond to the case history under consideration. A control group of twenty psychologists tried the same thing, and the project was proctored by two other psychologists. The statistics were compiled by a professional statistician. The results? They showed that sixteen of the twenty astrologers predicted better-than-chance in the over-all sense.

Psychologist Clark concluded: "These results would seem to suggest that astrologers, using only the horoscope—that is, a geo-centric map of the Solar system as it appears at the moment of birth—can make better-than-chance identification of individuals and at a high level of confidence. It demonstrated that astrologers in performing this task, have exhibited a clear and unmistakable tendency to move in the direction of correct judgment.

"The experiment tells us nothing about the manner in which the astrologers have made use of the horoscopes or the techniques which they have applied to them. It does infer, and quite strongly, that such a technique exists and is worthy of the study of scientists in every field, especially psychology."

Is it any wonder that, at times, those of us in this field get a bit discouraged? That we are skeptical about the intentions of astronomers who claim they really have investigated the subject and now want to speak out about it? I have, on many occasions, debated with astronomers over radio and television—and I can assure you that they have never presented any facts to back up their claims against the subject.

But, first, let us complete the strange saga of the Dr. Bok affair.

After the meeting of Junior Astronomers in New York City there was plenty of havoc, as we know, in Harvard circles generally, and among astronomers specifically. The wrath was turned toward Dr. Bok for his "fantastic" statements regarding co-operation in connection with astrological research. The pressure was applied.

In a letter addressed to "The Astrologers present at the meeting of November 22," Dr. Bok wrote the following words (dated December 2, 1941):

When I came to New York on November 22 for a lecture to the Junior Astronomy Club, I had no idea that I was to address an audience in which the leading astrologers of the nation would be present. I had made some notes for the lecture, but after my return to Cambridge it seemed advisable that I write these down in some detail. I have asked Mr. Rothschild, of the Junior Astronomy Club, to send each of you a copy of this summary. It represents my considered opinion and I would appreciate it if you would quote me from the summary only.

There is one point on which the summary puts a somewhat different emphasis than which I gave in my talk. As Mr. Grant pointed out, we are "friendly enemies" and such we shall probably remain for quite a while. In view of this it seems that I would make a mistake in associating myself closely with astrologers. I shall, therefore, not wish to write directly for publication in any astrological magazine, simply because the "enemy" aspect might be too easily forgotten or misconstrued.

I am interested in seeing tests made of astrological predictions of various kinds. As far as I am personally concerned, I shall be glad to look as carefully as time permits into such analyses as may be presented, but for the same reason that I have given above, I shall prefer not to join a committee with astrologers among its members.

I believe that by doing this we shall be able to keep the issues between you and me clearly drawn.

I am glad that I have had an opportunity to meet several of you personally.

Very sincerely yours,

BART J. BOK

The summary of the talk, stressed in the letter by Dr. Bok, was only an apology for what he actually said, for what occurred, for the promises he made, for the expectations he expressed regarding greater harmony and co-operation between astronomers and astrologers.

After receipt of Dr. Bok's letter and "summary" of his November 22 lecture, Ernest Grant wrote him as follows, in a letter dated December 13, 1941:

My dear Doctor Bok:

I have received a copy of your letter of December 2, addressed to the "Astrologers present at the meeting of November 22," together with your "Summary of a Lecture before the Junior Astronomy Club."

Frankly, I am stunned at its content. In comparing it with a stenographic transcript of all that was actually said, it is difficult for me to understand your reversal from the attitude you presented in your discourse. I have commended many of the things you recommended to my astrological friends and have indicated to them my belief, that aside from their previous experiences they need have no fears that evidence which they might make available would be misused. What am I to say to them in the light of this communication?

At the time of your lecture, you made no request for withholding quotations from the address you delivered. Now, almost four weeks later, comes your request to quote you only from the summary. I'm afraid it arrives too late, for the actual address has been quoted widely.

Please let me know what has caused this change in your viewpoint.

Sincerely and cordially,

ERNEST A. GRANT

So, for all practical purposes, ended the affair of Dr. Bart J. Bok.

XVI

ASTROLOGY AND LITERATURE

I have stated often, as did the late John J. O'Neill, that astrology is a rich treasure-vein of knowledge. Our very language, the words we use, can be traced to astrology, to the planets, to man's attempt to find his place in the universe by correlating his activities, personal cycles with the ever-changing planetary patterns. Being a writer and being interested in the language and in what has been created by great writers, this particular aspect holds great interest for me. Others have made some remarkably complete studies. I have made some small contribution in the study of one modern writer and the use of astrology in his works. I think it important for all students and astrologers to be aware of this phase of the subject; awareness, I believe, leads to greater understanding, to dimension, growth. It is just as unwise for astrologers to be limited as it is for those orthodox individuals who constantly take pop-shots at the subject. We must, in other words, not compound the errors of our opposition.

An important part of my reason for writing this book is not only to provide ammunition against the opposition, but also to broaden the knowledge of astrologers—to spark their interest, to enable them to go further, to grow, to be aware and enlightened. Thus, let me share with you some of the adventure that comes with a greater awareness of the tremendous role astrology has played in our language, our literature, our culture which, to a large extent, is derived from the writings of the great.

There are, to my knowlege, three major works in this area. My own book on the subject—*Henry Miller: His World of Urania*—might be said to constitute a fourth. But let us leave that until later, for it is the latest work. The first one is *The Medieval Attitude Toward Astrology* (particularly in England), by Theodore Otto Wedel of Yale University, published in 1919. The second is *The Star-Crossed Renaissance* (the quarrel about astrology and its influence in England), by Don Cameron Allen of Duke University, published in 1941. And the third work in this area is *Tamburlaine's Malady* (and other essays on astrology in Elizabethan drama), by Johnstone Parr of the University of Alabama, published in 1953.

These three works represent a vast amount of creative research by non-astrologers, tracing the influence of astrology in English literature.

Wedel points out that, "The literary interest in astrology, which had been on the increase in England throughout the 14th Century, culminated in the works of Gower and Chaucer. Although references to astrology were already frequent in the romances of the 14th Century, these still retained the signs of being foreign importations. It was only in the 15th Century that astrological similes and embellishments became a matter of course in the literature of England."

Most of these innovations were due to Chaucer rather than to Gower. But Gower, too, perceived the artistic possibilities in the use of astrology—and he did make use of these in his retelling of the Alexander legend.

Chaucer used the subject as an artist would, as a writer—finding the "language of astrology" fresh, new, able to revitalize his words and meanings. Chaucer, as Dr. Wedel pointed out, used astrology for dramatic and literary force. In Wedel's words, "His originality in employing astrology for poetic purposes is incontestable, and is, perhaps, unrivaled in the entire realm of medieval literature."

The Wife of Bath, for one example, ascribes her amorous disposition to her horoscope: "Myn ascendant was Taur, and Mars therinne." Hypermenestra obtained her beauty from Venus and Jupiter. And Chaucer attributed her death in prison to Saturn. And so on—the symbols represented by the planets and the signs taking hold, being part of the language, so much so that the greater writers and dramatists of the times could utilize them much in the manner that a modern playwright can use terms, such as "suppressed desires," without fear that his audience will not understand. Readers of Shakespeare, Spenser and Ben Jonson realize the truth of this—know, as Don Cameron Allen points out—that a survey of European attitudes toward astrology during the years 1475–1625 shows that all men of this time "believed" in astrology. The arguments centered about the abuses of the subject.

The literature of astrology is as vast as the history of man, as Allen states in his preface to *The Star-Crossed Renaissance*. Of course Shakespeare, through the characters in his plays, often gives us examples. There are the "star-crossed lovers" of *Romeo and Juliet*. And Lear is made to cry in despair:

> *It is the stars*
> *The Stars above us, govern our conditions;*
> *Else one self mate and make could not beget*
> *Such different issues.*

Allen tells us, in his section on astrology and English literature, that "The Philosophy of the literary men of the English Renaissance was in many ways the philosophy of the moderate astrologers."

He adds: "As most of the Elizabethan and Jacobean authors accepted the basic tenets of the moderate astrologers, it is not surprising to discover that they all seem to know something about the technicalities of astrology.

Not only did they "know something," but astrology, as Johnstone Parr points out, "was reputedly entwined in the lives of men in the 16th Century; many of the various branches of this science were frequently employed by the Elizabethan artist in the creation of his works."

Shakespeare's plays include more than 100 separate astrological allusions. Parr tells us that "All of the astrological predictions in Shakespeare's plays are fulfilled." But Shakespeare, and his characters, are also aware of man's free will. Helena, in *All's Well*, states:

> *Our remedies oft in ourselves do lie,*
> *Which we ascribe to heaven. The fated sky*

> *Gives us free scope, only doth backward pull*
> *Our slow designs when we ourselves are dull.*

In *Julius Caesar,* of course, Cassius tells Brutus that the blame for being an "underling" lies not in the stars, but in oneself:

CASSIUS: *The fault, dear Brutus, is not in our stars.*
But in ourselves, that we are underlings.

In *All's Well,* Shakespeare's characters Helena and Parolles have this dialogue:

HELENA: *Monsieur Parolles, you were born under a charitable star.*
PAROLLES: *Under Mars, I.*
HELENA: *I especially think under Mars.*
PAROLLES: *Why under Mars?*
HELENA: *The wars have kept you so under, that you must needs be born under Mars.*
PAROLLES: *When he was predominant.*
HELENA: *When he was retrograde, I think rather.*
PAROLLES: *Why think you so?*
HELENA: *You go so much backward when you fight.*
PAROLLES: *I am so full of business, I cannot answer thee acutely.*

Parr claims, "There are few places in Elizabethan or Jacobean drama where words are used more effectively than in these passages. Although they show a minimum knowledge of astrological technicalities, they doubtless exhibit the most *artistic* use of astrology in the Elizabethan and Jacobean drama."

Francis Bacon, said to be the father of modern science, summed up his attitude toward astrology in his essay in philosophy, "De Augmentis Scientiarum." Bacon made clear he was in favor of what he termed "sane astrology," meaning he was against fatalism and was in favor of more research, more reason. He said:

The last rule (which has always been held by the wiser astrologers) is that there is no fatal necessity in the stars; but that they rather incline than compel. I will add one thing besides (wherein I shall certainly seem to take part with astrology, if it were reformed); which is, that I hold it for certain that the celestial bodies have in them certain other influences besides heat and light; which very influences however act by those rules laid down above and not otherwise. But these lie concealed in the depths of Physic, and require a longer dissertation.

Don Cameron Allen states that "Bacon's position is clear. His attitude towards astrology is so liberal that he can be claimed as a partisan of the art."

Literary men of Renaissance England adhered to the philosophy of moderate astrologers. This seems to disturb many of our critics, our professors. Instead of taking the time to look into the subject, the majority of them—including Parr, Wedel and Allen—attempt to explain away this fact. It is a fact, that they admit. But this does not shake them into granting that, after all, there might be something worth looking into. Nevertheless, their presentations are enlightening, worth reading and studying—and quoting, which we have taken the liberty, to some extent, of doing in this chapter.

XVII

HENRY MILLER

Part of the adventure involves the many rich areas of human experience which astrology unearths: the many great, creative people whose lives and whose works touch on the subject and thus, directly or indirectly, intermingle with the life of the astrologer. One is apt, understandably, to receive the impression that it is all battle, controversy, debate. That is not so, although the clash of ideas lends spice and instills vitality, once one learns to grow, to mature beyond the immediate discouragement, the gloom, the feeling of frustration when the doors are shut in the face of astrology.

One soon learns that not all doors are shut. Those that open admit air that is refreshing, air that one enjoys breathing. Through astrology, doors have opened for me that led to some of the most brilliant, creative, entertaining, delightful, warm and dynamic people of our time. And to some of the most controversial persons, too—not necessarily in their relation to astrology, but because their works have challenged their time, have perceived future times.

One such individual is Henry Miller. He is perhaps the world's most "forbidden" writer. He is a Capricorn, born December 26, 1891, 12:30 P.M., in New York City. I have already written much about him, in my book *Henry Miller: His World of Urania*. I do not, here, intend to give a history of Miller, his works, the acclaim and condemnation which have surrounded such books as *Tropic of Cancer, Black Spring, Tropic of Capricorn*. Henry Miller is a prolific, prophetic writer who, through his great body of work, has made use of astrological symbolism, although he is not an astrologer in the accepted or ordinary sense. In fact, he was not aware of the great use he had made of astrology, the numerous references he had made to the subject: the reliance upon the symbols to enlarge his language—to electrify his sense of communication. I knew it and was impelled to check all of his work or as much as I could—and thus began the adventure, the correspondence, the book I did which amounted to "The Astrology of Henry Miller."

I had not yet met Miller when I wrote the book, but by the time it was finished our correspondence was voluminous. And I was able to state in my preface:

The body of the specific references to astrology made by Miller in his books, essays and stories, serves as a kaleidoscope of color, as bright and as dark, as gay and as sad as any planet or astrological symbol. Viewed as a spectrum, the astrology of Henry Miller is a rainbow on earth, "our mother the earth," as he might say. For, with Henry Miller, one does not need to look to the heavens for rainbows: the hues, the shades, the blazing brightness is here, right here, where we can see the colors, where we can hear the music of the spheres.

Perhaps my explanation of Miller's "horoscopic brush strokes" will serve to best illustrate the role of astrology not only during the time of the Renaissance but in modern literature as well.

For Miller, the planets, the Sun and the Moon become symbols, part of the language, something he takes for granted. Even the quotations he chooses, to illustrate the works of men like D. H. Lawrence, abound in this kind of symbolism.

As an example, in his random notes on Lawrence, he tells of the Sun, the cosmos: "Start with the Sun and the rest will happen." Miller calls this the important line, "the really cryptic line." He says that Lawrence, from the very beginning of his development as a thinker, stressed the Sun.

In astrology, the Sun represents the masculine, while the Moon is the feminine. Lawrence, as Miller says, speaks of men being the Sun, the positive, of the Moon being the negative or feminine.

Miller tells us: "Lawrence had always looked upon the Sun as the source of life, and the Moon as the symbol of non-being. Life and Death—like a mariner he kept before him constantly these two poles. 'He who gets nearer the sun,' he said, 'is leader, the aristocrat of aristocrats. Or, he who, like Dostoyevsky, gets nearer the Moon of our non-being.' "

Still speaking of Lawrence, Miller says: "He saw man as a seasonal phenomenon, a Moon that waxes and wanes, a seed that emerges out of primal darkness to return therein." Still referring to Lawrence, Miller notes: "From an insignificant microcosm, but recently separated from the animal world, he (man) eventually spreads himself over the heavens in the form of the great *anthropos,* the mythical man of the zodiac."

At other times, Miller is more obvious in his references. Speaking of himself in *The Wisdom of the Heart,* he says: "I am the equal signs, the spiritual counterpart of the sign Libra which was wedged into the original zodiac by separating Virgo from Scorpio." And he says in a letter, "Astrology . . . is a subject especially stimulating and rewarding for a writer. It . . . amplifies his unilateral approach to things, his reliance on word-language alone."

Henry Miller makes colorful use of the planetary symbols for his word language. In *Black Spring,* he gives us what he calls "a few horoscopic brush-strokes" of himself: "I am Chancre, the crab, which moves sideways and backwards and forwards at will. I move in strange tropics and deal in high explosives, embalming fluid, jasper, myrrh . . . and porcupines' toes."

In the second volume of *Hamlet,* he makes this prediction: "By the year 2000 A.D. we will be definitely under the influence of Uranus and Pluto. The word Communism will be an obsolete expression known only to philologists and etymologists. We will be under the sway of tyrants and breaking ground for the new anarchy which will come in with Aquarius, circa 2160 A.D. There won't be any more A.D., as the symbol will cease to mean anything. We shall have a wholly new calendar before we definitely enter the sign of Aquarius."

Miller uses the Sun and Moon as basic symbols: "A man lives with dead Suns inside him or he goes out like a flame and lives the life of the Moon. Or he disintegrates entirely and throws a flaming comet across the horizon."

Miller, like the writers of the 15th Century, feels a kinship with the planets, the Sun, the Moon, the entire Solar system; he can "use" these as symbols—he relies upon them, to a great extent, for communication, for word-language. He sees the symbols of astrology in analyzing Lawrence. The same is true when he examines the work of Anais Nin. In *The Cosmological Eye,* he speaks of the diary of Anais Nin: "The diary is not a journey towards the heart of darkness, in the stern Conradian sense of destiny, not a voyage *au bout de la nuit,* as with Celine, or even a voyage to the Moon in the psychological sense of escape. It is much more like a mythological voyage towards the source and fountainhead of life—I might say an astrologic voyage of metamorphosis."

Miller can be funny, sad and very perceptive when he talks about the planets, about the Sun and Moon. The imagery he creates strikes with a beautiful-ugly force; his *Tante* Meilia had an obsession for the Moon: ". . . she was perpetually reaching for it with her two hands. I remember the first time she reached for it, the night she went daft. Never did the Moon seem so remote to me. And yet not hopelessly remote! Eternally out of reach, but only so by a hair's breadth, as it were."

Jupiter he regards, "according to astrological lingo," as his benevolent diety. His description of Saturn, appearing in *The Colossus of Maroussi,* is a classic. Miller takes off from a standing-still position and soars.

Again and again, Miller is able to "get the feel" of his subject by using planetary symbols. He has an instinctive understanding of what astrology is all about—and in this he has a kinship with the great Elizabethan and Jacobean authors. He reveals this intuitive understanding when he says, "With Hitler Pluto came out in the open." And again, "The birth of Man follows closely the birth of the heavens. With the birth of a new type of man a current is set in motion which later enables us to perceive that he was merely the foam on the crest of a mighty wave."

Not scientific, perhaps, but it gets to the heart of the matter. That's the way the poet, the writer, prefers it. Astrology for Henry Miller is poetry—a poetry of the universe. He shies away from its scientific uses. He prefers it as a basis for riotous comedy, such as in "Astrological Fricassee," appearing in *Remember to Remember.* Astrology, for him, becomes the gloom of Saturn or the luck of Jupiter. Astrology to Henry Miller is both poetry and the poet, the poet Rimbaud: "It was an affliction which poisoned him both at the Zenith and Nadir of his being. In him Sun and Moon were both strong. . . . His life as a poet, which was the Lunar phase of his evolution, reveals the same quality of eclipse as his later life of adventurer and man of action, which was the Solar phase."

Later in his book on Rimbaud, *The Time of the Assassins,* Miller puts it this way: "We of the fixed stars have rejected the message of the wanderers in the sky. We have regarded them as dead planets, as fugitive ghosts, as the survivors of long forgotten catastrophes. How like the wanderers of the heavens are the poets! Do they not, like the planets, seem to be in communication with other worlds. Do they not tell us of things to come as well as of things long past, buried in the racial memory of man?"

Miller is not only a great writer, but also an outstanding person, one who has achieved a true wisdom. He is a wise man who knows how to laugh and live.

Later, I did meet him. And what I had written about him held up. This "idol" had no feet of clay. Both of his feet were solid, on the ground, even though his creative vision takes us soaring to planetary heights.

Henry Miller had no reason to desire an association with astrology. Those familiar with his life, with the struggle and the controversy surrounding his works, know very well he has enough problems of his own. Nevertheless, he more than co-operated with me on the project which was to become the book relating his work and his life to astrology. His foreword to that book is a view of the subject by one of America's great men of letters. It is a poetic, yet realistic view—or, as perhaps we should say, a realistic view because it *is* poetic—with the majestic, panoramic sweep only a Henry Miller could provide.

XVIII

ALDOUS HUXLEY AND
DR. GUSTAF STROMBERG

I think that by now I have made the point that astrology is not only a controversial area of human thought, but also an adventure: it leads to the future, as well as telling us much about the past and the present, including ourselves, persons in the news, celebrities, loved ones, associates, friends. Astrology is rich in the best sense of the word, offering much if only we will but give it even a little of ourselves.

Why, then, you are entitled to ask, have so few prominent scientists come out for the record with favorable statements on the subject? I asked that question of one of the world's most distinguished philosophers and authors.

"What," I asked Aldous Huxley, "would modern scientists say if a member of their group came out in favor of astrology?"

Huxley smiled a little and replied: "They would say, 'Here is a great scientist with a foible.' "

A great author thus succinctly answered the question. To me, it was evident from Huxley's answer and from his expression, that he felt the attitudes of scientists today do not reflect progress, but rather a retrogression to Nineteenth Century materialism.

I had told Huxley about Jung and his interest and work in connection with astrology. The author of *Brave New World,* thin and graying but mentally alert and perceptive, his creative powers strong, his sense of humor delightful, his inner vision penetrating even though his "physical" vision was failing, indicated he would not be at all surprised if orthodox science would accept Jung as the great psychologist he was, but would, in turn, ridicule his "attachment" to astrology.

Huxley thought it a good example, not only of the attitude of science toward astrology, but also of orthodox science toward knowledge in general. Scientists might be willing to concede that a man like Jung is great, in a very real way—that is, so long as he "sticks to the line." But once his ideas stray too far from accepted points of view, it would be quite natural to expect even his staunchest admirers to label him the victim of a foible.

In making his statement, Huxley was not necessarily coming out as a "believer" in astrology. But he was making an excellent point. His intention was clear; he felt that astrology is worthy of scientific study. He also believes that scientists, with attitudes existing today, are not likely to give the subject the consideration it deserves. Thus, he felt that condemnation of astrology by orthodox scientists is not worth very much as far as serious thought is concerned.

Astrology has been attacked in some quarters because it is basically a scientific art rather than a pure physical science. It is difficult, if not impossible, to confine man to a laboratory and to say, for example, that each and every time transiting Mars conjoins a native's Sun he will meet with an accident. If that were possible, then astrology would be a pure physical science. However, it is possible—and has been repeatedly demonstrated—to measure cycles of events (even thoughts) which will occur to the subject under various planetary aspects. It is possible that the native will suffer an accident when Mars transits his natal Sun; but it is also likely that his affairs will suffer an "accident" due to a sudden, Mars-type change of pace which demands quick action. I knew Huxley would understand this difference and he did. I discussed the subject with him and with Dr. Gustaf Stromberg, an eminent astronomer. The time was January 27, 1954, in Los Angeles. I had brought the two men together in co-operation with the Public Affairs Department of the Columbia Broadcasting System. That afternoon, we were to hold a roundtable discussion in which James Crenshaw, a reporter on the then *Los Angeles Herald Express* (now the *Herald Examiner*), would also participate. The subject was to be psychic phenomena.

But during this luncheon meeting—and on other occasions which followed—I was concerned with astrology: Huxley's view of the subject and also the attitude of Dr. Stromberg.

As I say, the famed writer did not find it difficult to accept the fact that astrology was no less valid because it was not fatalistic. He had previously stated:

In human life, unique and unrepeatable events are of cardinal importance. When we try to reduce men's diversities to identities, we run the risk of gross over-simplification in theory and even the worse risk of totalitarian dictatorship in practice.

We had better admit, then, that there will probably never be a completely adequate Science of Man. There are all sorts of useful partial sciences dealing with generalities and averages—such as economics and actuarial statistics, sociology and comparative religion, various brands of psychology. But there is no genuine anthropology, no full Science of Man, in which the uniqueness of human beings takes its place along with their likeness, the irreducible diversities along with the unities. The art of living is still an art and is likely to remain one indefinitely.

Those words, by Huxley, should go a long way toward quieting those who insist on a fatalistic astrology (exact predictions)—and in the next breath attack the subject for what they term its fatalistic doctrine.

Astrology, basically, is the Science of Man, which Huxley called for; it is, in the philosopher Emerson's words, "Astronomy brought down to earth and applied to the affairs of man." Astrology, like the art of living, is an art, though a scientific one. It, too, is likely to remain one indefinitely.

Huxley was always willing to discuss astrology with me. And on this afternoon, our first contact, he was making his contribution to our exchange of thoughts on the subject. It was his belief that human beings are not isolated individuals, but are connected with each other—this connection, most likely, being through their minds. That is why I pointed out to him that Dr. J. B. Rhine, in his famous extrasensory perception experiments at Duke University, has discovered that twins obtain better results "sending" and "receiving" thoughts than do persons not related. The astrological significance here is obvious. Similar horoscopes equal a greater connection, more sympathy between persons. In many instances, the horoscopes of members of the same family form a pattern which cannot be attributed to chance alone.

I also explained to Huxley about the signs of the zodiac, how each of the twelve signs is associated with one of the four elements known to the ancients: Fire, Earth, Air and Water.

It was when I pointed out that the Water signs (Cancer, Scorpio, Pisces) are considered fruitful, receptive, impressionable and perceptive, that Huxley was immediately able to see the possibility of applying the astrological technique to telepathic or ESP experiments.

When the Moon transits through the Water signs, subjects might be expected to come up with higher ESP scores—for during those periods of time, the minds of men should, generally speaking, be more receptive to outside thoughts and influences.

Listening was Dr. Stromberg, the astronomer. His contributions to his own science are recognized around the world. As a member of the scientific research staff of the Carnegie Institute's Mount Wilson Observatory, he achieved international renown. But, unlike most astronomers, Dr. Stromberg's interests are not limited. He has compiled data pointing to the survival of human memory and consciousness after bodily death. This has included the analytical examination of data on certain "living fields" which seem to have their roots in a nonphysical world, a world beyond the realm of space and time. Many of his findings are contained in two books, *The Soul of the Universe* and *The Searchers*. These two volumes have had much impact upon scientific thinking throughout the world.

"For many years I attacked astrology," he told me. He smiled when I replied, "Dr. Stromberg, you are the first astronomer I ever met who admitted he *could* be wrong."

"There are problems," he said, "which astrologers must solve and present for themselves." He added, "There has long been a belief that the menstrual period of a woman coincides with a lunar cycle. If that could be proven to be a fact, it would go a long way toward helping establish astrology."

Dr. Stromberg also expressed keen interest in experiments performed at the Methodist Hospital of California, in Los Angeles, which tend to prove that more babies are born during the Full Moon than during any other time period. Both he and Huxley were fascinated, too, with the RCA experiments.

Huxley, sympathetic with my efforts to gain greater recognition for astrology, said that part of the problem is that young persons today are too inclined to accept the "pigeon holes" which have been carved out for them.

"We must," he declared, "seek the cracks in the wall." Huxley went on, "It is in those cracks that we will find our real knowledge."

Textbook knowledge, he implied, is one thing, but it is not designed to replace intellectual curiosity, the desire to move away from the status quo and to find out for ourselves.

"What we need," Huxley told me, "are more rebels." The "rebels" he referred to, of course, are men who would not hesitate to look into the truths offered not only by astrology, but also by a study of other "borderline" subjects.

Unusual as Huxley's remarks were, they were matched by Dr. Stromberg's. He told me he is, after long years of study, convinced that the human personality and memory survive after bodily death. After hearing this, I told him: "Those of us interested in astrology have a hard enough time attracting the interest of scientists. I just wonder what *your* fellow scientists think of your findings. I am curious about their reactions."

Dr. Stromberg merely shrugged and smiled. He seemed to indicate he would like the acceptance of other scientific workers, but he would not wither and fall from the vine were it not forthcoming.

Of Stromberg's ideas and writings, Albert Einstein once wrote: "Very few men could of their own knowledge present the material as clearly and concisely as he has succeeded in doing."

I never met the late Albert Einstein, although I had an interview scheduled with him at Princeton, New Jersey, shortly before his death. I told this to Dr. Stromberg, who did not seem surprised that Einstein possibly might have been receptive toward astrology.

When I first met Huxley and articulated my interest in astrology, he was extremely interested.

"It is a strange subject," he said.

"It is even stranger to me," I said, "that scientists who should know better are so unscientific in their approach to it."

"Well," answered Huxley, "the reason most scientists are inclined to veer away from astrology is that it falls in the philosophical realm."

Then he added, "But, as for myself, I have found that the great truths exist in this 'philosophical realm' rather than in materialistic conceptions.

As we continued to talk, I became more and more aware that Huxley was an expert on past and present activities in connection with psychic phenomena. The author of *Point Counter Point, Ape and Essence, Science, Liberty and Peace* and *The Doors of Perception* was anything but a limited man. He was a humanist in the fullest, best sense. His mind was not only open, but was perceptive. His familiarity with "borderline" subjects astounded me. It was an easy familiarity, not strained, not embarrassed. He didn't look over his shoulder to make sure the "establishment" was not within earshot. Believe it or not, I have talked to some individuals, high in the academic and literary world, who did just that—the old fear, the academic prejudice being very much in evidence. But it certainly was not there where Aldous Huxley was concerned.

It was when he mentioned Dr. Charlotte Wolfe, a medical doctor in Vienna, who has devoted her life to the study of the human hand, that I suggested an astrological experiment.

Earlier, I had told Huxley about the belief that extrasensory perception would be more evident when the Moon was transiting through the Water signs: Cancer, Scorpio, Pisces. He thought it would be a good idea to experiment along these lines. And, now, he was telling me that Mrs. Huxley was a serious student of hand reading. He was curious to know how astrology might be tied in with the human hand. I told him of my published findings, which utilize the four elements of Earth, Fire, Air and Water. The experiment consists of attempting to determine an individual's Sun sign by the general size and shape of the hand.

For example, the square, thick hand would fall under the Earth trinity of Taurus, Virgo or Capricorn.

The oval-shaped hand, one featured by fleshy or "water" features, would come under one of the Water signs: Cancer, Scorpio, Pisces.

Fire signs (Aries, Leo, Sagittarius), theoretically, should produce conic or cone-shaped hands.

Long, tapering, artistic hands would suggest the Air trinity: Gemini, Libra, Aquarius.

With practice, it might be possible first to determine the proper trinity and then to pick the right Sun sign from the group of three.

For example, when examining a person's hand—finding it to be thick, square-shaped, one would expect the person to be born under one of the Earth signs: Taurus, Virgo or Capricorn. The odds of "guessing" the sign thus are reduced from 12 to 1 to 3 to 1.

I have had some success with this technique, but certainly not 100 per cent, perhaps because the Ascendant or Rising Sign (based on time of birth) also enters into the picture.

Huxley was enthusiastic about the concept of being able to select birthdates by the native's hand. He told me how he and Mrs. Huxley were, in a large way, responsible for Dr. Wolfe's career as one of the world's most distinguished hand analysts. As a refugee, she had managed to escape with her life from Hitler's Germany. It was in France that she met the Huxleys. They had watched her and personally experienced her demonstrations of hand reading. Finally, they became her unofficial sponsors. Later, Huxley wrote the introduction to one of her books.

The Huxleys had also been unofficial sponsors for Dr. Tera Bey, a director of Lebanon's largest hospital. I personally witnessed a demonstration at the Philharmonic Auditorium in Los Angeles. A medical man, Dr. Bey astounded our own physicians by controlling his pulsebeat.

One group of doctors checked the beat on his left hand, while another group kept count on his right. At will, Dr. Bey changed the rate of the beat, first on one hand, then the other. He appar-

132 MY WORLD OF ASTROLOGY

ently experienced no pain when our doctors stabbed him with needles, pins and knives.

His demonstration of telepathy was the most remarkable I had ever witnessed. While a medical doctor merely thought of a certain action, Dr. Bey performed it. When I mentioned this to Huxley, he told me of experiments he had witnessed which were even more extraordinary.

I believe that as knowledge of secret powers which exist in man are uncovered, astrology will also find its place. The "cracks in the wall" Huxley referred to will be opened wide—and within will be found knowledge which is destined to replace the narrow confines of stuffy "pigeon holes."

Both Dr. Stromberg and Huxley agreed that, in a scientific discussion of astrology or psychic phenomena, it is necessary to remain free of preconceived notions.

The problem, they pointed out, has been largely overcome in psychic phenomena. Previously, it was nearly impossible for a group of scientists to discuss the question without becoming emotional. The very words—Stromberg and Huxley told me—words like "telepathy" and "clairvoyance"—made the faces of many red with anger.

Then the scientists discovered the answer to the problem. They headed all psychic phenomena under the title *Psi*, which is merely the twenty-third letter in the Greek alphabet. It stands for psychology, psychic phenomena, etc. Now, by discussing *Psi* instead of psychic phenomena, minds are kept open and intelligent discussion becomes a reality instead of just an ideal.

Dr. Stromberg and Huxley were inclined to feel that astrology, too, might benefit—not necessarily by a name change—but by the utilization of a scientific symbol. In this manner, the subject could be brought up in academic circles and some progress might be made.

Perhaps this is the answer. Which symbol could be used for astrology? This, certainly, is an intriguing question. For all of us are interested, including the American Federation of Astrologers and readers, students, professional astrologers.

What do you think?

XIX

CASTING THE HOROSCOPE

We come now to that portion of our study where, if we don't already know, we learn how to actually cast a chart or horoscope or Nativity. Let me assure you that this is more difficult to explain than it is to accomplish. This is the mathematical part of astrology, or the astronomy of astrology. It has nothing to do with interpreting a chart, which is the astrology of astrology.

Some astrologers enjoy the mathematical portion of the work. Others perform the task because it is a necessary one. Some astrologers are experts at delineating a chart, others not so expert.

Naturally, the most important and creative part of the work is the *interpretation* of charts, of transits over those charts. Many people complain that they simply cannot learn to cast a horoscope—perhaps because the explanations have not been clear, the rules not succinctly set forth—perhaps, too, because those attempting to learn become too easily discouraged and do not stay with the job. I would rather study and interpret a chart than cast it. So, I can sympathize with those students who cringe at the prospect of setting up a horoscope. But let me state that there is great satisfaction in finally learning, once and for all, what a horoscope is and how to correctly cast it.

To help us get off to a good start, I have asked my colleague, Carl Payne Tobey—an excellent mathematician as well as an astrologer—to explain and instruct, which he very ably does in the following pages.

WHAT IS A HOROSCOPE?
HOW DO YOU PRODUCE ONE?

by Carl Payne Tobey

A horoscope is merely a map of the heavens for a given moment, showing the earth in the center, with the various planets and solar bodies around it in their proper positions. To erect, or draw, such a map, one needs certain tools. We'll list them as a basic chart showing the earth in the center, a Table of Houses, an ephemeris, and of course, something to write with.

Since astrologers have to draw so many of these charts, pads of charts for this purpose are made available and sold to astrologers. A simple copy of such a chart is given here. You will note that the small inner circle represents the earth. The outer circles may be regarded merely as a border of the picture or graph of the heavens about to be drawn.

You will note that the space around the earth is divided into twelve parts. This is for purposes of measurement, to help us gain a more accurate picture and place bodies of the heavens in correct positions.

You will need to know what a Table of Houses is. You will need to know what an ephemeris is, but we will explain these terms before you need to employ them.

First, we want to talk about *time*. So long as you deal with astrology, you deal with time. There are various kinds of time. Clock time is all right so long as you remain at one position on the earth's surface. If you go any distance, the time factor begins to complicate itself.

When it is noon in London, it is 7:00 A.M. in New York and 4:00 A.M. in Los Angeles. However, this is Standard Time. It is merely an agreed-upon time.

NAME

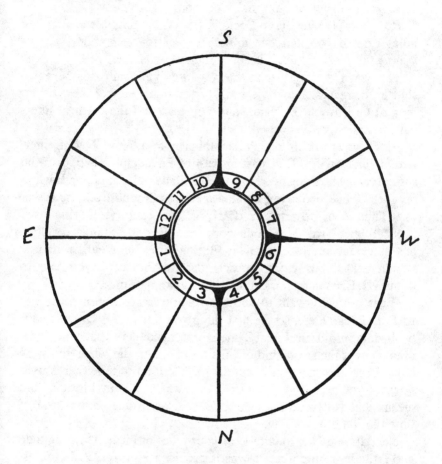

Next, we have True Local Time. You think of noon as being when the Sun is overhead. That conception is True Local Time. True noon or True Local Time is when the Sun is 90° or one quarter of a circle from the horizon at a point due east or west—in other words, halfway between the eastern and western horizons.

This is not necessarily noon when we are using Standard Time. It is noon only if you happen to be at a Time Zone Center. Yuma, Arizona, uses Mountain Standard Time but is not at a Time Zone

Center. When clocks say it is noon in Yuma, the Sun is not half-way between the two horizons. When True Local Time at Yuma is 11:24 A.M., the clock says that it is noon.

Roughly speaking, True Local Time is one minute later fourteen miles east of you and one minute earlier fourteen miles west of you. A mile east of you, it is about four seconds later.

This was the kind of time that was used until railroads began to shorten distances. Now, we have twenty-four Time Zones, beginning at Greenwich, England, and going around the earth at intervals of 15°.

At 75° west longitude, Philadelphia is at a Time Zone Center, and all territory for 7½° east or west of Philadelphia is part of the same zone. All of this territory uses Philadelphia Time, or Eastern Standard Time. However, some areas jump around from the use of one Time Zone to another. Early in this century, Florida used Central Standard Time, but now uses Eastern Standard Time, meaning that accepted noon in Florida is an hour earlier than it was in 1915. Thus, before you can draw a horoscope, you have to know WHEN a person was born, in what kind of time.

What we really want to know is when were you born according to True Local Time, so the first thing you must do is convert your birth time into True Local Time. First, make sure that your birth area is using the same kind of time today that it did when you were born. If not, correct your birth time to the kind of time that is used now. If you were born at 7:00 A.M., in 1900, in Florida, that means that you were born at 8:00 A.M. according to the kind of time Florida is now using.

Next, look up the longitude of your place of birth. The longitude and latitude of important towns is provided in a Table of Houses. If your birth town is not given, select the town closest to it.

The rule for changing over from Standard Time to True Local Time is quite simple. One degree changes the time by four minutes. If you are east of the Time Zone Center, add four minutes per degree. If you are west of the Time Zone Center, deduct four minutes for each degree.

New York is 1° east of Philadelphia, so you would add four minutes if born in New York. Pittsburgh is 5° west of Philadelphia, so you deduct 5 × 4 = 20 minutes. True noon in Pittsburgh is twenty minutes later than in Philadelphia.

By following these relatively simple rules, it is not difficult to know when you were born in True Local Time. Follow the rules carefully.

That is one step. Now we must deal with another kind of time. As soon as you start dealing with space, earth time is not going to be satisfactory, because earth time does not apply when you are out in space. So what kind of time are we going to use now?

We have to convert to Sidereal Time, which means *star time*.

A day is twenty-four hours long, and we think of the earth rotating on its axis once in twenty-four hours. That is only relatively true. It does if we are considering only an earth-sun relationship. Otherwise, it rotates once in twenty-three hours and fifty-six minutes. In other words, if a certain star is directly overhead from where you are at midnight tonight, it will again cross that point overhead tomorrow night at 11:56 P.M., and each night it will be there four minutes sooner. The earth has turned all the way around on its axis in twenty-three hours and fifty-six minutes.

Then why is a day twenty-four hours in length? Why isn't a day twenty-three hours and fifty-six minutes?

The discrepancy comes because of the fact that, in addition to turning on its axis, the earth is traveling through space in its annual trip around the Sun. In twenty-four hours, while the earth has turned around once, it has moved through space about 780,000 miles. Thus, when we look at the Sun tomorrow, its relation to the fixed stars is not quite the same as today. Its position appears to have changed in the heavens by almost a degree.

If the earth could remain stationary in space but continue to rotate on its axis, a day would be twenty-three hours and fifty-six minutes. Since it does not, when the earth has turned on its axis once, it has to turn one additional degree to point to where the Sun appears today instead of where it was yesterday. From the time a star crosses overhead until it crosses again is a Sidereal Day, but there is an extra Sidereal Day in a year. Instead of being 365.25 days, a year is 366.25 Sidereal Days. People uninterested in what's out in space do not have to think about such things, but the moment you become interested in the outer world, these are things you must know.

Just as a Sidereal Day is shorter than an earth day, a sidereal hour is shorter, a sidereal minute is shorter and a sidereal second is shorter by the same ratio. There are twenty-four sidereal hours and four sidereal minutes in an earth day.

First, we had to know what time of day you were born. Then, we had to know the True Local Time of day when you were born. Now, we have to take the next step. We have to know at what Sidereal Time of day you were born. Whatever the Sidereal Time is at noon today, it will be four minutes later at noon tomorrow. However, whatever the Sidereal Time may be at noon today in London, it will be close to the same at noon all over the world. If the Sidereal Time is 4:06 at noon in London, then it will be approximately the same at Denver when it becomes noon in Denver. There will be a deviation, but halfway around the world, the difference will amount to only two minutes. We can afford that degree of inaccuracy, because people do not record birth times that accurately. Most birth times are off by as much as 15 minutes. The best way of achieving accuracy is to correct the chart later, from events in a person's life.

When we are measuring a board, we use a ruler which is marked off in inches and parts of inches down to sixteenths of an inch. When we are measuring space around the earth, we divide the circle into degrees, and parts of degrees. We have 360° in the circle, and we divide each degree into sixty minutes. These are known as minutes of arc, not minutes of time. Then we divide each minute of arc into sixty seconds of arc.

A ruler has two ends, and we measure from one end to the other. A circle doesn't have these two ends, so we have to have an agreed-upon point somewhere on the circle that we are to employ as a starting point. As we go around the circle, we have no beginning or ending, and so we have to create one artificially. We do that by selecting the mathematical point where two imaginary lines cross.

A two-dimensional chart of the heavens has to be drawn in some plane of space. The horoscope is a chart of the heavens drawn in the plane of the ecliptic. The ecliptic is merely the plane of the earth's orbit around the Sun. The horoscope is a chart of the heavens you would see if you were at a point in space directly over the ecliptic North Pole. The earth has three different north poles, and they are all at different locations. The regular North Pole is that mathematical point that is 90° north from any part of the equator. If 50 men started from 50 different points on the equator and traveled north for 90°, they would all reach the same mathematical point, and that would be the regular North Pole of the earth. The north-south regular poles are at the earth's axis.

Next, we have the magnetic north pole. This is up in the eastern part of Canada, but it won't stay there. It moves around on the surface of the earth, and nobody knows what causes the motion or where it will go next.

The ecliptic North Pole is the one that is important in astrology. Where is the ecliptic North Pole? It is that mathematical point which is 90° north of any part of the ecliptic. It describes a circle on the surface of the earth in twenty-three hours and fifty-six minutes, or in twenty-four Sidereal Hours. This circle is known as the Arctic Circle. The Arctic Circle is the daily path of the ecliptic North Pole, and despite the fact that that's why it was originally placed on maps, I have never seen this mentioned in an astronomical or astrological book, and I never ran across an astronomer or astrologer who was aware of this fact. Astronomers usually think of it merely as the farthest-north point where the Sun is visible at noon on the first day of winter. North of the Arctic Circle, there is no place where the Sun is visible at any time of day on the first day of winter—all is darkness. On the other hand, on the first day of summer, you can see the Sun at any time of day anywhere above the Arctic Circle. You can see it at noon or at midnight. The ancient Greeks had this all figured out before they knew anyone, or ever heard of anyone, who had been above the Arctic Circle. Just as the Arctic Circle is the path of daily motion for the ecliptic North Pole, the Antarctic Circle is the daily path of the ecliptic South Pole. The Tropic of Cancer is the path of the Sun around the earth on the first day of summer, and the Tropic of Capricorn is the path of the Sun around the earth on the first day of winter.

The distance from the Arctic Circle to the regular North Pole of the earth is exactly the same as the distance of the Tropic of Cancer from the equator, with the same relationship existing between the Tropic of Capricorn and the Antarctic Circle.

If you stand right on the Arctic Circle, there will be a time every day when the ecliptic pole will pass right through you.

Now, we want a picture of the heavens for the moment you were born, and we want to see just how they would look if we were directly above the ecliptic North Pole at that moment. We mentioned determining a starting point, on the circle that is the ecliptic, from which to measure. We select the point where the circle of the ecliptic crosses the circle of the equator. We call this the Vernal Equinox, but we also call it O-Aries. We measure everything from that point.

Instead of numbering each section of the circle the way we number inches on a ruler, we give them names. These are what we call the signs of the zodiac. They go around the heavens, and they have to go around our chart. These signs run in the order: Aries, Taurus, Gemini, Cancer, Leo, Virgo, Libra, Scorpio, Sagittarius, Capricorn, Aquarius and Pisces. When we reach the end of Pisces, we are back to the starting point at 0° Aries. We have already stated that the circle is divided into 360°, and since there are twelve signs, that means that there are 30° to each of the signs.

Sidereal Time runs from 0 to twenty-four hours, instead of starting over at twelve hours. For this reason, we have no A.M. or P.M. involved in Sidereal Time. When the Vernal Equinoctial point or 0-Aries, the beginning of the zodiac, crosses overhead at the equator on a line drawn from the regular North Pole to the regular South Pole, the Sidereal Time is 0:00. That is the starting point. Understand that the zodiacal degree overhead at the equator is not necessarily overhead where you are. It will be the same twice a day, at 0:00 Sidereal Time and at 12:00 Sidereal Time, but at no other time of day.

In astrology, we use the term *Ascendant*. It is usually stated that this is the degree of the zodiac on the eastern horizon at birth, but this does not mean east as you think of east. This is celestial-east; celestial-east and earth-east are not synonymous.

Earth-east is 90° around the horizon from the earth-north pole, while celestial east is 90° around the horizon from the ecliptic-North Pole. At sunrise on the first day of summer, celestial-east is 23° north of earth-east, but at sunset on the same day, it is 23° south of earth-east. Celestial-west will then be 23° north of earth-west. This factor is changing all day, and it also changes with the seasons. Just as at sunrise on the first day of summer, celestial-east is 23° north of earth-east, at sunrise on the first day of winter, it is 23° south of east. You can verify this by observation. On the first day of summer, the Sun rises far to the north of east, but on the first day of winter, it rises far to the south of east. The Sun always designates the ecliptic.

You will visualize this if you realize that at sunrise on the first day of summer, the plane of the zodiac, the ecliptic, or orbit of the earth, comes over the horizon 23° north of earth-east, and traverses the sky from this northeasterly point in a southwesterly direction, crossing the western horizon 23° south of earth-west.

The degree of the zodiac at the Ascendant where you are will not be the same for someone 1,000 miles south of you. For that reason, we have to use *latitude of birth* as well as longitude. Let us give the reason.

At the first quarter of the Moon, you see half of it. That is the half on which the Sun is shining. The dark half is where it is night. Consider that line between the dark half and the light half.

Suppose you were out in space directly over where you are now, viewing the earth at sunrise. You would see it as you saw the Moon. Half of it would be light and half of it dark, and you would have that line between the dark and the light halves.

The important thing to note is that the line would not run from the regular earth north to south poles. It *would* run from the ecliptic North to ecliptic South Pole. These two poles are *always* at the ends of that dividing line.

Mexico City is due south of La Crosse, Kansas, but the Sun does not rise over both places at the same time, as many would suppose. On the first day of summer, the Sun will rise at La Crosse, Kansas, 48 minutes sooner than it will rise in Mexico City.

We can offer a greater extreme. Norman Wells, in northern Canada, is farther west than Los Angeles and yet the Sun will rise at Norman Wells on the first day of summer before it rises at Miami.

It is helpful to know these things, because when you do, you will understand an astrological chart. The above facts are why you need a Table of Houses.

A Table of Houses is a table that will show you what degree of the zodiac is on the Ascendant at any desired latitude at any given Sidereal Time.

Let us pause again and go back to finding the Sidereal Time at the moment of your birth. We have shown you how to determine the True Local Time when you were born. Now, you must convert True Local Time into Sidereal Time. This is when you will first need an ephemeris.

An ephemeris is much simpler than its Latin name. It is a timetable of the planet's places or positions for any day of any year. It is easy to obtain such data back to the year 1850, more difficult to obtain the data for previous years. It is also possible to obtain such data for several years into the future.

The ephemeris will also tell you the Sidereal Time at noon of any day. This is approximately the same for the same day of any year, being slightly off because of leap year and the imperfection of our calendar. This is usually the Sidereal Time at noon in Greenwich, England, but the difference for some other place is too little for too great attention. You can use Sidereal Time at noon for Greenwich. You merely look at the ephemeris for the date of your birth, go to the column that gives Sidereal Time at noon and copy the figure given.

There is another factor to watch. An ephemeris published in more recent years may give the Sidereal Time at midnight instead of the Sidereal Time at noon. You will have to make sure which your particular ephemeris presents—noon or midnight. Otherwise, if you are drawing a horoscope for someone born at noon, you may discover that it will show the Sun where it should be at midnight. In fact, this is something you should always check. After you have placed the Sun in a horoscope, you should see if it is where it should be. You know it should be at the eastern horizon at sunrise, overhead at noon, at the western horizon at sunset, and beneath the earth at midnight.

Unless all this is very clear to you, read it again. If necessary, read it half a dozen times or until it is clear. Once you learn this, you will never have to cover this ground again and the information will serve you for the rest of your life.

Once you know the Sidereal Time at noon, which you merely take from that column in the ephemeris, you are ready to find the Sidereal Time for the time of birth. If the person whose horoscope you are drawing was born exactly at noon, True Local Time, you can use the time given in the ephemeris. Otherwise, you have to add to, or subtract from, that given figure. If the birth was *before* noon, you subtract. If it was *later* than noon, you add. How much do you add or subtract? However much the birth *was* before or after noon. If the birth was at 1:00 P.M., which is an hour *after* noon, you add an hour, so that if the Sidereal Time given in the ephemeris is 7:22, you add an hour and make it 8:22. If it was at 11:00 A.M., which is one hour before noon, you deduct an hour and make it 6:22. It is as simple as that, but most people manage to complicate it because it has never been properly explained to them.

Now, take a look at the blank chart that accompanies this chapter. You see a circle divided into 12 equal parts. Again, this is merely the custom of dividing the circle into sections (like inches on a ruler) for purposes of measurement.

The left of this chart represents east and the right west, but in this case, it is ecliptic-east and ecliptic-west, instead of ordinary east and west. Where the horizontal line touches the border of the chart at the east is the mathematical point we call the Ascendant. Just as we selected 0-Aries as a starting point for measurement within the zodiac, in this chart we select the Ascendant as the starting point for measurement purposes.

You see how the chart is divided into 12 equal parts. These are called Houses. This is an odd term, dating back thousands of years. We use the word House no differently than we use the word inch on a ruler. So, we have 12 "Houses." Starting at the Ascendant, we number these in a counterclockwise direction, down and around. We call them the 1st House, the 2nd House, etc., around to the 12th House.

You have learned how to determine the Sidereal Time at birth. With that information, you now turn to the Table of Houses. Turn to the section of the Table of Houses that deals with the particular latitude of your place of birth. Go down the columns of Sidereal Time until you find the figure closest to the Sidereal Time you are seeking. From there, move over to the column labeled Ascendant or "Asc.," and it will give a degree of the Zodiac opposite the Sidereal Time you have determined. Place that figure on the chart at the Ascendant. Pay no attention to any other figures given in the Table of Houses. We will explain why presently. In other words, ignore all the other columns except the ones headed Sidereal Time and Ascendant.

Now, put the other signs of the zodiac around the chart in the order we have furnished them. The spaces are called the Houses, and the lines between the spaces are called the House *Cusps*. The line at the beginning of each House is considered as the Cusp of that House. The Ascendant is considered the Cusp of the 1st House. The next line down is the Cusp of the 2nd House, etc.

Here, we will pause to explain why we ignore everything else to be found in the Table of Houses.

The type of chart used by astrologers throughout the world at the beginning of this century was never employed by the ancient astrologers. Where did it come from and why?

In the 13th Century, a lad known by the name of Regiomontanus began using a new kind of a chart. From a mathematical or astronomical viewpoint, the chart didn't make much sense. Instead of putting the zodiacal degree 90° west of the Ascendant on the 10th Cusp, he kept the Ascendant, as we have explained it here, and then, at the 10th Cusp, he placed the degree of the zodiac that was at the equator on a line drawn from the earth north pole through the place of birth, south to the equator. In other words, to find the Cusps of the 1st and 7th Houses, he employed the ecliptic and the ecliptic North and South Poles as his frame of reference. He made his calculations from there, but to find the Cusps of the 4th and 10th Houses, he employed the equator and the earth north-south poles as a frame of reference. When he finished his chart, he had a picture of nothing that ever existed in the heavens. If he was going to try a new system based on the earth directions instead of the celestial or ecliptic directions, he should have done so with Ascendant and all the rest of the cusps, but he didn't. He merely created a monster which has plagued astrology ever since.

Nevertheless, his system was almost universally adopted. In the next century, Campanus tried to correct it, but he didn't do any better. He merely changed the method of finding Cusps for the 2nd, 3rd, 5th, 6th, 8th, 9th, 11th and 12th Houses. In the Fifteenth Century, this was changed again and the Placidian System was adopted. This was just as bad, from an astronomical, mathematical or factual point of view. At the beginning of this century, nearly all astrologers were using the Placidian System of erecting a chart. A few were still using the other two systems. Nobody was using the system of the ancients.

No person who has a clear three-dimensional conception of astronomy, the heavens and the Solar system could use any one of these three types of charts without realizing that they do not give a true picture of the planetary positions. The planets are just not in the positions shown in such a chart. A planet may be shown at the 10th Cusp when it is far away from the 10th Cusp. The planet is placed at the 10th Cusp on the assumption that if the 10th Cusp is 10-Aries and the planet is at 10° Aries, the planet is on a line drawn from the earth north pole through the place of birth to the equator, but the planet may be north or south of the ecliptic or zodiacal plane, and this is north or south in a celestial or Zodiacal direction—not toward the earth-north or earth-south poles. It is off in an entirely different direction. It can make an error in the position of a planet in the chart of as much as 22°.

All right, you have placed the signs of the zodiac around the 12 Cusps of your chart. Whatever degree of a sign is on the Ascendant, place that *same number* on each of the other cusps. If the

Ascendant is 13–Cancer, the 2nd Cusp will be 13–Leo, the 3rd Cusp, 13–Virgo, etc.

You now have a chart showing just how the earth posed within the zodiac at the moment of birth.

Next, the planets must be placed in this chart.

Your Ephemeris gives the position of each planet. Now, all you have to do is place them in the chart. If the Ascendant is 13-Cancer and you find Neptune at 20-Cancer, you place Neptune just below the Ascendant in the chart, and you write beside it, "20-Cancer." If Uranus is 2-Aquarius, where would that go in the chart? You have 13-Capricorn on the 7th Cusp and 13-Aquarius on the 8th Cusp, and 2-Aquarius is between those two points, so it would go in the 7th House.

When you get over to the faster-moving bodies, Mercury and Venus, you may want to correct them. The birth may have been 12 hours after the time for which the ephemeris was calculated, and during that time, Mercury or Venus may have moved into another degree. These are matters you can take up later, when you require such accuracy. Until you advance further, you may do better to simplify things and not go into such detail.

When you come to the Moon, you will have a more serious problem. The motion of the Moon in one day can range from less than 12° to more than 15°.

If the ephemeris was calculated for noon at Greenwich, figure out how long the birth was *before* or *after* that time. If you want relative accuracy, add a degree to the Moon's position for every two hours after noon at Greenwich, or deduct a degree for every two hours before noon at Greenwich.

A better and easier way to do this is to figure out what time it is at the birth location when it is noon at Greenwich and consider the ephemeris as having been calculated for that time at the place of birth. For example, when it is noon at Greenwich, it is 7:00 A.M. in New York, 6:00 A.M. in Chicago, 5:00 A.M in Denver and 4:00 A.M. in Los Angeles. If you happen to be in California, figure that the ephemeris was computed for 4:00 A.M. in Los Angeles, because it actually was, for that is the same moment as noon in Greenwich.

Let us go over the important features again. Follow the rules in this order:

1. Determine recorded time of birth.
2. Make certain the custom of recording time has not been changed between the time of the birth and now, in that particular locality.
3. Convert given birth time into True Local Time.
4. Convert True Local Time into Sidereal Time.
5. From Table of Houses, determine Ascending degree of zodiac for correct latitude involved.
6. Place signs of zodiac around other Houses, after marking degree and sign of zodiac on Ascendant.
7. Look up planetary positions for the date of birth in the ephemeris. Place them in chart.
8. Correct Moon position.

That you may better understand these rules, let us have an example. Let us cast a horoscope, that of Sydney Omarr. He was born on August 5, 1926, 10:27 A.M., Eastern Standard Time, at Philadelphia, Pennsylvania. If we look up the longitude and latitude of Philadelphia, in a Table of Houses or on a map, we will find that it is 40° north latitude and 75° west longitude. Because 75° west is the *center* of a Time Zone, we do not have to make any correction to gain True Local Time, because True Local Time and Eastern Standard Time at this point are one and the same. If it was at 76° west longitude, we would have to deduct four minutes, or if it was at 74° west longitude, we would have to add four minutes to get True Local Time. Thus, the first three rules stated above have already been covered and taken care of, and we can go to Rule 4, which tells us to convert True Local Time into Sidereal Time.

Using an ephemeris, turn to August 5, 1926, where the first column on the page tells us that the Sidereal Time at noon for Greenwich is 8:53. If we wanted to be technical, we could add one minute to that to get the Sidereal Time at Philadelphia, which is almost one quarter of the way around the world, but it isn't worthwhile. That much of an error won't make any difference. You can employ the Sidereal Time just as it is given in the ephemeris. Your greatest error won't be over two minutes, and it will always be very doubtful whether a birth time given is that accurate. If you can get any birth time within four minutes, you are doing as well as necessary for practical purposes.

We know that the Sidereal Time at noon was 8:53. Omarr was born at 10:27 A.M. That is one hour and 33 minutes before noon:

> 12:00 Noon
> 10:27 A.M.—birth
> _____
> 1:33 hours and minutes before noon.

Don't lose sight of the fact that if he had been born after noon, we would have done this differently. Suppose he had been born at 10:27 P.M. That is 10 hours and 27 minutes after noon.

We take the Sidereal Time at noon (8:53) and we deduct that 1 hour and 33 minutes from it. Thus:

> 8:53 Sidereal Time at noon
> 1:33
> _____
> 7:20 Sidereal Time at birth.

Again bear in mind that if the birth had been at 10:27 P.M. instead of A.M., we would have done it in this fashion:

> 8:53 Sidereal Time
> 10:27
> _____
> 19:20 Sidereal Time at 10:27 P.M.

We go to Rule 5, which tells us to determine Ascending degree of zodiac for correct latitude from Table of Houses.

Buy a Table of Houses. Note that each page is divided into three sections. Turn to the page showing latitudes 40°, 41° and 42°. We are interested in the first of these three sections headed 40°, because the birth was at 40°. If the birth had been at 45°, we would have to seek another page of the Table of Houses, and since Sidereal Time runs from 0 to 24:00, it requires twelve pages to present the figures for just one latitude. We are concerned only with the page required for this horoscope. Now, go down the column, looking for the figure 7:20, the Sidereal Time for birth of Omarr. We come to 7:18:01 and then 7:22:18. You will find three figures each time. The first is hours, the second is minutes and the third is seconds. Forget the seconds. Few birth times are that accurate. In other words, 7:18:01 means seven hours, 18 minutes and one second. The figure we want is 7:20, and we have to choose between 7:18 and 7:22.

Now, go over to the column labeled Asc., which is the abbreviation for *Ascendant*. Forget all the other columns. We are not going to use them. At 7:18, we find the Ascendant given as 15:34, and at the top of the column, we see the symbol for Libra (   ), meaning that at 7:22, the Ascendant is 15° and thirty-four minutes of Libra. At 7:22, we find the Ascendant at 16:25 Libra.

Thus, in the four-minute interval between 7:18 and 7:22, the Ascendant moves fifty-one minutes. That means it would move half that in two minutes. It would move 25.5 minutes. If you want accuracy, you can add 25.5 minutes to 16:25, the figure given for the time before the one we want, and we get 15:59.5 Libra, within a half minute of arc of 16-Libra, so we are safe to use 16-Libra as the Ascendant.

Following instructions, we place 16–Libra at the Ascendant of the chart as shown in Illustration 3, and we place the other signs around the chart in their proper order, and when we have done this as shown, we have covered Rule 6.

Rule 7 tells us to look up planetary positions for the date of birth in the ephemeris and copy them into the chart.

Turn to the page from the ephemeris for August, 1926. If we go down to the *5th of the month*, we have the positions of all the planets and can copy them into the chart. When we do that, we have what we see on page 150.

We now turn to our last rule, Number 8, and it tells us to correct position of the Moon. The ephemeris gives the Moon position for noon Greenwich, which is 7:00 A.M. in Philadelphia. Thus, from 7:00 until 10:27 A.M. is three hours and twenty-seven minutes. The ephemeris gives the Moon at 8° and nine minutes of Cancer at 10:27 A.M., Philadelphia Time. In that time the Moon would move about one and three quarters of a degree, which would

NAME _____

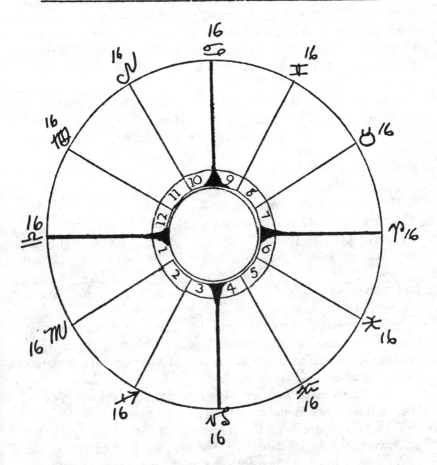

place it at 9° Cancer. It wouldn't quite have time to reach 10° Cancer.

There, you have it—the horoscope of Sydney Omarr.

ONCE OVER—LIGHTLY!

Now that Carl Payne Tobey has explained and illustrated—let us go once over it lightly.

Here is how to find True Local Time:

1. Birth hour according to Standard Time.

2. Degrees birthplace is east or west of Standard Time Meridian in use at birth.

3. Multiply this number of degrees by four minutes; it equals . . . (Add if birthplace is east of this meridian, subtract if birthplace is west of this meridian.)

NAME

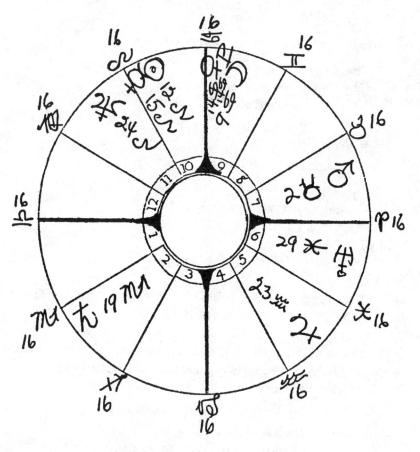

HOROSCOPE OF SYDNEY OMARR

4. Gives True Local Time of Birth.

Here is how to find Sidereal Time (S.T.):

1. Sidereal Time at Greenwich for noon previous to birth.
2. Correction of 10 seconds for each 15° of longitude. (Add if west longitude, deduct if east longitude.)
3. Interval between previous noon and True Local Time of birth.
4. Add correction of 10 seconds per hour of interval.
5. Gives Sidereal Time (S.T.) at birthplace at birth hour.
6. Nearest S.T. in Table of Houses.

Here is how to find Greenwich Mean Time:

1. True Local Time of birth.
2. Degrees east or west of Greenwich.
3. Multiply this number of degrees by four minutes; it equals
. . (Add if west longitude, deduct if east longitude.)
4. Gives Greenwich Mean Time (G.M.T.).

To correct planetary positions, especially that of the Moon:

1. Sign.
2. Coming noon position (after G.M.T.).
3. Previous noon position (before G.M.T.).
4. Travel in 24 hours.
5. Logarithm of Travel (Table of Logarithms to be found in back of ephemeris).
6. Permanent logarithm (found by checking interval of Greenwich Mean Time to nearest noon).
7. Sum of Logarithms.
8. Travel during interval (Direct planets: add to previous noon position if G.M.T. is A.M. Retrograde planets, reverse this rule).
9. Gives position of planet.

There you have it. To repeat—the process is much more difficult to explain than it is to do. Do it; at least try it.

If you haven't tried before, keep these pages open—get your horoscope blanks and ephemeris and Table of Houses—and go along step by step. If possible, have a professional astrologer check your progress and your final chart.

I am sure that, once you have made the effort and have cast your horoscope, you can send your birth data and the chart for "checking" to the American Federation of Astrologers, at 6 Library Court, S.E., Washington 3, D.C. Explain that you are trying to learn—and find out if what you have done is correct. The AFA is extremely co-operative and always willing to help sincere students along the road of astrology.

XX

THE LANGUAGE
OF ASTROLOGY

When consulting an ephemeris, you will soon discover that *astronomical* symbols are used to denote the planets and signs. You should become familiar with these symbols, which are as follows:

Aries ♈, ruler Mars ♂

Taurus ♉, ruler Venus ♀

Gemini ♊, ruler Mercury ☿

Cancer ♋, ruler Moon ☽

Leo ♌, ruler Sun ☉

Virgo ♍, ruler Mercury ☿

Libra ♎, ruler Venus ♀

Scorpio ♏, ruler Pluto- ♇

Sagittarius ♐, ruler Jupiter ♃

Capricorn ♑, ruler Saturn ♄

Aquarius ♒, ruler Uranus ♅

sub-ruler Saturn ♄

Pisces ♓, ruler Neptune ♆

We have traveled far along our journey. But the path continues. It continues to the point of learning the most important lesson, a lesson one must gain, to a large extent, through experimentation— self-knowledge. What I mean to say is that interpreting a chart is an art, depending much upon the background and skill—and hard work and practice—of the individual. Once a chart is set up, the astrologer looks at it and sees the symbols of the signs and planets: now, those symbols must be interpreted, based on Houses and signs, on *aspects* (distances) between the planets. We have already seen how RCA utilizes the aspects to forecast magnetic storms. We have, I hope, realized that these symbols represent planetary patterns which can be interpreted for the purpose of coming up with valid information: about the character of the native, about past, present and future indications.

Once again, let me stress that the best way to begin interpreting the meanings of the planetary positions is to regard the planets as symbols for an emotion or activity, just as each House, or section of the chart, is associated with certain activity and just as each sign is connected with specific characteristics. For example, if a certain sign or planet is part of the 1st House, that House is modified or intensified in its meaning by the sign and planet occupying it.

Always keep in mind, presuming that this is a "learning" stage, that the planets constantly move, and these movements are called *transits*. Thus, the Moon transiting through a native's 1st House would stress his personality, would be the marker of a cycle enabling him to take new steps in new directions. The Moon is a "quick mover," staying in one sign approximately two days, so it is used as an indicator of brief or daily cycles.

The slower-moving planets mark major or longer cycles. We will be going into this phase of our study shortly. But we now know that the birth chart is *fixed*. The planetary positions are "frozen." The birth chart is our starting point, our over-all frame of reference. The current positions of the planets are transits and are, in effect, placed on top of the birth chart, so we can compare the current positions of the planets with the birth planets (aspects). Saturn might be in the 5th House of a birth chart. Transiting Saturn might be in the 10th House. And just as we can compare the current positions of the planets (transits) with the birth positions, we can project (check future positions through the use of the ephemeris) into the future. We can see where the planets will be and thus what the future indications are apt to be; also, we can go back to the past, five-ten years ago, and determine what the indications were at *that* time. We can check our indications of the past with the actual events and so determine our accuracy.

Using our system of key words or symbols, let us now briefly indicate the activities associated with each of the 12 Houses:

FIRST HOUSE: Beginning of life, the personality, the impression the native makes on others. This is a very important part of the horoscope—the Ascendant.

SECOND HOUSE: Money, income, the ways the native has of accumulating material goods.

THIRD HOUSE: Brothers, sisters, short journeys, ideas, need to communicate, writing, degree of versatility.

FOURTH HOUSE: Property, father, environment, security or lack of it, home life in later years.

FIFTH HOUSE: Pleasure, relations with members of the opposite sex, romance, children, speculation, extravagance, creative drive.

SIXTH HOUSE: Health, work, fellow workers, persons who serve the native, accidents.

SEVENTH HOUSE: Marriage, contracts, legal affairs, partners, the way the world is apt to look to the native, public relations and contacts.

EIGHTH HOUSE: Legacies, bequests, money received through insurance, property, goods, death.

NINTH HOUSE: Long journeys, foreign countries, dreams, psychic experiences, education, invention, attainment, academic matters, publishing, creative writing.

TENTH HOUSE: Profession, honors, ambitions, standing in community, fame, recognition for past efforts, mother, involvement with affairs of government.

ELEVENTH HOUSE: Friends, hopes and wishes, attainment, pleasure, ability to socialize.

TWELFTH HOUSE: Restrictions, secrets, hospitals, confinement, fears, periods of feeling unable to take direct action, undercover experiences.

Planets transiting through any of the 12 Houses would emphasize the activity depicted by the particular House. Mars, for example, going through the 2nd House would mark a period of time when the native should be on guard against impulsive tendencies to be extravagant in money matters. He might be tempted to spend in order to accumulate goods he really does not require. Saturn, on the other hand, going through the same sector would have a "heavy" influence, and money affairs would appear "bogged down." And other activities are emphasized by the other planets—

depending on their symbolic meanings—as they transit the Houses of the horoscope.

Each planet has its own rate of speed, its individual cycle. Thus, some transits (cycles) are quick: the Moon moves through all of the signs in approximately twenty-eight days, remaining in each just about two and one half days. The Sun (as viewed from the earth) takes a year—it is in each sign about one month. Here is a convenient table:

SUN: One year to circle the Zodiac (actually, of course, the earth is moving around the Sun).
MOON: Takes 28 days to cover each sign.
MERCURY: Takes 224½ days to travel around the Sun.
MARS: One year and 322 days (the time it takes to cover each of 12 signs).
JUPITER: 12 years (remains in each sign one year).
SATURN: 29½ years.
URANUS: 84 years.
NEPTUNE: 165 years.
PLUTO: 248 years.

Note that Saturn, for example, would be in one sign approximately two and one-half years before moving on to the next sign. A transit of Saturn marks a major cycle. It is the planet which brings tests of responsibility, makes one grow or perish. Saturn, in the 4th House, might mark a time when the native—much as he would like it otherwise—is going through a period of relative obscurity. He is learning about value, security—the things that count, such as home, family, the protection that comes from knowledge based on experience.

This, in part, is the language of astrology, a language "born" almost at the same time man learned to communicate; an ancient language which has stood the test of time, century after century. The language of astrology is universal. Its symbols do for students around the world what the symbols of algebra, calculus and the higher branches of mathematics do for mathematicians; they tell a story—a never-ending one—of life on this planet and of the way men act and react throughout their lives. The language of astrology is, as we have said, part of medicine, of history, of literature; it is rich, meaningful, a treasure vein of knowledge, with the only limit being the individual skill and creativeness of the person "reading the signs."

This must be emphasized. The person doing the "reading" must, if he is to be a credit to astrology and to himself, become familiar with the planets, the Houses, the signs as meaningful symbols. One learns key words. One learns by checking charts against actual events, comparing charts to lives. One learns by experimenting, reading and remembering. The interpretation of charts should be something you will revere, not only as revealing much to the native, but as an act which is also self-revealing to you. I want you to become so familiar with the symbols that when you see Mars in the 3rd House, in Aries, it will *mean* something, not just *look* like something. I want you to begin looking at and interpreting charts as a whole, not in separate parts, which is what you will be doing in the beginning. As you progress, each aspect, each indication, each meaning, will lead you on to other factors, until the complete horoscope—the complete person—is viewed. This is what marks the professional, the skilled astrologer, and separates him from the amateur.

See the chart as a pattern, a wheel which goes round and round—let one step lead to another until you not only are telling of likely events, but of likely responses to events; until you are telling of character and the way that character is capable at times of modifying events or heightening them.

An outstanding British astrologer, Margaret E. Hone, puts it this way:

"In order to become an astrologer, a student must perfect himself in his technique and apply himself to gaining experience. These two objects are gained by familiarizing himself with *the essential natures* of the planets in their manifold ecliptical relationships, and by watching these in their embodiment in the lives of people, in business, and in political and world events. His results are obtained empirically. They are not easy to classify."

XXI

THE PLANETS

The symbolism of the planets and the Houses should become second nature, and each individual should add to them, based on the experience he gains from actual practice and further study. An understanding of the planets helps us to a greater understanding of the over-all pattern of our existence, gives us greater knowledge of universal, national and personal rhythms.

Neptune thus gives us illusions, and those illusions can be molded and made practical. First comes the idea, the illusion—this is followed by the reality. Neptune is inspiration and imagination. It can, on the negative side, be deception. Without the qualities symbolized by this planet, life would be cold, materialistic. Neptune's symbolic message is necessary for beauty. But it should not be used to promote pure fantasy. Self-deception is the danger of Neptune; one must draw the line between the constructive and the destructive aspects of all the planets, including Neptune.

Pluto brings upheaval, often despair, because the old has been wiped out and a new concept has been born. It is often difficult to abandon the old and steer toward new, progressive roads. Pluto tells of the necessity for courage to try the new, to pull ourselves out of hopeless grooves. Pluto can be destructive, but unpleasant experiences often help us eventually to appreciate peace and tranquility. The wreckage of Pluto is symbolic of the phoenix, a miraculous bird in Egyptian lore, believed to live for 500 years, only to be consumed in fire by its own act. However, the phoenix rises again in youthful freshness from its own ashes and becomes an emblem of immortality. Pluto thus offers a lesson in hope. Pluto is the chance for a comeback. Pluto points out that often the old must be torn down in order to make way for the new—Pluto is wreckage, often because we so desire, in order that we can start anew and rebuild. Pluto has been related to better conditions, in labor and other fields, but only after many heads were smashed and people attained a new dignity and a new unity.

The Moon, of course, provides visible beauty, and its various phases remind us of the cycles of life. There are ups and downs, moods, periods of glory and times of despair. Symbolically, the Moon is associated with family and permanent ties, with the things in life that make the individual want to succeed, not only for his own sake, but for the sake of security for his family. The Moon offers a lesson of consideration for others; it impresses on the consciousness the fact that careless action not only causes misery, but also blinds our eyes to existent beauty.

If you take too big a jump, you are in danger of falling. That, in one way, can be said to be the lesson of Mars. Mars is action, restlessness, impatience, fury, the desire for imposing one's will, by force at times. A study of the symbology of this planet teaches us that life cannot be beautiful if we rush and push and step on others in a frantic effort to be first, to obtain material success. Mars, negatively expressed, makes us want to know the answers too quickly. Negative Mars is superficial knowledge; the flash-in-the-pan, the slick, shiny object with no real substance. Patience is the lesson of Mars—one sometimes must wait for the really worthwhile things. Life, to use the words of the old radio soap operas, can be beautiful if you pay heed to the symbol of Mars—the arrow pointing upward. Look up to the future. Do not live in the past and expect to succeed.

Man's love for woman is one of the most beautiful things in this life, and it is symbolized, to a large extent, by Venus. This planet teaches the lesson of love; it is associated with beauty, luxury, appreciation for the finer things in life. On the negative side, we are warned of the dangers of excess and extravagance. Lustful pleasure can lead to an individual's downfall as surely and as swiftly as it led to the fall of the great Roman Empire. Put simply, too much of anything ceases to be good. The lesson of Venus is one of restraint. Restraint can prevent wars, havoc, destruction; it can prevent heartache; it can outline beauty and heighten your appreciation for the better things in life. There are many worthwhile things all around us if only we will but seek. To do this, you must be healthy in mind and body. You must be prepared, educationally and emotionally.

Man, having been entrusted with thinking apparatus, is responsible for his acts. He has more than instinct; he has a mind that works. Mercury is the symbol of thought, of ideas. The brain sends messages—the healthy body obeys. Mercury is quick, and so you must be when it comes to accepting life's challenges. You must not shrink back; come forward and as a thinking, intelligent being, accept the right and try to reject the wrong. This requires perception, which is an excellent key word for Mercury. You cannot depend merely on the physical senses. There is rhythm and beauty to be perceived; there is intelligence to be developed; there are sharp wits to be appreciated. Physical man is one small part of life; the mental realm is higher, more refined—although the physical aspects, as depicted by Mars and Venus, and by the 5th House, are not to be ignored. Yet, to fully comprehend, to perceive physical joys, one must have the harmony of Mercury, *mental harmony*. This is well illustrated through the 3rd and 9th Houses of the horoscope. The 3rd House, as we know, symbolizes the short journey, writing, flashes of insight which we often term "ideas." But the 9th House (symbolic of the "higher mind") develops the creative aspects of writing, turns ideas into sound philosophies, brings an appreciation of what has been written, gives us understanding. The 9th House promotes greater journeys into learning. Mercury starts with the "lower mind" and enables the individual to grow, to mature to the "higher mind."

The "giver of life" is symbolized by the Sun, the center of our Solar system. Sun-sign indications or "readings" are, perhaps, the most popular aspects of astrology. The Sun depicts basic characteristics, the character and the personality. It tells us "where we live." Later, when we go into a delineation of the various Sun signs, we will review some of the basic characteristics indicated by the Sun. The symbolism of the Sun is that of *purpose*—co-ordination and rhythm in nature. Our lives, too, have a basic rhythm, and astrology teaches us to find the "rate" of our own rhythm, and to go with instead of against it.

One of the major obstructions in the way of beauty is a negative attitude. Complaining is a path to unhappiness; a realization, on the other hand, of our many assets, our potentialities, is the road to peace, accomplishment and contentment. Jupiter is symbolic of the abundance of wealth and beauty open to man if he will but observe the wonders and opportunities surrounding him. Jupiter is wealth, not only in material goods but also in knowledge. Jupiter is associated with the 9th House, which represents higher learning. Jupiter is big (the largest planet), in a symbolic as well as in a material sense. Jupiter is cheer, luck. Jupiter helps us find beauty by advocating a constructive attitude based on cheerfulness, gratitude for what we possess. Jupiter is abundance; it overcomes the petty, urges man to become really big. Not many do. And when this occurs, his fellow men do not always recognize his growth. It sometimes is for the generations that follow to celebrate him, to study his teachings, to recognize his true greatness, his *bigness*. To be small is the opposite of Jupiter. It is to permit prejudice to rule. It is the enemy of reason, of the higher mind. To be small is to think that one is better or worse because of color or difference in methods of worship. Jupiter is the attainment of wisdom. It is money, success, but also the recognition that success is not aways dependent upon material goods.

Saturn brings tests, responsibility; it is the symbol of time and the tests of time; it is lasting value and it is representative of trial, tribulation, of growing and maturity. It is the opposite of the get-rich-quick approach. Responsibility is unpleasant to many persons because they have lessons to learn: the lessons that Saturn presents. Saturn brings restrictions, even upon freedom—the freedom to hurt others and to limit the free action of others cannot be considered freedom in the best sense. Those who cannot realize this have not learned the lesson of Saturn. There is supposed freedom of the press, for example, but there are also libel laws to protect individuals from abuses. Saturn, thus, is freedom to act within a defined area. One must recognize limitations, which is where Saturn enters the picture. To work, to struggle, to undergo hardships and to persist until the goal is achieved—this too is Saturn. All of the planets carry symbolic messages. Some are more sharply defined than others. Saturn, it seems, is very clear—and the astrologer who grasps Saturn is well along the way of understanding and interpreting the complete chart.

Uranus, like Saturn, has definite messages and meanings, carries specific indications. Saturn is time and testing; Jupiter is abundance; Mars is action—Uranus is surprise. Uranus is eccentric; it is publicity, sudden change, abrupt announcements, decisions. It is progressiveness, farsightedness, a willingness to pioneer. The planet symbolizes space travel, electricity, radio, television, entertainment—friends who are interested in occult subjects. Uranus tells us not to be afraid of the new. Life can be dull if you insist your way is always the right way. Uranus urges experimentation, testing, listening to various theories, no matter how farfetched they may seem. It is the rallying cry against going backward, the opponent of the reactionary.

All of the planets are associated with the various zodiacal signs: Mars with Aries; Venus with Libra and Taurus; Mercury with Gemini and Virgo; Moon with Cancer; Sun with Leo; Pluto with Scorpio; Jupiter with Sagittarius; Saturn with Capricorn; Uranus with Aquarius and Neptune with Pisces.

Thus, Aries persons must pay particular attention to the message or symbolism of Mars. They must become aware of the wisdom of waiting instead of rushing in where wiser persons fear to tread. Taurus and Libra persons are cautioned by Venus to avoid over- or self-indulgence. Mercury's lesson applies to the Gemini- and Virgo-born. They must strive to develop their sense of perception and to use it intelligently. Those born under Cancer will find life more worthwhile if they apply the lesson of the Moon and overcome the tendency to brood, to be overprotective. Leo natives learn from the Sun: to be thorough instead of flashy. Sagittarians, with Jupiter as a guidepost, should be "big" in the best sense and sweep away petty annoyances. Capricorn individuals, with Saturn as their symbolic ruler, must learn that time is something to consider, that tests should be met and welcomed as healthy challenges. Aquarians, with Uranus as a guide, can welcome the unusual, can experiment and encourage friends to confide their unusual interests and theories. For Pisces persons, Neptune provides a clear picture of the beauty which inspiration and imagination can provide. But this gift must be used constructively lest beauty be clouded by deception.

ARIES (Mar. 21 to Apr. 19): FIRST SIGN. MARS.
TAURUS (Apr. 20 to May 20): SECOND SIGN. VENUS.
GEMINI (May 21 to June 20): THIRD SIGN. MERCURY.
CANCER (June 21 to July 22): FOURTH SIGN. MOON.
LEO (July 23 to Aug. 22): FIFTH SIGN. SUN.
VIRGO (Aug. 23 to Sept. 22): SIXTH SIGN. MERCURY.
LIBRA (Sept. 23 to Oct. 22): SEVENTH SIGN. VENUS.
SCORPIO (Oct. 23 to Nov. 21): EIGHTH SIGN. PLUTO.
SAGITTARIUS (Nov. 22 to Dec. 21): NINTH SIGN. JUPITER.
CAPRICORN (Dec. 22 to Jan. 19): TENTH SIGN. SATURN.
AQUARIUS (Jan. 20 to Feb. 18): ELEVENTH SIGN. URANUS.
PISCES (Feb. 19 to Mar. 20): TWELFTH SIGN. NEPTUNE.

XXII

THE HOUSES

There are twelve Houses, just as there are twelve signs. Every department of human activity falls under one of these Houses. As with the planets and signs, we must become familiar with the Houses; we must enlarge upon basic meanings. As one develops skill, the Houses, like the planets, take on a rate of vibration, a rhythm, each one part of the whole. Thus if the 1st House represents the native and his personality, the 2nd House tells us how the native is apt to earn his living, how he is to accumulate material goods, and what form those goods are to take before being transformed into money. If the 3rd House represents, as it does, brothers and sisters, then the 4th House, which is *the 2nd from the 3rd,* tells us how the native's brothers and sisters obtain their money, their income. The 4th House also, of course, represents the native's security, his home, his old age, his eventual maturity and his father.

What we are trying to say here is that the Houses, beside their *basic* meanings, can be interpreted with refinements—mostly utilized in Horary astrology, which is yet another branch of this scientific art. Horary astrology is the art of answering direct, specific questions by taking the time (birth) of the query and setting up a map for the question. Thus is a related but different branch from Natal astrology. It is a fascinating subject and, after the student has mastered the techniques of Natal astrology, I would strongly urge that he familiarize himself with other branches: Horary, Mundane, astro-meteorology, medical, etc. In a Horary map, for example, if the native asked about an affair he suspected his mate were carrying on with another individual—one would look to the 5th from the 7th House because the 7th House represents the marriage partner. The 5th House represents love affairs, as differentiated from legal ties.

And so it is with all of the sections, or Houses. They are all related and all have basic meanings. But as the astrologer develops his skill, these meanings and indications are elaborated—they are refined until the astrologer becomes an analyst, an artist, interpreting with the skill of a master diagnostician.

Technically, the Houses are divisions of the heavens as seen at any point of time at any place on earth—with a corresponding division of the invisible heavens, beneath the earth. The meanings of the Houses are modified by the planets within them, by the aspects the planets make to each other.

It is best, at the start, to know the difference between a zodiacal sign and a House. The sign Aries could be on the cusp (starting point) not only of the 1st House, but the 2nd or 3rd, or any of the 12, equally divided (we are using the Equal House system) sections of the chart. The signs are the celestial divisions of the heavens. The Houses are 30° divisions relative to the geographical location (birthplace) of the native. The rotation of the earth causes the planets to pass through all 12 Houses during 24 hours. The sign rising or ascending in the eastern angle of the Houses at birth is on the cusp of the 1st House.

If the time of birth is unknown, the Sun-sign degree as given in the ephemeris for the month, day and year of birth is placed on the cusp of the 1st House. Actually, a Solar chart is a chart set up for sunrise. It is this kind of chart which is utilized in the forecasts printed in popular astrology magazines. Thus, without the time of birth, a Leo individual would have Leo on the cusp of the 1st House, Virgo on the 2nd, Libra on the 3rd, and so on through the 12 signs. We are now interested in interpretation.

The 1st House depicts the personality, the outward appearance of the native. It tells us how the individual is likely to react to a situation just as its opposite, the 7th House, relates information concerning public reaction to activities by the native. The first section of the horoscope is the impression made by the native. With Mars there, the native is active, dynamic, tends to be impatient, at times angry at slight provocation—often with himself for not attaining goals quickly enough. The Moon in the first section would incline the native toward moodiness, procrastination. Neptune here is indicative of a tendency toward self-deception, "negative dreaming" as opposed to creative thinking. The Sun, traditionally speaking, tells of a native with a "sunny disposition." Jupiter would be indicative of an expansive personality, one who is inclined toward extravagance.

Of course, as in all forms of interpretation, no one indication should be taken alone—the chart must be compared as a whole. This must be emphasized. But we do need a starting point, a place to begin our interpretation of the horoscope. In effect, that is just what the 1st House is. Venus in the 1st sector reveals the native has, on the positive side, an appreciation for the "good things in life." Negatively, the native becomes selfish, wants possessions and comforts, and does not always think it is necessary to earn these nice things. Mercury, in the main, is regarded as "neutral." But Mercury in the 1st section denotes one who wants to express ideas, often through writing—sometimes through lecturing. Mercury here stresses activity, communication—at times this position tells of carelessness, a tendency to speak before all the facts are known. Pluto in the 1st represents the native whose personality is an outstanding factor in success—or failure. People tend to be suspicious at first encounter, perhaps a bit frightened, because of the native's apparent intenseness. These persons seldom do things halfway—it's all the way or nothing. Saturn here indicates responsibility early in life—often because the parents have separated or one of the parents died while the native was young. Saturn here indicates one who is serious, often "asking for punishment." These persons must cultivate a sense of humor and must learn to choose friends and places with great care.

Uranus in the 1st House represents one who attracts attention, publicity and, on the negative side, notoriety. These people act quickly, sometimes carelessly—they seem prone to emotional and physical "upsets." They can be vital, magnetic, attractive. But they must learn that attracting attention is only half the story—being able to fulfill promise and potential is the other, most important half. The 1st House represents action, personal appearance, disposition and manner. The Moon in this section is indicative of a native who can deal successfully with women, one who is quite conscious of personal appearance and can commercialize on this knowledge. Often, such an individual has a kind of "moon-faced" appearance. This at times is also true of one born under Cancer (Moon ruler), or one who has Cancer rising or on the cusp of the 1st House. The Moon in the first sector reveals one who is responsive to public reaction—and would make a fine entertainment or social director. Also, the Moon here is indicative of one who is subject to numerous moods at a fast, furious pace. A sense of balance becomes the key to greater potential for success and happiness.

The 1st House is the manner of approach. It also has much to do with vitality, health, personal habits. The 1st House is what we are and what we hope to gain. It is contact with the public and the appearance we make. It is a starting point; from here we go on to grow, mature, develop.

The 2nd House has much to do with the native's desires. He "starts" from the 1st sector—his personality is evident. Now, he wants to add to what he possesses. Basically, the 2nd House represents money, income, possessions. It is the means of fulfilling desires materially.

The 2nd House represents the native's desire—his need for fulfillment. Often, before full development is achieved, this need is based largely on material goods. This House represents financial standing, possessions, movable property, earning and spending capacities, the manner—or lack of it—in which the native fulfills obligations and potential. Thus, Jupiter in the 2nd House appears to bring the element of "luck," of expansion. One with Jupiter here is never satisfied merely to be "secure," but must constantly reach out, expand. Jupiter in this House position represents the financier, the individual with the big deal just around the corner. Whether that corner is successfully turned depends much on the remainder of the chart—other indications, characteristics. Jupiter here is "pleasant" in the sense that dealing with or being with successful persons is pleasant. One with Jupiter here can be relied upon to do the most with the least—but when the "big deal" falls through, it falls hard. All the way or nothing may be one way of describing Jupiter in the 2nd House. But this position bounces back, ready for another fling.

Saturn, on the other hand, takes time. Saturn in the 2nd House can deny the material goods, can represent frustration. But in the long haul, this position brings with it greater appreciation for what is gained. Saturn here depicts a native who builds for the future— and must be willing to forego some immediate luxuries.

The Moon in the 2nd House presents a picture of one who often is tempted to embrace superficial values. This native spends his money on bright, shiny "objects." Where Jupiter here would be planning on expansion, the Moon in the second sector thinks, basically, of obtaining, not multiplying or expanding. The Moon here is one who must gain or make money by appealing to the public imagination. In other words, this native often charms by his very financial inconsistencies. He attracts publicity; people obtain pleasure from reading about his exploits. This is not as good as one might imagine for long-range projects—but exciting while it lasts!

The Sun in this position is quite favorable. The personality is integrated where needs are concerned. The native is able to distinguish between desire and actual requirements. This position often "attracts" money where Jupiter here has to "drum it up." Mercury gains money-making ideas through reading and other forms of communication. This is a very good position for traveling salesmen, for those who "make a pitch" over television or radio, or who help others do so through advertising programs.

Pluto here (2nd) depicts one able to turn liabilities into assets. This individual could prosper in antiques, in hobbies featuring photographic restoration or historical projects. Mars in this position basically reflects one who is impatient, even furious, if his expectations are not met quickly. Action is the key. The lesson to be learned is that quality sometimes is not so "quick" as one would desire. This native requires guidance—money tends to "burn a hole" in his pocket.

Uranus in the 2nd attracts many who are only too willing to

help the native take a chance—with *his* money. Unorthodox methods of achieving gain appear best suited for one with Uranus here. Neptune, on the other hand, indicates one who gains behind the scenes. In fact, with Neptune here, the native would be well advised to be as practical as possible. Otherwise, the tendency is to reach a bit beyond the legal limit. Neptune tells of imagination in connection with earning power—but also is indicative of deception. This native must check associates with care—and must not listen to promises of schemes enabling him to gain riches rapidly. Venus here is indicative of financial gain through promotion of luxury items. The native, however, may have such a love of luxury himself that he tends to eat up his profits. This is generally a favorable position, but some solid strength and will power are required.

The 3rd House is associated with brothers, sisters, neighbors, the mind, ideas, short journeys, communications, the ability to take apparently unrelated facts and blend them into a complete story. It also has to do with memory, publicity, advertising, quick changes, travels for purposes of renewing family contacts. Just as the 1st House represents the "I," the personality, and the 2nd House is what "I do" to bring in the source of income, the 3rd House, basically, represents relations with family members, the ideas and interests which come about as the result of having earned the right to indulge in hobbies. It is the mind in a basic sense; it is the House of ideas, sensory impressions, humor, the ability to appreciate what one can obtain through his earnings.

Saturn here can bring depression. In the nativity, the "permanent" Saturn inclines the native to take a dark view of persons, events, potentials, ideas. The native has a lesson to learn: the mental attitude affects almost everything, from appetite for food to appetite for living. Saturn here demands practicality, but does not always have the means to steer along such an even course. The native should be encouraged to take a "lighter" view. Uranus here, by contrast, needs to learn some lessons in practicality. It is a House position which indicates one who gets on a horse and rides off in all directions at once. It indicates unusual relations with friends and family members; it depicts much travel, and a tendency to waste time, money and ideas. On the positive side, however, this position brings friends who aid the native in fulfilling desires through travel, publications, the writing of unusual material (often comedy). It is a very unusual position—and the native would tend to be one whose ideas, actions, reactions are considered "far out."

Jupiter here can almost be considered a "gift." The native has intense desire for higher education—both in the academic sense and in life in general. This is an individual who possesses what some term "mother wit"—basic natural wisdom, or "horse sense." On the negative side, Jupiter in the 3rd tends to have eyes bigger than his stomach (speaking, of course, in the poetic sense!); it causes the native to embrace too many, too quickly.

Neptune in the 3rd is difficult to satisfy because what is available does not seem worth attaining. Neptune in this position deals in illusion. It is an excellent position for a magician or illusionist, for this individual is in love with the intangible. He should promote constructive outlets, such as the arts, including writing, painting, acting, theatrical production and designing. Pluto here indicates that ideas are intense; nothing is done halfway. These persons are best suited for very progressive forms of education, for labor relations, for pursuits which demand the courage of one's convictions.

Mars in the 3rd promotes general restlessness and impatience. On the positive side, it brings about a native who demands direct action. Here is the person who is forthright—not always diplomatic, but dynamic, direct and able to obtain results. What the results *are* is the question! For this individual 3rd tends to let the chips fall where they may. The personality and the ideas of the native are closely allied. Here is a native who believes in what he is doing—sometimes too intensely. The pitfalls are obvious. The native's outlook should be broadened, or he should be toughened. The hard knocks are there—the danger of excessive speed, especially in traffic, also is evident. This chart is one of action—and one which could be involved in danger brought on by inattention to details.

Mercury in the 3rd is the natural mark of the communicator, the traveler, the critic, the native who brings to our attention the many interesting things taking place around us. He is not necessarily an artist in his own right, but one who can appreciate and criticize the artistic efforts of others. He is an excellent conversationalist, but often "talks out" emotions before they can be "captured" as scenes for any kind of important creative output.

Venus here reveals that the native gets what he wants through promise. He "looks good," he shows "class." Taken alone, this position does not tell us what chances the native has for fulfilling that promise. Other parts of the horoscope must be examined, blended, interpreted as a whole. But Venus here certainly brings to the native an appreciation for the finer things in life—gives him ideas about luxury, beauty, art, treasure, fulfillment of desire. It is physical and mental. He is handsome. She is lovely. But is there anything to back this beauty up? That is the question. Of course we are not talking about physical beauty. The 3rd House deals mainly with the *ideas* of the person, not with his appearance. But the ideas attract to him people who tend to think he is "beautiful." That's where the potential, the promise comes in—a very fascinating position to interpret and observe.

The Sun in the 3rd House is a position which attracts "bright" people, is one which brings the native in contact with intelligent, creative individuals. The Sun here is a good position (all other factors considered). It is indicative of a basically optimistic outlook. It means that the native is predisposed toward the right decisions at the right time. It makes one capable of adjusting. The Moon here, on the other hand, is a position which creates doubts but also promotes a healthy intellectual curiosity. The family of the native says he takes too many chances and should settle down. But, basically, this position (Moon in the 3rd) is one which makes intriguing, mysterious personalities.

The 4th House is indicative of where the native lives, his residence, his anchor, his security, his sense of being. This is the section of his chart which can relate to well-being, or to a feeling of being tied down. It is an important, sensitive point in the chart. All astrologers wishing to render creative, useful interpretations must take time with this House. In a sense, the 4th House is *time:* the time it takes to get established; the time necessary to recognize contributions made by the father or head of the family; finally, the time it takes to gain maturity necessary in the expression of adult love. The 4th House precedes the 5th, which has to do with romance, love, relations with members of the opposite sex. We have not yet approached that point. We remain in the 4th sector. We are preparing, getting ready, getting established. The 4th has to do with another kind of time: with memories. It is what we learn from experience, or what we fail to absorb from the past lessons we have studied. The 4th is domesticity, home, the father, the native's early life, his childhood, the character of his home environment; it has to do with lands, houses, estates, leases, real estate transactions. It is our preparation for how we react to life in general—a vital section of the chart.

While the 3rd sector tells us something of the native's *memory,* the 4th deals with his *memories.* The difference is in time and effect. The 3rd is fleeting—a knack of remembering, including facts and figures, such as might be required in a quiz game. But the 4th is concerned with memories, as related to experience. It is solid, it is time, the land where one lives, the way he establishes his character, the memories which help mold him into an adult. He is preparing to share love, home, life itself. He is part of what his environment and the dominant member of his family have made him.

Mercury here shows many persons entering and leaving the home: the native is one whose elders may well have had literary contacts. Sometimes there was much moving about in early life—a feeling of being far from settled. This depends, of course, upon the remainder of the chart. But Mercury in the 4th (other factors considered) brings with it a need to explore before settling down; it makes the native one who wants to try different lands, environments, homes—one who visits and is visited by relatives who travel a great distance. The native's ideas, very often, are extremely conservative—he can be very stubborn. Once he makes up his mind to do something, come hell or high water he proceeds. He often knows he's on the wrong track—but the quest now is a challenge and at times turns into a crusade.

The Sun in the 4th is favorable for dealing in real estate; it also is indicative of one who can be poetic where the home and family are concerned. Here are favorable indications in connection with parents, with ultimate security.

The Moon here stresses loyalty to family, to land, to country—the native feels genuine pleasure in making "a place" for loved ones. This native has a sense of humor, but not such a good sense of satire. At times he actually seems to be playing a role—one which can make him appear ridiculous. On the positive side, the Moon here is a refreshing kind of loyalty and dependabiliy; it can indicate skill at making a profit in connection with sight-seeing tours or travel aimed at viewing old or famous homes, museums, etc. Comfort in old age is indicated—and a fondness for antiques which could be turned into a profitable hobby or business. The Moon in the 4th is excellent for dealing with mothers in general: this native would make an excellent "front man" for a children's photographer, a children's clothing store, etc.

Venus here typifies caution where permanent ties, such as marriage, are concerned. It sometimes depicts a late but happy marriage. The native likes to eat and has to watch his weight, for he tends to go to extremes in eating, drinking—the luxuries of life. He needs a place to come home to.

Mars in the 4th tells of stormy sessions in domestic life. There are many changes, many dangers, including fire. The native must carefully observe transits over this position. His best therapy: learn to bring order into life. Self-discipline is required. He must set an example himself instead of demanding that others do so. His personality, at times, feels blocked or shut in; he wants to get away from it all. But he must finally learn that one does not run away from himself. On the positive side, the native is willing to fight for country, home, possessions. He attracts persons with "fiery" ideas, very creative individuals who are full of life—so much so, they often break things, including valuable possessions!

Pluto in the 4th sector indicates one who needs to have his authority recognized in his home. And he would like to extend this "home" to a large area. Difficulties in connection with home life and childhood are indicated—the kind which often put a chip on an individual's shoulder. He goes around subconsciously daring the world to "knock it off."

Jupiter here indicates one who enjoys the feeling of expansiveness in his home. He does not like a closed-in feeling. Venus, on the other hand, might enjoy this kind of closeness. Jupiter loves fine surroundings with lots of space. Benefits are indicated through real estate, but the native must avoid extravagance and attempts to gain too much for too little, and too soon. Jupiter here wants gain so much that, on the negative side, the native becomes greedy. Saturn, by contrast, is willing to wait, often too long in a quest, a need to feel secure. The native often surrounds himself with old books or antiques and makes his home resemble a museum or auction site. There are problems shown in connection with environment and parents, including the possible separation of parents or early death of one.

Uranus here paints a picture of eccentric home life, including a very unusual parent. There is the lack of an "anchor"; the native does not trust himself to be happy in his home life. This may make marriage a special problem. The need for friends, laughter, parties in the home is indicated. On the negative side, Uranus here is indicative of a basic weakness, the fear of being alone. Neptune in the 4th has illusions concerning "ideal" home life. The native has many lessons to learn, and often comes down to earth with a thump. He tends to attract persons who deceive him in his own home (he falls for a salesman's line very easily). He benefits through music and artistic endeavors in the home—he should not concentrate on dealing in homes or real estate. This indicates one who attracts unusual experiments in his home, including séances.

The 5th House is one which should absorb the serious astrologer's interest. It is the section of the chart associated with sex, love, and children; creative expression and endeavors; amusement, change, variety; the willingness and ability of the native to give of himself. The 5th House is the sex drive; it also is related to long-range accomplishments, including education. Kinsey found that sex activity and higher education are indeed connected. An active 5th House—one indicating great sex activity at a relatively early age—might be interpreted as one which discourages higher education. Kinsey studied five brothers, particularly their sexual behavior at the age of 16. Four of the brothers were "active" and did not go on to college. The "inactive" (by comparison) brother did go on to a university. This should indicate that the 5th House tells not only of affairs of the heart, but how these activities affect much of the life pattern. A "healthy" 5th House leads to happiness in various departments of life. This is one in which the native is not restricted, does not have to prove himself, but can accept and give love.

Saturn here creates friction and restriction. Thus the astrologer should encourage greater freedom—should be sure the native does not begin hating the father image, authority, law. The astrologer no longer should be one who merely "shows off" by telling a native with Saturn here that he has had difficulty in self-expression, that the love act often leaves him feeling incomplete. The creative astrologer, perhaps with the aid of a qualified psychologist, must help the native understand himself—must help him free himself of myths, restrictions, taboos. Freedom where love and sex are concerned represents, to a great extent, over-all freedom, fulfillment and happiness. Saturn here paints a picture of timidity, of delay, of self-denial. Note to the astrologer: Find out what has caused the native to attempt to punish himself through self-denial.

The 5th House represents children, recreation, pleasure, emotional and romantic tendencies. Jupiter here is good: when other chart indications confirm, it brings "luck," the ability to speculate and show a profit. It attracts the native to children, can make him a successful publicist—especially in connection with amusement parks, theaters, etc. The 5th House is drama, the theater, in the sense that skilled actors manipulate emotions for the entertainment and enlightenment of vast audiences. Jupiter here represents a love of grandeur; it makes one sensuous. The 5th is the time in life when we are ready to offer love, to receive it—to bring with our love some kind of shelter, protection, maturity. (We have passed through the "experience" of the 4th).

Pluto here depicts interest in sports. Thus the native could be an athlete (other factors considered) or would be successful in writing about athletic events. A love of gambling is indicated—and a "lucky" object is desired. Sometimes the "object" is represented by the mate. This native is not easy to live with, but he seldom shows a desire to change.

Mercury here intellectualizes—he often substitutes thought for action; the Sun here, however, is strong (positive) and is a wonderful indication of popularity, adulation and success in dealing with members of opposite sex. The native is self-indulgent, has way with children and attracts numerous affairs of the heart.

The 5th reveals our mode of emotional expression. With Uranus here, it is one that is sensational and at time leads to adverse publicity. There is a tendency to have many love affairs and to attract eccentric lovers. Neptune is indicative of self-deception where love is concerned. The native tends to idealize, to seek perfection. He wants a kind of love often found only in cheap motion pictures: nonreal, where no powerful feelings come into play. He shouldn't gamble. He has a tendency to brood and be moody, to think "if I only had done this or that" . . . instead of starting at once to make his life better and happier, more productive. Venus here is passionate, loves life and people, and can be successful in "painting" people as a writer, artist or theatrical producer. A gain is indicated through children, perhaps as a publisher of books or a producer of plays for children.

Mars here is ardent, nothing halfway; it is impulsive, often throwing away happiness because of lack of discipline. Mars here gives in to temptation too easily. The native needs an outlet, love and creative endeavor. He is an excellent competitor but a terrible loser. The Moon in the 5th House often brings early success and publicity; it indicates a native who "makes a splash." He has an excellent sense of drama, and is good at dealing with children, including teaching. The Sun here is a wonderful indication of success, a tendency to dominate in affairs of the heart—one who has the vitality to make loved ones physically happy.

When comparing charts, it is very important to note which planets fall into the native's 5th from another chart. For example, a native with Leo on the cusp of the 5th—compared to a native with Saturn in Leo—would have "another person's" Saturn in his 5th. This is not so good, as we know, where freedom in connection with love is concerned. This technique of comparison should, of course, be used with all the Houses and in connection with the over-all chart. But the comparison technique is of special importance in connection with the 5th House. Here is a suggestion: begin interpreting your chart (or the native's) by closely observing the 5th House; start with the sign on the cusp of the 5th, the planets in the 5th, the zodiacal and House position of the ruler of the 5th, the aspects made to and by the ruler of the 5th, the aspects in relation to planets in the 5th. Study the 5th House and find out what it is all about—and you will have learned much about the emotional life and potentials of the native.

The 6th House represents service, clothing, pets, physical well-being or lack of it; it reveals the native's capacity to render service, to work with associates and to express appreciation for being served. It is the kind of security one feels as a result of making loved ones happy; it is the gain obtained from loving and being loved. It has to do with a job rather than a *profession,* which is depicted by the 10th House. The 6th tells us something about the physical constitution of the native and his relations with everyday people, including those who serve him in various capacities. The Sun here tells a basic story of determination; faithfulness; regard for health, beauty and vitality. The Moon in the 6th is indicative of numerous job changes, indecision in connection with work. The native is apt to give the impression of being restless or cranky, but he is very considerate of those who work for or serve him. Pluto paints a picture of one who constantly sides with the underdog—it marks one interested in labor movements, union activities. He is not afraid to stick his neck out. Mercury, on the other hand, can cause one to be too conservative—inclined to have fine ideas, but needing a push in carrying through on creative thinking.

Venus in the 6th tends to attract the native to artistic endeavors; he is very good at promoting and selling luxury items. Success is indicated in creating services for women. The native tends to want love on his own terms—he is not very willing to make emotional adjustments. Mars here is more significant; the native can be rash, can drive himself to illness by setting too fast a pace. He can alienate those who work for or with him by a display of irritability and impatience. He can be accident-prone if other areas of the chart indicate problems which are not faced and resolved.

Jupiter here depicts a native who is basically giving, generous, willing to offer the benefit of the doubt—he is interested in charity drives and would make a good public-relations director of a philanthropic project. This is an excellent indication for organizing workers; the native gets the most from the least because he knows how to keep morale high. He would make a good vocational guidance advisor.

Saturn here attracts the native to large organizations, including government work. But he tends to get bogged down in details. It is best to urge him to see a project as a whole rather than in bits and pieces. He must learn to accept constructive suggestions and change the course of action when it leads to a "dead end." Uranus here shows one who is original, inventive, can think of different methods of accomplishing a project. He is suited for advertising agency work, for a publicity office, for directing specific projects. He doesn't fare too well when restricted to only one way of doing things. He is at his best when his versatility is permitted to find expression.

This is not the best House position for Neptune. The native encounters unusual, even peculiar conditions in employment and has experiences he often prefers to keep to himself. This leads to brooding and, if unchecked, to actual physical illness. He needs to have his sense of humor activated; he must learn to appreciate his own foibles—and those of others. The key is maturity.

The 7th House is opposite from the 1st; it is that section of the horoscope relating to partnerships, the public, the way the world looks to the native—it is that point arrived at when the native is ready to accept the added responsibility of a mate, marital in some cases, a business partner in other instances. The 7th House represents individuality as opposed to personality, symbolized by the 1st House. The 7th represents human relations and how we meet them. Uranus here would tell us of one likely to become involved in numerous sudden relationships: that planetary position (taken alone) is indicative of more than one marriage, of divorce, sudden decisions and unusual environment because the people the native attracts are out of the ordinary. Unusual reactions from the public are indicated: this is a good planetary House position for a publicist, but not so good for one in public relations. In other words, Uranus in the 7th is fine for flash, sensationalism, putting over an idea or a scheme, but not so good for the institutional type of campaign aimed at promoting confidence and an image of permanency. If there is anything Uranus in the 7th is not, it is permanent. Uranus here is odd, subject to change, the spotlight of attention: at times the activities of the native resemble harmless antics. At other times (depending upon transits and how they aspect 7th House Uranus) the actions "bring the house down," cause the public to cry, "Shame! Shame!" The serious astrologer, noting this angular position of Uranus (7th like the 1st, 4th and 10th Houses is on one of the angles of the horoscope), cautions his client against entering into bizarre agreements.

The 7th House is related to the outcome of lawsuits, of opposition, of efforts to gain public attention. The 7th House is persistence, perfection, the "perfect" blend, the partnership, the marriage, the public reaction to our efforts; it is relations with people whose signatures we require for sales, success, the "big break." It is legal and covers "enemies," fines, mistakes, the rectification of errors based on lack of experience. It is marriage and the number of marriages—it is the "legalizing" of love, it is public sanction; the 7th is a fascinating section of the chart and covers challenge, mergers, legal affairs, competitors, the effect of our actions upon the public. Pluto here pushes the native toward great independence, gives him a strong desire for freedom; it inclines him toward a dominant marital or business partner. This individual sometimes places his trust in the wrong persons—giving others the same amount of freedom he personally appreciates. The native must be taught to be discriminating, to choose with care, both in business and personal affairs. The 7th House is justice and the law—in a small and "large" sense. It is, if one is inclined to be metaphysical, *Karma,* and therefore that section of the chart which, to a great extent, pays us back for past efforts. The Sun here is "pleasant," in that others are attracted to the native, and he tends to bring happiness where partnerships are concerned. Jupiter is similar, indicating a generous, wealthy marriage partner—and success where mergers and partnerships are concerned.

Neptune brings about unusual conditions relating to 7th House affairs, including a marriage partner considered "weird," psychic, mediumistic—it has much to do with deception, and the native is advised to check fine print in all legal matters. Neptune here could mean a mate who is physically handicapped, for the native tends to attract situations in which people "lean" on him. Saturn could attract a morbidly sensitive mate; the native may have to learn from experience where marriage, public relations or legal affairs enter the picture. At times, disparity in age, temperament, outlook and ambition are quite evident where native's "partner" is concerned.

Mercury here inclines to changes, doubts, a temptation to "put something over" on the world—including his partners. Venus is harmony and indicates success, with great attraction for the law as a hobby or profession. This native could attract a beautiful mate, all other things in chart being equal (good aspects to Venus in 7th, etc.).

Mars here is impulse—the impulse to get married, to close a deal, to make one's influence felt, to obtain early success—to keep moving. Mars here reveals partnerships, relations which break and leave emotional wounds. It attracts a dominant mate, someone who wants to tell the native "what's best." And the native feels he "should be told." He feels inadequate, and the astrologer must check other portions of chart, especially the 5th House, to determine the cause for this feeling of lack. Mars here is a native who has to prove himself. He has to receive public acclaim, to be assured and reassured of his ability, his talents, his prowess in all fields.

The Moon in the 7th represents popularity with the public—often the native is tempted to make things smooth rather than to pioneer new trails. He needs discipline. Otherwise, he fluctuates from one mission or person to another. He is not ready for marriage until a degree of maturity is assured. He tends to attract persons of great sensitivity—and unless he is ready to make some concessions, the relationship "blows up."

The 8th House is associated with secrets, with sex, with the creative and "life force"; it is that section of the chart which represents release—release from frustration, fear, superstition—it is the end of inhibition, it is rebirth—it is the area of life experience which marks the time when the old is torn down to make way for the new. It is revitalization. The 8th House is the money of the partner or wife, money which is in the form of hidden assets. It is a difficult section to interpret; it is money belonging to other people; it is inheritance; it is money one has earned, perhaps without knowing it. The 8th House is power and responsibility; it represents emotional steam, hidden assets, feelings which smoulder "undercover." This section is the occult, the hidden, the subtle, the "boiling point." It has been called the section dealing with death, with money one gains through the death of another person. It can be the transmutation of tragedy into power. It is the financial relationship of *others* to the native: the others being a partner or the world in general. The 8th House represents the native's financial responsibility toward others—promises and potential that are kept or fall apart. It is also a section relating to the creative powers, to sex, but in a more definite, heavy-handed manner than in the 5th sector.

Pluto here can be militant, demanding—can also be fearful of the future, of responsibilities. On the positive side, Pluto is willing to tear down financial plans and structures in order to make way for the new. Negatively, Pluto hangs on to the past—even to a losing proposition—because of fear of the future and its challenges. Pluto in the 8th is resistance, but often the kind that melts too quickly. This means the native is influenced by associates and their promises. He may resist change—but if those around him are convincing about the future being "rosy," then the native stops resisting. This is an unusual part of chart to examine because the 8th in itself is mysterious, filled with dark, deep drives and frustrations. And Pluto *itself* symbolizes the type of experience we are never quite prepared for, because it is unique, threatening, yet with an over-all promise of holding the solution to all problems. So, Pluto here gives us the native who can be at once reactionary and ultraprogressive. Pluto in the 8th needs to grow up and become self-reliant and realize that heaven on earth can be here if we utilize our assets to the best of our ability and permit our spiritual side to flourish. Otherwise, this native (other things being considered) can wander through life looking and never being satisfied—no matter what or whom he finds.

The 8th House is the House of mystery—it is that section covering the unknown, stretching to include what man fears and what he reveres. Saturn here tends to give us a native who seeks to deny himself. He seeks companionship among those who complain and brood—but who do not necessarily take any direct action to relieve the conditions which cause the brooding. Saturn here is one who may marry "below his station," who must earn his own way or be disappointed in what is left him, given him or awarded to him. No financial shortcuts (other things in the chart being equal) are evident here, unless we find Jupiter in the 5th well aspected, which would then indicate some kind of windfall is indeed a possibility.

Jupiter here, in the 8th, reveals gains through resourcefulness—the competent handling of money—and unusual, "healthy" contacts made as the result of an unusual hobby. Gain through the mantic arts is indicated.

The Sun here is powerful, giving the native tremendous creative energy. The astrologer should urge him to find an outlet for this energy, possibly through writing, acting and other pursuits which challenge the drive possessed by the native. Taken alone, the Sun here is favorable, for it brightens an otherwise dark corner. Just as Neptune helps offset the materialistic side through spiritual expression, the Sun gives the native a bright, humorous outlook in money matters, earning power and other activities which many consider anything but a pleasure to pursue. Neptune does not lend humor (as does the Sun to the 8th), but does temper the harsh, materialistic necessities with a warm, spiritual glow. This native is intrigued with religion, life after death, the occult and the "borderline" sciences, including dowsing, ESP, hypnotism. He may have the ability to perceive the future and to be "psychic" about the past.

Uranus here (in the 8th House) is indicative of unusual conditions involving money belonging to partners, and of tremendous attraction to the occult. The key is balance. Otherwise, the native tends to give in to superstition and fear, and to sit back and wait for his boat to come in, loaded down with riches. The native has a unique sense of humor but does not always put it to good use. He is apt to offend friends by poking satirical fun in their direction. If he could put this kind of humor on paper, in the form of cartoons or stories, it might prove very profitable.

The Moon here gives the native the feeling that security is the thing most needed. He saves for the future, he invests—and, at the same time, he can also complain that others are having all the fun. He denies himself out of a sense of duty. The native must overcome a tendency to store chestnuts merely for the sake of storing. The key is greater relaxation, a broadening of interests. He can attract women investors, and must not take advantage of their trust—if he does, trouble ahead! He is very interested in subjects others may consider morbid, such as suicide, causes of death and burial information, especially where costs, trends, public opinion and desires are concerned.

Venus here lays emphasis on money—marrying for money or for a better social position. Venus is luxury and beauty and desire; it is sensuousness and "deep-down" drives. The combination can be too much if allowed to run over into too rich a cream. In other words, the native must not give in to his appetites in too complete a sense. This includes excess eating, drinking, physical love in a manner leading to promiscuity. Mercury here can make one sly, a schemer, can tell us of a native able to get what he wants *when* he wants it, including sex. The trouble is that he doesn't always enjoy what he thought he wanted—once he does obtain it. He needs to mature, to display greater discrimination, to realize that he possesses, in a manner of speaking, a magic lantern. He needs but "rub" (think, put ideas into motion, slyly scheme, or in some other fashion set his sights) that lantern and he has what he thinks he requires. But he must be guided toward "right" thinking. Otherwise, Mercury here is like a child given all the candy he asks for—he eventually makes himself sick and comes to despise what he once loved.

Mars here is strife, possibly concerning a partner's money. The native doesn't care about what other people think he should do with his money. Conversely, he often feels quite capable of entering disputes involving other people's money or public funds. He is not good at long-range saving. The astrologer should attempt to guide this native along lines leading to a greater regard for future security.

The 9th House is higher education, metaphysics, logic, the structure of our lives, the meaning of our existence. It is the abstract; it is intuition, inspiration, dreams, visions; it is religion, higher thought processes, publishing, communication over long distances, long journeys as opposed to the short journeys symbolized by the 3rd House (opposite of the 9th). The 9th represents legal affairs, relatives by law, vast distances, journeys of the mind as well as physical journeys overseas. An "active" (one with numerous planets) 9th House *activates* these aspects of life. Jupiter is in an excellent position here—giving the native a brilliance which attracts students, followers, admirers—and attracts *him* to success as a writer, publisher, student of the law, and of the way people think, and the way they act toward each other. The native is a natural humanitarian. He has worldwide contacts, activity in connection with foreign lands; he has to do with advertising and public relations, and propaganda in its best sense. Jupiter here indicates a toleration for beliefs of others; it makes for fine writing, publishing, and attraction to sports and the outdoor life.

Mars here may require caution during travel, caution in that the native speaks and writes on impulse rather than as a result of real knowledge. He is enthusiastic and independent, but tends to be fanatical once he gets hold of an idea or religious concept. Saturn tends toward orthodoxy, conservatism, the upholding of established principles, while Pluto is willing to throw away the good with the bad in order to get started again. The native tends to feel he has all the answers. The astrologer must guide him along lines which develop a love of ideas for themselves, rather than blind adherence to one concept, idea or method. Much travel is indicated—and connection with unusual causes and publications.

The Moon here is the dreamer, the creator, the artist, the man who often seems to be "above and beyond it all." He must learn to come down to earth so that he actually communicates instead of merely relating ideas and experiences abstractly. The Sun here tells of noble motives, but a sense of practicality is often found lacking. Venus creates such a desire for harmony that the native appears to lack "fight." Mercury is the writer, traveler, publisher, the propagandist, the lecturer—the individual who gets from one place to another, from one idea to another, often without stopping long enough to absorb true values. The native must be taught reverence for basic principles. He must learn the rules before breaking them.

Neptune here provides love of beauty and indicates long journeys overseas, a mystical attitude toward religion—and, on the negative side, a complete lack of appreciation for material needs. Uranus indicates surprises where legal, religious and travel affairs are concerned. The native possesses unusual drives, ideas, desires. Often he changes his mind on a moment's notice; he is subject to inspiration, passionate beliefs in unorthodox causes—and is quite willing to accept public scorn in order to continue toward his goal. The astrologer must help the native recognize his goal, once it is reached.

The 10th House represents career, ambition, aspirations, standing in the community, authority, willingness to work for a goal, an ideal—inventiveness related to profession. It represents the native's business, professional activity, position in society—what he is capable of attaining. It is that section of the chart which has to do with drive, ambition, determination; it summarizes the native's relationship to the world in which he lives through his occupation, achievements, advancement along the lines of endeavor he has chosen. Saturn here makes for work, gives the native determination to continue working until he achieves his goal. Jupiter indicates recognition, just as the Sun brings fame, at times early in life; Uranus brings unusual conditions in connection with an occupation, while Neptune takes the native along strange paths and introduces him to people who delve into the unknown.

This House deals with those in authority—the "boss," the dominant individual in the native's professional life. It also represents the mother, just as the opposite, the 4th, depicts the father.

The 10th House is business and the influence the native exerts in his own circle, his own time. This House also reveals what the native thinks of his own abilities. Neptune could mean self-doubt, self-deception, a view that is nonmaterialistic, while Jupiter is indeed materialistic, and the Sun requires publicity, adulation. The Moon here is indicative of changes where profession and goals are concerned—help from women is indicated. A native with the Moon here is in touch with the people, is able to "feel the pulse" of the public. This is good for publicity, exploitation, promotion, advertising. Mercury here is apt to give us a native who demands speed, from himself and others. Often this leads to superficial efforts and makes one a reporter rather than a writer, a talker instead of an individual who accomplishes things. It makes one active, but the act of being busy is not necessarily constructive. Saturn is more permanent, more reliable in the long run. Pluto here makes one willing to fight authority, to battle the orthodox, to try new methods, to be attracted to new professions—the native tends to be impatient; he wants others to recognize him as an authority, perhaps before he has earned that right.

Mars here is one whose personality is a driving force. The native wants to be dominant, wants attention, wants to make a name for himself. On the negative side, he is belligerent, and takes needless chances in order to draw attention to himself. This native is dynamic and positive—often stubborn, militant, attracted to force and power, with a desire to manipulate people and events. The competent astrologer must find out the why of this militancy. It may involve domination or lack of supervision by one of the parents. The parents may have been separated by death or divorce. Mars here is definite, so much so that it is unlikely to exist as a pattern in the native's life unless there is a definite reason (hunger for love, hunger for authority, need to be understood). If unable to move armies or crowds, the native "moves" mechanical objects or works with steel; he could be a surgeon or construction worker. But he never is satisfied merely to be "moved" himself. He is only "moved" toward greater events, greater opportunities, a greater niche in life.

Venus here depicts a great desire for social acceptance. The native is generally regarded as popular with women. He knows how to appeal to the love of luxury in people, and could succeed in the manufacture or sale of luxury items. A fortunate relationship is indicated with one parent or an individual in authority. The native tends to attract those who can help him—he needs to learn, to a greater extent, how to help himself. The public likes him; he is popular. But he may never, unless other areas of chart so indicate, do anything "valuable." This position is not one for pioneering into new areas. Instead, it is one which enjoys the "good life." The native does not necessarily want anything else; all must be smooth—love, career, health, money. Naturally, this is not always possible—Venus in the 10th has many lessons to learn. A more earthy attitude is perhaps the best therapeutic course for this native.

The 10th House brings us into contact with people and situations connected with professional activity. In turn, there are social contacts. The 10th is the base from which we dive into social intercourse. It is our "contact" with the world—and it represents how a certain part of the world—business—views us. What we make of ourselves is largely answered by this area of the horoscope.

The 11th House represents hopes, wishes, desires, friendships, social contacts—the native makes professional contacts through the 10th and through these, he moves on to social intercourse. Jupiter here is fine; it denotes expansion of interests, an ever-growing circle of friends and great popularity, so much so that there is a distinct possibility of actual fame and fortune. Jupiter here is travel in connection with friends, is generosity, social reformation; on the negative side, the native is one who becomes a typical "tennis bum," professional house guest, host who is "paid for his services."

The 11th House is the native's social position; it represents the persons he attracts. Neptune here denotes attraction to and from those who deal in behind-the-scenes activity, from motion picture and television production to "productions" in the séance room. The 11th House represents ideals, social relationships, humanitarian projects in the form of action, as opposed to ideals in connection with 9th House activity. The native depends on friendships to sustain him if Uranus is here: the native's ambitions, achievements are tied up in a "wish world." Uranus knows no bounds, no limitations; it spreads friendships, wishes, hopes far beyond the "normal" into uncharted areas. Uranus here brings strange friends, unusual persons into the native's "inner circle." He may have an original way of expressing himself, of offering to help people. He is often involved in unusual love-sex relationships—and is subject to a fetish of being "different." A good astrologer, all other things being equal, attempts to teach the native that being different merely for the sake of being different is a waste of time and energy. The 11th House is companionship, sociability, the ability to adjust to society, to comprehend social mores. It represents social alliances, stepchildren, income from business (being the Second House from the 10th). The 7th is what shows, what the public sees. The 11th is what the native wants the people to see. The 9th is internal, the real thoughts and aspirations of the native. The 11th, in this sense, is not so important, but important in that most of us have to live within a society, and *how* we do it provides keys to our character and thus to our "destiny." The 11th House is an index to personal desires, while the 5th tells of our emotional needs, our need for love-fulfillment, for sex gratification. In comparison to the 5th, the 11th House is platonic. Mercury here attracts literary friends—those who publish, write and sell books, magazines, etc.

Mercury here shows a respect and desire for culture: it attracts the native to teachers, to original teaching methods, to the sale and production of textbooks and teaching aids. The 11th House wants to share, and with Mercury here the native shares knowledge.

The 11th House is that part of us which is "open" to influence. Friends enter the picture: our guard goes down to an extent. We are helped or hurt, depending upon our 11th House planets, the aspects to them, or the position of the 11th House ruler and its aspects. Pluto here warns of a need to maintain balance—the tendency is to go to extremes in giving of ourselves. Pluto can "tear us apart" or provide the greatest pleasure. But one can become "addicted" to this type of activity—the native is apt to have friends who run his life, who become too dominant an influence. There is nothing halfway about Pluto. The attractions, the sexual feelings, the emotional hunger the native experiences is part of his chart which requires great care and attention. Pluto here shows us a native who is intense about loyalties; he must be taught that others, if given the opportunity and if temptations are placed constantly in front of them, will take advantage of his loyalty. He must be made more practical in his approach to friendships, ideals, loyalty to causes, people and movements.

The Sun here would make one attractive to members of opposite sex. He would attract celebrated friends. The native prides himself on "right thoughts, right friends." His hopes and wishes become challenges—and unless they are fulfilled, he tends to brood. He must be taught to reach for what he can achieve, not for conditions which are out of his reach. There is no quick fame—he should be learning the fundamentals, the basics—or once an opportunity is achieved, he tends to be only a "flash in the pan."

The Moon here shows that the native's security, to a great extent, depends upon friends and the kind of hopes and wishes he creates for himself. He is popular but with different groups at various times. Loyalty is a quality he wants in others—but he must learn how to personally express loyal feelings. He makes changes without thinking about the effects they will have on others. The key is improved relations with others, including members of opposite sex—a greater sense of consideration. The native is popular with women. He can "get his own way," and then he wonders if that's what he wanted in the first place. He needs someone around on a "steady" basis. But before he recognizes this basic fact, he makes dozens of mistakes and makes numerous changes which cost him materially and emotionally.

Venus gives us evidence of a "romantic nature," one who seeks beauty but often finds that life is not made up merely of the beautiful—it contains also the "bad," the blemishes. The native attracts artistic friends; he can gain through the arts and has affairs of the heart with those persons engaged in theater, music, writing, the arts in general. He must learn to face the fact that not everyone is talented—and some merely are fooling themselves and perhaps fooling the native—perhaps deliberately. A realistic approach is best for one with Venus in the 11th.

Saturn here reveals that the native succeeds best through contacting business associates or prospects via social affairs. Many of his friends are professional people; but the native tends to work at being friendly and must learn to gain joy, not only business assets, from friendships. He is reserved, can't seem to "let go."

He wants "release" but also feels held back by responsibility. Sexual problems are indicated. Examine the complete chart. Find out whether all of the horoscope indicates this "tightness." Then with the competent aid of a qualified psychologist, work to "release" the native. Help him to live and love. Help him to get the real thing instead of merely going through the motions. The same condition might exist with Saturn in the 5th, with certain key differences. It is important to the native to feel liked, respected—and he often does things for effect rather than because he gets a "kick" out of doing them. Get him to loosen up!

Mars here tells of attraction by dynamic action. The native may tend to be dominating, however. This creates problems with those who don't like the idea of being dominated. He attracts those with mechanical ability and has connections with institutions, hospitals, the military. Mars here is not halfway—friends are either friendly or the kind that fight, argue, debate and eventually cease being friends. The amount of happiness native is able to achieve depends upon his ability to learn that all is not black or white, but that there are shades in between, and that right and wrong can be abstract conceptions—that what is right for one individual can possibly be wrong for another one. The astrologer should attempt to help the native broaden his concepts, should encurage him to read and engage in hobbies which enlarge his scope of experience.

The 12th House, like the 8th, is associated with mystery, undercover pursuits, behind-the-scenes activities; it also is related to secret fears, past responsibilities, coming home to "face the music." It is that section of the chart associated with hospitals, institutions, shut-ins, exiles, enemies real or imagined.

The 12th House is limitation. It is what we have earned or failed to earn—the payoff. Pluto here tells us the native often is reluctant to change course, is apt to hang on to an idea much in the manner of a fanatic. The "payoff" here is one who feels that he truly knows the answers . . . "if only *they* would listen." The native needs to be "taken out" of himself. He is secluded in the sense that very few, if any, persons really know him. He must "unlock" himself and overcome fear of the world in general. The fear often is expressed in a pugilistic manner, a striking out at unknown enemies.

The Sun gives us a brighter picture, but tells us the native has idealized the sexual state of affairs. What he seeks is his own kind of perfection. He must be taught some of the actualities of life. He requires greater confidence and the realization that others, too, share some of his ordeals. He often prefers to work for institutions rather than individuals and often is quite successful in this kind of endeavor.

The Moon here is good for publicity in connection with hospitals, prisons, etc. The native tends to be over-sensitive about his background, family, nation. He can be extremely provincial. He often fears to tread on strange ground (including foreign lands). He needs to realize that moods can be beautiful, if transformed into creative endeavors. Otherwise, he turns to brooding and finds only solitude, loneliness, depression.

Neptune in the 12th is the man of mystery who usually is kindly, but whose kindness is suspected. Here is the native who wants to give, share, help the underdog, but whose methods often appear underhanded. He loves the mysterious; he may become a member of a secret organization because he adores the romance of mystery. Once he finds a cause, organization or ideal to fight for, he is difficult to stop. But, alone, he becomes morbid and sad; he dreams and broods and constantly waits for his "ship" to come in.

Uranus is fascinating here; it represents a desire to break through to new ground, to snap the straps of limitation, to bring about social reform, to meet and understand various people, including foreigners. This is wonderful for social work, for rehabilitating those who have suffered tragedies; this native is ideal for administrative work in hospitals, publishing companies, motion picture studios and prisons. He is the magician who entertains his audience by breaking out of restraints. Offstage, he is also unusual, smashing conventions and announcing to the world that what appears unfortunate and helpless only appears so—he fights for the underdog. His fortunes suffer reverses; he goes up and down, but he *goes*.

The 12th House brings limitations and inhibitions—and as such represents areas where we want to find greater freedom. Jupiter here is good, for it in itself is the symbol for expansion. Jupiter in the 12th represents a resourceful native, one who is charitable, willing to take chances on trusting less fortunate individuals. The key is generosity. Once the native becomes afraid of the future or afraid to spend on what he feels is a worthy project, he is not complete. He needs to be needed, to give, to watch his efforts flower into success. He is, to a certain extent, very much dependent on how others react to him.

Mercury here is the analyst of other people's trouble; he needs to learn to analyze himself. Venus is beauty, but a special and protected kind, one not meant to be shared with everyone. It tends to get the native involved in secret affairs, including those involving married people. He must learn that anything so special, so secret, may be too secret for him to know. He cannot flout convention and morality and thus hurt others without risking emotional and other wounds.

Mars here is indicative of disputes involving organizations such as insurance companies, hospitals, police stations, etc. It also includes the military: the native seems to take some kind of strange delight in "bucking" organizations and organization men. Saturn here may be the opposite: the native is tied down to organization, work, respectability, institutions. His professional dignity is all mixed up in his emotions with happiness and contentment. He must be taught to separate fact from fiction, job from play, life from an imitation of life. He is almost morbidly sensitive about being made a fool of, and tends to be fearful of going it alone.

A good astrologer helps this native to cultivate hope, confidence, a sense of humor.

This has been a brief summary of the 12 Houses and the shadings given the meaning of each House by the planets deposited in them. The skilled astrologer is one who combines the various factors in the chart, who realizes that the "ruler" of one House, placed in another, "colors" that House and planet meaning.

XXIII

PLANETS IN THE SIGNS

Now we are ready for a brief glimpse of the meanings of the planets in the signs. Most casual observers already are familiar with the indications of "Sun signs," the Sun in the various zodiacal signs. And so we will cover this area in the manner which has proven most popular: with humor, example and special hints; in this case, special hints for men and women about each of the signs. Of course the Sun-sign meanings are, as we should be well aware of at this stage, colored by the House position of the Sun, by the aspects, by the fact that other planets are or are not in the same sign occupied by the Sun.

After analyzing the Sun-sign indications, we will also cover the Moon and planetary positions in the 12 signs. We have provided information enabling the reader to cast his own horoscope, to consult an ephemeris and thus discover where the planets were when he was born—which signs the planets occupied. But, for those who have not yet taken this step, or hesitate to do so for various reasons, including lack of time or inclination, we provide, in the appendix, tables which are of great value: they enable anyone to find out where the planets were when he was born. He has only to consult the proper table.

For the student who *has* cast his chart or at least consulted an ephemeris for the year of his birth, the tables serve as a convenient checkpoint. If the student finds he has Saturn in Taurus—and the tables agree—he indeed knows he is making progress and accurately following instructions.

With the tables one is able to find out where each of the planets was at the time of his birth. For the Moon, an ephemeris will have to be consulted. But for the Sun and the planets we get the information we seek—and begin, with the information provided in this chapter, to actually *interpret* a chart or horoscope.

Let us continue to keep in mind that no one House or sign position must be taken *alone* but rather combined, integrated, synthesized into a creative picture of the whole. In this manner, we develop skill and maturity in delineation. For example, we have mentioned the planetary indications in the various Houses. Let us remember that the House meanings, indications, potentials are colored, modified or emphasized by the sign on the cusp of the House. Thus, Scorpio on the cusp of the 1st House would represent more power and passion than, let us say, Libra or Virgo. The interpretations of the planets in the Houses must be added to or subtracted from, in connection with the *sign on the cusp of the House* under consideration—and in connection with the sign in which the planet is placed. Mars in Scorpio in the 1st House obviously represents something different from what Mars in the 1st in Libra would represent. In the latter instance, the sense of balance and beauty would be a fiery element in the native's makeup. He would demand action, would fight for the underdog—and perhaps would battle to make life more beautiful for his clients, neighbors, fellowmen. Doing so would be part of making his own life more meaningful. But Mars in Scorpio in the 1st House would present us with the picture of an intense individual, one who is tempted to go to extremes, to act impulsively, to give vent to his feelings and perhaps suffer as a result. We must also consider which House the planet is ruling or signifying. Mars in Libra in the 1st would be the significator of the 7th House (Aries), and as such would point even more to the native's sense of justice, his fighting of legal battles, his insistence on a fair deal for the people he represents and for the world in general. Mars in Scorpio in the 1st House would mean that Mars is significator of the 6th House (Aries) and would indicate that the native gives his best at full steam and expects the same of others. He often is too demanding, both of others and himself, and is subject to extreme fatigue or illness brought on by too fast a pace. So we must remember to look at the chart as a whole—the planets in the Houses, the sign on the cusp of the House, the House which the planet signifies.

Now let us present a brief analysis of the planets, the Sun and Moon in the signs. Remember, convenient tables are provided in the appendix so you can determine which signs the planets occupied in your own and other birthdates under consideration. But be sure to obtain an ephemeris and follow instructions on how to cast a horoscope. Then the tables need merely serve as checkpoints for your accuracy in setting up the chart.

Let us begin with the Sun signs. Then we will proceed to the Moon, and to each of the planets in each of the 12 signs.

Remember, because the Moon changes signs at so rapid a rate, the tables will not give the Moon-sign position. However, we will provide interpretations of the Moon in the 12 zodiacal signs. To find out *where* the Moon was when you were born, it will be necessary to obtain an ephemeris for your year of birth and to follow instructions provided in previous chapters.

XXIV

SUN IN ARIES

(*March 21–April 19*)

FOR MEN ONLY—

This is not the kind of woman you can lead around in circles: she usually wants to know where you are taking her and she has some ideas of her own on how to get there! She can be temperamental, headstrong and independent, and exude a kind of charm and sex appeal based on a blending of arrogance and pride. She is quite a woman: you can't force or push her, but neither should you fear her. At least, never let her know you're afraid!

This woman wants to think, to analyze, to arrive at her own conclusions. Let her do so, but tell her when you think she's wrong. Remember, the Aries woman can stand criticism. In fact, she can stand almost anything except being ignored. She requires a fair exchange of ideas, emotions, reactions.

You can win your way with this woman by being diplomatic. She is conscious of appearance, her own as well as yours. She is Martian, fiery in nature, spirited to the point of being domineering—if you let her be! With her, it is all the way or nothing. She can be as cold as ice or as warm and comforting as any man could desire. It is up to you to bring out the best in this woman. She admires qualities of leadership and is willing to follow once you gain her confidence. But if you disappoint her—look out! You will have to start your winning campaign all over—from the beginning.

Never permit this lady to think you're an easy catch. Let her work for your approval—make her strive to please you. This takes great skill on your part—but the results will be worth the time and trouble!

Be wary when she becomes bossy. An Aries woman wants a man, not an individual who is lc oking for a mother. Nothing discourages her more than always being able to have things her own way.

If your sign is Pisces, this woman is fortunate for you in financial affairs. You are physically drawn to her if your sign is Sagittarius. She stimulates you mentally if you are an Aquarian. Libra men are attracted to this woman, but it is often a case of opposites attracting opposites. Aquarius, Gemini, Leo and Sagittarius are men of the zodiac usually involved with the Aries woman. Men born under Cancer and Capricorn might be well advised to look elsewhere!

The Aries woman often is striking in appearance; she appears aloof but the fires of yearning and passion are there—if you are the right man. If you are, these hints should prove of great value. Good luck!

Famous women born under Aries include Joan Crawford, Mary Pickford, Gloria Swanson, Claire Boothe Luce and Lily Pons.

FOR WOMEN ONLY—

The man born under Aries can be dominant, inventive and very impatient! He'll keep you hopping unless you teach him to wait. This man's bark is worse than his bite. But please do not get the idea that you can train him as you would a dog—he will rebel every time. He is constantly seeking new ways, new persons, new ideas. You'll have to keep up with the times if you want to keep the Aries man.

If you were born under Pisces, the Aries man helps you financially. You are physically attracted to Aries if your sign is Sagittarius. You are mentally stimulated by Aries men if your sign is Aquarius. Women born under Leo, Sagittarius, Aquarius and Gemini can find harmonious relationships with Aries men. Libra women are fascinated by Aries men but could find the relationship punishing. Women born under Cancer or Capricorn should think twice before becoming involved with this zodiacal man.

In dealing with this male, try to keep his chin up. Once he

begins to sag, he is heading for defeat. See to it that he gets plenty of exercise and encouragement. Tell him he's good. The more he thinks you appreciate him, the more he will return the compliment.

Being interested in an Aries man is akin to taking a new lease on life. His temperament is fiery, his drives are strong, his ambitions are great; his capacity for love is enormous. Knowing this, do not attempt halfway measures. Decide either that you want him and will fight to keep him—or forget him entirely.

An Aries man can be militant, determined and obstinate. Once he gets rolling—even down the wrong road—he tends to keep in motion and in the same direction. You will have to be tactful in order to make him change his ways and his motives. Otherwise, he will fight you every inch of the way.

You get around him by showering him with compliments, affection and common sense. Remember, if you go about it the right way, this man will listen to reason. Never dare him; he will take you up on it. On the other hand, don't try to outsmart him by daring him to do one thing because you really want him to do the opposite. He's very likely to see through the ruse!

An Aries man is an adventure seeker; it is not easy to harness his powers. His thinking, often brilliant, is just as often erratic. He will take a chance and worry about the outcome later. He is ambitious but once he finds a niche it is difficult to urge him on. He is more successful at fighting his way to the top than he is when it comes to securing his position through creative moves aimed at still greater success.

This man plays hard and works hard; often he runs himself down. For the woman who wants him, close attention to these hints can prevent many a heartache and numerous headaches as well!

Famous men born under Aries include Charlie Chaplin, Harry Houdini, Lowell Thomas, James Branch Cabell, and Dr. Wehrner von Braun.

XXV

SUN IN TAURUS

(April 20–May 20)

FOR MEN ONLY—

Taurus women are generally hungry for experience as well as for food. They like the good life. But they are willing to give as well as take. These women can be very affectionate but don't try to take advantage of them. They can see through a phony. Be frank with them. Tell them where you stand and what it is you want—it's very likely they'll size you up and come to a decision in your favor.

The secret is simply to be aboveboard; women of this zodiacal sign respond to good taste and understanding. Any flim-flam draws their fire as well as their ire. Here is another important hint: know when to draw the line at giving in to their whims. At times, like a crying baby, they will test you—to see just how much they can get away with. Let them go so far, then pull in the reins.

These women are earthy in temperament; there is a tendency for them to become careless in the way they look. When you first meet them, their taste is impeccable. But after a while they appear to let down. Make sure you are treated as well as a stranger would be! Don't be a stuffed shirt, but do refuse to put up with curlers in the hair and rumpled dress or manners.

This lady can be lucky for you financially if you were born under Aries. You are physically attracted to Taurus women if your own sign is Capricorn. If you are a Pisces man this woman stimulates you mentally. Generally, the best signs for Taurus are Capricorn, Virgo, Cancer and Pisces. As a Scorpio man, there is bound at one time or another to be a Taurus woman in your life—

whether for keeps or not is another question. If you were born under Leo or Aquarius, there may be many difficulties in your relationships with Taurus women.

This lady can entice, appease, attract, magnetize, hypnotize: she is seductive, pleasantly lazy, Venusian, obstinate and charming. If you want to run the gamut of emotions, she is for you.

The way to assure happiness with a Taurus woman is to make sure you know what it is you really want. She'll help you to get it! But if you are not positive, she can be a worrisome thing—a Taurus woman needs a man. If you think you're up to it—go right ahead and good luck.

Remember: don't try to force issues. This woman has a keen sense of beauty and awareness. She may be troublesome at times, but she is generally worth it.

Famous women born under Taurus include Shirley Temple, Anita Loos, Simone Simone, Janet Blair and Charlotte Brontë.

FOR WOMEN ONLY—

This man likes luxury but he wants you to be practical about it! He likes style and he appreciates the best of everything. Yet he wants a woman who can also keep an eye on the budget. So, if you are interested in a Taurus man—you have a fascinating challenge, an over-all one that will keep you on your toes, the kind of challenge which is vital enough to make you aware of life. This man can be easygoing but it isn't wise to wave the red flag in front of the bull.

He is earthy in temperament. If you were born under the zodiacal sign of Aries he is lucky for you in money matters. If you are a Capricorn person, you will be physically attracted to the Taurus man. If you were born under Aquarius, this man helps you in the fulfillment of your ambitions. If you are a Pisces woman, the Taurus man acts as a mental stimulant. Women born under Capricorn and Virgo are harmonious as far as Taurus men are concerned; so are Cancer and Pisces women. Scorpio women are attracted to Taurus men but only time can tell the final outcome of such a relationship. Women born under the zodiacal signs of Leo and Gemini must exercise caution in their dealings with these men.

Taurus men can be stubborn; when they make up their minds to go along certain paths it is difficult, if not impossible, to make them turn a corner. These men have to be won over with kindness, even guile. They are not always easy to live with—they enjoy the basic things: eating, sleeping, loving, fighting, mating, etc.

If you are looking for perfection, please bypass the Taurus man. On the other hand, if you desire a very human man then go full speed ahead in your campaign to nab him.

Don't try to corral this man; he won't stand for being fenced in. He wants plenty of room. He will want to come back to you, he will need and desire your affection; but he wants to find this out for himself. He doesn't want lectures. He wants love with a capital L.

Famous men born under Taurus include astrologer Carl Payne Tobey, Joe Louis, Perry Como, Lionel Barrymore, and James Mason.

XXVI

SUN IN GEMINI
(*May 21–June 21*)

FOR MEN ONLY—

A Gemini woman, if you are not careful, is liable to grow on you; you acquire a taste for her, just as some people do for lima beans or buttermilk or spinach or grits and eggs. If you want to win and keep a woman born under this sign—you will have to be in good physical and mental condition. She will lead you a merry chase. You will be exasperated; your nerves will tingle, sometimes with joy, at other times simply because you're becoming an emotional and physical wreck. Apparently she's worth the trouble. Gemini women are popular. They are charming. They can be seductive. They can even, on occasion, be reasonable!

A must here is a sense of humor. Without it, you may as well give up. If you are going to pursue, or be pursued by, a Gemini woman, you must know how to laugh. This lady is on the go; she wants to know and be seen and she wants to ask questions and to break the bubble of pomposity wherever she finds it. Sometimes, she talks too much!

If you were born under Taurus, this woman could be lucky for you financially. If you are an Aquarian, you find the Gemini lady physically attractive. You are also attracted to Gemini women if you were born under Leo or Aries. Libra men are drawn to Gemini women, as are Sagittarians, though the latter is usually a matter of opposites attracting opposites. You may have a rough road ahead with Gemini women if you are a man who was born under Virgo or Pisces.

Gemini women can exhibit a disturbing habit: they laugh at the wrong times. There is a romantic moment—you wish to say or do something sweet—and Gemini is laughing.

When you get used to them, Gemini women can become indispensable. However, once you let them realize this, you're in for trouble! Treat them lightly: the more you take Gemini women seriously, the more you are apt to suffer. Obviously, they have their excellent points. One of them is the stuff of life and living: there is nothing halfway about them. It is all the way or nothing at all. They can be daring, lovely, witty and, at times, devastatingly funny.

You have a job on your hands if you are involved with women of Gemini. But it could indeed be a pleasant job—nice work if you can get it!

Famous women born under Gemini include Judy Garland; Tobe Davis, fashion designer; Hedda Hopper; Wally Simpson; and Anne Frank.

FOR WOMEN ONLY—

This man is versatile, alert, charming and blessed with loads of energy. No matter what the weather, he is willing to go out, to be on the move, to experiment, to satisfy his curiosity. He may tire you, but you must not complain. That is the secret hint: never let him know when you are brooding or worrying. He may agree that you have a right to be sad but, in reality, he expects you to keep your chin up, to keep smiling, to be disgustingly healthy. Complaining or nagging is one sure way to lose a Gemini man.

These men can be deceptive; often they are testing, probing, trying to find out what you are really made of, whether or not you are sincere. They are, like Gemini women, airy in temperament. They are idealistic; when forced to face practical issues, they are often downcast, hurt, bewildered—or at least give that impression.

A Gemini man must be convinced of your loyalty. Once he is, he is yours: you can ask for and receive anything he is capable of giving. But as far as he is concerned, it is you first—first you show your loyalty and love, then perhaps he'll come around!

A Gemini man is elusive, quick with his hands, artistic, restless, with a tendency to scatter his forces. It is best for you to make him believe that you are many-sided. Once he feels he has figured you out, he is apt to shrug and go on to his next love.

Gemini men are lucky for you in money matters if you were born under Taurus, Aquarius women are physically attracted to Gemini men. If you were born under Leo or Aries, you will find that these men keep turning up in your life—and the same may apply if your sign is Sagittarius. Libra women often find themselves involved with men of Gemini. Women born under the signs Virgo and Pisces are apt to make problems for themselves by pursuing these men.

Gemini men can talk their way into and out of almost anything. Listen to them but remain skeptical; and keep a Mona Lisa smile on your face. That definitely helps!

Famous men born under Gemini include Walt Whitman, Ralph Waldo Emerson, Gene Tunney, Bob Hope and Herman Wouk.

XXVII

SUN IN CANCER

(*June 22–July 21*)

FOR MEN ONLY—

Cancer women are lovely and often lonely; they reach out for love and affection. Often, when their desires for security are not fulfilled, they stray. They seek and experiment. However, if you can give this woman love, if you are willing to make a home for her, she will usually prove faithful, loyal, warm and exciting. Besides, she is a good cook!

Men, this woman likes to aid loved ones. Here is a good hint: ask her for advice! Don't always follow it—but ask, anyway. Include her "in." To shut a Cancer woman out is to invite trouble.

If you are interested in keeping your Cancer woman—pay attention to the home. Domesticity becomes a key word, along with bigger and better household furnishings. But don't think she is satisfied merely to be kept busy around and in the house. She wants to share your life, not merely wait on you.

She is highly emotional, being of the Water element. Her intuition is highly developed. She can usually perceive when something of importance is about to occur. She has a tendency to brood and worry; she requires constant assurance and reassurance in love and is not satisfied with a peck on the cheek. She wants sincerity and plenty of affection.

Don't try to fool this woman. Place your cards face up and then let her make up her own mind. If she loves you, she will fight in your corner. This is true no matter what the odds. She is a valuable ally. She can make life worth living as long as you are loyal. Once you are not, you begin a chain of events that could boomerang.

If you are a Gemini man, this woman can be fortunate for you with money. Basically, she is thrifty. But she is apt to be able to save on so-called "little" things while being very generous with her money (and yours) when it comes to larger expenditures. If you are a Capricorn man, you will be attracted to this woman; the outcome of your relationship, however, is questionable. You should have harmonious relations if you were born under Scorpio, Pisces, Virgo or Taurus. Caution must be exercised in relationships with Cancer women if you were born under Libra or Aries. If you are a Taurus man, this woman can stimulate you mentally and help you arrive at profitable ideas.

If you are looking for a woman who can make a home for you, she is for you. But never take her for granted!

Famous women born under Cancer include Janet Leigh, Leslie Caron, Mary Baker Eddy, Anne Morrow Lindberg, and Susan Hayward.

FOR WOMEN ONLY—

Be sympathetic with the Cancer man—but don't spoil him! He is more emotional than the average man; he is sensitive to his surroundings and to your moods. And he has plenty of moods of his own, too. It is said that Cancer men love the home and good food. But the truth of the matter, most likely, is that he appreciates homemaking efforts, including the talents that make up a skillful chef. He does not require a palace or a queen, but he insists upon undivided loyalty. With this insistence there is a lurking suspicion that all could not be as good as it looks; he feels someone, somewhere, is doing something he or she should not be doing. This makes him unhappy!

This is not the easiest man to love. He is an idealist; he expects to make mistakes himself but he is astonished when a loved one slips in any manner. His standards are high; he is patriotic, loyal; he doesn't mind fighting with members of his own family. He enjoys a good family quarrel: it clears the air! But let an outsider say something about a person he loves—then he fights.

He is a moody man and the best hint is this: recognize that his moods are expressions, nuances of his feelings, character, hopes, dreams. Don't try to pull him out of his thoughts. His ambitions are based upon ideas. He realizes that fulfillment of dreams depends upon his ability to outmaneuver or outthink competitors. Once this man declares his love for you, he is apt to be pretty serious about it.

Avoid sniping at him. Keep your head—give and take—don't ask for special favors or privileges. This man appreciates honesty and frankness; he cannot tolerate whining. Remember, he is the one who seeks sympathy—to ask him to give you too much is to make him think that maybe he's with the wrong woman!

If you are a Gemini woman he is good for you financially. Pisces women are physically attracted to Cancer men. Aries women find that they have many obstacles to overcome in their relations with these men—yet Cancer men spur their ambitions, help them achieve their goals. If you are a Pisces, Scorpio, Virgo or Taurus woman—you should pay close attention to these hints, for there is likely to be such a man in your life! It might be best for Capricorn women to think twice before encouraging a relationship with this man. The same applies to women born under Libra and Aries.

This man appreciates women and the finer things in life. The better he has it the more discriminating he becomes. He fears ridicule, and the quickest way to lose him is to laugh at him.

Famous men born under Cancer include Art Linkletter, Ernest Hemingway, Yul Brynner, Mike Todd and Calvin Coolidge.

XXVIII

SUN IN LEO

(*July 22–August 21*)

FOR MEN ONLY—

Leo women have a flair for the dramatic: they abhor the humdrum, the ordinary, the routine. These women believe in living life as if a spotlight were turned on—they are not always exhibitionists but they certainly want you to be aware of them. A touch, a gesture, an expression—a secret signal—these all are important to the woman born under this zodiacal sign.

If you want a really good hint concerning the feminine Leo, just remember to *recognize* her. She wants and needs recognition. Be aware of her presence. Stand up when she enters the room. Smile in a special way; let her know that what you do is done especially for her. You can win her and hold her if your manner is regal. Carried to extremes, of course, this could be ridiculous. You must use your judgment. The Leo woman helps you to become familiar with the finer things of life. She is in rhythm, with the nuances of life. Life, to her, is living. It is motion, animation—the opposite of drudgery, of repeated action leading to a rut.

A Leo woman is in love with love: romance is as essential as food and drink. Affection is a necessity. Her personal magnetism is strong: she attracts members of the opposite sex. It is all right to be jealous as long as you don't let her know it. Be calm and cool. Admire her. Once you lose your temper or show weakness by being obviously jealous, you begin to lose out with this lady. Let her win you! Make yourself a fascinating challenge. Indeed, a man learns a great deal by being involved with a Leo woman. The involvement may tire him, but he learns and lives and loves.

If you are a Cancer man, this lady can be fortunate for you in money matters. If your birth sign is Aries, you will most certainly find this woman physically attractive. Gemini men are stimulated mentally by her; almost all men, including Aquarians, are intrigued. Her nature is fiery; she is passionate, giving and usually generous. If you maintain an air of mystery, she is practically yours for the asking. If you are a Gemini, Libra, Sagittarius or Aries man, you should find this a good relationship. Leo women appeal to you and you ring a bell with them. It might be best, if you are a Scorpio or Taurus man, to be wary in your dealings with Leo women. There are many obstacles to overcome and the trouble may not be worth it. No one will blame you for trying, though!

Famous women born under Leo include Mae West, Edna Ferber, Lucille Ball, Gracie Allen and Dorothy Parker.

FOR WOMEN ONLY—

If you're looking for secret hints concerning Leo men, then you automatically mark yourself as an unusual woman. This is not to say you are necessarily a wise woman—but certainly unusual! It seems that Leo men attract persons—especially women—with unique personalities, talents, problems, etc. A Leo man is fiery and romantic; he demands attention and can become jealous, offended or aloof if he feels you regard him as anything less than kingly. He tends to be inflexible and seeks—generally to your surprise—stability. He likes to get around and to be seen and heard, but he wants to return to the lair and be cuddled, cooed at and reassured.

A Leo man is never satisfied merely to be great: he wants to be told so. He is attractive to women; he seems to draw them like flies. He doesn't mind if you're jealous—he even enjoys it. But he does not like you to make scenes. The best way to hold the interest of this man is to be quietly dramatic. He is fascinated by subtle women. If you shout, you are lost. But try wiping away a tear, then holding up your chin as if nothing happened. Make sure, however, that he sees you! He'll melt; he'll change from a lion into a purring kitten. A Leo man can be taken advantage of; he enjoys being the center of intrigue. You can lead him to a trap and even make him fall in. But, unless you keep him interested, he will get up and get out.

He is a natural showman; he likes the theater but he dislikes theatrics. He admires beauty but shies away from the obvious: from women who use too much makeup, from women who cry openly, from women who laugh too loud, from women who steal the limelight. He is a man of tremendous pride; you can win him and woo him and do almost anything you want with him if only you will remember to compliment him. He wants to be proud of you but he wants you to keep your place as a woman. He believes in equal rights for men and women but he wants you to believe that he is just a little better. He wants you to be independent but to completely depend upon him. He is a rather impossible person, but at least you've been warned!

He's good for you financially if you were born under Cancer; you are attracted to him if you are an Aquarian, an Aries, a Sagittarian, a Gemini or a Libran. It might be best to take Leo men very lightly if you are a Scorpio or Taurus woman. If you are an Aries woman you will find Leo men physically attractive.

Famous men born under Leo include Aldous Huxley, Cecil B. DeMille; Bernard Baruch; Robert Taylor; George Bernard Shaw; Alan Leo, astrologer; and Llewellyn George, astrologer-publisher.

XXIX

SUN IN VIRGO

(*August 22–September 22*)

FOR MEN ONLY—

Virgo women are discriminating, often regal, very often tiresome in their pursuit of cleanliness and, more often than not, aware of the details of any project you might be considering. This woman appreciates money in the bank and is not at all adverse to seeing the ring on her finger. Promises are fine; she will appreciate the fact that you are well meaning. But she does demand results. In so doing, she is capable of bringing out the best in you. She is mercurial, earthy, energetic, full of plans; she is ambitious, not only for herself but also for you.

One of the best hints is this: do not underestimate her. She knows what she is about. She can set a goal and overcome the most tremendous odds. She is an invaluable ally; she will not let you down if you take her into your confidence.

If you are seeking some kind of half-relationship, she is not the woman for you. But if you are serious, willing to go all the way for her, accept her as a full partner, then she can be a wonderful asset.

If you are a Leo man, she can prove fortunate for you financially. If you were born under Taurus, this woman attracts you physically. If you are a Taurus, a Capricorn, a Scorpio or a Cancer, then your relationships with Virgo should prove harmonious. Pisces men, although attracted to these women, do not always make a go of it with them. If your birth sign is Saggitarius or Gemini, it might be best to set your sights on some other woman.

Virgo women want to know where they stand. It doesn't help to beat around the bush with them. If you are kidding, or if your purpose is a night of fun, come out and state the case. That way, the Virgo woman respects you and you'll probably have more fun than would otherwise be the case.

These women have a genuine interest in serving the public; they are dedicated workers and seldom know the meaning of fear or defeat. They are natural fighters and their goal is truth. It doesn't matter what traditions fall before them in their quest; the important thing is to reach the goal.

You had better look elsewhere if it is a "Betty-Bop" girl you want. However, if it is a woman who is intelligent, loyal, frank, discriminating, thorough and wryly humorous, you have picked the correct one in Virgo.

One more hint: confide in her and you will assure her that you are sincere. Keep things from her and she will suspect the entire framework of your character and your motives.

Famous women born under Virgo include "Grandma" Moses, Jane Addams, Shirley Booth, Sophia Loren and Greta Garbo.

FOR WOMEN ONLY—

The Virgo man is demanding; he asks that you prove yourself, that you be willing to sacrifice when necessary. He is not apt to be a "sugar-daddy." He knows the meaning of work and the value of money. He is discriminating, not easy to fool; he is the kind of man a woman can depend upon for security. But if you are not willing to give as well as receive—then it would be best for you to forget the Virgo man.

This man likes to feel he is worthy; integrity is a key word. He applies his own standards to others, including you. He will not tolerate deception.

His mind is quick; he is mercurial and earthy. He usually says what he means and he usually means well. This, however, is not always apparent. At times, he may appear hypersensitive, overcritical. These are things you should know if you are interested in a Virgo man.

He is practical, honest, fair; he is also basically shy—it is difficult for him to express his true feelings. He is not the kind of happy-go-lucky fellow that others immediately accept. This is one of his problems. Learn to read between the lines; try to understand that sentiment is something he has trouble expressing. This man is conservative in the way he expresses himself; there is plenty of reserve in his makeup. You will have to be patient and loyal.

If you are a Leo woman, he can help you financially. If you were born under Taurus, you will find this man physically attractive. He stimulates you mentally if you are a Cancer. Harmonious relations are likely if you are a Taurus, Capricorn, Cancer or Scorpio. You are attracted to him if you were born under Pisces, but it is apt to be a case of opposites attracting each other. Trouble with this man is indicated if you are a Sagittarian or a Gemini.

This is not a pretentious man; often you will have to help him build confidence. He needs a woman who has faith in him, who can appreciate his patience and willingness to work toward and achieve important goals.

In all, the Virgo man often proves his value; he is a good bet for a long, solid relationship. If you are looking for lots of laughs and little permanence, this is not the man for you. But if you want to build for the future, you've found your man.

Famous men born under Virgo include H. L. Mencken, Robert Benchley, Walter Reuther and Van Johnson.

XXX

SUN IN LIBRA
(*September 23–October 22*)

FOR MEN ONLY—

These women possess charm. In fact, it is very likely they can charm you into anything! They are generally intellectual, idealistic, "airy" in nature, sensitive and greatly aware of beauty. Being beautiful is of the utmost importance to this lady; she is Venusian, has natural finesse, is desirable and makes a delightful hostess. If you want to win this lady, avoid coarseness. Appeal to her sense of justice, of good, of beauty. If you are blunt, if you rush things, if your language or your manners are not up to par—then you'd better wait. You simply are not ready for the Libra woman.

She needs affection and love. She must have faith in you and your motives. Her principles are paramount in her life—she is not likely to compromise. There is a tendency for her to withdraw; if she has been hurt emotionally she isn't likely to stick out her chin. Thus, patience on your part, mingled with understanding, is essential.

This woman balances one thing against the other: she appreciates money and luxury, but compares those advantages to character and stability. She is creative and appreciates that quality in others. She doesn't enter a relationship with the idea that it might end tomorrow. She looks to the future—and you now have fair warning. Do not become involved with this woman unless your intentions are serious. Living, for her, is an art. As a companion she is most desirable. When she gives you her heart, you will realize you have something to treasure. She is liberal, graceful and possesses a sense of freedom.

Love is as important as food for this lady. Her surroundings are important. Carelessness in taste is one way to lose her. She has her faults and one of them is being affected to an extreme by where she is, by manners, etc. Often she is apt to bypass something or someone worthwhile because she insists so highly on manners. Her keys are romance, partnership, marriage, independence, beauty. Her moods can be all the way up or all the way down; she exhibits a tendency to say "show me," while neglecting to prove her own abilities and motives.

She is worth winning, but expect evasive action—and never push too hard for direct answers. There is no black and white with her; there are shades of good and bad and you may as well get used to that idea.

She can be lucky in money matters for you if you are a Virgo. If you are a Gemini man, you are physically attracted to this woman. Harmonious relations are indicated if you are a Gemini, Aquarian, Sagittarian or a Leo. If your sign is Aries, you are attracted to her but there are apt to be numerous disputes. Many obstacles are indicated if you are a Capricorn or Cancer man.

Famous women born under Libra include Helen Hayes, Rita Hayworth, Ina Claire, Deborah Kerr and Annie Besant.

FOR WOMEN ONLY—

This man is considered highstrung. In reality, however, it is not so much his nerves, but his sense of awareness, his keen convictions, his drive for justice and independence. He likes proportion in all things and is very apt to notice bulges in the wrong places! He isn't the easiest man in the world to live with, but he is appreciative and seldom asks the impossible—he just requires that you strive toward that goal!

He needs to be told how good he is; flattery is a necessity. This does not mean he is egotistical; it does mean that he requires someone to share in his triumphs, someone who appreciates him. He has more of a sense of humor than you might first realize; his natural bent is toward intellectual subjects—he is nobody's fool, though at times he may act like one.

It is important for you to avoid irritability; the Libra man adores a woman with an even temper, one who can laugh in the face of adversity. He is appreciative of talent, art, literature, music: he will encourage hobbies, even if such encouragement costs him money. This man demands refinement; he is a man to whom culture is important. He is a good catch but it takes quite a run before the chase is over. He is apt to demand perfection but will settle for less—provided you "understand" him. Convince him you are on his side and the world is yours for the asking!

If you are a Virgo woman this man is good for you financially. If your sign is Gemini, you are physically attracted to him. Leo women find him especially stimulating as far as ideas and ambitions are concerned. He is good for you if you are a Sagittarian, a Leo, an Aquarian or a Gemini. He fascinates Aries women, too. But if your birth sign is Capricorn or Cancer, there could be a number of obstacles to overcome in your relations with the Libra man.

Any breach of good taste is offensive to this man. He is a social being, demanding manners, grace, charm and dignity. And don't be shocked if, despite his demands upon you, he himself breaks every rule by arguing with guests, challenging their ideas, and causing them to look at him goggle-eyed as he presents what may appear to be outlandish theories. The Libra man is an individual, if nothing else!

His key word is challenge. He loves expressions of originality and when he argues, it is for the sake of bringing out the best in the thinking of others. He is not always easy to understand, but he would never knowingly hurt you.

Famous men born under Libra include Oscar Wilde; Dr. J. B. Rhine; Ed Sullivan; Dwight Eisenhower; Hereward Carrington, authority on psychic phenomena; and Russell Birdwell, public relations expert.

XXXI

SUN IN SCORPIO

(*October 23–November 21*)

FOR MEN ONLY—

Scorpio women are emotional, affectionate, often passionate; they are willing to tear down the past in order to build for the future. Tradition takes a back seat when it comes to the promise of better things tomorrow. These women have an air of mystery, are often considered psychic; it is difficult to know them completely, for they change as circumstances demand. A man involved with a Scorpio woman is not always going to have an easy time—but it will be exciting and he will know he's alive.

Do not seek relations with these women unless you are strong, willing to change your opinions, able to adjust, and unless you have a basic respect for members of the opposite sex.

This woman is dynamic, even explosive. She can lose her temper one minute and resemble a purring kitten the next. You are stepping on a merry-go-round when you begin to court a Scorpio woman. The pace may be dizzying—but if you ask for it you have no right to complain.

This woman can be fiercely loyal; she demands a great deal, but she also has much to give. She knows her way about the practical aspects of living. This may puzzle you, for one day she can discuss finances like an expert, and the next day she is willing to follow a whim or a hunch instead of charts or facts. She is not easy to understand. It is best to close your eyes and enjoy the changes she is bound to make in your life. If you are the nervous or oversensitive type, please seek another woman!

This woman possesses personal magnetism; she is physically

attractive. She doesn't do things halfway. She gives of herself or holds back completely. She represents a challenge. She often enjoys a battle; when she believes the cause is right, nothing can deter her from a fight. She can be forceful, dynamic, dominating. Her willpower is admirable except when it fades into obstinacy.

This woman likes secrets. Don't try to know all there is to know about her. If you ever, by some accident, actually succeed, she will lose interest in you and that will be the end of your relationship.

If you are a Libra man, she could be lucky for you in money matters. You are physically attracted to this woman if your sign is Cancer. She stimulates you mentally if you are a Virgo. You also harmonize with the Scorpio woman if you were born under Capricorn, Pisces or Cancer. Taurus men are attracted, but the attraction could turn out for the worse. Obstacles are indicated should you be an Aquarius or a Leo.

Famous women born under Scorpio include Sarah Bernhardt, Hedy Lamarr, Hetty Greene, Linda Christian and Marie Dressler.

FOR WOMEN ONLY—

Don't expect this man to say one thing and mean something else. He has a knack or gift of seeing through pretense, of knowing what others are really like; he can perceive, delineate, render shrewd analyses of persons and subjects. He is a tough one to fool and if you are not up to it, you had better look elsewhere. Scorpio men are physical, yet emotional; they require love in its poetic sense, yet can be animal-like, even brutal. But the brutality does not stem from cruelty. Rather, it is brutality in a basic sense: brutal frankness, brutal honesty, and so forth. Nothing halfway here; these men can fight and win. They set a goal and can go underground or arise and fly like an eagle to attain it.

Do not attempt to reform this man. He knows what he wants and usually has sound reasons for acting the way he does. If you want to lose him, start correcting his manners, his speech; if you want to keep him—try to understand and sympathize.

The Scorpio man is forceful, direct, independent, often aggressive. He is likely to be a man of action. If you want to impress him, you will have to do more than talk or make promises—he likes results.

If you are a Libra woman, this man can be good for you financially. Virgo women find Scorpio men mentally stimulating. If you were born under Cancer, this man is physically attractive to you. He seems to be a good catch if you were born under Virgo, Capricorn, Cancer or Pisces. You are attracted to him in many ways if you are a Taurus woman, but numerous obstacles have to be overcome. Women born under Aquarius and Leo often find such a relationship impossible.

This man can be very jealous. Often he appears a little too careful in money matters. On the positive side, however, this characteristic is really an expression of desire for security. A Scorpio man does not forget a wrong. He is a good person to have on your side; bear this in mind before you try insulting or ridiculing him. He makes a formidable foe.

A Scorpio man is capable of hard work and hard play. At times, his appetite appears insatiable. He is not an easy man to size up or analyze; sometimes he is like a quick-change artist, looking and acting one way today and another way tomorrow.

If you want this man, you will have to meet and pass numerous tests. Once the examinations are over, however, you may well feel the trouble was more than worthwhile.

Famous men born under Scorpio include Edward A. Wagner, astrological magazine editor; Martin Luther; Burt Lancaster; Dr. Jonas E. Salk; and Theodore Roosevelt.

XXXII

SUN IN SAGITTARIUS

(November 22–December 21)

FOR MEN ONLY—

The Sagittarius lady is an idealist; honesty and frankness are key words. She is loyal; her love is a very real thing and she doesn't want to make light of it. This is a noble lady; when she makes up her mind to do something it gets done, despite often overwhelming odds. Her decisions are swift; sometimes impulsive actions cause her difficulty. If you want this lady, you must stress integrity. Respect comes first—then love grows, at least as far as she is concerned.

She must always have a goal in front of her; it could be an overseas journey, a book she is going to write or read, any ambition, but the future must be there before her: she is not one to live on past memories or scrapbooks.

This woman is proud, refined; she is sensitive, often disturbed by comparatively minor matters. Don't attempt to pressure her: it is best to let her decide, to make up her own mind, to take the initiative. She is fiery in temperament; her outlook is universal, philosophical. At times she does go to extremes. But if you are able to win this lady, you will have attained a great deal. Her assets far outweigh her faults.

If you were born under Scorpio, this lady is good for your finances. You should have a harmonious relationship with the Sagittarius woman if your own sign is Leo, Aries, Aquarius or Libra. You are attracted to her if you are a Gemini, but the outcome of such attraction is dubious. Obstacles in such a relationship are indicated if your sign is Pisces or Virgo. You are physically attracted to Sagittarius women if you are a Leo.

A Sagittarius woman is exciting, yet gives the impression of being shy. She presents a challenge. You want to know her, to have her express her true feelings. In other words, this woman is difficult to resist! One important hint is this: be honest—state your business, your intentions—don't attempt coverups, false promises, statements. Another hint is that this lady appreciates the outdoors and sports, and is drawn to men who are kind to animals.

She will bring out the best in you and will try to earn your respect. The Sagittarius woman is something special. Study these hints and apply yourself. She's worth the trouble!

Famous women born under Sagittarius include Lillian Russell, Irene Dunne, Marion Davies, Fay Bainter and Julie Harris.

FOR WOMEN ONLY—

If you are the kind of lady who wants only to stay indoors, then you had better forget the Sagittarius man. He is open in his nature and he likes to be out in the open. He wants to share things with you: his likes and dislikes, his hobbies, interests, hopes, aspirations. This is a man who will make you know you are a woman. And he'll make you live up to it!

This man dislikes petty persons; he will help you to grow and will expect you to be a big person. If you do not succeed, his initial attraction may turn to revulsion. The best hint is to follow your true feelings, even your intuition. By being honest, even impulsive, you can win this man's sympathy and understanding.

Basically, this man is trustworthy. He may not always do things in the way you expected, but he gets them done. He keeps his promises. You can feel secure with him. During a time of emergency, he acts. He thinks quickly; he is fiery in temperament and has a knack for seeing the situation as a whole. Often, he does not take the time to explain his actions. These are the times when you must have faith in his judgment. It would be a mistake, for example, to nag, to question, to doubt, to undermine his motives.

If you are a Scorpio woman, this man is lucky for you in matters of finance. He stimulates you mentally if your sign is Libra. You are physically attracted to him if you are a Leo. There are some obstacles if you are a Pisces, but these are the obstacles which lead to inspired action and help you obtain your ambitions. Generally, you harmonize with the Sagittarius man if you were born under Leo or Aries, Aquarius or Libra. There is attraction if you are a Gemini, but it may well be a case of opposites attracting opposites. Caution in such a relationship is advised if your sign is Pisces or Virgo. As stated, Pisces women need some of the Sagittarius fire, but there could be too much of a good thing.

Sagittarius men do not pull their punches; you can trap them but, if so, they will withdraw to such an extent that you will be left more alone than if you actually were alone. Sagittarius men want to learn: by reading, experimenting, questioning, traveling, writing, examining, probing. If the kind of life you want is a "sit still and be quiet" kind, then the Sagittarius man could only make you unhappy, and vice versa.

You catch him with color, charm, wit: you intrigue him by asking fantastic questions. You make him lose interest by being too conventional in your outlook, ambitions, questions.

This man wants companionship; he wants to share his experiences, adventures. By all means, stick to your views, your individuality. He may appear to rebel—but the one quality he admires in a woman, above all else, is independence.

Famous men born under Sagittarius include Arthur Brisbane, Winston Churchill, Eric Sevareid, Edward G. Robinson and Walt Disney.

XXXIII

SUN IN CAPRICORN

(December 22–January 20)

FOR MEN ONLY—

This is an earthy woman, not necessarily demonstrative. But she will not run out on you; she may appear aloof, cold, disinterested, but the fire of passion runs through her veins and she is a woman in the best sense of that word. Look for someone else if you want the frivolous, if you desire someone who can give you a "line." This woman has something to offer to someone who is concerned with the future. She is not for you if you are merely dabbling, experimenting, looking for an interlude.

There is energy and strength here; this woman can perceive your character, can know you and love you and be loyal to you. But she does expect you to be a man. This woman is apt to be cautious; she isn't easy to win. She also has a tendency to be curious about the bank account. This is because she is aware of the future, is concerned about tomorrow as well as today. She can accept challenges, is able to work, is disciplined, prefers to avoid sensationalism and publicity, possesses great determination and usually finishes what she starts.

She is all of the above—but she is not cold. She may appear so, but once she feels you may be the one for her, she is as warm as a Venus-Mars conjunction. She is earthy in temperament; she is basically independent, original in her thinking—and can break from tradition as easily as some persons drink a cup of coffee. It is not always easy for her to do so; the Capricorn woman does have a tendency to hang on to the familiar, to be classical, to adhere to a set line of action. Yet, when necessary, she can break habit patterns. That is a key word with her: necessity. She meets emergencies, she does what is necessary, including the making of sacrifices. She can give up luxuries for loved ones.

If you are a Sagittarius man, she can be lucky for you in money matters. Virgo men find this woman physically attractive. She is good for you if your sign is Scorpio, Pisces, Taurus or Virgo. You are attracted to her if your zodiacal sign is Cancer, but there are many problems to overcome in such a relationship, just as there are if your sign happens to be Aries or Libra.

This woman is not satisfied to be buried, hidden or relegated to second fiddle. She has her own thoughts and wants to express them. And she most certainly deserves to be heard. This woman has much to offer. If you feel you are not quite ready for her—why not wait until you've really become a man?

Famous women born under Capricorn include Jane Wyman, Rebecca West, Ava Gardner, Loretta Young and Gladys Swarthout.

FOR WOMEN ONLY—

This man may start slowly; but you can bet your life that he'll be around at the finish! He is earthy, possesses a keen sense of awareness, is human and warm, and can be depended upon to help the underdog and to fight for loved ones. At times you may have to prod him, to make him live up to his capabilities—but you will not have to ask for consideration. He would never knowingly hurt you.

This man is more sensitive than you might at first suspect: he often laughs at himself, shrugs off sympathy and gives the impression of being immune to pain. However, he is not only personally sensitive, but transfers this sense of feeling to others; he can look at you, and at others, and somehow know when things are not right. This produces a dissipating effect; he tends to wear down, to worry more about others than about himself. One's first reaction, of course, is admiration for this man's apparent nobility. However, if you are really interested in his welfare, you should encourage him to face his own problems. The Capricorn man sometimes seeks an "out." He busies himself in helping others instead of putting his shoulder to the wheel with his own problems. An important hint is this: let him talk about himself and help him to help himself. This will almost assure you of winning him!

Tact is important in dealing with this man. He may sound brash, he may appear tough—but when it comes to women he expects them to be tactful, loving, tender and aware of his particular charms. The Capricorn man constantly builds for the future: he may not always be aware of his struggle for recognition, but it is a part of him and you must recognize it if you are to be happy with him.

Ambition is keynoted here, although he may deny it. He is not always sure of what he wants to attain—but he is going somewhere. Having a successful association with him means having faith; forget this man if you are looking for quick rewards. The relationship must be rewarding as a whole if it is to mean anything at all. Once you hook up with this man, you may find yourself hooked for good!

If you are a Sagittarius woman, this man could prove fortunate for you financially. If your birth sign is Virgo, you are physically attracted to him. He is good for you if you are a Scorpio, Pisces, Taurus or Virgo. You are drawn to him if your sign is Cancer, but the outcome of such a relationship is not predictable. Many obstacles are indicated if your sign is Aries or Libra.

Famous men under Capricorn include Henry Miller, Woodrow Wilson, Steve Allen, J. Edgar Hoover and Rudyard Kipling.

XXXIV

SUN IN AQUARIUS

(*January 21–February 19*)

FOR MEN ONLY—

You can lead a horse to water but . . .

So the saying goes and it most certainly applies to an Aquarius woman. This lady can be as fixed and determined as any person you've ever met, but you can win her if you follow these hints:

1. Since she is idealistic and airy in temperament, take her bluster and show of pugnaciousness with a grain of salt. Smile at her, make her realize that no matter what she thinks, you *are* her friend. She appreciates and understands friendship, perhaps above all else.

2. Let her know she is not the only person with Uranian interests. Tell her about a few of your own, including astrology! Let her know that you are on her side when it comes to bucking tradition and caring for the underdog.

3. This might be the most important hint of all: be charming and imaginative in entertainment plans; remember, she lives in a world where dreams can—and often do—come true. If you are drab in manner, in entertaining, in presenting your ideas and ambitions—she is likely to think you a fool—or worse, a bore. Knowing this lady could change your life for the better. She is a stimulus in the manner that cold, bubbly wine is—and before you know it she'll go to your head!

This woman does like to have her own way. When she is right, let her. But when you feel she is in error, fight her every inch of the way! She enjoys a good fight; it has a tonic effect on her and she will look at you with new respect. She'll lead you in circles if she

228

can get away with it. Tell her where you stand, what it is you want and expect of her, and you will be on the way toward a happy, fruitful relationship. She loves the unusual. She wants you to be daring, dashing. Admittedly, this can be tiring; but the lady is worth it!

An Aquarius woman can bring out the best in you. Her own poise, mental and physical, can be an inspiration. It can also be damned irritating! That's part of the inspiration: being inspired to think of ways to shake her up.

If you are a Capricorn man, she can be lucky for you in money matters. Sagittarius men find this woman mentally stimulating. Libra men are physically attracted to the Aquarius woman. She is good for you generally if you are born under Aries, Sagittarius, Libra or Gemini. If you are a Leo man, you find this woman fascinating but difficult to get along with; it might be best to consider closely before embarking upon a permanent relationship. Many obstacles are indicated if you are a Taurus or Scorpio man.

In all, the Aquarius woman is loyal, is a wonderful person to take your problems to, is able to help you to help yourself. There are likely to be very few dull moments with her. Her intuition is developed to a fine hone; she can usually sense what the future holds.

Famous women born under Aquarius include Blanca Holmes, astrologer; Gertrude Stein; Lana Turner; Marian Anderson; Kay Boyle, writer; Tallulah Bankhead; and Evangeline Adams, astrologer.

FOR WOMEN ONLY—

Sometimes this man's mind is so much on the future that he tends to overlook the present completely! Make sure he doesn't forget you. Let him be aware of your presence. Make yourself a part of his plans, for he is constantly planning, dreaming, inventing, devising, prophesying. He is airy in temperament, fixed, determined at times to the point of being stubborn. He isn't always easy to get along with, and he can be a bully—absentminded: but those are negative sides of his nature. On the positive side, he is worth working to catch!

This man has a tendency to make dreams come true. He can fight and work against odds. But he needs someone to have faith in him: you can fill that role. Please do not expect the Aquarius man to be perfect: he has faults, loads of them—and he can be exasperating. However, he is generous, reasonable, willing to help, to listen to your problems, to offer intelligent, sometimes sage, advice. He practices what he preaches, too. You have to teach him to be practical. If left to his own devices, he might give everything away. He experiments, makes friends with persons others are apt to consider mere cranks.

He is willing to pioneer, to accept challenges, to lead a life of adventure and risk. Is that what you want? If it isn't, it would be better to forget these hints and to find yourself another, safer, more reliable individual. This man is not apt to fit into any pigeonhole: he tends to sprout wings and to fly high.

This man possesses the ability to learn without formal study: his knowledge could be described as subjective or intuitive. His learning and abilities are not academic: he learns by doing, feeling, experimenting, making as many mistakes as any beginner, yet displaying a master's "feel" for a subject. The Aquarian man is concerned with hopes, wishes, friends, loyalty, promises: a broken promise can mean a broken relationship as far as he is concerned. Here's an important hint: do not say one thing and do another. No matter how innocent or noble your intentions, this man can interpret your word to the letter and if you break that word, it is a serious affair with him.

He is lucky for you in financial affairs if you are a Capricorn; he attracts you physically if your sign is Libra; he is stimulating to you mentally if you are a Sagittarius woman. He is generally good for you if you are a Gemini, Libra, Aries, or Sagittarian. You are drawn to him if your sign is Leo. There are obstacles to overcome in such a relationship if you are a Taurus or Scorpio woman.

Famous men born under Aquarius include Abraham Lincoln, Jack Benny, Franklin Delano Roosevelt, Thomas Alva Edison and Clark Gable.

XXXV

SUN IN PISCES

(*February 20–March 20*)

This woman appreciates kindness and consideration above almost anything else: you can win her by being sympathetic. However, once you do, she is apt to be possessive, has a tendency to want to "take over." In a way, this could be pleasant: Pisces women are lovely, poetic, emotional, giving, generous: to have a woman such as this want you all to herself is not too hard to take. On the other hand, if you are basically independent you will soon resent her. This brings us to the all-important hint: when dealing with Pisces women, be frank, open and honest to the point of confiding your secrets. This appeals to her and gains her confidence. Once this is accomplished, she is not likely to hold so tight to the reins. The secret hint, in other words, is to give the Pisces lady confidence in *herself*. She has a tendency toward self-doubt, often expressed in her possessive attitude.

If you want to be happy with a Pisces woman, don't hold back. No matter how terrible the truth, it is better to tell it. This lady is a fighter as well as a poet: she has a few secrets of her own, some contacts or ideas which, if utilized, might well pull you out of difficulties. She is not an easy woman to understand; she often changes with the scenery, with the situation—as if nature had given her a strange power to face any situation, no matter how pleasant or awful.

You will want to shield her, protect her; but time and again she will prove that she is tough, able to take it. Then, in almost the next moment, she once more will become the gentle, leaning dependent Piscean. One of her great assets is a sense of humor: she will laugh when you most need to hear the sound of laughter. Give her confidence, warmth and love—and you will be amply repaid.

These women are extraordinary when it comes to psychic power: they can see through a falsehood, they can tell what the next move will bring, they can read your motives with crystal clarity. In a way, living with a Pisces woman is similar to living with a lie detector. It is a wonderful feeling of vindication—when the indicator points to "truth"—but the feeling of depression is severe when the needle points the other way.

One more hint: despite her hunches, her psychic abilities, her sympathy for the underdog, this woman has plenty of common sense. Don't attempt to play upon her weaknesses.

She is lucky for you in money matters if you are an Aquarian; she stimulates you mentally if your sign is Capricorn; you are physically drawn to her if you are a Scorpio man. She is generally good for you if your zodiacal sign is Scorpio, Cancer, Capricorn or Taurus. There is attraction if you are a Virgo, but it is a case of opposites attracting each other. Caution is advised in this relationship if you are a Gemini or a Sagittarian.

Famous women born under Pisces include Elizabeth Barrett Browning; Anais Nin, writer; Dinah Shore; Elizabeth Taylor; and Cyd Charisse.

FOR WOMEN ONLY—

One of the best hints is to go slow with this man. Don't push or force issues. Be subtle. Plan carefully. Ingratiate yourself with him, make yourself a part of his life and work. He will soon ask your opinions, he will confide in you. He is a sensitive soul if you take it easy. If you push, force, demand, he will stand up to you and show you the door. He is not the easiest man to be with, but he may well be one of the kindest and most considerate.

Gentle methods can capture this man's heart; he does have a tendency to be self-indulgent, and forceful arguments can send him into a protective shell, where he will be quite satisfied to commiserate with himself. If you abhor daydreaming, then find another man. The Pisces male is imaginative, often highly creative, and he is a dreamer if ever there was one.

He is emotional, Neptunian, at times mediumistic in that he appears to be inspired from out of the blue. He has flashes of insight, and these first impressions are often not only correct but ultimately prove profitable! This man is never completely contented. It is important for you to be aware of this trait. Otherwise, the tendency would be for you to blame yourself, or to blame him. The characteristic is ingrained, it is part of the man—it is a healthy discontent. On the highest or most creative plane, it could be termed "divine discontent." He is not satisfied to rest on past performance; he strives for improvement. Often he appears abstract: you are tempted to complain that there are problems to be attended to close at home—this instead of dreaming of a Utopia. But you have been forewarned: the Pisces man is a dreamer, but he is *not* a schemer.

When he decides he loves you, it is with all his heart. If you are a Cancer or Scorpio woman, or if your sign is Taurus or Capricorn, you will be most appreciative of this man. Virgo women are drawn to him but such a relationship often produces conflict. Many obstacles are indicated if your sign is Gemini or Sagittarius. He is good for you financially if you are an Aquarius woman. You are physically attracted to him if your sign is Scorpio. He stimulates you mentally if you are a Capricorn.

This man's greatest fault, perhaps, is a tendency to be too trusting: he sees persons and situations the way he wishes or would like them to be instead of in actuality. This is part of his charm, however. It is one of the things that could make you love him.

He is wonderfully considerate of those who are weak or ill, or who need help. He will seldom disappoint you when it comes to qualities of integrity or sympathy.

Famous men born under Pisces include Manly Palmer Hall, philosopher-astrologer; Albert Einstein; Harry Belafonte; Rimsky-Korsakov; Enrico Caruso; and Edwin Raphael, 19th Century astrologer.

XXXVI

THE MOON

In *Aries,* the Moon stresses independence, drive—a need for self-assertion. The Moon in this, the first zodiacal sign, tells us the native's personality is colored by a desire to get at the truth, which can be abstract. It can be a symbol, something to aim for rather than to attain. Maybe the truth is constantly out of reach. The Moon in Aries is not discouraged, but continues the quest. In a way, this makes for idealism and high principles, but not necessarily for concrete results. The Moon here may cause others to lose patience with the native—because he is forever concerned with what should be, instead of "making do" with what exists.

The astrologer, of course, must combine the indications for the Moon in Aries with the House position occupied by the Moon. Such a combination means using the art of synthesis. And this, as we continue to repeat, is the backbone of the art of astrology.

So the Moon here stresses a seeking of the truth as the native sees it. What kind of "truth" does he see? It could be that he sees the truth only as it is convenient for him to see it. This, of course, depends upon other factors in the chart, including aspects and House positions. But, taken alone, the Moon here makes for one who can fight for the truth as long as the "truth" is of practical value—concerning his home, his future, his security. "Truth" here can be narrow and limited. The native inclines toward a headstrong attitude, one which can bring about conflicts, resentment, envy and actual physical battles if the temper is not controlled.

This native must learn to develop his abilities through study, experience, perhaps travel. Then he must stress an enlargement of his horizon, a wider point of view—and self-improvement. This is not a crusading kind of drive to improve others—it could merely be a negative expression of the Moon in Aries. Let this native first improve himself and his own life; then, perhaps, he can inspire others to greater accomplishments. There is a tendency here to be selfish, headstrong, so sure of being right that the vision is narrowed down and only limited pictures are observed.

These people have plenty of push, drive and energy. They can fight for what they believe to be right—and they refuse to be pushed around. They have great potential, especially in inventiveness and originality.

In *Taurus,* the Moon indicates that the native has a good idea of what he thinks he desires: he tends to become overinterested in material things, luxuries, and can become bogged down with possessions. At times he has an obsession with collecting things. He is not necessarily a self-starter—he requires stimulation. This comes in the form of an aggressive partner or friend; or it can take the form of actual stimulants, including alcohol. He is attracted to the physical, passionate—he wants to be admired, needs attention and feels there is not so great a need for action if it makes one uncomfortable. The native has the ability to bounce back, to ride with the blows of fate, and to shift and adjust until he is secure.

The Moon in Taurus paints the picture of one who can be determined to the point of obstinacy. Idealism in itself will not move him—but it will show him where he can gain, help himself or make his position more secure. He is reserved, but loves the "good life," including parties, excellent food and drink. His intuitive intellect, finely honed, has great "staying power."

The Moon here takes what comes, analyzes it to suit his own needs and then "lives with it." This includes relations with members of the opposite sex. Some key words are voluptuous, indolent, and self-indulgent.

On the positive side, this lunar position gives the ability to appeal to popular tastes, to adjust to changing social conditions and capture the imagination of the public. The native is romantic, appreciates what he possesses, and can make a little go a long way.

The astrologer would do well (all other factors in chart being considered) to encourage the native to look beyond the immediate to make full use of a fine sense of what people want, need and are capable of obtaining. With the Moon in Taurus, the native should be encouraged to read, to broaden his horizons, to realize that indeed "a house is not necessarily a home."

The Moon in *Gemini* is indicative of one who is mentally alert, keen on self-expression—perhaps a literary buff, a reporter, one who can tell a good story, is adaptable, versatile and has a tendency to scatter his forces. Seems to move about constantly—if not physically, then certainly mentally. He can see various points of view, but doesn't often go too deeply into any one subject.

He can be perceptive, can hit at the truth in a lighthearted manner; he would make a good satirist, for he is flexible, tends to doubt the seriousness of his own acts, intentions, statements, writings. He would make an excellent humorist, but when things are not going just right, he is inclined to nervousness, brooding, self-suspicion, doubt, envy, and perhaps even a "persecution complex."

He is articulate, seldom at a loss for words; but he might spread himself too thin, at times becoming involved in absurd causes, attracting "tricky" friends, flirting with the underground or passing a bit of money under the table.

He possesses a great amount of curiosity, but once he finds the answer, or thinks he has, he tends to lose interest. He does not have the staying power of the Moon in Taurus but he is a better self-starter—more active and more likely to do something about changing an unpleasant situation.

Self-control is essential. Greater self-discipline is also necessary if the native is to be more than merely an attractive but superficial individual.

The native finds it fun to use his hands skillfully, such as in sleight-of-hand; he is fond of short journeys, getting around and contacting people. He would make an excellent salesman, is capable of living by his wits, is willing to experiment with an occupation.

His strong points: versatility, curiosity. His weak one: a tendency to be superficial and flashy rather than thorough and knowledgeable.

The Moon in *Cancer* takes himself seriously, feels he is "destined" to fulfill a certain role, is loyal to family tradition, or at least to family members. He may battle them himself, but will brook no interference from outsiders. He must learn to think of how outsiders feel, think, react.

There is "unconscious" selfishness evident. The native appears to feel that others are too sensitive to accept favors or show appreciation. The astrologer should attempt to make him see the situation as it exists and to see persons in light of their everyday problems. The Moon here depicts one who seems, somehow, to believe that others truly understand what he means by some kind of osmosis. The native should be taught greater respect for hard, cold facts, including the economic ones. He needs to be taught to have greater interest in what others think, feel, need, hope, dream and aspire to accomplish.

The native reacts inwardly, he takes a kind of fierce pleasure in brooding, pondering the "toughness" of the world in general and his associates and friends in particular. His family and security mean much—but he often appears to do everything in his power to endanger his chances of success. He is a puzzle, but an interesting one—he wants to know himself and the world. He is creative, sensitive, strong in the belief that he is "special"; but he seems fated to wander in many directions. He wants comfort in his home but tends to complain if things go too smoothly.

The native, a bit like the Sun in Leo, needs an audience, wants to impress others and requires recognition, but is suspicious of the source once it is received. He can do more to harm himself than any enemy would dream of doing.

His need for a creative outlet is evident: he would make a good writer, painter, one who deals in an unusual manner with liquid, food and with the thoughts of others. He can be found in news, advertising and public relations, and in affairs connected with security, marriage advice and real estate.

He is a complicated individual, although he will deny it, insisting he is simple and easy to get along with if only others would understand him. The astrologer's job is to make the native play his part in the role of understanding—including family, finances, and members of the opposite sex who want to receive as well as give a feeling of well-being. The Moon in Cancer is sociable, emotional, changeable and sensitive to the point of being psychic.

The Moon in *Leo* makes the native want to give the impression of nobility. In desiring to present such a picture, his very actions and thoughts often do become noble. This native has drive and ambition; he wants to better himself. Security in itself does not satisfy him. Ambition is a key word here. Like the Moon in Taurus, he loves luxury. But there is more "fire" to his makeup—he is dashing, popular with the opposite sex and tends toward extravagant gestures. He is prone to "emotional hangovers."

The Moon in Leo tends to sit in an "ivory tower." He tells himself he is merely an interested spectator. But very often he becomes more involved in situations than the actual participants.

The astrologer must know that the native has an inner feeling of strength. He doesn't call on it because he feels it is there whenever he needs it. This could create the kind of situation which is hopeless—something like this: the writer who begins to hang out in "dives." He tells himself he is there to gather material. But soon he is one of the local characters—providing instead of gathering stories. The Moon in Leo requires discipline; otherwise he slips into the easiest path, never really living up to his potential. The tendency here is toward "snobbery." The rules are fine, he is apt to feel, but they don't necessarily apply to him. He will associate with anyone but keep a part of himself to himself. On the positive side, he holds something in reserve. On the negative side, he thinks he is holding something in reserve. A fine point, admittedly, but it could create disillusion, dissipation and unhappiness.

Generally, the native is honorable, generous with time and money. He needs to feel he is special. In dealing with members of the opposite sex, he seeks one who finds him charming, irresistible. He shows appreciation of and ability in artistic, creative fields, including music, painting, poetry. He loves to explain, display and criticize the arts. He is never satisfied with burying his "light" in a bushel.

In *Virgo,* the Moon position stresses the intellectual approach. Where the Moon in Leo would be content to feel, the Moon here finds it necessary to understand. This native wants his family (and the world could be his family) to adjust to what he can understand!

The astrologer can readily see that this creates some difficulties. He must learn whether the native's range of understanding is narrow or wide. The stress is on sincerity, a job well done, powers of discrimination. The native can be fussy, stubborn and demanding, but he never asks others to do what he himself would not do. He tends to be a censor. If he doesn't feel something is good to read or see, he feels it is logical to assume it is not good for others. The astrologer must work to help the native broaden his vision, open his mind and welcome new experiences.

The native is excellent when it comes to analyzing. Difficulties arise when he analyzes to such an extent that he is frozen into periods of absolute inaction. He wants to *know:* but this drive toward knowledge can shut out the intuitive intellect; it can make the native ultraconservative. Indications here are good for teaching, reporting, analyzing reports, statistics.

He feels tremendously gratified when others ask questions, ask his opinion, or show appreciation for his efforts. He is easily taken advantage of by those shrewd enough to play on his need for affection, appreciation, understanding.

The native is loyal, persistent; he possesses the desire to overcome obstacles and arrive at a goal. Here the astrologer has an important key: the native *must* have a goal. Nothing discourages him more than aimlessness. He often is intolerant of those who are "abstract," who do not appear definite enough, or who are "waiting for the right time." The Moon in Virgo needs to be busy. He consults, he reports, he makes trips, he writes letters, he arranges meetings. He is a wonderful agent, detective, diagnostician, technician, host—if the party is for a reason.

He wants to be of use. He admires others who are dedicated and tends to ridicule those who can relax. What is the astrologer to stress? Taken alone, he views the Moon in Virgo as an indication of one with tremendous potential. The native can make himself reliable and needed, but can find himself buried in a maze of details, overlooked for the promotions, the "bigger" things, including the kind of fulfillment which brings greatest personal happiness. The native, reacting negatively, is finicky about food, sex, new experiences.

He needs to learn to loosen up. Then he becomes discriminating in the best sense: he recognizes quality and enjoys what he has, instead of constantly reaching out for something else.

In *Libra,* the Moon finds expression in public relations, advertising and law. He is also found in real estate, in constructing buildings for sports contests, etc. The native has vision—he sees beyond the immediate indications. He possesses the charm to win his way to select circles, and can convince investors that he has his finger on the pot of gold at the end of the rainbow.

He wants to be in on events and happenings, including news and rumor. He is fond of people, is gracious, can be a remarkably good host. He has fine taste when it comes to furnishings, food and wine—contingent on his background and other factors in his horoscope.

In Libra, the Moon position inclines the native toward successful partnerships, including marriage. Often he is described as being elegant. There is (as in case of Moon in Taurus) love of luxury, the "good life," companionship, conversation, exchange of ideas.

He is basically gentle and understanding, and attracts others to him with their problems. This is one reason he would succeed as a lawyer, public relations counselor or advertising expert. He tends to see the best in others, and this could lead to disillusionment—he might be attracting those who seek to take advantage of his good nature.

The native works well with others; much of his success (or lack of it) depends upon the people he attracts. The astrologer, knowing this, must prod the native toward a greater degree of selectivity. He must be taught to exercise care in granting his trust, confidence, material goods. The native thirsts for society, people, places and challenges. He needs these things and must choose the best, or choose to the best of his ability.

Grant Lewi has called this a "Cinderella position" because the native is capable of making hopes and wishes turn to realities. He can overcome odds to rise to the top. He rises above his environment. He seeks beauty, refinement—and does all in his power to be worthy of these things. The astrologer must also stress the necessity of recognizing desires when they appear. Otherwise, the native simply daydreams and achieves nothing but an introverted kind of vision.

He should be encouraged to read and to seek higher education, even if in night school or through church or social organizations. He is sensitive, inclined to brood.

He requires those close to him to have faith. He must learn to attract those whose "faith" is worth striving to acquire!

The Moon in *Scorpio* is intense, dynamic, perhaps best described as "all the way or nothing at all." The native is self-reliant, serious, often described as a penetrating person. He is attracted to the hidden or the occult; he may be a detective, or extremely fond of mystery and attracted to the solution of crimes. He is very energetic—at times abrupt, acting on impulse, especially in connection with members of the opposite sex. Once he starts, there is no stopping him. He gets up steam and goes on, moving forward, digging deep, leaving broken hearts, disillusionment. But this is the negative response to the Moon in Scorpio—and these people, in the long run, hurt no one as much as they injure themselves.

On the positive side, the Moon in Scorpio native inspires confidence, creates solutions to touchy problems, provides for the security of loved ones; he is virile, passionate, speaks out for his principles and can be found battling for the underdog.

The astrologer must watch for one basic trait—a tendency to go to extremes in eating and drinking and in affairs of the heart. This is no halfway person—the Moon here is complete and committed.

The native has strong convictions; once he has been convinced, it is difficult if not impossible to change his mind. He can be irritable on the negative side—or creatively angry on the constructive side. He must find a creative outlet for his energies or his emotions build up, spill over and burn himself and others.

The native seems to possess extrasensory perception or at least a highly developed intuitive sense. He can perceive when something of importance is about to occur. He can look at an individual and size him up—he can gaze deep, sense when the entire story has not been told. He can annoy people, get under their skins. He is expert at making others lose their control—and thus blurt out what was supposed to be a deep, dark secret.

The native is intense, and reaction to him is the same—either one of great fondness, or near hate. The Moon here has great attraction for members of the opposite sex. Alan Leo says it favors marriage in a male horoscope, but threatens disharmony in the married state. The Moon in Scorpio is indicative of money by inheritance, marriage or partnership (8th House influence—Scorpio being the natural 8th sign of the zodiac—the 8th House being the *second from the 7th House*).

The native apparently must learn by experience. Like Rasputin, he perhaps feels one cannot be saved unless he has sinned. He is very serious, needs to develop a sense of humor and throw aside the idea that he is some kind of secret martyr.

There are no light bruises for this native. When misfortune occurs—he takes it hard and personally. He may even feel fate has it in for him—quite a fascinating lunar position!

In *Sagittarius,* the Moon tells of much activity, physical and mental—of high ideals, of travels both physical and mental. The native wants to learn, to spread knowledge; he wants to give of himself and attracts people with trouble, inspiration, and a message to impart to the world. He can be buried in the ambitions and problems of others to his own detriment if he does not take care to avoid such a situation. He loves adventure and creates idols which, at times, prove to have feet of clay—he is a natural student and is attracted to reading, writing, publishing, advertising, publicity and understanding various peoples of the world. He is generous, charming, fond of the outdoors and of animals, and wants to discover things and people.

He has much imagination—which on the positive side leads to solid, creative expression. On the negative side, this leads to daydreaming, procrastination, unorthodoxy merely for the sake of being different. The native is frank, expresses himself clearly, is able to combine irony with humor—he loves to tell stories, to recall past events; he is attracted to history as a hobby and profession.

The native tends to feel limited. He would like to soar to the heights—but there is danger that he will be aimless, soaring merely to get moving, to create changes, to feel free, to toss off the weight of basic responsibilities. Much travel is indicated, including overseas—and the native often becomes an expert on another country, even if he never actually visits the nation in question.

He is inclined to be restless. Thus, numerous changes of residence are indicated. He also has changes of heart and emotions with members of the opposite sex. He is difficult to understand because he does not, in the long run, find himself easy to comprehend. His moods and interests are subject to change. He is in constant need of mental stimulation. The purely physical soon bores him. He is attracted, first and foremost, by the intellect—by another person's ability to express himself.

Much talent is indicated along lines of philosophy—much interest in the subject of religion, even if the native is not a religious individual in the orthodox sense. He is attracted to mysticism—he wants to find out about the lives of men who changed the world. Thus, he would make an excellent researcher, teacher, writer. He wants to publish, to spread information and knowledge. He can be found in advertising, creating propaganda, and is also the constructive critic of the efforts of others.

He either has two occupations or a hobby which so absorbs him that he might as well have two fields of endeavor.

The astrologer must help him learn some of the hard facts of life—learn the value of money and strive to be more practical in his outlook.

In *Capricorn,* the Moon indicates one who is earthy, tends to be materialistic, ambitious, very sensitive about his standing in the community. The native takes responsibilities seriously but is much too aware of what others think about his efforts. He needs to devote more attention to his loved ones; he must learn that impressing others is secondary—the important thing is to have self-respect.

He can handle authority and expects others to do as he says, not as he does. He thinks of himself as tough, practical, stubborn, and determined. He is embarrassed at displays of emotion.

The astrologer needs to instill confidence in him—the confidence to attain his goals. Otherwise, the Moon in Capricorn becomes depressed, frustrated, resentful. This is a fascinating lunar position because the native inwardly feels he is chosen for the role of leadership. If he doesn't attain it he chooses one of two courses. The first is that of putting forth greater effort. The second is that of throwing his hands up in the air in a futile gesture. The astrologer, naturally, must encourage the first course.

The native serves the public and is served, demands and receives prestige. This takes time, but this individual has time on his side—if only he can be made to realize it. He is often accused of being cold or materialistic. Members of the opposite sex are forever trying to reform or change him. The more the effort is made, the more he resists, despite outward appearances or promises.

There are indications of a difference in age or social position of the marriage partner; some difficulties are experienced in this area. The native may marry for money and then miss love. His parents experience difficulty—there may be separation, or early death of one parent.

Obstacles must be regarded as challenges; the native thrives on controversy, being true to himself, and is attracted to those who have overcome odds to achieve their goal. He feels, inwardly, he must fulfill his destiny.

He comes to the attention of the public. Some people swear by him—others *at* him. He is attracted to power for the sake of power, not necessarily money. He wants prestige as some people want money and needs recognition as some require alcohol. He must be himself and not attempt to play someone else's role. This is a "tough" lunar position because the native is demanding and must meet numerous demands.

With the Moon in *Aquarius,* the native is generous, broad-minded, attractive to members of the opposite sex and popular in general, but he often lacks the strength to be practical enough to fulfill his hopes and wishes. He loves applause and praise but secretly doubts that he is really as capable as others might imagine him to be. He needs to be determined but should avoid being stubborn. He must learn to accept criticism and not constantly seek the company of those who flatter him.

The native is interested in social mores; he wants to improve world conditions but often neglects his own neighborhood or family.

There are numerous contradictions in his nature. He recognizes these and they cause him more than a little concern. The road to Hell, as they say, is paved with good intentions. Perhaps this very well fits the Moon in Aquarius. No doubt he wants to do good. But in trying, he steps on toes, is often harsh in his efforts to get in a position where his influence will be felt. He needs to feel he is helping others—and in trying to do so often convinces people they are not really as happy as they think.

He is attracted to "far out" subjects, including astrology, magnetism, dream interpretation, psychology, sociology, social theories, hypnotism, television, space flights, etc. He is given to fantasy, fascinated by science fiction (even though he may profess to be "above it all"). He is very sensitive—and if the Moon is in poor aspect to the Sun, may have an eye defect.

He is considered unconventional—and he is proud of it! His public image is that of a humanitarian who often makes himself appear ridiculous by going the long way around.

The astrologer's task is to make him realize that his first duty is to make himself happy. He must help himself before he can really earn the respect of others.

In *Pisces*, the Moon indicates the native is restless, sensitive, impressionable, subject to brooding and changes of mood, and fond of travel, yet needing an anchor, a place to remain in happiness and contentment. He can be self-indulgent; also very capable of sensing moods in others, even of perceiving their thoughts. He can be found working behind the scenes, including behind a camera, or in institutions, hospitals, etc. He looks constantly for some kind of Shangri-la and dives into seclusion when hurt—he wonders when others will recognize the loftiness of his motives.

He is only truly appreciated when he appreciates himself and this is not accomplished unless he lives up to his highest ideals. There appears to be no middle ground.

He tends to be too easygoing. too willing to change the course of his action if obstacles appear, too willing to back down. The astrologer must help him see the folly of making so many "zigs and zags."

The native is fascinated by the occult—he is called "psychic" by many of his friends. It is necessary for him to adhere to the highest principles. Otherwise, he begins to suspect his own motives and then his entire framework of confidence crumbles like a house of cards. He is affected by the moods and feelings of others, and can be sent into a fit of gloom by observing family members as they quarrel.

He wants to be surrounded by happiness—but cannot seem to put his finger on his own salvation. His worst enemy: indecision. His best friend: confidence in his own ideals.

XXXVII

MERCURY

In *Aries,* Mercury tells of one who reacts quickly, is sensitive, perceives artistic values; appreciates originality; is delighted by skill, talent and creativity; and is capable of offering criticism on the highest level. The astrologer must help the native to become something more than merely clever. He needs to learn the value of being thorough, determined—creative rather than merely headstrong.

Indications are that the native is fluent in speech. Grant Lewi makes the point that sound is very important to the native, and he should strive to live amid "agreeable" sounds. The native, thus, would be attracted to music and should be encouraged to develop his sense of music appreciation. He reacts to first impressions and must avoid acting completely on impulse. He has an active imagination but requires direction, discipline and realization of his own potential.

In *Taurus,* Mercury tells of one who gains more from sight than sound: he gains much from reading, from visual demonstrations, from watching, observing, absorbing knowledge. He may appear slow to learn, but once his lessons are learned, they stick. He can be obstinate, but also loyal. He has strong likes and dislikes—but generally the native is diplomatic. He can smile at you—but it is not easy to know what he is thinking. He appears to be slow in speech, but this is because he measures his words.

In *Gemini,* Mercury keynotes versatility, a tendency toward scattering forces. The native is inventive, has wit and humor, is capable of acquiring knowledge through travel and reading. He tends to be nervous because he "takes on" the problems and foibles of those around him. It is important for the astrologer to make the native realize the importance of his surroundings. If they are not orderly, the native's thoughts wander—he becomes discouraged and depressed. If, on the other hand, his surroundings spell out discipline and orderliness, then the native begins to think clearly and his work reflects this state of mind. Often he is in love with life, but can find it difficult to remain faithful to one person. It is possible for the native to love more than one individual at the same time.

He can break with convention and announce he is willing to let the chips fall where they may. But inwardly, there is apt to be confusion, for that sense of the orderly cannot be denied. The astrologer must help the native realize this apparent contradiction and come to terms with it.

Mercury in *Cancer* is described by a major keyword: Adaptability. The native adapts himself to his surroundings—but he can tend to fall into a rut instead of trying to change anything. He may know what he should do, but is simply too adaptable. He is discreet and realizes that others are loyal to their beliefs, their families, their countries—without this necessarily making them right in their feelings. Mercury in Cancer shrugs off combat; his attitude is one of live and let live. But when conditions demand change or action, he is perturbed, often at a loss; he begins to brood, whine and complain.

Mercury here has a tendency to personalize his surroundings; the people he meets; the things he sees, hears, smells, tastes. The astrologer's task, obviously, is to help the native draw his mental forces together, make them work for him, refuse to take second best merely because it is convenient. His family is important to him and so is a feeling that his loved ones are happy, even if far away. His mind is retentive; he loves the old and established. He is fond of antiques and fine old classics in literature, and has what might be termed an intellectual interest in food.

In *Leo,* Mercury gives us a native who is apt to be subjective—he takes a known fact and applies it to his own life, thoughts, feelings, personal symbols. He takes the large view, doesn't like to think in bits and pieces, wants to see the project as a whole. He sees persons in relation to their lives, their abilities, their accomplishments. This native sometimes is overwhelmed with the difference in what he thinks he desires and what he actually surrounds himself with—including the people he loves and is loved by. He constantly criticizes himself, quietly, for not having the very best: he never doubts he is capable, but blames this minor mistake, that lack of appreciation, and so on down the line, until the series of links appears endless. Grass usually appears greener to Mercury in Leo, but he feels, somehow, that his ship is coming in, and that in the not too distant future he will be playing the tune and others will be dancing to his rhythms. Takes only time and determination, he feels. He is often arrogant, making others feel he thinks he is superior. He thus pushes people from him and then, so often, wonders why others don't recognize his great charms. It never occurs to him that perhaps he hasn't really been so charming after all!

He often is bored, and doesn't make too much of a show of trying to appear interested. He feels he has a little extra to offer—and maybe he has. But the astrologer must make him realize that just thinking, feeling, believing are not enough—he must get down to the work of living, of being happy, of creating, of displaying the talents, charms, powers he *knows* he possesses. This is a very significant Mercury position and the astrologer's job here is an enormous one.

In *Virgo,* Mercury tells of a native who can be sharp but brittle. He can be aware, sensitive and alert, but subject to quick or mercurial changes and to an early breaking point. He needs to be made "softer." The astrologer must teach him to develop a greater attitude of acceptance. Perhaps the native analyzes too often, too much—and by the time he finishes, the flavor, the joy of whatever activity he is engaged in has gone. Because of self-criticism, he breaks down his own confidence, yet is surprised when others express a lack of confidence. He pushes too hard; he wants results, yet is skeptical when they finally materialize. He is cautious, prudent and versatile, and has good intuition—but he has to be so simply is not taken.

sure before taking a step that, in numerous instances, the step

He can be methodical, so much so that subjects and persons take on a "dry" flavor. The astrologer must encourage a greater degree of relaxation and confidence.

The native is fond of work which enables him to digest facts thoroughly and come up with conclusions. This is an excellent indication for an accountant, mathematician or individual in charge of seeing that others receive the best for their money. He can also be found teaching, in photography, reporting, radio and television. This native is sincere but tends to find himself with too many irons in the fire—and not enough fire. He is neat, careful about food, often afraid to let himself go in relations with members of the opposite sex.

Mercury in *Libra* is sensitive, artistic, socially aware, politically mature, attracted to the arts, able to transform the commonplace into the beautiful. The native is creative and attracts to him those engaged in creative activities. He thinks along lines of balance, justice, a blending of many elements into a whole.

His mental pursuits are broad—he sees potentials better than actual details. He is sometimes accused of being absentminded. But, very likely, the truth of the matter is that he sees or remembers only what is necessary for him to remember, rather than allowing his mind to become cluttered with details.

He wants things in order, but is not necessarily an orderly individual. He knows how to appeal to the public in general but is often puzzled when dealing with individuals. He possesses good taste and favors quality over quantity—he does not appear attracted to bargains.

In *Scorpio,* Mercury indicates one who is sensuous, able to perceive hidden meanings, shrewd, curious; he tends to be suspicious, but his suspicions usually have foundation in fact. He is capable of understanding high finance; fascinated with the stock market, he draws charts in an effort to understand various trends. This native knows how to appeal to the opposite sex—and would gain much by selling specific items such as clothing to either sex. He sees through false claims and people who make them.

The astrologer must teach the native to overcome his fear that greater security is constantly required. Often, no matter how good his financial position might be, he worries, and can make himself miserable over little things while neglecting important projects.

In *Sagittarius*, Mercury paints a picture of one who is fond of sports, tries to live by the Golden Rule, is fair, wants to impart or share knowledge, and is fascinated by travel, publishing, and the formation of public opinion. Indications are excellent for advertising, public relations, writing, producing, political campaigns, creating of editorial policy.

The astrologer must help him to see the obvious. He tends to be idealistic to the extent that others take advantage of him, and must learn to be more practical—otherwise he is in for disillusionment, especially with members of the opposite sex. He will battle for freedom of speech, but can be so concerned with the right of *others* to speak that he is "shut out." He must be taught to concentrate, finish projects and to take care of personal needs before worrying about the needs of strangers.

Mercury in *Capricorn* can be earthy, warm, giving, trusting, and capable of seeing only the best in others. This can lead to some situations which are sad, costly and enervating.

The astrologer's job is to help the native to use his abilities, including intuitive intellect. Perhaps, on the other hand, the real task is to have the native heed the message his common sense sends rather than disregarding facts and hoping for the best. He is industrious and works toward his goal, but doesn't always know in which direction the goal lies. He must be more discriminating and suspicious, and call upon personal resources rather than trusting those who perhaps are not trustworthy.

In *Aquarius,* Mercury is oriented toward helping large groups, working with organizations, making friends for unpopular causes. The native is idealistic and expects others to live by the Golden Rule, but often is in contact with those who don't have much of a social conscience.

He is attracted to metaphysical subjects, is intuitive, will often act in a manner which causes him to be labeled unorthodox. He attracts friends who follow unusual careers, including aviation, theater, astrology, exploring. He makes friends because he expresses an interest in what others are doing. On the negative side, he becomes so fascinated with others that he neglects his own personal appearance, thoughts, ambitions, hopes and wishes.

He loves to gather information, inform, improve conditions, improvise, create, attract members of the opposite sex; he wants to be popular, but requires popularity on his own terms. He promotes subjects which do not necessarily have the approval of the masses. He needs to be well rounded; he must study all sides of a question and be very well informed, or he falls into the trap of seeing persons and situations only as they might ideally exist.

In *Pisces,* Mercury presents the picture of a native whose fears may prove to be his greatest assets. Once the native recognizes fear as a challenge he overcomes it and becomes a dynamic, useful member of society. Otherwise, he is obsessed by lack of security, lack of confidence, and by a feeling of unworthiness.

He must face issues squarely, be willing to admit mistakes and to accept credit for a job well done. He should be helped to overcome false modesty. This native must learn to speak out, to stand up for his convictions. He is able to analyze the problems of others but is shy about calling the shots on his own difficulties. He is fascinated by secrets, would make a wonderful historian because he enjoys digging for facts. He is receptive to the needs of others but must be helped to help himself.

XXXVIII

VENUS

In *Aries,* Venus is an emotional antenna—the native is sensitive, aware of how others feel and react. He wants to love and be loved—romance is the key. Without romance, he withers, becomes discouraged, broods, worries, complains.

The astrologer's job is to help him discover the romance that is everywhere, available, ready to be grasped and enjoyed. The native tends to be too romantic about romance! He often doesn't recognize the real thing and is taken in by the phony, the imitation.

Venus in *Taurus* paints the picture of strong emotions—the native is more intuitive than intellectual. There is a need for greater self-control of his emotions. He tends to give of himself too much and thus is "taken in." He must learn to think as well as feel. The astrologer should help him realize that he cannot be all things to all people. He feels he needs things, people, emotions—when, in actuality, what he may need is a more simple, direct approach to life and its problems and joys. He is physically attractive and responsive to physical attraction. This trait can spell trouble if it goes unchecked.

In *Gemini,* Venus is attracted to travel and romance in connection with travel—the native is able to shower affection on many, but personally demands loyalty and faithfulness—quite a contradiction!

He must learn what he really wants, must strive for greater maturity. He can be a gay and stimulating companion—can know a little about a lot of subjects and be an excellent conversationalist. Yet he can be very lonely! The astrologer should help him develop a sense of awareness and humor. The native, if he channels his forces, can be a bright, happy individual. Otherwise, disappointment is the key word.

In *Cancer,* Venus paints the picture of a native who wants security in love. His needs are basic: shelter, love, protection, the best for his loved ones. His standards are high but the drive, fire and ambition to obtain his desires often is lacking. The astrologer must "shake him up" to his potential. The native is sentimental and sincere; he feels silly wasting time on people or things which do not interest him. Thus he tends to arouse antagonism among those who feel he merely is being rude.

In *Leo,* Venus provides us with the natural showman—the individual who can turn the commonplace into the magnificent, who can make us see the beauty, the emotion, the sex appeal in what generally might be regarded as the everyday. Emotional experiences are dramatized; the native seldom feels anything halfway; he is intense, his responses are spontaneous, impulsive. But he is aware, sensitive, knowing, capable of appreciating fully the physical aspects of life: eating, loving, drinking, sleeping, waking, walking, basking in the sun.

His chief danger is letting his emotions become mechanical, jaded, insensitive because of abuse or overindulgence. He is extravagant, on the negative side, fond of social display; he can become so actively interested in appearances that he finds himself too tired to enjoy the object of his attention.

In *Virgo,* there is a very different story. Venus here wants discretion, needs to feel his emotions are treated as something rare and delicate. Often he becomes involved with inferiors and finds that instead of tenderness, he is treated with reckless abandon. The native is conscientious about his reputation but becomes entangled with those who have secret troubles and are liable to scandal. He has an organized code of conduct, but others may have their own codes—leaving him "up in the air." Special attention is required so that he understands the reason for his confusion.

In *Libra,* Venus tells of a native who is idealistic, whose emotions are direct, who has a love of beauty—one who is sensitive and easily hurt, but who nevertheless continues to see the romance surrounding him. He usually gives others the benefit of any doubt—he seeks justice and truth, and responds to the finer instincts. He needs, at times, to be brought back down to earth and to face realities. He has a strong desire for peace, order and harmony; he yearns for knowledge, is philosophical, attracted to art and creative endeavors. This native is able to attract people to his special charity, cause or interest—and is fascinated by the law (man-made) and by the laws of nature. He can be highly spiritual and thrives on affection.

Venus in *Scorpio* must learn to overcome possessiveness and jealousy, an intense kind of love nature which leads, if unchecked, to unhappiness and even to violence. The native attracts unusual friends, likes to move about, to travel, to speculate on how he can gain through marriage or partnerships. He must learn to be worthy of luxury instead of dreaming about it, demanding it. He talks one way but often acts conversely. Unless the native is careful, he can be taken advantage of by a lover who appeals to his basic, physical nature. Gain is indicated by secret alliances—but his drive for improvement, for added possessions, can be so strong that real happiness is something he regards as only an illusion. He may marry more than once; he tends to take the path of least resistance and must make an effort to avoid extravagance, gambling, promiscuity.

The astrologer has a job cut out for him: he must help the native to realize that deeper meanings lie under most events, desires, persons. The native must learn to place more value on the spiritual and on himself as an individual, and must avoid trying to possess things or people merely for the sake of possessing.

In *Sagittarius,* Venus is indicative of one who is likely to become involved in numerous affairs of the heart but is generous and really *intends* to be loyal. The native tends to love things which are not easily obtainable. Thus he is in danger of attaching himself to persons who care so little that the native is exploited, even humiliated. The astrologer must help him overcome what might be an inner desire to be punished.

The key here is perspective. The native must see things as they exist in relation to his own life. Once he recognizes the reason for his actions, he gains inner illumination. He tends to follow his emotions blindly; this leads to bumps, bruises and emotional involvements which create depression.

In *Capricorn,* Venus tells of a native who is adaptable, moves with the times, is able to make adjustments, strives to make his loved ones happy and secure. There are basic disappointments, but he thrives on them and accepts them as challenges—nevertheless, he does not go unscathed. Gain is indicated from foreign travel and legacies. He must be wary of those who "talk a good game" but have little to offer. Otherwise, he becomes involved with individuals who use and insult him, and then complain because he appears cold or indifferent.

Venus in *Aquarius* tends toward generalities rather than specifics. This includes the native's response to love, romance, emotions and inner drives. He must be taught to be an indvidual; he should learn to demand something in return for his efforts, affection and trust. Otherwise, his tendency is to attract those who demand sacrifice but would not think of giving anything in return.

He attracts artistic friends and is attracted to beauty but must learn that beauty *is* only skin deep.

In *Pisces,* Venus feels a great need for self-expression but often finds it difficult to get his point across. The native is subject to being misunderstood though generally he is kind, sympathetic, easily impressed. He is philanthropic, attracted to work in connection with institutions; he helps the underdog, has friends among those who are weak or afflicted with emotional or physical difficulties. He gains pleasure through secret affairs of the heart, is attracted to the occult and tends to resign himself to his fate—he is not always fortunate in affairs of the heart.

The astrologer must help the native overcome a tendency to be indolent, satisfied merely with existing instead of living life to its fullest. He is more vital in helping others than in aiding himself. He must become less modest, more direct, a bit more determined to better his own position. His greatest need: more ambition, and greater appreciation for the material things in life.

XXXIX

MARS

In *Aries,* Mars makes the native restless, dynamic; it is indicative of originality, daring, a healthy ego, but one which, if permitted full play, could indicate a native who feels that only *his* thoughts, feelings and comforts are of any importance. He is independent and enterprising, and has a keen appreciation for his own best interests.

He must learn to control his temper and impulses. Though inventive, he is sometimes in so much of a hurry he neglects details, leaves himself open to ridicule and can be prone to accidents. The astrologer's job is to help him gain a broader scope, envision new horizons, channel his energy and be more patient.

In *Taurus,* Mars points to passion, giving vent to emotions and involvement with those who bilk him by appealing to those emotions. The native's chief asset is perseverance. He works for security and drives toward his goals, real or imagined. Keeping on the move, he alienates many because he seems self-centered. He should strive for a more tactful approach and adopt an attitude of tolerance for others' foibles. He often thinks of love and money together—he is inclined to the physical, the creature comforts, and feels others must be worthy of his attentions. He must be taught not to bear grudges or brood about injustices.

Mars in *Gemini* gives the native an active, restless mind; it makes him want to change things, to bend situations to his own will. He likes action, but tries too hard, too soon. The astrologer can teach him the value of concentration and the necessity, at times, of making adjustments instead of insisting that the world adjust to him.

Mars in Gemini is adventurous, but once the chase is over he doesn't enjoy the victory as much as he should. This includes numerous areas of life: sex, food, money. Thus, there are numerous affairs, a general restless nature, dissatisfaction with home life.

Mars in *Cancer* battles for security, has a tendency to disagree with family members; the native is torn between loyalty and desire to be free and independent—the leader of all he surveys. He respects authority but feels that authority belongs in *his* hands. He wants to lead from behind the scenes; he wants to be the family head in the large sense of the word "family."

The astrologer must help the native overcome his fears in regard to security. Free expression and humor are to be encouraged—while a kind of behind-the-scenes timidity is to be discouraged. He must come out and say what he thinks.

In *Leo,* Mars is a symbol of great creative energy—the native is restless, anxious, dynamic, forceful; at times he pushes himself to such an extent that he frightens people, including members of the opposite sex.

He possesses a great degree of personal magnetism; he both repels and attracts. His personality is reflected in his creative endeavors. His personal touch is on almost everything he does. He tends to be self-centered and doesn't believe anything is of real importance unless he, personally, feels its effects. He is impulsive and acts with haste but seldom repents, because he is alert for a second chance. There may be battles with loved ones and the danger that the excitement he finds in these clashes could blossom into psychological disorder.

In *Virgo,* Mars tells of a native who is shrewd; he appears impulsive, but his actions are well planned, designed to bring about greater security.

He wants a system: any kind. He doesn't favor doing anything merely for the sake of pleasure or impulse. He wants to be an individual in every sense, but fears he will be relegated to obscurity. He wants to analyze: he wants to feel there is sense to what he's doing, even if it appears to be sheer folly. The astrologer must teach him the lesson of cooperation, and help him appreciate constructive criticism, encouraging him to be thorough, to have faith and to avoid spectacular actions which lead not to riches but to embarrassment and loss.

Mars in *Libra* succeeds in appealing to the public's desire for an easy life, concentrating on luxury and beauty—the native does so with vehemence. He is concerned with success, popularity, public appeal—and with attracting to him the material goods which, he firmly believes, make life worth living.

A social urge is evident. The native needs people and wants people to need him. He wants to be the center of attraction, but the more popular he becomes the more danger there is that he will attract those who eclipse him. The astrologer must make him understand this, must guide him toward maturity, creativeness, appreciation of the talents others possess. He possesses the gift of "survival." He remains, although times may change. The impression he makes upon the public is one of youthful vigor and inventiveness.

Mars in *Scorpio* is perceptive but drives himself harder than he would drive anyone else. The native is passionate, determined, attracted to people he does not really respect. He has great magnetism and draws persons who want to love, live, move, chase and be chased. He is not given too much time for relaxation!

The astrologer must help him find peace through personal fulfillment and teach him the lesson of true relaxation. He must help the native obtain a greater degree of self-discipline, self-control. There is much power and creativity here—hopefully, it can be used constructively.

In *Sagittarius,* Mars reveals a need for activity, both in exercise and sports, and intellectually.

The native wants to be able to spread his views, to take the initiative in publishing, advertising, in getting to know people of many lands. But his true desire is to have others know him. He is capable of high accomplishments; he has the drive and creative energy to fulfill his desires. But the key is channeling the energy and being observant. Mars in Sagittarius looks afar; he stresses ideals and often misses the point because he neglects the details, the proper apprenticeship, the basics, the techniques. He feels, somehow, this is beneath the level toward which he is striving.

The astrologer must help him take a more practical view, help him realize that getting to the top requires climbing, not mere soaring.

The native loves travel, adventure; he craves being part of the "inner circle," wants to be active in influencing the thoughts, the mores of his times. The astrologer should help him realize that control of some of his impulses would be healthy, would help him along the road of greater fulfillment.

Mars in *Capricorn* gives us a native who is ambitious and patient. There is a contradiction here if the native merely waits. But, on the other hand, there is strength; the native may be waiting for the right time—building, creating, doing what must be done, being true to his own high principles—and only then making his move. Mars in Capricorn could utilize some of the characteristics of Mars in Sagittarius. And Mars in Sagittarius, most certainly, could well observe Mars in Capricorn for some valuable lessons. The native here has control, discipline; he can be a leader and can rest easy in the knowledge that time, instead of running against him, is on his side.

Mars in Capricorn is almost fanatic about "doing his duty." He feels responsible for himself, his family and members of the community—and, as a result, is often imposed upon, his time taken up with problems that others shove on his shoulders.

In *Aquarius*, Mars gives us the native who is idealistic, active with organizations; he is sensitive, often impatient with the failure of others to "see the obvious." The astrologer must help him to avoid becoming so bogged down with group tasks that he neglects his own problems, his own job and ambitions. Organizational ability is indicated; the native has the fire to inspire others, to make friends for various causes—including the unpopular ones.

His views, generally, are not of the orthodox type; this leads to battles with authority, including parental authority. He tends to become set in his ways, but seldom loses touch with humanity—he would rather hurt himself than injure others.

Mars in *Pisces* is a clue to a determined lack of concentration.

This means the native, quite deliberately, tends to be "watery," moving about from one area to another; he is content to taste a little here and a little there, without absorbing the full flavor.

The astrologer must help him to see what he is missing. Otherwise, the native actually may be proud of his superficiality; he may feel he is being fashionable, but in so being may be missing out on the vital aspects of life—love and the fulfillment which comes from handling responsibility creatively. He does not want to be enthusiastic about his "secret life," meaning his true desires, his inner voice, his attractions, his natural inclinations.

If he has proper rest, timing, pacing, he can overcome many obstacles. But the trick is to make him realize this and want to do his best. He is sympathetic and fights for the rights of others. The native must be taught that he himself must also be strong and free—he must learn to "heal himself." He should be helped to transform his dreams into realities, to practice economy instead of waste, to use what he has instead of gambling it away.

JUPITER

In *Aries,* Jupiter tends to create an air of overoptimism. In the best sense, the native is cheerful—attracts friends and symbolizes courage and encouragement. In another sense, this planetary sign position leads to false courage, an optimism which is a kind of fool's paradise (being based on nothing more than wishful thinking) and extravagance.

The native should realize that only ability, study, preparation lead to ultimate accomplishment. He is ambitious, makes a wonderful public relations representative, has a knack of turning former enemies into friends. Jupiter in Aries symbolizes expansiveness, extravagance, attractiveness; he tends to create a superficial attitude, and must be taught that luck, even though it may ride with him for a time, cannot be counted on to "stick."

Jupiter in *Taurus* shows a gain through friends; it gives us the native who gains through hobbies, such as collections of books, autographs, stamps, etc. But hobbies or collections may well take over unless controlled. The native is weak when it comes to knowing when to stop. This includes eating and drinking, socializing, spending, promising things he is in no position to deliver, and believing the promises of others. He has faith in himself and others, but he may be so easygoing that drive, or followthrough, is lacking. He has the ability to enjoy himself, but often ruins his own chances by going too far.

In *Gemini,* the Jupiter position tells the astrologer of a native who scatters his forces, wants to expand too quickly, wants all the world to be "related," and demands recognition, but balks when it comes to the kind of serious research which gains solid recognition. He needs to learn the lesson of concentration. He has a marvelous sense of humor, but often laughs when he should cry. He needs to learn the lesson of being practical.

He reaches out for friendship, but the "friends" he attracts, very often, only make demands of him and are not at all willing or able to give anything in return.

In *Cancer,* Jupiter is proud and loyal; the native is susceptible to abuse from family members because he would rather be abused than be guilty of hurting a loved one. He likes the good things in life and wants to share what he has earned. Often, however, he shares too much—he goes out on a limb and has nothing to show for his efforts. Jupiter, as we know, is generosity, expansion, sharing, optimism. In Cancer, this applies to the native's attitude toward home and security. He wants his friends to share—but he often attracts those who share only in his bounty.

Jupiter in *Leo* is fortunate in love, speculation and dealings with children, the theater—creative endeavors. The native finds it necessary to like the persons he loves. This is not true of all individuals; some find it a pleasure to love those they do not like. But this native attracts to him those he not only likes, but can love. This can make up for numerous defects, and the astrologer would be wise always to consider this indication.

The native is popular, but leans toward extravagance. He meets and marries people with influence. He tends to give his all; when he is disappointed he goes to extremes—drinking, divorce, even violence. He needs a "stage" upon which to display his talents, and can never be truly satisfied behind the scenes.

In *Virgo,* Jupiter paints a picture of one who is discriminating when it comes to friends and pleasures. This often results in a bottling up of emotions. The astrologer's task is to help the native become less rigid, to help him remove some of his armor. He is philosophical; his critical tastes are finely honed. He is not so fortunate when it comes to speculation—he can "figure things out," but this does not apply to the racing form!

He is especially fortunate when it comes to developing his hobbies into professions. He is able to start with a little and make it grow. The astrologer should encourage him to be patient and confident—and to laugh at his own foibles.

Jupiter in *Libra* presents an extraordinary talent for spotting opportunity, for swaying public opinion, for winning friends and influencing people. The native tends to take too many things for granted. He tends to back down when the going gets rough. This is because it usually is smooth—and setbacks are something foreign to him. He needs to hear applause; he feels praise is more important than food. The astrologer must help him to see that principles, too, are important.

Gain is indicated through marriage, partnerships and projects which depend upon wide public acceptance. The native always needs to have a goal in sight and must be taught to create his own goal.

Jupiter in *Scorpio* tells of the native who has friends in the "underground"—he is attracted to the hidden, the occult, to the underdog. He is fortunate in investments and he gains through his faith in projects which start as "acorns" and grow into "trees." His emotions are deep; he can undergo much suffering if he feels his cause is right. Thus, the astrologer must help him develop powers of discrimination so that he is more likely to make wise choices.

He possesses enormous pride, often is entrusted with secrets, makes and spends great sums, thrives on challenge—but must be "cured" of creating defeats which he feels he is always capable of transforming into victories. In other words, he tends to make his path rougher than it should be, and for no other reason than the "exercise" this provides.

Jupiter in *Sagittarius* makes the native appear to possess keen insight; he invariably seems to know what is happening and what caused it to happen. His intuitive intellect is sharp. He is attracted to higher learning, but his knowledge is not based primarily on formal education. There is an expansiveness connected with him; it seems to cover all of his activities. He "leans into" a subject and absorbs it.

Benefit from overseas journeys is indicated. The native is attracted to games of speculation. He has faith in his own, personal kind of luck—and no amount of reasoning seems to discourage him. This is harmless, of course, if not carried to extremes. The astrologer must make certain the native does not try to substitute luck for work, knowledge and determination.

The native is idealistic, has a tendency to drift along with the tide. He should be encouraged to create his own opportunities and not merely wait, speculate and philosophize. He is attracted to sports and would be excellent as a sportswriter, thus combining literary talents with his "second love." He is not easy to corrupt; he will stick to his ideals in the face of adversity. But he does not seem to have enough *get-up-and-go!* He needs a push and very often gets it from his mate. Too often, after the "pushing" is finished, marital difficulties begin in earnest. It would be best for him to be a self-starter!

In *Capricorn,* Jupiter is a contradiction. The native wants to be generous, but also has a deep respect for security. He wants to travel but has a need for an "anchor," a place to stay, to feel secure. He wants to pioneer, but has enormous respect (or fear?) for tradition. He wants authority, yet hesitates to bear down in order to earn it. He has the ability to organize, manage, direct; he has great interest in challenges, things that seem far off in the distance—but when the challenges are met (or come closer) he seems to lose interest. The astrologer should help him to see the obvious, to keep his mind open, to remain intellectually curious and excited, or his life will sink into the morass of the conventional—and, eventually, he will drive loved ones away because he grows so sure of himself he becomes a downright bore.

Jupiter in *Aquarius* depicts the native whose friendships and "status" mean much—he does all in his power to win people, to please and charm them.

Jupiter in Aquarius is the humanitarian. In the broadest and most creatively mature sense, he wants people to be happy, pleased, content, productive. He joins organizations to help bring this about; he lends money, time and effort trying to practice what he preaches. On the negative side, he is extravagant, gives lip service to social work and merely broods about the plight of the downtrodden. He can be found working in conjunction with public projects. He is connected with the theater, financial institutions, with publishing houses, newspapers and magazines. His view is wide; he would make an excellent representative for a travel agency or a good "contact man" for a public relations firm. He is diligent and convincing; he possesses charm and a liberal point of view.

In *Pisces,* Jupiter represents the native who is kind, charitable, hospitable, sympathetic to problems of others—and often appears absentminded when it comes to solving his own troubles. He is much concerned with ideals, honor, "doing his best." He is in danger of attracting "inferiors" who become parasites, living off his good name and good will. This applies especially to relations with members of the opposite sex. The astrologer should help him put more "steel" into his makeup, help him overcome a fear of asserting himself.

The native doesn't often reveal his private visions, dreams, ambitions, feelings. Thus it is not easy to know what pleases him and what offends him. The astrologer would prove helpful if he encouraged the native toward a greater degree of self-expression. His friends are often connected with institutions such as hospitals, charitable organizations, etc. He works well with groups and is apt to become lonely and depressed when struggling alone. He has the ability to fulfill his ambitions, once he clearly defines them and discovers where they lie, and where they eventually are going to take him. He takes a great interest in reading, acquiring knowledge on his own, and then confiding in a few trusted friends. It is important that he find the proper environment. Otherwise he suffers, usually in silence.

XLI

SATURN

Saturn in *Aries* tends to make the native strive for responsibility and, at the same time, fear it. He appears serious, but could lack depth. He wants authority, respect, dignity; but he often finds the climb a bit tedious and depressing—just a little too much of a test. The astrologer must help him go after what he really wants and needs, not the glitter, the glamour, the power he imagines is possessed by a "big executive."

If the native is to succeed personally or professionally, he must work—success does not come easily. He must persevere; his outlook must be realistic. He tends to believe someone else has the secret key—and that only he, himself, is made to struggle. He must learn that time is on his side; that the older he gets, the stronger he becomes; that the more he tries, the more he learns. In this way he is most fortunate; he gains through his own efforts and eventually attracts the attention of the very persons he admires or is trying to impress.

Saturn in *Taurus,* like the man whose left hand doesn't know what his right is doing, often succeeds in spite of himself. The native tends to wait too long, to lack confidence, to brood over money matters, to trust the wrong people and accuse the right ones. He gains by being frugal, but often has to spend what he saved because his saving created an unhappy domestic situation. He is not easy to understand but is determined, able to collect facts and figures, stocks and bonds; he is capable of responding well under pressure. The astrologer must help relieve him of numerous anxieties concerning security, money and love. He must help him to open up and express emotions with a greater degree of freedom and enthusiasm.

In *Gemini*, Saturn gives us a native who is easily depressed and wonders when he will receive the affection he is so willing to give. He can meet misfortune through journeys and dealings with relatives unless he takes special care. He tends toward self-deception—he wants persons and situations to be a certain way and often sees them that way. The astrologer's task is to help the native obtain a greater grasp of reality. This is accomplished by helping him overcome his fear of responsibility and concentration—he must learn to finish what he starts, to tackle one project at a time; he must not spread his efforts too thin. He is capable of learning from experience but, if he is not wary, the experience can be depressing. His motives are fine but his methods, at times, are devoid of logic.

Saturn in *Cancer* tells of a native who may be so "married" to authority, age and experience that he is afraid to make a move of his own, fearful of striking out independently, hesitant about applying original methods. He must be given a greater degree of confidence, helped to break away, to realize that lessons of the past should be utilized for the future and not be regarded as chains against progress.

Grant Lewi has stated that this native may have a "parent fixation," and that the need for self-justification is the native's deepest driving force. This planetary position seems to create a lack, a denial in the home or with regard to the love of one of the parents. This lack is expressed by the native in his drive for security, love, pleasure; in his apparent deep respect for authority as he tries to "please" age and experience and thus win the love, the security that has been "denied" him. The astrologer must help him to feel he is worthy of love and is capable of succeeding in the face of heavy odds.

In *Leo,* Saturn may present some sexual problems; the native wants love and romance, but is restricted. This restriction may be the result of religious teaching, of circumstances, of physical disability. Saturn represents discipline—and in the natural 5th (sex, pleasure, speculation, children) House could present complications, mental problems, a feeling of being "tied in knots" when it comes to expressing the love nature.

In *Virgo,* Saturn indicates the native is discreet, perhaps over-cautious, and tends to blame a lack of vitality for his difficulties. Even if he is in perfect health he is apt to "invent" illness, discomfort if all doesn't go according to plan. Thus, he may have some disorder (stutter, bodily twitch, etc.) which could be aided by self-understanding and psychiatric and psychological means including hypnosis. The native is intelligent and able to see his own quirks—with encouragement from an astrologer, he may be capable of doing something to overcome them.

Saturn in *Libra* tells us of a native who would like his life to be in order, who wants the world to hand out justice rather than punishment. In seeking the ideal, he often runs into emotional storms; there are indications of more than one marriage, of disappointments in partners (both marital and business).

He has strength, ability and courage, but his public image is apt to be ultra-serious. He must pay heed to public relations and should take special care with legal documents, including birth certificates, passports, contracts.

He is not an easy person to really know; the astrologer must help him to know himself better. He makes his influence felt—and the key is to make it felt in a constructive manner. Otherwise he is accused of being prejudiced and narrow.

In *Scorpio,* Saturn tells of difficulties in relations with members of the opposite sex. The native attracts people from the "underworld." He is trusted by those with dark secrets. He is connected with inheritance, death, preparations for undercover assignments, etc. He is self-willed, and his peculiar tastes could lead to difficulties; he is constantly seeking better means of self-expression. He tends to become obsessed with the idea that sex fulfillment is denied him; he searches for the ideal partner and wastes energy, time and money. He must learn to be more practical, to get enough rest, to pay attention to his diet and health needs. If he does, then some (if not all) of his sexual problems can be overcome. He tends to act impulsively and later to regret his actions—but the regrets do not necessarily lead to constructive changes.

He may be bothered by a lack of funds, even though he has more than the average member of his community. The astrologer should help him to understand his motives. Otherwise, the native begins to rationalize, to justify the most bizarre acts and opinions.

Saturn in *Sagittarius* tells us that self-respect is essential for the native's sense of well-being. He doesn't mind failure as such, if it is accompanied by the gallant try, the knowledge he is on the side of the angels, the feeling that he is spreading valuable information and providing inspiration. He is philosophical, often interested in religion; he is capable of publishing works that "last," is concerned with the peoples of the world and regards himself as a humanitarian. At times, he is more abstract than solid, more interested in theory than direct action, concerned with people far away while neglecting those close to him; he can be so "hung up" on a theoretical point that he suffers loss due to delay, indecision and insistence upon adhering to outdated methods and policies. He tends to argue with those close to him and to smile at those who really don't care what he thinks. He needs aid in finding a more practical course—that of getting his message across without being concerned with whether it is interpreted in exactly the manner he prescribes. Otherwise, he gets fouled in a maze of details and worries; he needs to realize that people demand the right to examine, test, scold, praise or accept in their own way.

Saturn in *Capricorn* tells of the native whose greatest asset is his ability to climb from the depths, to overcome adversity, to ride out storms and eventually gain recognition. But he must be ready for adversity, not try to duck it. He gets where he's going by determination, grit, a stubborn kind of faith in himself. Otherwise he is not happy, never reaches his goal and is captured by the feeling that the world passed him by and gave him a good kick in doing so.

He is ambitious and could gain in foreign lands—he wants to succeed in spite of losses in personal happiness. The astrologer should help steer him away from the course of blind materialism, help him to realize his spiritual potential and remind him that the outcome of the game is not always as important as how it was played. The native is capable of handling responsibility and running his own business. He is not so good at taking orders, working for others and taking a subservient role.

In *Aquarius,* Saturn shows one who often permits his friends to give him advice which, if followed, proves costly. He learns his lessons the hard way; he wants to be attractive to members of the opposite sex and can be flattered into making a fool of himself.

He wants recognition and loyal friends, and tends to be extravagant in trying to convince people of his importance when, actually, a simple approach and sincerity would be a much better approach to permanent, fulfilling relationships.

Saturn in *Pisces* represents a native who appears bewildered by the outside world. He wants to break loose, to feel free, to express himself. But, often, he acts in an opposite manner; he gets "tied up" with institutions, organizations, commitments beyond his financial capabilities: he thus restricts himself to an even greater extent. The astrologer's job is to help him perceive the folly of some of his actions. It is important that the native realize he defeats his own purpose by accepting a defeatist attitude as a way of life. He can be identified as a chronic complainer and fatalist.

On the positive side, he can be a responsible member of the community who strives to improve conditions for the mentally ill, for the economically depressed. The key to greater happiness here is self-knowledge—acceptance of responsibility instead of being resigned to fate.

Saturn is of such extreme importance in astrology that it deserves further attention. For those interested in further study, I have provided it in a special study.*

* March 1948 issue of *Horoscope* Magazine, Dell Publishing Company.

XLII

PLUTO, NEPTUNE, URANUS

These planets remain in one sign for a long time—their significance applies to "the times," the generations, rather than to individual characteristics. Refer to the chapter on *The Houses* for a good indication of the interpretations of these planets in the signs: regard the 1st House as an Aries influence. The 2nd House would represent a Taurus influence, while the 3rd House would be Gemini, and so on down the line, covering the 12 Houses. It is never wise to confuse the signs and Houses. And it is absolutely necessary to remember that Pluto, Neptune and Uranus in the signs depict the tenor of the times, the characteristics of the generations, the mood, the society, the tempo. Naturally all of us are, to an extent, under the influence of the times in which we live. This being so, the sign positions of Pluto, Neptune and Uranus *do* provide some clues.

Uranus has been associated with astrology itself. It is one of the most fascinating planets for study, especially interesting because it produces, by aspects and transits, quick action and an element of surprise. New starts, broken precedents and divorce can be considered keys to the influence of Uranus, discovered in 1781 by the astronomer Herschel. Uranus is associated with Aquarius, and at present we are said to be in the "Aquarian Age," meaning we reach out for space, for other planets; we delve into the mystery of the life force itself.

Uranus takes seven years to transit through a sign and completes its trip around the zodiac in 84 years. The cycle of Uranus appears to have a peculiar relationship to the history of the United States. There is disagreement as to which sign is rising in the U.S.

natal chart. But a study of the Solar horoscope reveals some highlights. With Cancer on the cusp of the 1st House (July 4, the "birthday" of the U.S., gives us a Cancer Sun sign, which in a Solar chart becomes the 1st House), Aquarius becomes the 8th House of the chart. Thus, Uranus rules the section of the U.S. horoscope which governs "threat of death."

Gemini falls on the cusp of the 12th House, related to secret enemies and the like. Throughout the history of the U.S., whenever Uranus, ruler of the threat-of-death House, transits through the House of enemies (Gemini), the U.S. is involved in a war for its very existence. Uranus has passed through Gemini three times since the birth of the nation. The first time the transit occurred was during the American Revolution. It took place again during the Civil War; and in 1942, when Uranus once more entered Gemini, the U.S. was involved in World War II. Uranus enters Gemini again in the year 2026.

Uranus is related to a quick rise to fame or a drop in popularity. Many persons in the public eye have had sudden opportunity to display their talent. This has come after waiting years for a chance at success. In these cases, a favorable aspect from transiting Uranus to the natal Jupiter is usually in evidence. Just as the Uranus angle on Jupiter affects luck and success, that planet's aspect to the natal Venus brings love affairs—when unfavorable, broken engagements and divorce.

The same applies to natal Mars receiving Uranus aspects. When Mars is involved, the influences bring hasty, destructive action. Uranus applying to the Sun affects individuality, touches off channels of creative expression. Natives with transiting Uranus aspecting the Moon go through emotional ups and downs, depending on the nature of the aspect.*

* The subject of transits, thanks to the kind permission of Paul R. Grell, executive secretary of the American Federation of Astrologers (6 Library Court, S.E., Washington 3, D.C.), is covered in the Appendix in a unique and valuable manner. All of us must, of course, experiment and observe, and thus learn from observation the influence of the transits. But great aid is provided by Dr. Heber J. Smith, the teacher of Evangeline Adams. Dr. Smith's work on transits is distributed to members of the AFA, and Paul Grell has kindly given us permission to reprint that work. I would also

The Uranus House position is a key to the department of life where action of a sudden type occurs. A study of Uranus in this respect reveals vocational trends, tendencies which should be emphasized and other inclinations which should be controlled.*

recommend Grant Lewi's *Astrology for Millions* and *The Evangeline Adams Guide for 1933* as further valuable aids in understanding and interpreting transits (a dictionary of basic astrological terms also appears in the Appendix).

* For further study, see the author's articles: On Uranus, April 1948 issue of *Horoscope* Magazine, Dell Publishing Company; on Nijinsky, June 1950 issue.

XLIII

BASIC DICTIONARY OF TERMS

For advanced students, this section on basic terms is not required. But I hope we have taken with us on this journey a number of individuals who are meeting astrology, with some degree of open-mindedness, for the first time—and who intend to continue the journey, reading and rereading this work, plus others I have recommended, plus the numerous others they encounter. And it is for this new passenger—this individual who represents the future in astrology, that we present this brief basic dictionary. It should prove a convenient, quick reference source. And on the subject of dictionaries, permit me to recommend highly the James Wilson masterpiece, *Dictionary of Astrology,* published in 1885—perhaps one of the most colorful, informative, *personal* dictionaries ever produced. It is hard to find these days, but well worth the search. More easily obtained is the late Nicholas DeVore's *Encyclopedia of Astrology,* in itself a reference, representing a gigantic task on the part of DeVore—a scholar and a gentleman who encouraged me in astrology, not only through the words he spoke and wrote, but by the example he set of understanding and humanity.

Let us begin.

ANGLE. Any of the four cardinal points in a horoscope: the 1st, 4th, 7th, and 10th Houses. Considered significant and "strong." Angular signs are Aries (natural 1st sign), Cancer (natural 4th), Libra (natural 7th) and Capricorn (natural 10th). The Houses are referred to as angles, while the signs are referred to as Cardinal signs.

ANGULAR. Reference to a planet in one of the angles—in the 1st, 4th, 7th or 10th Houses.

ASCENDANT. The degree of the zodiac on the eastern horizon at the moment of birth—often referred to as the Rising Sign.

ASPECT. Angular relationships between the planets. Favorable aspects considered to be the sextile (60°, or two signs apart) and the trine (120°, or four signs apart). Unfavorable aspects are the square (90°, or three signs apart) and the opposition (180°, or six signs apart). Thus, a planet in Aries is in opposition to one in Libra. A planet in Aries is sextiled to one in Gemini, is squared to one in Cancer is trined to one in Leo. For the Sun and Moon, a 10° orb is allowed. For the planets, approximately 8° of separation is permitted. Thus, a planet 12° in Aries would be out of orb to a planet 29° in Gemini; the orb would be too wide for the sextile aspect to be in effect. The conjunction is referred to by many astrologers as an aspect: when two planets are in the same sign. In addition, there are minor aspects: the semi-sextile (one sign apart); the semi-square (one and a half signs apart); the sesquiquadrate (four and a half signs apart); and the quincunx (five signs apart).

COMBUST. When a planet is closer than 5° to the Sun. This term is most apt to be utilized in Horary astrology.

CULMINATION. Used, at times, to indicate the completion of an aspect: a planet's arrival at exact conjunction, sextile, square, trine or opposition to another planet. Also, the arrival of a planet at the Midheaven, which is the cusp of the 10th House.

CUSP. A line—imaginary—separating a sign from adjoining signs, separating a House from its adjoining Houses. The lines we utilize to divide the circle of the horoscope into 12 sections could be described as the cusps. Thus, an individual born when the Sun was leaving one sign and entering another is said to be "born on the cusp." He thus has some of the characteristics of each of the two signs in question.

DIRECTIONS. Generally, the progressing of birth planets to future positions by various methods: this is an attempt to obtain a glimpse of future cycles, indications, guidance for the native. Known also as progressions. In this work, we have utilized transits (see Appendix) because we find they "work." Transits are based upon the actual motions of the various planets. But directions and progressions are based on a theory of motion. This is fascinating and should be "meat" for the student's hunger for experiments. But, to begin with, we suggest the use of transits—merely a comparison of current and future planetary positions in relation to the birth map or horoscope.

DOG DAYS. A period lasting 40 days, from July 4 to August 11. Regarded by the ancients as the hottest period of the year. And by some moderns as the "silly summer season." Ancients reckoned the commencement of Dog Days from the heliacal rising of Sirius, the Dog Star.

DOG STARS. Sirius and Procyon.

DOUBLE-BODIED SIGNS. Gemini, Sagittarius and Pisces. Their symbols represent two figures: Gemini, the Twins; Sagittarius, half-man and half-animal; Pisces, the two fishes. In interpretation these signs are often said to signify a native who has a dual nature, is often at odds with himself. Some researchers state that a double-bodied sign on the cusp of the 7th House (see chapter on *The Houses*) is indicative of more than one marriage. A double-bodied sign on the cusp of the 5th House might, therefore, be regarded as an indication of twin offspring.

ELECTIONAL ASTROLOGY. A method of choosing the best time to begin a project, to make an appointment, etc. In a way, we "elect," or choose, the birth chart of an enterprise including marriage, building, investing, launching a ship, moving, etc. For success in business Jupiter ideally would be "elected" in the 10th House, and so on. We would not want Mars in the 3rd House for a safe journey. Nor would we want Saturn in the 7th when we sign a contract, etc.

ELEMENTS. Fire (Aries, Leo, Sagittarius); Earth (Taurus, Virgo, Capricorn); Air (Gemini, Libra, Aquarius); and Water (Cancer, Scorpio, Pisces).

EPHEMERIS. An almanac listing the positions which the Sun, Moon and planets will occupy on each day of the year—their longitude, latitude, declination. The astronomer's ephemeris lists these positions in heliocentric terms; the astrologer's ephemeris lists the positions in geocentric terms.

FIRE SIGNS. See Elements.

FORTUNA. Part of Fortune. A point that bears the same relation to the Rising Sign that the Moon bears to the Sun. It occupies the same House position in a horoscope that the Moon has in a Solar chart. Its symbol is a cross within a circle and is utilized by astronomers to represent the earth. Many astrologers regard the position of the Part of Fortune as significant. Others practically neglect the Part of Fortune. It is said to indicate the department of life (House) that will be most fortunate for the native. If the Part of Fortune is in the 9th House, for example, the native could be financially successful in publishing, writing, traveling or activities connected with travel.

FRUITFUL SIGNS. The Water signs (see Elements).

GRAND TRINE. Two planets trined to each other—and both trined by a third planet.

HELIACAL RISING. When a planet or star, after being hidden by the Sun's rays, again becomes visible: rising with the Sun.

HELIACAL SETTING. A star is overtaken by the Sun and is not visible because of the Sun's rays. Heliacal rising or setting of the Moon: when lunar body is within 17° of the Sun. Other stars, planets: when within 30° of the Sun.

HORARY ASTROLOGY. A chart is set up for the "birth of a question." This is a fascinating branch of astrology. The native asks the question and the astrologer notes the time. A figure (horoscope) is cast and the astrologer interprets it, based on rules of Horary astrology. Best modern reference: *Problem Solving by Horary Astrology,* by Marc Edmund Jones. I regard this art (Horary astrology) as a marvelous aid to interpretation and I have had some remarkable results. Evangeline Adams (*The Bowl of Heaven*) relates her own system of Horary astrology. She noted the time of the question, set up the Ascendant and Houses based on time and then inserted the native's birth planets in those Houses.

HOUSES. See section on *The Houses.*

MUNDANE ASTROLOGY. Having to do with nations and national trends rather than with individuals and individual cycles. The horoscopes of nations. There is also astro-meteorology, dealing with the weather. And there is medical astrology, dealing with health and disease in connection with planetary positions and movements.

NATIVE. The individual whose horoscope is under study.

NATIVITY. The horoscope, the birth moment when the native first inhales.

NODES. Point where a planet crosses the ecliptic out of south into north latitude is called its North Node. Where it crosses into south latitude it is called the planet's South Node. The Moon's North Node is called the Dragon's head and its symbol is similar to the symbol used for the zodiacal sign Leo. The South Node of the Moon is referred to as the Dragon's Tail and its symbol is similar to the symbol of Leo, upside-down. We have not utilized the nodes to any great degree in interpretation but we suggest the student experiment and read more on this subject.

ORBS. The space between planets aspecting one another. See Aspect.

RADICAL. Pertaining to the horoscope of birth. Radical planets, thus, would be "birth planets." In Horary astrology a "radical figure" is one which can be properly used for arriving at a judgment, an answer to a question. A figure that is "not radical" indicates, in the Horary art, that the question cannot be judged properly, perhaps because it is premature, or too late, or for a variety of reasons.

RECTIFICATION. An art within the art of astrology—that of correcting the time of birth by using the events in the native's life to coincide with planetary positions, aspects, etc. The process of verification or correction of the birth moment or ascendant degree of the horoscope.

RETROGRADE. When a planet apparently moves backward: apparent backward motion in the zodiac of certain planets when decreasing in longitude as viewed from the earth. When Mercury is in Retrograde (as depicted in the ephemeris by the letter R), communications are said to be disrupted, red tape results, errors in paper work, etc. Not a good time for mailing manuscripts, for planning journeys, for getting to the bottom of a problem.

RISING SIGN. Sign rising on eastern horizon at the moment of birth.

RULER. Planet associated with sign. Thus, Mars is said to "rule" Aries. Taurus is the sign associated with Venus, and thus Venus is the "ruler" of Taurus, as it also is of Libra. Mercury rules Gemini. The Moon rules Cancer. The Sun rules Leo. Mercury rules Virgo. Venus rules Taurus and Libra. Pluto rules Scorpio. Jupiter rules Sagittarius. Saturn rules Capricorn. Uranus rules Aquarius. Neptune rules Pisces.

TRANSIT. The movements of the planets, utilized to depict cycles, based on the relation of transits to birth planets of native. See Appendix.

XLIV

WHO'S WHO

It is obviously impossible to list all of those who have made contributions to astrology not even a small portion. But we can list some.

There are two astrologers who have, in different ways, helped the art, helped to a tremendous extent, *given.*

One is Carl Payne Tobey, whose statistical research and writings, whose integrity have helped keep alive astrology as a science and an art. He is one of this country's great astrologers. His original research has earned the respect of astronomers, as well as that of fellow astrologers.

Another is Edward A. Wagner, editor of *Horoscope* Magazine, the largest astrology magazine in the world, published in New York by the Dell Publishing Company. Wagner printed much of my early work. He encouraged me but also offered much constructive criticism. His high journalistic standard has raised the standards of astrology. He has done this by insisting on quality in *Horoscope,* and by rewarding it when he finds it. Since 1946, his career has run along two lines: astrology and meteorology. After his discharge from the Army Air Force in late 1945, he set up his own weather business, furnishing pictorial maps and forecast data to newspapers, television and radio stations. He is a past president of the Ohio Astrological Association, a member of the Astrologers' Guild of New York and the American Federation of Astrologers, and a Corporate Member of the American Meteorological Society.

The late Llewellyn George and the late Alan Leo were also influential. The combined works of these two astrological authors make up a library in themselves. We all owe much to them; their names are immortal in the annals of astrological history. So, too, is the name Grant Lewi, former editor of *Horoscope* Magazine, English literature professor at Dartmouth, author of *Astrology for the Millions* and *Heaven Knows What,* plus two novels. We have already told something of Evangeline Adams' contribution in the special section devoted to her.

The list is long. It includes Marc Edmund Jones, a prolific author, whose *Problem Solving By Horary Astrology* stands as a modern masterpiece. There is also the late Cedric W. Lemont, who helped obtain legal status for astrology in Ohio, just as Evangeline Adams did in New York.

There is Ernest Grant, of Washington, D.C., long an official of the American Federation of Astrologers, whose efforts have helped keep astrology alive and kicking, through "good" days and "bad" ones. And there is the present executive secretary of the AFA, Paul Grell, who is a tireless worker, trying to spread the best of astrology around the world.

The list includes Charles E. Luntz, whose work, *Vocational Guidance by Astrology,* is highly recommended. The works of Robert De Luce are also to be commended, as are those of Dane Rudhyar, perhaps one of the most erudite of modern astrologers, a contributor to numerous journals, and among other works, author of the highly recommended *The Astrology of Personality*.

No attempted list of "Who's Who" would be complete without the name Louis De Wohl, who told the British what Hitler's astrologers were telling him! The late De Wohl was a brilliant novelist as well as an astrologer. He became a captain in British Intelligence, where he utilized his astrological knowledge in the war effort. Later, he was decorated. Articles, books and acknowledgments from high British officials proved beyond the question of a doubt that the British (like Hitler!) used astrology. But, of course, the British, so we are told, were using De Wohl's services because of the knowledge that Hitler employed astrologers. This is a story in itself, perhaps a book: there is not room here to detail this fascinating chapter in the history of astrology, in the history of our time, in the history of World War II. Part of it has been chronicled in a series of articles by De Wohl, which appeared in *American Astrology* Magazine—and can be obtained by writing to Mrs. Paul G. Clancy, editor and publisher of *American Astrology,* 148 Larchmont Avenue, Larchmont, New York. Other aspects of the story are to be found in *The Man with the Miraculous Hands,* by Joseph Kessel, published in paperback by the Dell Publishing Company, New York, and in *The Rise and Fall of the Third Reich,* by William L. Shirer, obtainable in paperback edition from Crest Books, New York.

It is impossible to cover all who belong in any "Who's Who in Astrology," but certainly Paul G. Clancy, who founded *American Astrology* Magazine, belongs—and so do the following: Nona Howard, Blanca Holmes, Dorothea De Luce, Elizabeth Aldrich, Charles A. Jayne Jr., Elbert Benjamine, Doris Chase Doane, Edna L. Scott, Vivian Robson, Margaret Hone, Hugh MacCraig, Margaret Morrell, Sidney K. Bennett, George J. McCormack, Edward Johndro, Charles E. O. Carter, Mabel Leslie-Fleischer, Dal Lee, James Wilson, Alfred Pearce, Philip W. Rhys, Harold McDougal, Louise G. Mench, Keye Lloyd and Dr. W. M. Davidson.

All of us owe a debt of gratitude to those mentioned. To those who *should* have been named, space limitations and perhaps a faulty memory or simple lack of knowledge on my part are the reasons.

It is my fervent wish that this book may in some small way help add to the list, may inspire others along this adventurous, controversial, yet rewarding path that is astrology; may in some manner help create the future names for an astrological "Who's Who."

APPENDIX

WHERE WAS JUPITER WHEN YOU WERE BORN?

The following table will give you the position of Jupiter at the time of your birth:

DATE		ZODIACAL SIGN
1/01/1890 to	2/24/1890	Capricorn
2/25/1890 to	3/07/1891	Aquarius
3/08/1890 to	3/16/1892	Pisces
3/17/1892 to	3/24/1893	Aries
3/25/1893 to	8/20/1893	Taurus
8/21/1893 to	10/19/1893	Gemini
10/20/1893 to	4/01/1894	Taurus
4/02/1894 to	8/18/1894	Gemini
8/19/1894 to	1/01/1895	Cancer
1/02/1895 to	4/10/1895	Gemini
4/11/1895 to	9/04/1895	Cancer
9/05/1895 to	2/29/1896	Leo
3/01/1896 to	4/17/1896	Cancer
4/18/1896 to	9/27/1896	Leo
9/28/1896 to	10/27/1897	Virgo
10/28/1897 to	11/26/1898	Libra
11/27/1898 to	12/25/1899	Scorpio
12/26/1899 to	1/18/1901	Sagittarius
1/19/1901 to	2/06/1902	Capricorn
2/07/1902 to	2/19/1903	Aquarius
2/20/1903 to	2/29/1904	Pisces
3/01/1904 to	8/08/1904	Aries
8/09/1904 to	8/31/1904	Taurus
9/01/1904 to	3/07/1905	Aries
4/08/1905 to	7/20/1905	Taurus
7/21/1905 to	12/04/1905	Gemini
12/05/1905 to	3/09/1906	Taurus
3/10/1906 to	7/30/1906	Gemini
7/31/1906 to	8/18/1907	Cancer

8/19/1907 to	9/11/1908	Leo
9/12/1908 to	10/11/1909	Virgo
10/12/1909 to	11/11/1910	Libra
11/12/1910 to	12/09/1911	Scorpio
12/10/1911 to	1/02/1913	Sagittarius
1/03/1913 to	1/21/1914	Capricorn
1/22/1914 to	2/03/1915	Aquarius
2/04/1915 to	2/11/1916	Pisces
2/12/1916 to	6/25/1916	Aries
6/26/1916 to	10/26/1916	Taurus
10/27/1916 to	2/12/1917	Aries
2/13/1917 to	6/29/1917	Taurus
6/30/1917 to	7/12/1918	Gemini
7/13/1918 to	8/01/1919	Cancer
8/02/1919 to	8/26/1920	Leo
8/27/1920 to	9/25/1921	Virgo
9/26/1921 to	10/26/1922	Libra
10/27/1922 to	11/24/1923	Scorpio
11/25/1923 to	12/17/1924	Sagittarius
12/18/1924 to	1/05/1926	Capricorn
1/06/1926 to	1/17/1927	Aquarius
1/18/1927 to	6/05/1927	Pisces
6/06/1927 to	9/10/1927	Aries
9/11/1927 to	1/22/1928	Pisces
1/23/1928 to	6/03/1928	Aries
6/04/1928 to	6/11/1929	Taurus
6/12/1929 to	6/26/1930	Gemini
6/27/1930 to	7/16/1931	Cancer
7/17/1931 to	8/10/1932	Leo
8/11/1932 to	9/09/1933	Virgo
9/10/1933 to	10/10/1934	Libra
10/11/1934 to	11/08/1935	Scorpio
11/09/1935 to	12/01/1936	Sagittarius
12/02/1936 to	12/19/1937	Capricorn
12/20/1937 to	5/13/1938	Aquarius
5/14/1938 to	7/29/1938	Pisces
7/30/1938 to	12/28/1938	Aquarius
12/29/1938 to	5/10/1939	Pisces
5/11/1939 to	10/29/1939	Aries

10/30/1939 to	12/19/1939	Pisces
12/20/1939 to	5/15/1940	Aries
5/16/1940 to	5/25/1941	Taurus
5/26/1941 to	6/09/1942	Gemini
6/10/1942 to	6/29/1943	Cancer
6/30/1943 to	7/25/1944	Leo
7/26/1944 to	8/24/1945	Virgo
8/25/1945 to	9/24/1946	Libra
9/25/1946 to	10/23/1947	Scorpio
10/24/1947 to	11/14/1948	Sagittarius
11/15/1948 to	4/11/1949	Capricorn
4/12/1949 to	6/26/1949	Aquarius
6/27/1949 to	11/29/1949	Capricorn
11/30/1949 to	4/14/1950	Aquarius
4/15/1950 to	9/14/1950	Pisces
9/15/1950 to	12/01/1950	Aquarius
12/02/1950 to	4/20/1951	Pisces
4/21/1951 to	4/27/1952	Aries
4/28/1952 to	5/08/1953	Taurus
5/09/1953 to	5/23/1954	Gemini
5/24/1954 to	6/11/1955	Cancer
6/12/1955 to	11/16/1955	Leo
11/17/1955 to	1/17/1956	Virgo
1/18/1956 to	7/06/1956	Leo
7/07/1956 to	12/11/1956	Virgo
12/12/1956 to	2/18/1957	Libra
2/19/1957 to	8/05/1957	Virgo
8/06/1957 to	1/12/1958	Libra
1/13/1958 to	3/19/1958	Scorpio
3/20/1958 to	9/06/1958	Libra
9/07/1958 to	2/09/1959	Scorpio
2/10/1959 to	4/23/1959	Sagittarius
4/24/1959 to	10/04/1959	Scorpio
10/05/1959 to	2/29/1960	Sagittarius
3/01/1960 to	6/09/1960	Capricorn
6/10/1960 to	10/24/1960	Sagittarius
10/25/1960 to	3/14/1961	Capricorn
3/15/1961 to	8/11/1961	Aquarius
8/12/1961 to	11/03/1961	Capricorn

11/04/1961 to	3/24/1962	Aquarius
3/25/1962 to	4/03/1963	Pisces
4/04/1963 to	4/11/1964	Aries
4/12/1964 to	4/21/1965	Taurus
4/22/1965 to	9/20/1965	Gemini
9/21/1965 to	11/16/1965	Cancer
11/17/1965 to	5/04/1966	Gemini
5/05/1966 to	9/26/1966	Cancer
9/27/1966 to	1/15/1967	Leo
1/16/1967 to	5/22/1967	Cancer
5/23/1967 to	10/18/1967	Leo
10/19/1967 to	2/26/1968	Virgo
2/27/1968 to	6/14/1968	Leo
6/15/1968 to	11/14/1968	Virgo
11/15/1968 to	3/29/1969	Libra
3/30/1969 to	7/14/1969	Virgo
7/15/1969 to	12/15/1969	Libra
12/16/1969 to	4/29/1970	Scorpio
4/30/1970 to	8/14/1970	Libra
8/15/1970 to	12/31/1970	Scorpio

WHERE WAS MARS WHEN YOU WERE BORN?

The following table will supply the zodiacal sign of Mars for the particular day and year when you were born:

DATE		ZODIACAL SIGN	DATE		ZODIACAL SIGN
1890			3/08 to	4/19	Taurus
			4/20 to	6/03	Gemini
1/01 to	2/28	Scorpio	6/04 to	7/19	Cancer
2/29 to	6/16	Sagittarius	7/20 to	9/04	Leo
6/17 to	7/21	Scorpio	9/05 to	10/21	Virgo
7/22 to	9/23	Sagittarius	10/22 to	12/07	Libra
9/24 to	11/04	Capricorn	12/08 to	12/31	Scorpio
11/05 to	12/16	Aquarius			
12/17 to	12/31	Pisces	*1892*		
			1/01 to	2/24	Scorpio
1891			2/25 to	3/13	Sagittarius
1/01 to	1/25	Pisces	3/14 to	5/06	Capricorn
1/26 to	3/07	Aries			

DATE	ZODIACAL SIGN	DATE	ZODIACAL SIGN
5/07 to 11/08	Aquarius	4/12 to 5/21	Pisces
11/09 to 12/27	Pisces	5/22 to 7/01	Aries
12/28 to 12/31	Aries	7/02 to 8/15	Taurus
		8/16 to 12/31	Gemini

1893

1/01 to 2/10	Aries		
2/11 to 3/28	Taurus	**1897**	
3/29 to 5/13	Gemini	1/01 to 3/21	Gemini
5/14 to 6/29	Cancer	3/22 to 5/17	Cancer
6/30 to 8/15	Leo	5/18 to 7/08	Leo
8/16 to 10/01	Virgo	7/09 to 8/25	Virgo
10/02 to 11/16	Libra	8/26 to 10/09	Libra
11/17 to 12/31	Scorpio	10/10 to 11/21	Scorpio
		11/22 to 12/31	Sagittarius

1894

1898

1/01 to 2/13	Sagittarius	1/01	Sagittarius
2/14 to 3/27	Capricorn	1/02 to 2/10	Capricorn
3/28 to 5/09	Aquarius	2/11 to 3/20	Aquarius
5/10 to 6/22	Pisces	3/21 to 4/28	Pisces
6/23 to 8/18	Aries	4/29 to 6/06	Aries
8/19 to 10/12	Taurus	6/07 to 7/18	Taurus
10/13 to 12/30	Aries	7/19 to 9/02	Gemini
12/31	Taurus	9/03 to 10/30	Cancer
		10/31 to 12/31	Leo

1895

1899

1/01 to 3/01	Taurus	1/01 to 1/15	Leo
3/02 to 4/21	Gemini	1/16 to 4/14	Cancer
4/22 to 6/10	Cancer	4/15 to 6/15	Leo
6/11 to 7/28	Leo	6/16 to 8/05	Virgo
7/29 to 9/13	Virgo	8/06 to 9/20	Libra
9/14 to 10/30	Libra	9/21 to 11/02	Scorpio
10/31 to 12/11	Scorpio	11/03 to 12/13	Sagittarius
12/12 to 12/31	Sagittarius	12/14 to 12/31	Capricorn

1896

1900

1/01 to 1/22	Sagittarius		
1/23 to 3/02	Capricorn	1/01 to 2/28	Aquarius
3/03 to 4/11	Aquarius	3/01 to 4/07	Pisces

DATE	ZODIACAL SIGN	DATE	ZODIACAL SIGN
4/08 to 5/16	Aries	**1904**	
5/17 to 6/26	Taurus	1/01 to 1/19	Aquarius
6/27 to 8/09	Gemini	1/20 to 2/26	Pisces
8/10 to 9/26	Cancer	2/27 to 4/06	Aries
9/27 to 11/22	Leo	4/07 to 5/17	Taurus
11/23 to 12/31	Virgo	5/18 to 6/30	Gemini
		7/01 to 8/14	Cancer
1901		8/15 to 10/01	Leo
1/01 to 3/01	Virgo	10/02 to 11/19	Virgo
3/02 to 5/10	Leo	11/20 to 12/31	Libra
5/11 to 7/13	Virgo		
7/14 to 8/31	Libra	**1905**	
9/01 to 10/14	Scorpio	1/01 to 1/13	Libra
10/15 to 11/23	Sagittarius	1/14 to 8/21	Scorpio
11/24 to 12/31	Capricorn	8/22 to 10/07	Sagittarius
		10/08 to 11/17	Capricorn
1902		11/18 to 12/27	Aquarius
1/01	Capricorn	12/28 to 12/31	Pisces
1/02 to 2/08	Aquarius		
2/09 to 3/17	Pisces	**1906**	
3/18 to 4/26	Aries	1/01 to 2/04	Pisces
4/27 to 6/06	Taurus	2/05 to 3/16	Aries
6/07 to 7/20	Gemini	3/17 to 4/28	Taurus
7/21 to 9/04	Cancer	4/29 to 6/11	Gemini
9/05 to 10/23	Leo	6/12 to 7/27	Cancer
10/24 to 12/19	Virgo	7/28 to 9/12	Leo
12/20 to 12/31	Libra	9/13 to 10/29	Virgo
		10/30 to 12/16	Libra
1903		12/17 to 12/31	Scorpio
1/01 to 4/19	Libra		
4/20 to 5/30	Virgo	**1907**	
5/31 to 8/06	Libra	1/01 to 2/04	Scorpio
8/07 to 9/22	Scorpio	2/05 to 4/01	Sagittarius
9/23 to 11/02	Sagittarius	4/02 to 10/13	Capricorn
11/03 to 12/11	Capricorn	10/14 to 11/28	Aquarius
12/12 to 12/31	Aquarius	11/29 to 12/31	Pisces

DATE	ZODIACAL SIGN	DATE	ZODIACAL SIGN

1908

1/01 to 1/10	Pisces
1/11 to 2/22	Aries
2/23 to 4/06	Taurus
4/07 to 5/22	Gemini
5/23 to 7/07	Cancer
7/08 to 8/23	Leo
8/24 to 10/09	Virgo
10/10 to 11/25	Libra
11/26 to 12/31	Scorpio

1909

1/01 to 1/09	Scorpio
1/10 to 2/23	Sagittarius
2/24 to 4/09	Capricorn
4/10 to 5/25	Aquarius
5/26 to 7/20	Pisces
7/21 to 9/26	Aries
9/27 to 11/20	Pisces
11/21 to 12/31	Aries

1910

1/01 to 2/22	Aries
2/23 to 3/13	Taurus
3/14 to 5/01	Gemini
5/02 to 6/18	Cancer
6/19 to 8/05	Leo
8/06 to 9/21	Virgo
9/22 to 11/06	Libra
11/07 to 12/19	Scorpio
12/20 to 12/31	Sagittarius

1911

1/01 to 1/31	Sagittarius
2/01 to 3/13	Capricorn
3/14 to 4/22	Aquarius
4/23 to 6/02	Pisces
6/03 to 7/15	Aries

7/16 to 9/05	Taurus
9/06 to 11/29	Gemini
11/30 to 12/31	Taurus

1912

1/01 to 1/30	Taurus
1/31 to 4/04	Gemini
4/05 to 5/27	Cancer
5/28 to 7/16	Leo
7/17 to 9/02	Virgo
9/03 to 10/17	Libra
10/18 to 11/29	Scorpio
11/30 to 12/31	Sagittarius

1913

1/01 to 1/10	Sagittarius
1/11 to 2/18	Capricorn
2/19 to 3/29	Aquarius
3/30 to 5/07	Pisces
5/08 to 6/16	Aries
6/17 to 7/28	Taurus
7/29 to 9/15	Gemini
9/16 to 12/31	Cancer

1914

1/01 to 5/01	Cancer
5/02 to 6/25	Leo
6/26 to 8/14	Virgo
8/15 to 9/28	Libra
9/29 to 11/10	Scorpio
11/11 to 12/21	Sagittarius
12/22 to 12/31	Capricorn

1915

1/01 to 1/29	Capricorn
1/30 to 3/09	Aquarius
3/10 to 4/16	Pisces
4/17 to 5/25	Aries

DATE	ZODIACAL SIGN	DATE	ZODIACAL SIGN
5/26 to 7/05	Taurus	4/15 to 5/25	Taurus
7/06 to 8/18	Gemini	5/26 to 7/08	Gemini
8/19 to 10/07	Cancer	7/09 to 8/22	Cancer
10/08 to 12/31	Leo	8/23 to 10/09	Leo
		10/10 to 11/29	Virgo
1916		11/30 to 12/31	Libra
1/01 to 5/28	Leo		
5/29 to 7/22	Virgo	*1920*	
7/23 to 9/08	Libra	1/01 to 1/31	Libra
9/09 to 10/21	Scorpio	2/01 to 4/23	Scorpio
10/22 to 12/01	Sagittarius	4/24 to 7/10	Libra
12/02 to 12/31	Capricorn	7/11 to 9/04	Scorpio
		9/05 to 10/18	Sagittarius
1917		10/19 to 11/27	Capricorn
1/01 to 1/09	Capricorn	11/28 to 12/31	Aquarius
1/10 to 2/16	Aquarius		
2/17 to 3/26	Pisces	*1921*	
3/27 to 5/04	Aries	1/01 to 1/04	Aquarius
5/05 to 6/14	Taurus	1/05 to 2/12	Pisces
6/15 to 7/27	Gemini	2/13 to 3/24	Aries
7/28 to 9/11	Cancer	3/25 to 5/05	Taurus
9/12 to 11/01	Leo	5/06 to 6/19	Gemini
11/02 to 12/31	Virgo	6/20 to 8/02	Cancer
		8/03 to 9/18	Leo
1918		9/19 to 11/06	Virgo
1/01 to 1/10	Virgo	11/07 to 12/25	Libra
1/11 to 2/25	Libra	12/26 to 12/31	Scorpio
2/26 to 6/23	Virgo		
6/24 to 8/16	Libra	*1922*	
8/17 to 9/30	Scorpio	1/01 to 2/18	Scorpio
10/01 to 11/10	Sagittarius	2/19 to 9/13	Sagittarius
11/11 to 12/19	Capricorn	9/14 to 10/30	Capricorn
12/20 to 12/31	Aquarius	10/31 to 12/11	Aquarius
		12/12 to 12/31	Pisces
1919			
1/01 to 1/26	Aquarius	*1923*	
1/27 to 3/06	Pisces	1/01 to 1/20	Pisces
3/07 to 4/14	Aries	1/21 to 3/03	Aries

DATE	ZODIACAL SIGN	DATE	ZODIACAL SIGN
3/04 to 4/15	Taurus	**1927**	
4/16 to 5/30	Gemini	1/01 to 2/21	Taurus
5/31 to 7/15	Cancer	2/22 to 4/16	Gemini
7/16 to 8/31	Leo	4/17 to 6/05	Cancer
9/01 to 10/17	Virgo	6/06 to 7/24	Leo
10/18 to 12/03	Libra	7/25 to 9/10	Virgo
12/04 to 12/31	Scorpio	9/11 to 10/25	Libra
		10/26 to 12/07	Scorpio
1924		12/08 to 12/31	Sagittarius
1/01 to 2/19	Scorpio		
2/20 to 3/06	Sagittarius	**1928**	
3/07 to 4/24	Capricorn	1/01 to 1/18	Sagittarius
4/25 to 6/24	Aquarius	1/19 to 2/27	Capricorn
6/25 to 8/24	Pisces	2/28 to 4/07	Aquarius
8/25 to 10/19	Aquarius	4/08 to 5/16	Pisces
10/20 to 12/18	Pisces	5/17 to 6/25	Aries
12/19 to 12/31	Aries	6/26 to 8/08	Taurus
		8/09 to 10/02	Gemini
1925		10/03 to 12/19	Cancer
1/01 to 2/04	Aries	12/20 to 12/31	Gemini
2/05 to 3/23	Taurus		
3/24 to 5/09	Gemini	**1929**	
5/10 to 6/25	Cancer	1/01 to 3/10	Gemini
6/26 to 8/12	Leo	3/11 to 5/12	Cancer
8/13 to 9/28	Virgo	5/13 to 7/03	Leo
9/29 to 11/13	Libra	7/04 to 8/21	Virgo
11/14 to 12/27	Scorpio	8/22 to 10/05	Libra
12/28 to 12/31	Sagittarius	10/06 to 11/18	Scorpio
		11/19 to 12/28	Sagittarius
1926		12/29 to 12/31	Capricorn
1/01 to 2/08	Sagittarius		
2/09 to 3/22	Capricorn	**1930**	
3/23 to 5/03	Aquarius	1/01 to 2/06	Capricorn
5/04 to 6/14	Pisces	2/07 to 3/16	Aquarius
6/15 to 7/31	Aries	3/17 to 4/24	Pisces
8/01 to 12/31	Taurus	4/25 to 6/02	Aries
		6/03 to 7/14	Taurus

DATE	ZODIACAL SIGN	DATE	ZODIACAL SIGN
7/15 to 8/27	Gemini	6/02 to 7/14	Gemini
8/28 to 10/20	Cancer	7/15 to 8/29	Cancer
10/21 to 12/31	Leo	8/30 to 10/17	Leo
		10/18 to 12/10	Virgo
1931		12/11 to 12/31	Libra
1/01 to 2/15	Leo		
2/16 to 3/29	Cancer	**1935**	
3/30 to 6/09	Leo	1/01 to 7/28	Libra
6/10 to 7/31	Virgo	7/29 to 9/15	Scorpio
8/01 to 9/16	Libra	9/16 to 10/27	Sagittarius
9/17 to 10/29	Scorpio	10/28 to 12/06	Capricorn
10/30 to 12/09	Sagittarius	12/07 to 12/31	Aquarius
12/10 to 12/31	Capricorn		
		1936	
1932		1/01 to 1/13	Aquarius
1/01 to 1/17	Capricorn	1/14 to 2/21	Pisces
1/18 to 2/24	Aquarius	2/22 to 3/31	Aries
2/25 to 4/02	Pisces	4/01 to 5/12	Taurus
4/03 to 5/11	Aries	5/13 to 6/24	Gemini
5/12 to 6/21	Taurus	6/25 to 8/09	Cancer
6/22 to 8/03	Gemini	8/10 to 9/25	Leo
8/04 to 9/19	Cancer	9/26 to 11/13	Virgo
9/20 to 11/12	Leo	11/14 to 12/31	Libra
11/13 to 12/31	Virgo		
		1937	
1933		1/01 to 3/12	Scorpio
1/01 to 7/05	Virgo	3/13 to 5/13	Sagittarius
7/06 to 8/25	Libra	5/14 to 8/07	Scorpio
8/26 to 10/08	Scorpio	8/08 to 9/29	Sagittarius
10/09 to 11/18	Sagittarius	9/30 to 11/10	Capricorn
11/19 to 12/27	Capricorn	11/11 to 12/20	Aquarius
12/28 to 12/31	Aquarius	12/21 to 12/31	Pisces
1934		**1938**	
1/01 to 2/03	Aquarius	1/01 to 1/29	Pisces
2/04 to 3/13	Pisces	1/30 to 3/11	Aries
3/14 to 4/21	Aries	3/12 to 4/22	Taurus
4/22 to 6/01	Taurus	4/23 to 6/06	Gemini

DATE	ZODIACAL SIGN	DATE	ZODIACAL SIGN
6/07 to 7/21	Cancer	6/14 to 7/31	Leo
7/22 to 9/06	Leo	8/01 to 9/16	Virgo
9/07 to 10/24	Virgo	9/17 to 10/31	Libra
10/25 to 12/10	Libra	11/01 to 12/14	Scorpio
12/11 to 12/31	Scorpio	12/14 to 12/31	Sagittarius

1939

1/01 to 1/28	Scorpio		
1/29 to 3/20	Sagittarius		
3/21 to 5/23	Capricorn		
5/24 to 7/20	Aquarius		
7/21 to 9/23	Capricorn		
9/24 to 11/18	Aquarius		
11/19 to 12/31	Pisces		

1943

1/01 to 1/25	Sagittarius
1/26 to 3/07	Capricorn
3/08 to 4/16	Aquarius
4/17 to 5/26	Pisces
5/27 to 6/06	Aries
6/07 to 8/22	Taurus
8/23 to 12/31	Gemini

1940

1/01 to 1/02	Pisces
1/03 to 2/16	Aries
2/17 to 3/31	Taurus
4/01 to 5/16	Gemini
5/17 to 7/02	Cancer
7/03 to 8/18	Leo
8/19 to 10/04	Virgo
10/05 to 11/19	Libra
11/20 to 12/31	Scorpio

1944

1/01 to 3/27	Gemini
3/28 to 5/21	Cancer
5/22 to 7/11	Leo
7/12 to 8/28	Virgo
8/29 to 10/12	Libra
10/13 to 11/24	Scorpio
11/25 to 12/31	Sagittarius

1941

1/01 to 1/03	Scorpio
1/04 to 2/16	Sagittarius
2/17 to 4/01	Capricorn
4/02 to 5/15	Aquarius
5/16 to 7/01	Pisces
7/02 to 12/31	Aries

1945

1/01 to 1/04	Sagittarius
1/05 to 2/13	Capricorn
2/14 to 3/24	Aquarius
3/25 to 5/01	Pisces
5/02 to 6/10	Aries
6/11 to 7/22	Taurus
7/23 to 9/06	Gemini
9/07 to 11/10	Cancer
11/11 to 12/25	Leo
12/26 to 12/31	Cancer

1942

1/01 to 1/10	Aries
1/11 to 3/06	Taurus
3/07 to 4/25	Gemini
4/26 to 6/13	Cancer

1946

1/01 to 4/21	Cancer
4/22 to 6/19	Leo

DATE	ZODIACAL SIGN	DATE	ZODIACAL SIGN
6/20 to 8/08	Virgo	**1950**	
8/09 to 9/23	Libra	1/01 to 3/27	Libra
9/24 to 11/05	Scorpio	3/28 to 6/10	Virgo
11/06 to 12/16	Sagittarius	6/11 to 8/09	Libra
12/17 to 12/31	Capricorn	8/10 to 9/24	Scorpio
		9/25 to 11/05	Sagittarius
1947		11/06 to 12/14	Capricorn
1/01 to 1/24	Capricorn	12/15 to 12/31	Aquarius
1/25 to 3/03	Aquarius		
3/04 to 4/10	Pisces	**1951**	
4/11 to 5/20	Aries	1/01 to 1/21	Aquarius
5/21 to 6/30	Taurus	1/22 to 2/28	Pisces
7/01 to 8/12	Gemini	3/01 to 4/09	Aries
8/13 to 9/30	Cancer	4/10 to 5/20	Taurus
10/01 to 11/30	Leo	5/21 to 7/02	Gemini
12/01 to 12/31	Virgo	7/03 to 8/17	Cancer
		8/18 to 10/03	Leo
1948		10/04 to 11/23	Virgo
1/01 to 2/11	Virgo	11/24 to 12/31	Libra
2/12 to 5/17	Leo		
5/18 to 7/16	Virgo	**1952**	
7/17 to 9/02	Libra	1/01 to 1/19	Libra
9/03 to 10/16	Scorpio	1/20 to 8/26	Scorpio
10/17 to 11/25	Sagittarius	8/27 to 10/11	Sagittarius
11/26 to 12/31	Capricorn	10/12 to 11/20	Capricorn
		11/21 to 12/29	Aquarius
1949		12/30 to 12/31	Pisces
1/01 to 1/03	Capricorn		
1/04 to 2/10	Aquarius	**1953**	
2/11 to 3/20	Pisces	1/01 to 2/07	Pisces
3/21 to 4/29	Aries	2/08 to 3/19	Aries
4/30 to 6/09	Taurus	3/20 to 4/30	Taurus
6/10 to 7/22	Gemini	5/01 to 6/13	Gemini
7/23 to 9/06	Cancer	6/14 to 7/28	Cancer
9/07 to 10/26	Leo	7/29 to 9/13	Leo
10/27 to 12/25	Virgo	9/14 to 10/31	Virgo
12/26 to 12/31	Libra	11/01 to 12/19	Libra
		12/20 to 12/31	Scorpio

DATE	ZODIACAL SIGN		DATE	ZODIACAL SIGN
1954			*1958*	
1/01 to 2/08	Scorpio		1/01 to 2/02	Sagittarius
2/09 to 4/11	Sagittarius		2/03 to 3/16	Capricorn
4/12 to 7/02	Capricorn		3/17 to 4/26	Aquarius
7/03 to 8/23	Sagittarius		4/27 to 6/06	Pisces
8/24 to 10/20	Capricorn		6/07 to 7/20	Aries
10/21 to 12/03	Aquarius		7/21 to 9/20	Taurus
12/04 to 12/31	Pisces		9/21 to 10/28	Gemini
			10/29 to 12/31	Taurus
1955			*1959*	
1/01 to 1/14	Pisces		1/01 to 2/09	Taurus
1/15 to 2/25	Aries		2/10 to 4/09	Gemini
2/26 to 4/09	Taurus		4/10 to 5/31	Cancer
4/10 to 5/25	Gemini		6/01 to 7/19	Leo
5/26 to 7/10	Cancer		7/20 to 9/04	Virgo
7/11 to 8/26	Leo		9/05 to 10/20	Libra
8/27 to 10/12	Virgo		10/21 to 12/02	Scorpio
10/13 to 11/28	Libra		12/03 to 12/31	Sagittarius
11/29 to 12/31	Scorpio			
1956			*1960*	
1/01 to 1/13	Scorpio		1/01 to 1/13	Sagittarius
1/14 to 2/27	Sagittarius		1/14 to 2/22	Capricorn
2/28 to 4/13	Capricorn		2/23 to 4/01	Aquarius
4/14 to 6/02	Aquarius		4/02 to 5/10	Pisces
6/03 to 12/05	Pisces		5/11 to 6/19	Aries
12/06 to 12/31	Aries		6/20 to 8/01	Taurus
			8/02 to 9/20	Gemini
1957			9/21 to 12/31	Cancer
1/01 to 2/27	Aries			
2/28 to 3/16	Taurus		*1961*	
3/17 to 5/03	Gemini		1/01 to 5/05	Cancer
5/04 to 6/20	Cancer		5/06 to 6/27	Leo
6/21 to 8/07	Leo		6/28 to 8/16	Virgo
8/08 to 9/23	Virgo		8/17 to 9/30	Libra
9/24 to 11/07	Libra		10/01 to 11/12	Scorpio
11/08 to 12/22	Scorpio		11/13 to 12/23	Sagittarius
12/23 to 12/31	Sagittarius		12/24 to 12/31	Capricorn

DATE	ZODIACAL SIGN

1962

1/01	to	1/31	Capricorn
2/01	to	3/11	Aquarius
3/12	to	4/18	Pisces
4/19	to	5/27	Aries
5/28	to	7/08	Taurus
7/09	to	8/21	Gemini
8/22	to	10/10	Cancer
10/11	to	12/31	Leo

1963

1/01	to	6/02	Leo
6/03	to	7/26	Virgo
7/27	to	9/11	Libra
9/12	to	10/24	Scorpio
10/25	to	12/04	Sagittarius
12/05	to	12/31	Capricorn

1964

1/01	to	1/12	Capricorn
1/13	to	2/19	Aquarius
2/20	to	3/28	Pisces
3/29	to	5/06	Aries
5/07	to	6/16	Taurus
6/17	to	7/29	Gemini
7/30	to	9/14	Cancer
9/15	to	11/05	Leo
11/06	to	12/31	Virgo

1965

1/01	to	6/28	Virgo
6/29	to	8/19	Libra
8/20	to	10/03	Scorpio
10/04	to	11/13	Sagittarius
11/14	to	12/22	Capricorn
12/23	to	12/31	Aquarius

DATE	ZODIACAL SIGN

1966

1/01	to	1/29	Aquarius
1/30	to	3/08	Pisces
3/09	to	4/16	Aries
4/17	to	5/27	Taurus
5/28	to	7/10	Gemini
7/11	to	8/24	Cancer
8/25	to	10/11	Leo
10/12	to	12/03	Virgo
12/04	to	12/31	Libra

1967

1/01	to	2/11	Libra
2/12	to	3/31	Scorpio
4/01	to	7/18	Libra
7/19	to	9/09	Scorpio
9/10	to	10/22	Sagittarius
10/23	to	11/30	Capricorn
12/01	to	12/31	Aquarius

1968

1/01	to	1/08	Aquarius
1/09	to	2/16	Pisces
2/17	to	3/26	Aries
3/27	to	5/07	Taurus
5/08	to	6/20	Gemini
6/21	to	8/04	Cancer
8/05	to	9/20	Leo
9/21	to	10/08	Virgo
10/09	to	12/28	Libra
12/29	to	12/31	Scorpio

1969

1/01	to	2/24	Scorpio
2/25	to	9/20	Sagittarius
9/21	to	11/03	Capricorn
11/04	to	12/13	Aquarius
12/14	to	12/31	Pisces

DATE		ZODIACAL SIGN	DATE		ZODIACAL SIGN
1970			6/02 to	7/17	Cancer
1/01 to	1/23	Pisces	7/18 to	9/02	Leo
1/24 to	3/06	Aries	9/03 to	10/19	Virgo
3/07 to	4/17	Taurus	10/20 to	12/05	Libra
4/18 to	6/01	Gemini	12/06 to	12/31	Scorpio

WHERE WAS PLUTO WHEN YOU WERE BORN?

Starting in Gemini, back in 1890, Pluto remained there till 1913. The motion of this planet is very slow, and the exact time when it changed from Gemini into the zodiacal sign Cancer cannot be accurately calculated, since the planet wasn't discovered until 1930 and its actual speed is open to some question. It appears to have been in Cancer during September, October and November 1913, after which it retrograded back into Gemini until July 1914, when it again returned to Cancer. It may have retrograded back into Gemini during February, March and April 1915, but after that it was in Cancer until about September 1938, when it appears to have entered Leo until January 1939. It then appears to have gone back into Cancer until August 1939. Following that, it was in Leo until September 1957, when it entered Virgo. From April through July 1958, it retrograded back into Leo for a short spell, and it will now remain in Virgo until late 1971.

WHERE WAS NEPTUNE WHEN YOU WERE BORN?

From the beginning of 1890 until July 19, 1901, Neptune was in Gemini. It was in Cancer from July 20, 1901 to December 25, 1901. After that, it retrograded back into Gemini from December 26, 1901, until May 19, 1902. It re-entered Cancer on May 21, 1902, remaining there until September 22, 1914. It was in Leo from September 23, 1914, until December 14, 1914. From December 15, 1914, until July 18, 1915, it retrograded back into Cancer. Re-entering Leo on July 19, 1915, it remained there until

March 19, 1916, when it again retrograded back into Cancer until May 1, 1916.

From May 2, 1916, until September 20, 1928, Neptune was in Leo. On May 3, 1916, it entered Virgo until February 19, 1929, when it fell back into Leo until July 23, 1929. On the 24th it entered Virgo, where it stayed until October 3, 1942.

On October 4, 1942, Neptune entered Libra, staying there until April 18, 1943. After spending the interval from April 19 to August 2, 1943, in Virgo, it re-entered Libra on August 3, 1943, remaining there until December 22, 1955.

It spent the brief spell from December 23, 1955, to March 10, 1956, in Scorpio, retrograding back into Libra from March 11 until October 18, 1956. It remained in Scorpio until June 15, 1957, when it again went back into Libra until August 4, 1957. It has been in Scorpio since that date, and will remain there until 1970.

WHERE WAS URANUS WHEN YOU WERE BORN?

The following table will give you the position of Uranus at the time of your birth.

DATE	ZODIACAL SIGN
1/01/1890 to 12/09/1890	Libra
12/10/1890 to 4/04/1891	Scorpio
4/05/1891 to 9/25/1891	Libra
9/26/1891 to 12/01/1897	Scorpio
12/02/1897 to 7/03/1898	Sagittarius
7/04/1898 to 9/10/1898	Scorpio
9/11/1898 to 12/19/1904	Sagittarius
12/20/1904 to 1/30/1912	Capricorn
1/31/1912 to 9/04/1912	Aquarius
9/05/1912 to 11/11/1912	Capricorn
11/12/1912 to 3/31/1919	Aquarius
4/01/1919 to 8/16/1919	Pisces
8/17/1919 to 1/21/1920	Aquarius
1/22/1920 to 3/30/1927	Pisces

3/31/1927 to 11/04/1927		Aries
11/05/1927 to 1/12/1928		Pisces
1/13/1928 to 6/06/1934		Aries
6/07/1934 to 10/09/1934		Taurus
10/10/1934 to 3/28/1935		Aries
3/29/1935 to 8/06/1941		Taurus
8/07/1941 to 10/04/1941		Gemini
10/05/1941 to 5/13/1942		Taurus
5/14/1942 to 8/29/1948		Gemini
8/30/1948 to 11/11/1948		Cancer
11/12/1948 to 6/09/1949		Gemini
6/10/1949 to 8/23/1955		Cancer
8/24/1955 to 1/27/1956		Leo
1/28/1956 to 6/08/1956		Cancer
6/09/1956 to 10/31/1961		Leo
11/01/1961 to 1/09/1962		Virgo
1/10/1962 to 8/08/1962		Leo
8/09/1962 to 9/27/1968		Virgo
9/28/1968 to 5/20/1969		Libra
5/21/1969 to 6/23/1969		Virgo
6/24/1969 to Dec. 1974		Libra

WHERE WAS SATURN WHEN YOU WERE BORN?

The following table will give you the position of Saturn at the time of your birth.

1/01/1890 to 1/23/1890		Virgo
1/24/1890 to 6/27/1890		Leo
6/28/1890 to 12/26/1891		Virgo
12/27/1891 to 1/22/1892		Libra
1/23/1892 to 8/28/1892		Virgo
8/29/1892 to 11/06/1894		Libra
11/07/1894 to 2/06/1897		Scorpio
2/07/1897 to 4/09/1897		Sagittarius
4/10/1897 to 10/26/1897		Scorpio
10/27/1897 to 1/20/1900		Sagittarius
1/21/1900 to 7/18/1900		Capricorn

7/19/1900 to	10/16/1900	Sagittarius
10/17/1900 to	1/19/1903	Capricorn
1/20/1903 to	4/12/1905	Aquarius
4/13/1905 to	8/16/1905	Pisces
8/17/1905 to	1/07/1906	Aquarius
1/08/1906 to	3/18/1908	Pisces
3/19/1908 to	5/16/1910	Aries
5/17/1910 to	12/14/1910	Taurus
12/15/1910 to	1/19/1911	Aries
1/20/1911 to	7/06/1912	Taurus
7/07/1912 to	11/30/1912	Gemini
12/01/1912 to	3/25/1913	Taurus
3/26/1913 to	8/24/1914	Gemini
8/25/1914 to	12/06/1914	Cancer
12/07/1914 to	5/11/1915	Gemini
5/12/1915 to	10/16/1916	Cancer
10/17/1916 to	12/07/1916	Leo
12/08/1916 to	6/23/1917	Cancer
6/24/1917 to	8/11/1919	Leo
8/12/1919 to	10/07/1921	Virgo
10/08/1921 to	12/19/1923	Libra
12/20/1923 to	4/05/1924	Scorpio
4/06/1924 to	9/13/1924	Libra
9/14/1924 to	12/02/1926	Scorpio
12/03/1926 to	3/29/1929	Sagittarius
3/30/1929 to	5/04/1929	Capricorn
5/05/1929 to	11/29/1929	Sagittarius
11/30/1929 to	2/22/1932	Capricorn
2/23/1932 to	8/12/1932	Aquarius
8/13/1932 to	11/18/1932	Capricorn
11/19/1932 to	2/13/1935	Aquarius
2/14/1935 to	4/24/1937	Pisces
4/25/1937 to	10/17/1937	Aries
10/18/1937 to	1/13/1938	Pisces
1/14/1938 to	7/05/1939	Aries
7/06/1939 to	9/21/1939	Taurus
9/22/1939 to	3/19/1940	Aries
3/20/1940 to	5/07/1942	Taurus
5/08/1942 to	6/19/1944	Gemini

6/20/1944 to	8/01/1946	Cancer
8/02/1946 to	9/18/1948	Leo
9/19/1948 to	4/02/1949	Virgo
4/03/1949 to	5/28/1949	Leo
5/29/1949 to	11/19/1950	Virgo
11/20/1950 to	3/06/1951	Libra
3/07/1951 to	8/12/1951	Virgo
8/13/1951 to	10/21/1953	Libra
10/22/1953 to	1/11/1956	Scorpio
1/12/1956 to	5/13/1956	Sagittarius
5/14/1956 to	10/09/1956	Scorpio
10/10/1956 to	1/04/1959	Sagittarius
1/05/1959 to	1/09/1962	Capricorn
1/10/1962 to	12/16/1964	Aquarius
12/17/1964 to	3/02/1967	Pisces
3/03/1967 to	4/28/1969	Aries
4/29/1969 thru	1970	Taurus

WHERE WAS VENUS WHEN YOU WERE BORN?

When we supply you with the dates when planets are in the various signs of the zodiac, you should be conscious of the fact that the planet does not make its change exactly at midnight, when the day begins. To this extent, our tables can be inaccurate. If we say that Venus was in Pisces from March 5 to 28, you know it was in Pisces if you were born on March 6. If you were born on March 5, the time of day when you were born might make a difference.

Because the position of Venus almost repeats itself on the same day of the year eight years later, we can abbreviate our Venus tables. Otherwise, we could not get them into this book. The difference in Venus position on April 1, 1910, will vary from its position on April 1, 1918, by less than a degree—about 40 minutes of arc. Thus, the table covering 1890 through 1897 can be used for other years by following instructions for those years carefully. The following table will tell you where Venus was when you were born:

DATE			ZODIACAL SIGN
1890			
1/01			Sagittarius
1/02	to	1/25	Capricorn
1/26	to	2/18	Aquarius
2/19	to	3/14	Pisces
3/15	to	4/07	Aries
4/08	to	5/01	Taurus
5/02	to	5/26	Gemini
5/27	to	6/20	Cancer
6/21	to	7/15	Leo
7/16	to	8/10	Virgo
8/11	to	9/06	Libra
9/07	to	10/07	Scorpio
10/08	to	12/31	Sagittarius
1891			
1/01	to	2/05	Sagittarius
2/06	to	3/05	Capricorn
3/06	to	4/01	Aquarius
4/02	to	4/26	Pisces
4/27	to	5/22	Aries
5/23	to	6/16	Taurus
6/17	to	7/10	Gemini
7/11	to	8/04	Cancer
8/05	to	8/28	Leo
8/29	to	9/21	Virgo
9/22	to	10/15	Libra
10/16	to	11/08	Scorpio
11/09	to	12/02	Sagittarius
12/03	to	12/26	Capricorn
12/27	to	12/31	Aquarius
1892			
1/01	to	1/20	Aquarius
1/21	to	2/13	Pisces
2/14	to	3/09	Aries
3/10	to	4/04	Taurus
4/05	to	5/04	Gemini

DATE			ZODIACAL SIGN
5/05	to	9/07	Cancer
9/08	to	10/Q7	Leo
10/08	to	11/02	Virgo
11/03	to	11/27	Libra
11/28	to	12/22	Scorpio
12/23	to	12/31	Sagittarius
1893			
1/01	to	1/15	Sagittarius
1/16	to	2/08	Capricorn
2/09	to	3/04	Aquarius
3/05	to	3/28	Pisces
3/29	to	4/22	Aries
4/23	to	5/16	Taurus
5/17	to	6/09	Gemini
6/10	to	7/04	Cancer
7/05	to	7/28	Leo
7/29	to	8/22	Virgo
8/23	to	9/16	Libra
9/17	to	10/11	Scorpio
10/12	to	11/06	Sagittarius
11/07	to	12/04	Capricorn
12/05	to	12/31	Aquarius
1894			
1/01	to	1/08	Aquarius
1/09	to	2/12	Pisces
2/13	to	4/02	Aquarius
4/03	to	5/05	Pisces
5/06	to	6/02	Aries
6/03	to	6/29	Taurus
6/30	to	7/24	Gemini
7/25	to	8/18	Cancer
8/19	to	9/12	Leo
9/13	to	10/06	Virgo
10/07	to	10/30	Libra
10/31	to	11/23	Scorpio
11/24	to	12/17	Sagittarius
12/18	to	12/31	Capricorn

DATE			ZODIACAL SIGN	DATE			ZODIACAL SIGN

1895

DATE			ZODIACAL SIGN	DATE			ZODIACAL SIGN
1/01	to	1/10	Capricorn	6/01	to	6/24	Gemini
1/11	to	2/03	Aquarius	6/25	to	7/19	Cancer
2/04	to	2/27	Pisces	7/20	to	8/12	Leo
2/28	to	3/23	Aries	8/13	to	9/05	Virgo
3/24	to	4/17	Taurus	9/06	to	9/29	Libra
4/18	to	5/12	Gemini	9/30	to	10/24	Scorpio
5/13	to	6/07	Cancer	10/25	to	11/17	Sagittarius
6/08	to	7/06	Leo	11/18	to	12/12	Capricorn
7/07	to	8/13	Virgo	12/13	to	12/31	Aquarius
8/14	to	9/12	Libra				
9/13	to	11/06	Virgo	*1897*			
11/07	to	12/08	Libra	1/01	to	1/06	Aquarius
12/09	to	12/31	Scorpio	1/07	to	2/01	Pisces
				2/02	to	3/04	Aries
1896				3/05	to	7/07	Taurus
1/01	to	1/03	Scorpio	7/08	to	8/05	Gemini
1/04	to	1/29	Sagittarius	8/06	to	8/31	Cancer
1/30	to	2/23	Capricorn	9/01	to	9/26	Leo
2/24	to	3/18	Aquarius	9/27	to	10/20	Virgo
3/19	to	4/12	Pisces	10/21	to	11/13	Libra
4/13	to	5/06	Aries	11/14	to	12/07	Scorpio
5/07	to	5/31	Taurus	12/08	to	12/31	Sagittarius

1898   Use table for 1890 but deduct one day from figures as given. In other words, Venus entered Capricorn on January 1 instead of January 2.

1899   Use table for 1891 but deduct one day from dates as given.

1900   Use table for 1892 but deduct one day from dates as given.

1901   Use table for 1893 but deduct one day from dates as given.

1902   Use table for 1894 but deduct one day from dates as given.

1903   Use table for 1895 but deduct one day from dates as given.

1904   Use table for 1896 but deduct one day from dates as given.

1905   Use table for 1897 but deduct one day from dates as given.

1906   Use table for 1890.

1907   Use table for 1891.

1908   Use table for 1892.

1909   Use table for 1893.

1910 Use table for 1894.
1911 Use table for 1895.
1912 Use table for 1896.
1913 Use table for 1897.
1914 Use table for 1890 but deduct one day from dates as given.
1915 Use table for 1891 but deduct one day from dates as given.
1916 Use table for 1892 but deduct one day from dates as given.
1917 Use table for 1893 but deduct one day from dates as given.
1918 Use table for 1894 but deduct one day from dates as given.
1919 Use table for 1895 but deduct one day from dates as given.
1920 Use table for 1896 but deduct one day from dates as given.
1921 Use table for 1897 but deduct one day from dates as given.
1922 Use table for 1890 but deduct one day from dates as given.
1923 Use table for 1891 but deduct one day from dates as given.
1924 Use table for 1892 but deduct one day from date as given.
1925 Use table for 1893 but deduct one day from dates as given.
1926 Use table for 1894 but deduct one day from dates as given.
1927 Use table for 1895 but deduct one day from dates as given.
1928 Use table for 1896 but deduct one day from dates as given.
1929 Use table for 1897 but deduct one day from dates as given.
1930 Use table for 1890 but deduct two days from dates as given.
1931 Use table for 1891 but deduct two days from dates as given.
1932 Use table for 1892 but deduct two days from dates as given.
1933 Use table for 1893 but deduct two days from dates as given.
1934 Use table for 1894 but deduct two days from dates as given.
1935 Use table for 1895 but deduct two days from dates as given.
1936 Use table for 1896 but deduct two days from dates as given.
1937 Use table for 1897 but deduct two days from dates as given.
1938 Use table for 1890 but deduct three days from dates as given.
1939 Use table for 1891 but deduct three days from dates as given.
1940 Use table for 1892 but deduct three days from dates as given.
1941 Use table for 1893 but deduct three days from dates as given.
1942 Use table for 1894 but deduct three days from dates as given.
1943 Use table for 1895 but deduct three days from dates given.
1944 Use table for 1896 but deduct three days from dates given.
1945 Use table for 1897 but deduct three days from dates given.
1946 Use table for 1890 but deduct three days from dates given.
1947 Use table for 1891 but deduct three days from dates given.
1948 Use table for 1892 but deduct three days from dates given.

1949   Use table for 1893 but deduct three days from dates given.
1950   Use table for 1894 but deduct three days from dates given.
1951   Use table for 1895 but deduct three days from dates given.
1952   Use table for 1896 but deduct three days from dates given.
1953   Use table for 1897 but deduct three days from dates given.
1954   Use table for 1890 but deduct four days from dates given.
1955   Use table for 1891 but deduct four days from dates given.
1956   Use table for 1892 but deduct four days from dates given.
1957   Use table for 1893 but deduct four days from dates given.
1958   Use table for 1894 but deduct four days from dates given.
1959   Use table for 1895 but deduct four days from dates given.
1960   Use table for 1896 but deduct four days from dates given.
1961   Use table for 1897 but deduct four days from dates given.
1962   Use table for 1890 but deduct four days from dates given.
1963   Use table for 1891 but deduct four days from dates given.
1964   Use table for 1892 but deduct four days from dates given.
1965   Use table for 1893 but deduct four days from dates given.
1966   Use table for 1894 but deduct four days from dates given.
1967   Use table for 1895 but deduct four days from dates given.
1968   Use table for 1896 but deduct four days from dates given.
1969   Use table for 1897 but deduct four days from dates given.
1970   Use table for 1890 but deduct five days from dates given.

WHERE WAS MERCURY WHEN YOU WERE BORN?

Mercury is the fastest-moving planet; it changes its zodiacal sign more frequently than any body except the Moon. This fact makes it impossible for us to supply tables of its position in this volume. However, there are limitations as to Mercury's position at the time of your birth; it could be in only one of three signs. You can check those three signs, and you might recognize where your own Mercury belongs. Mercury is always close to the Sun. Much of the time, it is in the same sign with the Sun. When it is not, it can be only one sign away. By looking at the table of Sun positions given below, you can know that Mercury is either in the zodiacal sign of your Sun or one sign away, ahead or behind. Select your Sun sign from the next table, check Mercury in the three signs thus described. See which one you think "fits" you.

WHERE WAS THE SUN WHEN YOU WERE BORN?

The following table shows the average dates when the Sun passes from one zodiacal sign to another. However, the first and last date of each period can be in error, because the change does not come exactly on the same day of each year. The reason for this is that we employ a calendar that is imperfect. A year is not exactly 365 days, so we add a day every fourth year, calling it a leap year, but that isn't accurate either. A year is not exactly 365.25 days; it is shorter. The result is that our calendar is always getting out of kilter. As we go along from year to year, it becomes a little more inaccurate. A perfect year would be one based on the equinoxes or signs of the zodiac, but society does things differently. In order to try to "even" things, or make them balance, the extra day for leap year was left out in the year 1800 and again in 1900. This helped to correct things. However, the error is constantly increasing again, and we'll have to skip a leap year again before we can gain accuracy. We'll probably do it in the year 2000.

You must also realize that the Sun doesn't make its change from one sign to another exactly at the beginning of the day, or midnight. Midnight isn't even the same on different parts of the earth. Thus, the change has to come sometime during a twenty-four-hour period. Consequently, if you are born on a date like April 20, you could possibly have the Sun in either Aries or Taurus, but these signs are so different that you would probably recognize one as right, the other as inaccurate. There could be another angle. A Taurean might well have Mercury and Venus in Aries—or other planets in Aries. Then, he is somewhat a combination of the two. Many of the most successful Taureans are those with such a chart, because Aries supplies some initiative that Taurus lacks. If you are born at one of these fringe points, it might be well to have an astrologer calculate the exact position of your Sun. This rule applies to all the planets. Jupiter might change its sign at 2:34 P.M. People born before that time would have it in another sign. Yet, this will not be a problem 93 per cent of the time. Most of the time, it can be ignored. Unless you are born at the beginning or end of the periods furnished, you have no such problem. The table of Sun sign positions follows:

DATE	SUN-SIGN
Jan. 1 to 20	Capricorn
Jan. 21 to Feb. 19	Aquarius
Feb. 20 to Mar. 20	Pisces
Mar. 21 to Apr. 19	Aries
Apr. 20 to May 20	Taurus
May 21 to Jun. 21	Gemini
Jun. 22 to Jul. 21	Cancer
Jul. 22 to Aug. 21	Leo
Aug. 22 to Sep. 22	Virgo
Sep. 23 to Oct. 22	Libra
Oct. 23 to Nov. 21	Scorpio
Nov. 22 to Dec. 21	Sagittarius
Dec. 22 to 31	Capricorn

THE TRANSITS OF THE PLANETS

The material included in this chapter on the transits of the planets is the work of Dr. Heber Smith of Boston, who was the teacher of Miss Evangeline Adams.

It is reported that Mrs. Julie Pontin, the rival of Miss Adams, paid $150 for a typewritten copy of this material, and that it has never been reproduced.

The original material is presented herewith without any editing whatsoever; its style is inimitable; idioms of the late 19th Century are used, I want to thank the American Federation of Astrologers for making this material available.

THE TRANSITS OF THE PLANET MERCURY

The transits of Mercury are not over-important unless Mercury happens to become retrograde or stationary in important places, and yet the effects are quite marked, and when Mercury adds his influence to that of the other planets he greatly intensifies their effects. The transits of Mercury, in accord with the law that the transits of the minor planets over the major are identical in quality with the transits of the major over the minor, although differing in degree and duration to the various planets, will effect, chiefly, the mind and nervous organism and will refer to all matters in which the mind, objectively, is concerned. In a general sense, the unfavorable transits of Mercury indicate restless, irritating, worrying and harassing conditions, while the favorable transits indicate mental progress, balance, poise, personal content, mental harmony, right decision, and nervous normality, as well as well-directed action, and successful effort. The evil transits of Mercury are very unfavorable for nervous complaints, irritability, associations with people, and in cases of confirmed mental or nervous pathologic states and will do much to irritate and intensify such states.

Mercury to the aspects of Venus is not important, but in the favorable aspects, turns the mind in the direction of art, music, pleasure, gaity, somewhat stimulates the emotions, and aids to the sociability, and in the evil aspects, may do all this, but in a more marked degree.

Mercury in Conjunction, Square or Opposition to Mars—This aspect tends toward irritability, impulsive speech and expression and hasty and immature judgment. It is likely, on the one hand, to lead to quarrels, misunderstandings, anger and the exhibition of some temper, and may lead you to be too critical, impatient, sharp, and too free in the expression of your ideas. People should try and be diplomatic in their relations with others, patient with those who are trying in their behavior, and if they feel out of harmony with others and their conditions, it is likely to be their own fault, while these vibrations often bring criticism, involve one in arguments, disputes and unfavorable comment, and lead to things which one would have rather left unsaid or undone. The whole nature of the aspect is toward irritating the nerves and intensifying the mental action, and it is apt to bring you in contact with people and conditions which are very irritating and annoying—your correspondence is likely to be troublesome, others are likely to draw out of you expressions of anger and impatience, and your petty affairs are likely to become involved, confused or worrying. Do nothing precipitate, say nothing that is not well considered, write nothing you are sure will cause offense, and the less you have to do with correspondence, legal affairs and the operations of the mind at this time, the better. It is a poor time to write important letters, to make decisions of moment, and for thinking up new ideas.

The unfavorable aspects of Mars to Mercury are similar in effect and are likely to be even more marked, but quite identical in quality.

Mercury in favorable aspect to Mars—This aspect is favorable for travel, for mental matters generally, and more especially for those which require forceful expression, accuracy of definition, and that are intended to work some positive result. It is favorable for any form of physical activity, as it lends vigor, strength and vacility to the muscles. Otherwise, it is not important.

The favorable aspects of the planet Mars to the place of Mercury can be considered similarly, but as being rather more important.

Mercury in Conjunction or good aspect to Jupiter—The planet Jupiter has a special bearing upon finance and all constructive, useful, and beneficial operations in the Universe, and is the planet of preservation, of peace and harmony, and has a natural ruling over all things which are in their nature lasting, permanent and productive of the mental, spiritual and bodily as well as emotional comfort of the human race. For instance, in the physical world, Jupiter has a great deal to do with finance, which is the physical home and all its accessories. Therefore, the aspects of Mercury to

Jupiter produce hopefulness, confidence and faith in oneself, and makes the mental action positive, harmonious, constructive, in tune with the minds of others, and therefore disposed to listen to advice, to express diplomatically, tactfully and moderately, to act maturely, practically and with the very best sense of utility and worth. All the attributes of the planet Jupiter may be summed up in the one word "practical" as it is popularly applied to various human activities. Anything is said to be practical which is found to be productive of positive and appreciable good, and this is what Jupiter implies. This is a good aspect under which to write, to attend to correspondence, legal affairs, and to deal with people through the medium of the mind. Under this influence you are more reasonable, tolerant, kindly and less nervous, irritated and impatient than usual, and your mind is likely to be more open, more harmonious, more practical than at other times. This is a good aspect for the spirits, for your dealings and associations with other people, and it is one of the best under which to make important decisions, and especially those which concern your physical and financial well-being and your general status in the world. It is at this time that you will be sensible.

Mercury in evil aspect of Jupiter—is inclined to be too hopeful, too sanguine, too sure, and it is a poor influence under which to make important decisions, attend to important financial and legal affairs, and while it is a very important aspect, it may join its forces with others to make you act unwisely in these things. You are likely to "reckon without your host" and take too much for granted. It tends toward making promises you cannot keep, picturing things more favorable than they really are, and a species of misrepresentation which is not deliberate deceit but which arises from the fact that for the time your impression of things is too highly colored. In all practical matters be, therefore, conservative and don't be too sure of things turning out just as you want them.

Mercury in Conjunction and evil aspect to Saturn—This is a very depressing influence, and physically, first of all, inclined to nervous troubles, and aggravation of such things as neuralgia, rheumatism and kindred difficulties, which might already exist. (Not important enough to cause them.) You are likely to feel discouraged, unhappy, mentally out of tune, dull and somewhat pessimistic. Bad for correspondence, and you may receive letters which are unsatisfactory, certain unwelcome news or fail to receive the letters you are expecting. Be careful what you put in writing, and although you will be inclined to be sceptical, be sceptical of your own judgment, and make no important decisions until the aspect has passed. Give your attention to the most routine part of your business life and try to associate with people who are cheerful and optimistic. Try not to be too critical, sarcastic, or otherwise cranky.

Mercury in good aspects of Saturn—This influence is good for steady mental work, application and thought, and favors mental dealings with older people. It is slightly favorable for legal affairs, and particularly good for making important decisions in matters which will not mature hastily. It is not a very important aspect but good for concentration, continuity and deep thought.

Mercury in Conjunction and evil aspects to Uranus—These conditions are excitable, irritating, nervous and tense. You may be inclined to be sarcastic, impatient, irritable and very uncertain. Try and be diplomatic in your dealings with others, and sceptical of your own judgment. The tendency is to be impatient with forms, customs and accepted ideas, to want to think along new lines, and try mental experiments. It is very unfavorable for applications, routine work and a time when you may find it exceedingly difficult to stay by your usual work, accustomed opinions and maintain a steady line of conduct. This aspect is highly nervous, irritating to the mind which is inclined to search for new ideas, and to be very much dissatisfied with its usual problem (pabulum) and at this time you are very apt to have trouble with those with whom you are generally associating, as being under such intense vibrations you are apt to behave in an unaccountably restless, cranky manner, to be subject to changes of opinion and intention, and be rather unreliable. It is a bad time in which to make important decisions, and in case of the evil aspects, decidedly bad for correspondence and writing, or for dealing with people on the mental plane and you may be inclined to entertain unpopular views, indulge in eccentric forms of expression, and generally antagonize people, while in the case of the conjunction, if there are any good aspects to the planet Uranus radically or by direction, you may receive new ideas, which will be worth considering and be mentally active and keen. All the aspects mentioned are apt to bring sudden and unexpected meetings with people, unlooked for news or events mainly of a trifling nature, however, and as the general influence of the planet Uranus is rather explosive and productive at all times the unexpected things are apt to go queerly, matters become tangled and confused, and cause a certain amount of worry and petty annoyance, and your minor affairs are likely to "pile up" on you, and cause you to be worried, hurried and otherwise tied up in knots. Do not lay too much stress upon the simple transits of one of Mercury's positions over that of Uranus, as that will not be very marked, but should both Mercury's transit at the same time, say one square and the other in conjunction to Uranus, radical place or Mercury pass over that body in company with the Sun or Mars, the worry, confusion, and general tendency to confuse, disarrange and hurry will be rather marked. Always take into account the other aspects that may be made at the same time, as well as the radical or progressed positions of the planet which the transiting body might meet at the same time, as all these influences will be very modifying. For instance, if the Sun and Mercury transited the conjunction of Uranus and Mars was squaring Uranus at birth, the influence would be, of course, very potent, but should Uranus be trine to Jupiter and sextile to Saturn so that Mercury and the Sun made their good aspects at the same time as he made the conjunction to Uranus, then these favorable angles would in a great measure prevent the confusion and enable the person to control the situation to a great degree. Take everything into account, and of course, the chief difficulty lies in the fact that at any given time, there are so many elements to consider that it is very difficult to give a right judgment, but unless in the aggregate influences are decidedly unfavorable, it is useless to expect much trouble, and the contrary.

Mercury in favorable aspects or Conjunction to Uranus—if Uranus be well aspected—Favorable for travel, for thinking up new ideas, for correspondence, for speaking or writing for publicity, for any mental work and this is a good time in which to exercise the mind to its fullest capacity. Ideas that come to you at this time are likely to be of some value and while the aspect does not of itself favor financial affairs, practical or conservative departments of life, it is splendid for inventions, progress or ideas out of the ordinary. A good aspect under which to lecture, to meet interesting people of a mental nature, and if you have any important matters to attend to which require your brightest mental efforts, this is a good time to choose. Indicates quick action, rapid and accurate work and keen intuition.

Mercury in Conjunction or evil aspects to Neptune—A queer influence and not at all reliable. Look out for deceit, humbug and quacks in general, deceptive ideas, lies, fraud, and don't trust your judgments or other's candor. When Neptune is afflicted look out for treachery, underhand enmity, scandal and be careful what you say, sign or put in writing. Make no important decisions, think up no important ideas and consider the influence generally untrustworthy. It is a "woozy" aspect.

Mercury in good aspect of Conjunction to Neptune—where Neptune is well ASPECTED—Brings unusual ideas, sometimes, and is inspirational and psychic. You may meet peculiar people, especially of a spiritual or psychic type, and you may either receive or express unusual views. It is a subtle influence, leads to intuition, aids music, poetry and the arts, and in many cases, where Neptune is not prominent, it may pass without any appreciable influences. Where Neptune is powerful, it tends to strong and unusual impressions, mental illumination and interesting experiences. Don't expect much, if anything, of it unless other influences combine. In a general sense the unfavorable transits of Mercury tend to bring unsatisfactory news, unfavorable criticism, lies, deceit, treachery and worry, petty quarreling and disputes, uneven mental action, impaired memory, want of application, interfering influences and where Mercury makes transits over very much afflicted points, expect unkindness, unpleasant experiences with people, verbal and written attacks, severe criticism, scandal and the like.

THE TRANSITS OF THE PLANET VENUS

Favorable aspects of Venus to the Sun are very favorable for social affairs, for dealing in a social way with men, for pleasure and friendship, and are good times to plan everything of a social or artistic nature.

Favorable aspects of Venus to Mercury are good for the expression of the artistic faculties, for social amenities, for pleasant correspondence, for associations with people generally, and for one's personal happiness and content.

Favorable aspects of Venus to the Moon are fortunate for dealing with women and men, the wife or mother, for domestic affairs, for personal happiness and spirits, for pleasure, travel and health. It is a fortunate influence under which to interview women, to ask favors of them, and for dealing with the general public, and especially in an artistic or musical way or where one's personality counts. The conjunction of Venus with the Moon always brings very pleasant experiences through some woman, unless the Moon is vilely afflicted, and tends to the expression of the emotional nature, to indulgence, sensuality and physical enjoyment, especially where the Moon is in such signs as Taurus, Cancer, Scorpio and Capricorn.

Aspects of Venus to Mars—stirs up the emotional nature very strongly and tends to impulsive expression of the affections, sudden attacks of love, and sometimes "lovers" quarrels, which are likely to end in petty displays of emotion, and charming relapses into delightful "mushiness." It is a very good aspect under which to "raise the devil," with your inamorata in the hopes of getting things going. In a more serious vein, the sexual instincts need guarding under the aspect, and where there is plentiful interchange of these two planets at any time in a horoscope, whether by transit of Venus to Mars or the reverse, radical or progressed, the mind is inclined to seek affection, sympathy and love, and the person is in the mood for enjoyment. In the favorable aspects, there is plenty of magnetism, activity but less likelihood of folly, and more of satisfaction, and in the adverse aspects there is the tendency to force conditions, be very impatient, passionate and foolhardy and things are not likely to go as smoothly or satisfactorily.

Venus in conjunction or good aspect to Jupiter—This is one of the more fortunate minor transits. First of all it is favorable for artistic and social matters, a good influence under which to meet people, make friends, entertain or be entertained. Next it usually brings favors, kindness and gifts, and usually fortunate for financial affairs generally, money usually comes in under this aspect better than usual. Jupiter governs the most conventional and conservative, as well as the most permanent departments of life, and has a natural ruling over the home, relatives and family generally, and friends of long standing, so this influence is a very favorable one under which to visit relatives, the home, parents or old friends. One usually sees old friends at this time and sometimes meets them unexpectedly. It is exceedingly happy in its influence, and all matters of pleasures and enjoyment are sure to go rightly under this aspect. If you want to entertain, give a concert or display work of an artistic character, this is a good time to choose, and anything of this nature is sure to be satisfactory at this time. It is a good time in which to repair quarrels, patch up friendships or renew acquaintance, and you are pretty sure to get good treatment at the hands of others at this time. It encourages generosity, tends to expenditures, assists extravagance, makes one more careful of their dress and deportment, and while expansive in nature it is all in the direction and along the lines of conservatism. It is a good aspect under which to seek the friendship of the wealthy, and distinguished in society, and those in superior positions. It is favorable for any matters connected with the home, the family or the financial standing, and owing to the fact that under this aspect the financial and social are blended harmoniously, it is pretty good for anything and everything in the common run of things.

Venus in evil aspect to Jupiter—This is, par excellence, the aspect of social boredom. The influence of this aspect is to place you amid circumstances which are trying from the fact of their being formal, too conservative, too stiff and elegant for comfort, and with people who are too conventional, who are perhaps expensively dressed and appointed, richly caparisoned, so to speak but very uninteresting, and it tends to put you where you are dissatisfied, more or less chocked and hampered with too much ceremony and rich surroundings and it is inclined to lead to extravagance, display and ostentation and the feeling is apt to be that it was not at all worthwhile. It is a poor aspect under which to plan entertainments as they are likely to be more expensive than edifying, and for being entertained, as you are likely to wish yourself somewhere else. In case this sort of thing suits you, you are fortunate for this particular time, even if unfortunate when not so conditioned, but I have always found the evil aspects of Venus to Jupiter very annoying, barren, uninteresting and disgustingly decent. It is not an important influence because it brings nothing positively favorable, and is neither good for finance nor for anything else, and the only good thing about it is that it is good discipline for the disposition, as it puts you where you have to behave, whether or no, and where you would not dare to say one rotten word. It indicates fat ladies, well-filled dining tables, gilded cages and vapidly pleasant social intercourse, in which there will not be one word of real sense, or genuine feeling. On the other hand, while it inclines to decorum and engenders perfect deportment, you will be so horrified at the realization of the ideal, that you will probably swear never to be respectable again. It enforces correct costuming, and prompt replies to invitations, as well as rapid acknowledgment of favors received. In fact, it is a holy horror! Perhaps the best feature of this trying situation is that it does not last long, unless Venus is retrograde, in which case it is best to go to bed until it is over. People you meet under this aspect are likely to be optimistic and well nourished, have a great regard for the etiquette column in the Sunday paper and their idea of being devilish is only going to church three times on Sunday and if possible four. Their equatorial circumference is likely to exceed their polar diameter by more than the aesthetic standard requires. They are likely to welcome you with a fat smile, and be very much over-bolstered. In case Jupiter is radically afflicted, the type is not so pure, which makes one willing to put up with that calamity if for no other reason. For further particulars, refer to the "Book of Snobs" by one, Thackeray.

*Venus in good aspect to Uranus—also Conjunction—*We are

now able to breathe again. These are very magnetic vibrations, but very capricious. The unexpected is likely to happen in your social affairs. You may meet someone unexpectedly, make a new acquaintance; and the unconventional side of your nature will be to the front. It is a very interested time in which to plan social affairs, meetings and pleasures generally, and whatever takes place under these vibrations is sure to be diverting—thank God. This is a good aspect for artistic affairs, which are sure to be artistic successes, even if not financially so, which especially belongs to Jupiter, and it is a very active, inspiring aspect. If you want things to be very brilliant and interesting, this is the aspect for which to plan and especially if the contemplated function is in the least degree "Bohemian." *In case Uranus is afflicted at birth,* the conjunction inclines rather too much to unconventionality, and may provoke you to be a little indiscreet or regardless of conventions, which would be a lamentable thing. On the other hand, people you meet under this aspect (conj.) will be interesting characters, magnetic and fascinating, but in the case of the afflicted Uranus, unreliable, and if you put too much stock in them, you will be disappointed. The best way is to expect nothing of them, enjoy them while they last, which will not be long, and when they disappear magically, don't be disappointed. *In the case of the favorable aspect,* they are not so elfish and you may possibly see them again.

Venus in evil aspect to Uranus—This is a very unconventional influence, and erratic. Your emotions are very active, and you may feel disposed to act without the advice of Mrs. Grundy. May meet someone very interesting, but don't take them seriously, as the influence is capricious, and while you might seem to be getting along famously, it is likely to come to nothing in the end. The unexpected, sudden and unlooked for is likely to happen, and it is best not to plan too rigidly for this aspect, as your plans are likely not to come to pass. Be a little guarded in the expression of your emotional nature, and if you take chances, be a sport and don't wail if you have to pay the price. This aspect never brings anything permanent or satisfactory, but it is often provocative of alluring overtures and enticing promises. Try and be guided by reason and sound judgment, and don't let your feelings run away with you.

Venus in conjunction or evil aspect to Saturn—This is decidedly a nasty one. Plan nothing social for this time. You are likely to expect too much of your friends and you may feel somewhat dull, unhappy or slighted, and get your precious feelings hurt. If you are disposed to be jealous, now is the time for the exhibition of this charming trait, and misunderstandings, grouches, sensitiveness, wounded feelings, tragedies constructed out of vague imaginings, slight will not be so nice to you at this time, so be a sport and smile if it kills you. Your plans for pleasure are apt to go wrong, if it's only the weather. The one person you wanted to see won't turn up, the company will be dull and stupid, the arrangements poor, and the dinner beastly. The person you sit next to will be unattractive, your hair will not curl, your nose will be shiny and your hose holey. You will look your worst, behave your baddest, and have the satisfaction of realizing that you look at least forty years older than you are. You will act awkwardly, say yes when you mean no, and be studiously misunderstood. The friend you counted on will spend his smiles somewhere else, your rival will have a more fascinating frock and look indecently ravishing, you will not get the largest piece of pie, and you will have an extra bad attack of disjointed proboscis. You will not be the center of attraction, your smile will not dazzle as of old, and every mirror you gaze in will insult you unmercifully. It is a good time to stay home and mend the family linen. It is a propitious time for washing the week's dishes and dusting the family Bible. And it's dollars to doughnuts that all the ladies you call on will not be at home, and especially the one whom you always call "dear," the line will be busy when you want to talk to your twin sister, who, as you know, has just the most interesting something to tell you. Mr. Z, who is so clever and interesting, and understands you so well, won't be at Mrs. A's this afternoon to tea, so it's no use your going, and if you don't go, why of course, he will be there. Mrs. B, by the way, thinks she understands him as no other woman in the world ever could or did—the hussy. In short, and not to go through any further detail, it's a maddening influence, and the less you expect, the better. The best thing to do, as I have hinted, is to stay home, have a good shampoo, dig out the corners of the parlor floor, and mend your husband's socks. It is bad for social affairs, music, art or anything in the nature of sentiment, love or pleasure or gaiety, and unless there are very powerful contrary aspects, you may as well expect the worst.

Venus in good aspect to Saturn—This is a very negative aspect, and conduces your good behavior, discretion, and the association of older people, self-control and all these dull proceedings. It is a very meaningless aspect, and doesn't seem to bring much of anything, and probably, like most of the favorable aspects of Saturn, is more restrictive and controlling in effect than anything else. Venus and Saturn both negative in nature, nothing happens. On the other hand, it can act as a preventive in case of too much hilarity, a disposition to be kittenish or unquiet emotional states, and where this aspect exists, there is not likely to be any indiscretion. Saturn conceals, and governs things through prudence, reason and caution, and it is therefore a good aspect when considered as an offset to Mars and Uranus.

Venus in evil aspect to Neptune—This is a very misleading influence, tends to peculiar emotional states, psychic influences, and people you meet under this aspect are likely to exercise a very subtle influence over you, and charm you in some way which is not physical or superficial. It is, however, a rather treacherous influence and not to be relied upon. Act on this influence and you are apt to wish you hadn't and one of the most common effects of it is to make you think you are in love when you aren't, or make you think that someone else cares for you when they don't. It implies self-deception, sometimes, and people under this stimulus are apt to let their emotions lead them too much. If Neptune is well aspected, in the case of the conjunction, it may indicate at times a very subtle, spiritual and elevating influence, and in any case, always a fascinating one. But the thing is not to be taken in and not to pay too much attention to, or be guided by your feelings under this aspect. Wait till other aspects set in and see how you feel then. If the accompanying aspects were good and Neptune, as aforesaid, well aspected, then the conjunction sometimes indicates a very strong and profound influence. I have a very intimate friend, personally, and on the day we met, Venus was transiting his Neptune by conjunction, Neptune being well aspected to the Sun, Mercury, Jupiter and Uranus, and he told me that on the day he met me, he knew that we would be very great friends, and he plainly felt a very powerful influence at work. He has Neptune rising and is very psychic. We are enjoying a very unusual and very close friendship in which the mutual relationship has been most beneficial so far. But as a general rule it is misleading influence and needs careful watching, and in many cases, probably has little or no results. There is usually something queer about either the person or the process of meeting them, and in this case, the circumstances leading up to our meeting were decidedly peculiar.

Venus in the unfavorable aspects of Neptune—This is apt to be decidedly queer, unconventional, and with a touch of the romantic, the strange or the mysterious. It is not to be trusted, leads to unwise expression of the emotional nature and there is sure to be an atmosphere of deceit, double-dealing, masquerading or something of the kind. Don't trust people you meet where this is the dominant note in your horoscope at the time, as either they are misrepresenting themselves or you are deceiving yourself about them. Your sympathies are likely to be aroused and you are likely to be actuated by pity, compassion or some subtle psychic force which bodes no good or beneficial effects. Of course where this aspect happens to be the dominant note at the time, it is best to beware. When I say the dominant note, this would be the case, for instance, where the Sun was always transiting at the same time, or Mercury, or Mars, or where there was some important direction, especially of Venus or Mercury, to Neptune in the progressed horoscope, and more than one transit at the same time or where one position of Venus was transiting Neptune and the other Uranus, or its evil aspect or some such mix-up. Where the other aspects are very normal, then Neptune will do no more than throw an air of mystery around these things, or romance, and adds slightly to the flavor of the unusual, which may be just enough to make the combination interesting. Never look for marked effects unless there is some sort of concerted effect, for although I have tried to describe these aspects very carefully, and give them the right coloring, I have exaggerated in order to do so, and if they all worked out just as I have said, life would be too interesting to ever leave. The whole difficulty lies in the correct analysis of mixtures, and giving things their right proportions.

THE SUN

Sun in evil aspects or conjunction to Saturn—The periods when the Sun makes the conjunction or evil aspects of Saturn mark the most depressing times of the year, and especially for health and general business affairs. This is a very unfavorable time for any work of an initiative nature, and is only fit for working on matters already under way. It slows up the functions generally, causes one to be most susceptible to colds or any trouble which is the result of poor elimination, and one should avoid at this time getting over-heated and cooling off too quickly. One is apt to feel tired, dragged and somewhat lacking in "snap" if nothing more. If any important propositions are made to you at this time, be sure first of all, that they are prompted by sincere motives, and secondly that they are quite practicable. If the ordinary affairs of your life go along quite satisfactory at this time, you should be quite satisfied, even if you do not seem to be accomplishing anything great. If your own affairs are all right, you may be worried over the health or affairs of some member of your family, or some person intimate in your life, particularly of the male sex. If the Sun in making this transit, makes at the same time, the benefic aspect of Jupiter, Venus, Uranus, etc., especially Jupiter, whether by trine, sextile, conjunction, even opposition and quintile, or the opposition of the quintile—108 degrees, then the effect of that particular transit will not be so marked, and the worst period of the year will be brought out by another aspect of the transiting Sun to Saturn, at a point of the horoscope which does not meet good aspects. And so of all the transits.

Sun in evil aspects or conjunction to Uranus—This transit causes one to feel much stirred up and very intense, and it is a time when it takes little to throw you off your poise. In the case of the conjunction and where Uranus has evil aspects in the radix to

Mercury, the Moon or Mars, it is a very disturbed time indeed, and when everything is apt to go awry for a few days. If subject to nervous trouble, this aspect will intensify them or bring them out. Be very sceptical of all propositions made to you at this time, and if you have any new ideas of a radical nature for conducting your business or life at this time, be cautious about putting them into execution, and it will be better to wait and see if, after the passage of this transit, they will still seem to you as practical or attractive as they did. If you feel totally out of harmony, dissatisfied with your condition and with the people about you, restless, nervous and on edge, be patient, as it is a condition that will soon pass off. This aspect is apt to bring the element of the unexpected into the life, and events of a sudden and unlooked for nature are apt to happen. If you have any important matters under way, do not be surprised if they suddenly fall through at the last moment, as it is of the very nature of Uranus to bring disaster at the last moment.

Sun in good aspects of Uranus—including quintile and sesquiquintile, 108 degrees—This is a very favorable condition for having dealings with corporations, the government, and large enterprises out of the ordinary, and it is well to make the most of opportunities which lead up to you at this time. It is favorable for any work of an initiative character, inventing, untried enterprises, or asking favors of people of intellect, genius, attainment or power, and in a general sense, for anything of an unusual type. This transit brightens up the intuition, adds vim and snap to the activities, tones up the system, and is an excellent aspect under which to plan anything which needs special effort, and in the doing of which one needs all of one's inspiration and nervous force.

Sun transiting the favorable aspects of Saturn—This is not at all important in respect of the fact that Saturn is a restricting and negative force, and there is not likely to bring about any particular marked event of effect. It is an aspect of self-control, conservatism, caution and during the operation of which one has oneself in hand more or less and its influence will serve to tone down the effect of any Martial or Uranian aspect which might for the time be in force. It would be a favorable time for seeking favors from old people, for listening to advice, for attending to precautionary measures, and favorable for routine work, finishing up work that has been already begun, or attending to matters which are by their nature slow, heavy and monotonous. Favorable for matters which are by their nature connected with the earth, real estate, or old conditions. Whatever of good this aspect brings will be on account of its tendency toward control, moderation and caution, and by process of elimination rather than initiation of the opposite.

Sun in evil aspect of conjunction to Neptune—This is a very unreliable influence, and in all cases, except those where Neptune is a very utilized force, it is best to be sceptical of the people one meets at this time, any propositions made to you, and there is likely to be an element of fraud playing about you during its continuance. Your own ideas are likely to be impractical and un-reliable, and tinged with some emotional or altruistic streak which may be very pleasant to experience and very dangerous to take too seriously. In the case of the conjunction, however, where Neptune has favorable aspects in the radix, it might be well to attend to any ideas which come to you at this time, as in this case they are likely not only to be actuated by motives of a very high order, but also capable of fit and successful expression. In other cases, if at this time you feel peculiarly nervous, ill at ease, and depleted or depressed, try to get away from your accustomed surroundings, and from the people with whom you are normally most intimate, as there is something in your mutual magnetisms which need adjusting, and you are probably being unfavorably acted upon on the psychic plane. A brief change of surroundings and associations will be the best possible thing for you. At this time you are likely to be appealed to through your sympathies, and any propositions made to you under these vibrations are likely to be "bubble schemes," or an attempt, however laudable, to get something for nothing by appealing to the higher vibrations in you, so keep your eyes open, and carefully investigate any plans put before you, or any suggestions to reap a quick harvest, they will usually be either impracticable, founded on crazy ideas, or else deceptive, visionary or otherwise unsatisfactory, and above all, see that the person is not trying to pull the wool over your eyes.

Sun in favorable aspects to Neptune—A very subtle vibration and probably apprehended by very few individuals, and not of very great importance unless the horoscope shows Neptune to be active and vital. In this case it usually brings to bear aspiration of a very spiritual and transcendental order, throwing into activity the altruistic, devotional, unselfish and serving elements of the character, inspiring one to acts of kindness, charity, love of one's kin, etc., and it is the most favorable time for experience of a high order, whether purely psychic or emotional. Under these vibrations, one may experience ennobling sentiments, and undergo spiritual or religious phases but it all depends on the condition of the horoscope; and in a great many cases the more delicate the subtle essence of Neptune is quite lost among the coarser vibrations of Mars, Jupiter and Saturn. In practical ways, little can be said of it. Neptune works mainly on the psychic plane; but it would at least be well not to disregard any unusual influence which might enter the life at this time as it would be likely to be of some importance spiritually, and meant for one's higher development; and it is under aspects of this sort that inner experiences come.

Sun in favorable aspects to Jupiter—Just as Saturn marks off the most unfavorable periods of the life, and the Sun's transits to him, the most troublesome periods of the year; so the Sun's aspects to Jupiter point out the most favorable periods of the year from the material and general standpoint. These vibrations are magnetic, health giving, toning up the system; giving courage through confidence, faith, hope, ambition, strength and efficiency to the whole being. It is the time to ask favors of those in power; from the wealthy, from one's friends or relations and particularly the male sex, and at this time one naturally approaches people in such a manner as to stir the best in them. When one has confidence, one naturally inspires confidence. Accordingly, almost anything of a reasonable nature that one undertakes at this time will go through at this time satisfactorily; and it is an exceedingly good time for work of a constructive and an initiatory nature, and if you have any important financial matters to attend to, this is the best time in which to do so. Do not reject any propositions made to you at this time, and any people you may meet, so long as it is not in a purely social way, are likely to be friendly to you and favor your cause.

Anything that you commence at this time should go forward fairly well and any plans or propositions that come up to you are likely to prove important and beneficial, even if at first they may not appear so. This aspect is favorable for health and favorable for one's dealing with the male sex, as well as for the members of the family. In all respects the periods covered by the Sun's aspects to Jupiter will be the most fortunate and beneficial of the year, unless it should happen that the Sun forms at the same period the very evil aspects of the malefics; which will hardly happen at every transit; although it might start some of them especially where Jupiter is heavily afflicted, and when the Sun's conjunction will not bring the benefit that it should.

Sun in evil aspect to Jupiter—This cannot be considered a very evil aspect as it is not at all depressing or unhappy in its influence; for to the contrary it is very hopeful, confident, sanguine influence, but far too much so and in this lies the evil, for it inspires people to be too confident, too hopeful, too sure and to think that there is safety where there is really danger. It is therefore treacherous influence financially, although not indicating a severe loss; but nothing at this time is likely to turn out satisfactorily or according to one's wishes, and it is a transit under which one's expectations are likely to be disappointed through being too expensive. It is best not to trust people who bring you propositions at this time, they are likely to be impractical or misrepresented. The prospects may read well but there may be very little at the back of it. People at this time are likely to allay your fears, hold out promises and raise your hopes, but if they do so, be on your guard, as the aspect promises little. It is a poor time for an initiative work, and especially where money is involved, and it is likely to lead to eventual loss. It is a poor time for law and for legal affairs and in the case of the square or the opposition, where Jupiter is afflicted by Mercury at birth, it is indicative of litigation, endless worry and vexation, red tape, form, ceremony observance and all the time killers that can be thrown in the way of the unwary. It is a safe rule not to allow oneself to be drawn into any financial or legal affairs at this time, and to be most cautious where money is involved. If Jupiter is afflicted at birth by Uranus, Saturn or Mars, it is a time when serious loss may take place. On the personal side, this aspect means enthusiasm, unwise impulse, the tendency to make greater promises than one can fulfill and in a general way, a too great expansion of the feelings that may result in foolish expenditure, indiscreet generosity and in some cases religious mania or excitation. In a word, one should avoid at this time allowing one's self to be carried away by one's feelings, hopes or ambitions and expectations, which in this case, are likely to be unreliable and misleading.

Sun in the aspects to Venus—There are several aspects of minor import whose results are similar and sometimes several of them come at the same time. These are:

Good or bad aspects of

Sun	to Venus
Venus	to Sun
Mars	to Venus
Venus	to Mars

All these have the effect of rousing the emotional or sex nature, and making one more susceptible to beauty, music, art, the attractions of the opposite sex, amusement, pleasure, love of dress and finery, and making one more magnetic; and in the case of the favorable aspects, especially of Venus to the Sun and the Sun to Venus, it is a good time for planning social affairs, amusements, and for pleasures generally, or for arranging meetings with those for whom you care and with whom you wish to enjoy yourself. The evil aspects have all the effect of making one magnetic and putting one in the right mood for enjoyment, but under their influence things are not likely to go so smoothly, or to one's satisfaction, and one may be inclined to force issues, strain the natural order of circumstances in order to gain a point, or in some way to act foolishly and inadvisedly. The transits of the Sun to the places of Venus, geo and helio, radical and progressed are worth watching, for under the conjunction or even the trine or sextile, one sometimes meets people who play an important part in life; but if there are no important transits of the major planets operating on Venus at the time, and particularly of Uranus and Jupiter, nothing of note need be expected. However, very pleasant influences are always brought about by the Sun to the conjunction, sextile, trine Venus; Venus conjunction, trine, sextile Sun: and even Venus aspecting her own place by good aspects, while the aspects of Venus to Mars and the contrary, when good, increases the magnetism, promotes gaiety and lively amusement; and in the unfavorable aspects act very strangely on the emotional nature, and inclines to indiscretion and dangerous impulses. As a general rule, do not plan social matters, meetings with friends, and all things which concern pleasure, art, music, etc., on the bad aspects more than you can help and the more favorable aspects that you can find to the places of Venus, whether from the Sun, Mars, Venus or Mercury or those of Venus to Mercury and the Sun, and the Moon transiting a favorable aspect only concern things of a transitory nature, the really important things and lasting affairs come under the major transits.

Sun in evil aspects to Mars—Mars in evil aspects to the Sun— Mars here gives force and energy to the feelings. The native is inclined to adopt a too dictatorial attitude, to act on impulse, to use force, to try to drive things through regardless of the feelings of others, and as a result, quarrels, misunderstandings, and even violence may result, according to the horoscope. The thing to do is to try to keep in harmony at this time, to use patience and discretion, to avoid forcing issues, and whatever might be attempted at this time is likely to be founded upon impulses that are misleading. Conditions of unpleasantness, of great intensity are sometimes brought about through the transit of Mars to the Sun, but owing to the transient nature of that planet, they are short lived, and nothing should be done, no great alterations made, and no issue taken on this aspect—it always tends to cause people to do things for which they are sorry very soon after; and as soon as the Martial aspect disappears, they are apt to find that they had no good safe or sane reason for acting.

Mars transiting the Sun is an indication of quarrels, differences and misunderstandings with the male sex, and in the nativities of married women difficulties with the husband, or in others, with the father, lover or any male intimate in the life. It also indicates danger of accident, sometimes, and especially when making the transit while Uranus or Saturn are afflicting the Sun by transit at the same time. This planet in transit also is likely to bring about sudden attacks of illness of an inflammatory sort to aggravate evil conditions already prevailing, and while positive and vitalizing in its nature, it may result in those forms of ill health that are caused by fever, overactivity, excitement, overheating and the like. Never judge a transit of Mars as either dangerous or lasting unless either Saturn, Jupiter or Uranus are in aspect at the same time of the transit; as in the case of Roosevelt who had Uranus squaring the Sun and the helio Mars in conjunction the day he was shot. If Uranus had not been in aspect too, Mars would never have caused it. (T.R. had also a progressed secondary direction of Mars to conjunct helio Saturn radical on ascendant in Leo, very near square of the radical Sun at the time—according to the Nautical Almanac "EDM.E.P.") Mars transits the Sun two or three times a year, and it is only when some ponderable body assists, that danger really threatens. The other possible case is where, for instance, the radical Sun is afflicted by Mars, on the progressed horoscope by other planets; as events are caused (1) by violent concerted attack of planetary aspects to one point of the horoscope, (2) by attack of several planets in transit to several points of the horoscope, especially where it is possible to find more than one point of the horoscope, whether by direction or radix, that indicates a similarity of effect—as for instance, where the radical Sun might have the conjunction of Mars radically, and the progressed Sun the square of Uranus radically; and where both points were afflicted in transit by Mars, the Sun and either Jupiter, Uranus or Saturn, and especially the last two. The main point at issue being that the simple transit of Mars can do no more than stir up minor disagreeables, which, however, are very marked and threatening while they last. The transit of the Sun to Mars is similar in nature, but not as marked in effect. The radical place of Mars is not a vital point, though it is an afflicted one.

Sun in good aspect to Mars, Mars in good aspect to the Sun— not so important, and simply indicates the time when the vital forces are active, a good time for enterprises, for health, for pushing thru those things which require courage, energy and initiative. It distinctly favors health and would be a favorable period for the adoption of forceful or drastic measures; for operations or for any form of force. It is a good foil for the evil influences of Saturn and stirs up the activities, prevents too great a degree of stagnation, engenders a positive attitude, and is a tonic influence. It is neither so powerful, so lasting or beneficial as Jupiter, but it is a force of a similar sort, but more active, assertive and indicates activity and particularly physical activity.

Sun to Mercury—Mercury to the Sun—Not of importance, if Mercury is afflicted at time of birth then it becomes very important, and the nature of the influence will be in accordance with the particular aspect. It, of course, vitalizes and intensifies the mental action, and in the case where Mercury is fairly well conditioned, it gives force, energy and activity to the mind. It is then good for correspondence, for planning ideas, for all matters which concern papers and documents and legal affairs, but this will only be where Mercury is well supported, the very contrary being the case where it is not.

The Sun to the evil aspects of Mercury a worrying, fretful, restless and nervous aspect, tending toward change, movement, uncertainty and confusion and more especially of course, where Mercury is afflicted by Mars, Uranus or the Moon. Events are likely to become chaotic at this time, and matters mixed and tangled, with consequent indecision, hurry, confusion and strain. It is best not to make important decisions under this aspect, unless there are favorable aspects of Mercury at the same time, or unless the place of Mercury is very well aspected.

In a general sense, the Sun brings things to pass, although it is not the only influence which does so, but this much will be true; the Sun seems more or less, to concentrate the forces in the direction of his transits; that is to say, if matters of a more or less Martial character are under way, the transit of the Sun over Mars will precipitate things, and the same of any other. The transit of the Sun to afflicted points of the horoscope are very evil times, and it takes very powerful and positive aspects otherwise to mitigate the effects. If you have some particular or important matters pending, and it has to culminate at a time when the Sun is trining your Jupiter, it is equally good. It is not a good idea to commence things when the Sun is aspecting the malefics in your horoscope, and it is good to commence matters when the Sun has the favorable aspects of the benefics; or the favorable aspects of the malefics according to the nature of the matter. The transits of the Sun are very important, and very vital, which can be readily learned from the fact that the transits of the Sun over Saturn depresses everybody, devitalizes and brings things to a momentary standstill; whereas the transit of the Sun to Jupiter or his favorable aspects, does the contrary, and while the Sun is transiting the favorable aspects of Jupiter, everything goes well, unless at this particular aspects, the Sun meets the evil aspects of Saturn or Uranus, or a number of minor impediments. But, of the minor aspects, the Sun's are the most vital and important.

THE TRANSITS OF THE PLANET MARS

Mars in conjunction or evil aspect to the Moon—This stirs up the emotions and the senses, and in horoscopes that are uncontrolled may lead to excesses, petty violence, displays of temper and domestic brawls. It usually indicates trouble with or through women. You may be worried on account of some woman intimate in your life, or your domestic affairs may be unsettled and troublesome. You may have trouble with some woman, and at this time, it is necessary to exercise self-control and caution so as not to do so. Annoyance with or through women is the commonest concomitant of this aspect. It also can indicate some trouble with your health, and if the Moon is afflicted at birth it is likely to cause feverish complaints, functional troubles, or slight accidents. You are likely to be excited or angry, and it sometimes causes a journey or makes you want to travel.

Mars in favorable aspect to the Moon—not at all important.

Mars transiting the conjunction, square or opposition of his own place—This usually stirs up the energies, and under this aspect self-control, diplomacy and caution are needed. Where Mars is afflicted at birth, slight accidents are possible, especially where Mars afflicts Mercury, when trivial mishaps may occur through carelessness or recklessness. Where Mars afflicts the Sun at birth it sometimes causes slight cuts, abrasions or fevers. If Mars, at birth, is afflicted by Saturn or Uranus, then these times may bring accidents, but not as a rule, unless some other planet is transiting the evil aspect of the radical Mars, Saturn or Uranus at the same time.

Mars in conjunction or evil aspect of Jupiter—This is an aspect of impulse, expansion of the feelings, generosity, carelessness and recklessness in the matter of expenditure in finance. It indicates heavy expense, unsatisfactory purchases, extravagance, loss, theft and the inclination to take financial risk. It is the typical aspect of loss. Under this aspect, make no important purchases or you will find that you have not acquired what you really wanted, the article is not satisfactory, you have paid too much for it, or you have bought under impulse something you could very well have done without. Do not be careless about property as you may lose it or be robbed. Hold fast to your pocketbook. Don't speculate or take chances where money is concerned. In a general way, and outside of the financial consideration, which is the most important in the case of this aspect, don't be guided by your feelings, don't be too generous, too magnanimous, and avoid fanaticism, the over-expression of your sentiments, dogmatism. It is also an aspect typical of religious mania, so do not trust any sudden impulse to do quixotic or generous things, or make rash promises or you might find out that you have made a serious mistake, promised more than you can possibly perform, or otherwise committed yourself unwisely. Avoid legal matters; you will probably lose.

Mars in the good aspects of Jupiter—The favorable aspects of Mars to Jupiter tend to acts of generosity, courage, and heroism, to deeds which are prompted by nobility, high sense of duty, manliness and magnanimity; to largehandedness, to the free expression of the religious instincts, to proselytizing, to hospitality, kindness and tolerance towards enemies, and to all the deeds which befit the attitude of the strong and the able towards the weak and defenseless. It gives rise to any and every species of action which one naturally identifies with the true nobleman. It tends toward expenditure, but not toward loss.

Mars in the conjunction or evil aspect of Saturn—This is an aspect of great inharmony, and one is likely to feel bitter, abused or badly treated without due cause. It is apt to make things difficult, and for the time being your work may not go right, you may be subjected to treachery or jealousy, and you should be very careful not to place yourself in accidental situations. The temper under this aspect is a little fractious and troublesome, and the tendency to be revengeful and to brood over wrongs more marked.

Mars in conjunction or evil aspect of Uranus—This makes one feel disagreeable, and unless one exercises self-control the temper is likely to be troublesome and vicious, and antagonism is easily aroused. Accidents sometimes happen, and one's work is likely to go wrong, one is apt to feel reckless, act on very hasty impulse, and to take chanecs in a rather wild way. The utmost caution is always needed under this aspect.

Mars in conjunction or evil aspect of Neptune—This arouses the emotional nature and is apt to attract peculiar conditions. Where Neptune is afflicted at birth by the Moon or Venus the sense nature is much stimulated and the imagination very active. There may be a tendency to self-gratification, danger of indulging in drugs or narcotics, and states of great excitability. Where Mercury aspects Neptune at birth—this transit is rather hysterical and very emotional and it is hard to keep to one's work and to follow a settled course. The temper is strange, easily aroused, and quickly dispersed.

THE MAJOR PLANETS

The Major transits are the most important element in the science of prediction, and everything that can happen to the human being is determined, mainly, by these. The critical times in the period of transit will be those times when the Sun and Mars swing also into aspect with the superiors; as for instance, when the transit of Mars afflicts the body that is at the same time afflicted by Saturn and Uranus; these are very marked and very threatening. Even Jupiter in the evil aspects is dangerous in much afflicted nativities; and the combined transit of Saturn and afflicting Jupiter, or of Uranus and afflicting Jupiter, over heavily afflicted points in the nativity must be regarded with caution and suspicion.

It is very important that one never lose sight of the fact that most of the events of life are produced by combinations of transits, affecting radical and progressed places; and that no one transit over a single place is ever productive of important events; it is always the combinations that are of consequence.

The very marked periods of a person's life are produced by the coincidence of two or three important transits over two or three important radical or progressed places; the planets transiting being those that hold significant places in the natus; especially when angular or when the places tarnished are angular. The most marked effects are (in regard to a single department of life) when both the progressed and radical places of a planet, helio and geo., are either all afflicted at the same time or all benefitted at the same time. Also when both the radical and progressed ascendant are attacked at the same time, etc., when, for instance, all four positions of Mercury are so attacked with very little assistance from favorable angles, and Mercury is radically afflicted, the tendency of nervous disorder is very marked, and the mind is in a great state of confusion. When all four places of Venus are so attacked by the malefics at the same time, a period of great unhappiness or grief is likely. And finally, when Sun, Moon and Venus are all afflicted at the same time by transit, the consequences are likely to be very marked, indeed.

But when the radical Sun is afflicted by Saturn, the progressed Sun being at the same time benefitted by the transit of Jupiter—even though Saturn does afflict the radical Sun by this transit (evil aspect) then the consequence, at least as long as Jupiter assists the progressed Sun, are not likely to be all serious, unless the radical Sun is very heavily afflicted at birth and the progressed Sun is in a position that also meets several evil aspects. Jupiter, normally, is well able to ward off the worst effects of Saturn so long as he continues near the aspect, but it must be remembered at the same time that no planet *nullifies* the action of any other planet.

Suppose the radical Sun is squared in transit by Saturn and trined by Jupiter; each of these bodies will have its particular effect, and while the square of Saturn will bring some misfortune into the life; the trine of Jupiter will bring some good fortune which in the aggregate will greatly compensate for the evil done by Saturn. But will not really do away with the influence of that planet—Saturn will have his effect.

THE TRANSITS OF THE PLANET JUPITER

Jupiter in favorable aspect to the Sun—These are among the most marked periods of the life, when the health is good, the spirits above par, everything is prosperous, and new opportunities are arising; and Jupiter brings, when aspecting the Sun, times of recuperation, the attaining of one's object, financial improvement, and in all ways heads the ill effects of the malefics. Jupiter is in favorable aspect to the Sun during a very large proportion of a person's life, and especially when you consider that the progressed Sun has also to be taken into account.

First, it is favorable for one's dealings with the male sex. The father, the husband, or any man intimate in the life; and at this time the men associated with you closely are inclined to be happier, more fortunate, in better health and spirits, and kinder, more considerate, and beneficial to you. It is a general signification of health and prosperity to the male side of the family.

It is favorable to any man with whom you are associated in business or in any way that is not strictly social; and it is the best time in which to enter upon new relations with men, make partnerships, or to establish business connections. It usually brings into the life men who play a helpful and beneficial part in your destiny, and it also brings offers and opportunities in a business way to men, and sometimes offers of marriage to women. It is a splendid aspect under which to marry.

It is also favorable financially, one's money matters go along smoothly, and money comes in without delay, obstruction or trouble. It indicates freedom from delays and hindrances, and the clearing of the way for the accomplishment of ends. It always ushers in a better financial period, although if the radical Jupiter is afflicted at the same time by Saturn, the results from the financial standpoint may not be so marked.

It is also favorable for honors, attainment of position and power, bestowal of favors, advance in rank, and in a general sense will materially aid in bringing your plans to completion. Whatever you undertake under this aspect is likely to succeed. If you inaugurate new movements under it, they are likely to prosper. Friendships made at this time are likely to prove beneficial. Partnerships entered upon are satisfactory. For a woman, the men she meets and becomes interested in are likely to prove fortunate for her. Opportunities arising at this time should never be neglected and one should plan to take advantage of the periods of Jupiter to the fullest extent by putting oneself in line for meeting new people, by embracing opportunities, and by being open to suggestion and chances that arise during this aspect. It is a time when one can safely take a chance, and it is a very strong promise of sure success to enter upon an undertaking when Jupiter is making the approach to a sextile, trine or conjunction of the Sun.

For a woman, it works out the same way. Povided that she is in any sense professionally employed or in the business world; and as this is not usually the case, the aspect works out through her health and through her relations with the men with whom she is associated. It benefits the husband and all men who concern her intimately, even her sons (though you will regard testimonies gathered from the 5th for sons, the 3rd for brothers and 7th for the husband, etc.), and it indicates a period of success for them. It is the aspect par excellence of material prosperity, advantage, opportunity and success.

Jupiter in opposition or square to the Sun—This aspect, not usually noticed much by the astrologer, but certainly very important, is, in a general sense, favorable for health and spirits, making one cheerful, confident and optimistic; but it tends to surfeit, congestion, and dispose tissue and is not really and finally a favorable aspect at all. The case of the square, it has a very misleading trait, which has led the astrologer to attribute to the square of the radical Jupiter to the Sun the benefits that belong to the trine and the sextile; this arises from the curious fact that when Jupiter is squaring the Sun geocentrically he is quintile to the sun heliocentrically, and when he is quintile to the Sun geocentrically he is squaring the Sun heliocentrically, so that there is a double aspect, and it will be better to reckon the square as not so evil as the opposition, as the latter will have no compensating aspect. In the case of the square, there are likely to be present some of the effects of the good aspects and some of the effects of the bad, although, of course, the consequences of the quintile can hardly be as powerful as those of the conjunction, trine and sextile.

The tendency is toward the arising of opportunities that appear very favorable and in which one takes great stock and has high hopes, but the outcome is never satisfactory, there is often more expense than profit and hampering conditions. One is often obliged to put up with certain forms of limitation, particularly along lines of that species of circumstances where the conditions are outwardly favorable, apparently prosperous, and in which all the attendant incidents are well-appearing, but in connection with which one is dissatisfied, tied down and restless. One has to submit to authority of those who follow what one knows to be false standards, wrong or mistaken methods, to be annoyed by various harassing conditions, and always in such a way that the thing on the outside seems to be all right and has much to commend it. One of the chief concomitants is increased expense, misled ambitions and aspirations, ambitions directed in the wrong channels, and one finally finds out that one cannot get along that way.

This is a poor time for important financial matters, for entering upon new enterprises, for attempting to gratify one's ambitions, for expecting increase, advance and honors. It is also a poor time for legal affairs and for dealing with people of wealth and power, and while it may bring certain opportunities into the life, they are never very satisfactory.

Jupiter in conjunction and favorable aspect to the Moon—This is singularly fortunate for one's dealings with the public, for travel and for domestic affairs, for personal happiness, for one's relations with women, and usually at this time some woman plays a very important and helpful part in the life. It is very favorable for the health and affairs of the wife, mother, or any woman intimate in the life, and is a harmonizing, peaceful influence under which your private and personal affairs are likely to be well ordered, your senses under control, your instincts normal, and it favors conservatism, regard for the conventions, improved ways of living, well regulated habits, and good health. It is a very fortunate time in which to make domestic changes, and any made at this time are likely to be fortunate. It is a fortunate time in which to make the acquaintance of women, and favors and kindnesses are likely to come through them. Any woman entering your life at this time is sure to be beneficial, a good influence, and likely to assist you in some financial way. If your domestic affairs are at all involved, and, in the case of a amn, his matrimonial affairs, this aspect serves to straighten things out, and in every way it operates favorably upon the private life. At this time your emotional nature is more under control, your feelings are directed into more healthy and normal channels, and it is a time for reform, of reconstruction, and the abandonment of evil courses. It is, of course, especially favorable for the health of a woman. People whose business connects them with the general public will benefit at this time, especially politicians, and the like. It is a fortunate aspect under which to marry, for a man.

Jupiter in evil aspect to the Moon—Your domestic affairs at this time will be well-ordered, but you are likely to be hampered and interfered with at this time by influences which are too conservative, too conventional, and people who are too much taken up with the externals of life. You are likely to be compelled, for the time, to follow certain lines of action of which you do not approve and to hold yourself in check, and act in a more conventional manner than is your wont. It is unfavorable for the health and affairs of the wife or mother and domestic affairs are likely to be expensive, and there may be a tendency at this time for too much display, extravagance, and show. This is not a very important aspect, but quite annoying in some ways.

Jupiter in conjunction or favorable aspect to Mercury—Under this aspect, you will receive stimulus toward mental advancement, and particularly in the direction of making of practical use of the knowledge you have or of acquiring the more practical end of any subject, in which you may be interested. For instance, suppose that you are interested in Astrology, and you have the transit of Uranus over your Mercury, this will cause you to seek for new ideas, to extend the theoretical knowledge, and to know and understand more about the more difficult problems, to try experiments, enter upon research work, etc., but the aspect of Jupiter will cause to feel that you want, now, to bring all your knowledge to a practical standpoint, to make it useful and profitable, and since Jupiter is the planet of finance, and of practical constructiveness, you can readily see that it causes you to treat your knowledge in such a way as to make it useful, and so it does not mean the acquisition of new ideas so much as the ordering, application, extension and practical understanding of the old ones. You will increase your stock of useful knowledge, you will increase your efficiency and practical ability, and by the time the aspect has passed on, you will be in a better position to use the time and profit by the ideas you had. It causes one to study, to reach out for learning, to consult authorities, to reduce their ideas to system, to listen to the advice and counsel of others, to be more tolerant and more amenable to reason and less critical, less incredulous, and it usually brings someone into the life whose knowledge, advice and encouragement aid one in this task. It is a splendid aspect under which to take up definite courses of study, especially those prescribed by authority, and to reach out for mental honors. It favors writing, correspondence, and all legal affairs, it is fine for the judgment, it is a good time in which to make important decisions which will influence your future, and in every way it brightens up, vitalizes and makes efficient the action of the mind. It is a most important influence, a good aspect under which to speak or write, to publish, advertise, but the most important influence is what has already been mentioned, namely, to enable you to put your ideas into shape. Suppose a case—while Uranus was in aspect to Mercury, I would think up new ideas, investigate theories, invent and make them practical, put them in right shape for use, complete them, fill out all the details, and "market them." So, under this aspect, people are likely to improve their working methods, business men are likely to improve and put to rights office management and it is also a favorable aspect for one's relations with employees, especially clerks and the like. It frees one from worry, makes minor matters go smoothly, and means content, satisfaction and cheerfulness. It removes nervousness, irritability and fretfulness, gives confidence, sociability and causes one's relations with people generally to be more satisfactory.

Jupiter afflicting Mercury—This is a bad time for legal affairs and litigation, bad for making important decisions affecting matters of finance, and tends to loss, worry over money and property, and while not a disastrous aspect, or very evil, tends to a condition of affairs which is very unsatisfactory, because the mind is in a very sanguine condition and one's hopes and expectations will hardly be realized. It tends to wrong conceptions, causes one to be compelled to exercise the mind on matters which are hardly interesting or really profitable, associates one with people who try one's patience, and annoys one with their red tape, officiousness, conventionality, etc., and it is quite an annoying aspect. Unless Mercury is afflicted at birth or by direction, it is not necessary to expect much of this aspect. It is, however, unwise to enter legal matters, or undertake important correspondence or study under this aspect.

Jupiter in conjunction and good aspect to Venus—This is one of the most favorable transits that can occur in a minor way in the nativity. It brings new friends, pleasant social affairs, presents, favors, happiness, personal comfort and contentment, invitation, kindness and consideration from friends, and usually brings someone into the life who plays a helpful part, particularly in the way of stirring up and gratifying the better and more wholesome side of the emotional nature. It is a very healthy satisfactory influence, and tends towards relations which are at the same time perfectly in accord with the conventions and perfectly pleasant in every respect. It favors visits to old friends, intercourse with relatives, and one's home, and it is a very good aspect under which to visit old friends or relatives, to effect reconciliations, marriages, any and all social affairs, artistic affairs, and it indicates in the lives of the artistic, gain and success through their particular art. It always brings pleasurable and beneficial experience into the life and is socially constructive. This is the time to extend your acquaintance, to pick up friends, to broaden your social horizon, and to take up the broken threads of interrupted friendships, particularly will it be quite sure to bring some very pleasant influence into the life, whether male or female, someone who will minister to your pleasure, afford you considerable happiness, and in a general way make life happier for you. You will be in a mood for enjoyment, and yet inclined to seek normal and healthy forms of it, and its influence is strongly against any form of pleasure which is not wholesome. This will especially apply to the trine, sextile, and quintiles, as the conjunction, if it occur in a place where there are many afflicting aspects meeting, it may not be able to overcome the abnormal tendencies, but it will at least throw its influence in that direction. It is under this aspect that people take fresh courage, get younger and more spontaneous, attend to their dress and appearance, are more magnetic, more cheerful and more social and naturally seek the fellowship of their kind. It nearly always brings favors, kindness and *presents*. It is always wise to plan for some trip, important social affairs, important artistic matters, holidays, and journeys for pleasure. Visits to people of whom you are fond, marriages, when you see this aspect coming on, as no matters of this sort can go very badly under this aspect unless there are contradictory aspects of a very powerful sort.

Jupiter in evil aspect of Venus—If you refer to the contrary aspect, namely Venus to evil aspect of Jupiter, you will get the coloring of this, without the necessity of repeating all the details. It ushers in a period where you are apt to be associated with people who bore you with their overconventional attitude. You are likely to have a great many invitations, favors and even presents that you don't want and would rather be without, and it has a sort of stifling effect that a close room overheated has. Of course it is not in every horoscope that these effects come out quite so strongly, but that is the phase of the aspect.

Jupiter transiting conjunction or evil aspect to Mars—It seems to me that I gave you this, but in case not, here it is. This is expansive to the feelings and emotions, leads to acts of courage, unselfishness, religious enthusiasm, generosity and disregard for money and tends to extravagance, carelessness and sometimes loss. It is, in a general way, threatening financially, as all of Jupiter's aspects are to planets by square, opposition or semi-square, or an afflicted conjunction. I was robbed under the following configuration: Jupiter entering Scorpio opposite Neptune and Mars radical and square to Mercury, helio, with Saturn entering Taurus in opposition. It was through sheer carelessness, as I did not properly guard my things, and thought it perfectly safe to leave things exposed. The conjunction or favorable aspects to Mars are good for soldiers, doctors, surgeons and those who follow Mars professions, or are engaged in work of a dangerous, enterprising or arduous nature, where the principles of courage, strength and initiative are called out.

Jupiter in conjunction or good aspects to Saturn—This is not important and tends to economy, prudence and care in matters of finance. This aspect is restrictive, and produces nothing positive, but favors dealings with old people, things connected with old conditions, the earth, real estate, mines, house or land property, and is a very good time to start a bank account, enter upon financial matters with regard to one's distant future, etc.

Jupiter in evil aspects of Saturn—This is a slightly restricting unfavorable aspect for financial matters generally and is a delaying, hampering and interesting aspect. It slows down the benefic rays of Jupiter, and if Jupiter is making the good aspect to some part of the horoscope, meets this aspect, it must, to a large extent, prevent the full effect of Jupiter, and slow down his vibrations. It is an annoying aspect, but not of the greatest importance, as good aspects to the radical place of Jupiter can easily offset the influence.

Jupiter in good aspect or conjunction to Uranus—Favors financial gain through inventions, discoveries, new enterprises, corporations, etc., and sometimes brings money unexpectedly, and through peculiar means. If the place of Uranus is much afflicted, beware of the conjunction as it may bring sudden and unlooked for losses, and cause financial fluctuations of a very spasmodic order. Both to Uranus or Saturn, the good aspects of Jupiter sometimes bring inheritance or legacies. Jupiter in the evil aspects of Uranus is a very uncertain influence, and at this time money you expect may not come to you, or you may have strange losses or unexpected misfortune, in a financial way. The aspects of Jupiter to the superiors have these effects financially, but not in the degree that the aspects of the superiors to the body of Jupiter do. At the same time, while Jupiter squares or opposes Uranus, it is a poor time in which to take chances, speculate or play in games of chance where money is involved. The same when Jupiter afflicts Mars.

Jupiter in conjunction or evil aspects to Neptune—This awakes the altruistic side of the nature, makes one charitable and more unselfish, and one is likely under this influence to give to charity, to spend money on the needy, and to generally be "easy" and readily bamboozled. It is a very spiritualizing influence, and often awakens the religious side of the nature to a great extent. It leads in the direction of a purer and more spiritual form of belief and worship and inclines one to do all he can to make practical the spirit of Christianity. This in superior horoscopes, of course. Its chief danger, otherwise, is in its subjecting one to feelings of generosity and compassion which are apt to be misused and taken advantage of by others.

THE TRANSITS OF THE PLANET SATURN

As the chief instrument in the Universe of all the ills that flesh is heir to, Saturn easily takes the prize for making trouble, and his aspects, as he slowly wends his way around the horoscope, are always productive of some form of discipline, sorrow and affliction.

Saturn in conjunction or evil aspects to the Sun—First of all, this has a debilitating effect upon the constitution, lowers the vitality, and makes one susceptible to any diseases to which one is subject. It is a depressing and devitalizing influence, and one of the chief causes of ill health. The transit of Saturn in the first house of the horoscope is similar in this respect, lowering the whole vibratory rate of the individual. Nothing goes just right under this condition (to the Sun) and everything slows down, is delayed, and meets with obstacles and hindrances. It not only affects your own health, but is also evil for the health and conditions of the males closely connected in your domestic or business life. Sometimes it brings about marked changes and even deaths. Everything is retarded at this time, and in order to accomplish anything, you have to make more effort than usual and you are easily discouraged, easily tired, and often misunderstood and blamed for things for which you are really not responsible. It brings blame from superiors, and troubles in employment. It is wise at this time to take things about as they come and try not to force conditions at all. You cannot at this time be too careful whom you trust in a business way, and this is the very worst time in the world to initiate new ventures, start any important undertaking, or enter into any new relations with men. To a woman, it brings generally inharmony in the married life, trouble and misunderstanding with the husband, fiance or lover, and is a very bad condition under which to enter into relations with men, become engaged, married or enter into any agreement whatsoever. New men that come into the life are likely to turn out disappointing in the end. If nothing more, it brings some broken friendship thru misunderstanding. The best advice in regard to this aspect is the following: First, guard the health—see that you don't get run down, anemic, or below par. Second, don't force conditions, and when delays and obstacles spring up, don't try to sweep them away forcibly. Next, don't enter into partnership with a man or become engaged, married, or enter into intimate relations under this aspect, as he will bring you sorrow, responsibility, care and worry, and perhaps deceive you in the bargain. He is likely to be married, or in some way tied up so that he can't in any case really belong to you. Next, avoid misunderstanding with the men in your life at this time, and don't allow Saturn to make you too dissatisfied with existing conditions. This aspect does not necessarily affect the financial conditions although it may do so and will if Jupiter is also afflicted at the same time but usually the way it works is to make you dissatisfied with existing conditions, have trouble with men with whom you are associated, want to change your employ, and if married, sick and tired of your husband who won't be very magnetic, agreeable or pleasing under this aspect, and it would be very easy to make a great mistake. As soon as the aspect passes, things will readjust themselves. If men treat you wrongly, or unjustly, this will straighten out when the aspect is passed. Until then take the line of least resistance, be patient and wait for the dawn.

Saturn in good aspect to the Sun—Is very unimportant, slightly restrictive, tends to moderation, prudence, caution, may serve to hold back otherwise unfavorable conditions, and is wholly negative.

Saturn in evil aspect or conjunction to the Moon—This is also evil for the health, but in a functional way, and is likely to bring on troubles such as are signified by the Moon's sign at birth, or other planets which afflict this point. It is depressing and discouraging in a personal way, unfavorable to the domestic affairs, and productive of trouble with or through women. You may be anxious over the health or affairs of some woman intimate in your life at this time, such as the mother or wife, or else you may have trouble with or on account of some woman. Some woman may be jealous of you, take occasion to dislike you, treat you wrongfully, or abuse you, and at this time, no matters in which women are concerned in your life can turn out satisfactorily. You will be dissatisfied with your environment, either want to travel, or else do so, and it is always a heavy, dull, unhappy or uninspired period from the private and personal standpoint. There will be something in the home or private life which is a source of anxiety or unhappiness. Some woman may pass out of your life, and sometimes it brings the death of the mother or wife. It is always a bad time for a married man, and at this time his wife will be sick, disagreeable, or a cause of worry and trouble. In the case of women, they will also have trouble with or through their own sex.

A man should not marry under this aspect, or enter into relations with women, as in this case they will in the end prove a burden, bring unhappiness into their life, and play a restricting part. It is also evil for dealings with the public, as for instance, in the case of a politician, who depends on the public vote. It brings unpopularity, and sometimes, in the case of the afflicted Moon, disgrace. The women who enter your life at this time are bound to disappoint you, cause you worry, unhappiness and trouble.

Favorable aspect of Saturn to the Moon—is good for dealings with elderly women, tends to self-control, caution and prudence in private affairs and control of the senses. Not important.

Saturn in conjunction or evil aspects to Mercury—This is very disturbing to the mentality and depressing, too, and the memory and concentration are poor, while the tendency is to try very hard to overcome the obstacles, as Saturn is a plodder. It tends to pessimism, incredulity, and scepticism, unbelief, doubt, mental distress, and the careful examination of your mental outfit, with a view of throwing out whatever seems unfit. It causes people to change their point of view on many matters, to question matters they have held for a long time and during this aspect you are likely to be very uneasy, unhappy, rather subject to moods and the "blues." It tends to mental effort, hard study, and patient effort, which, however, results in little benefit unless there is some good aspect at the same time. At this time, avoid the law, litigation, disputes, and be careful of what you put in writing. Your correspondence is likely to be unsatisfactory, and it is well not to ask favors in writing, as you would be likely to put things in such a way that no good will follow. This aspect sometimes brings important changes and journeys. It also tends towards trouble with the voice, and colds in the throat and chest.

Saturn here sometimes brings someone in the life whose views and opinions have a very detrimental and worrying effect upon you, and owing to whom you get unsettled. You are bound, under this aspect, to have cause for worry, depression, and fear, and some circumstance is sure to come up to cause it. It may bring very serious and harassing conditions where Mercury is much afflicted at birth. It is a poor time under which to undertake studies, writing or speaking.

Saturn in good aspect to Mercury—Tends to mental continuity, patience, perseverance, careful and earnest study, and though quite negative, is good, but not very important.

Saturn in conjunction and evil aspects to Venus—This is one of the most disagreeable aspects in the whole range, but as you know, if the place of Venus is not afflicted, it will not work out in full force. It causes a person to be more sensitive, easily slighted and more exacting with those around them than is usually the case, and you will be led to feel that people do not care for you as much as they should, etc. One expects too much of their friends, and when they are not able to meet your demands, you may feel hurt, become indifferent, and disconnect yourself from any of your old friends and acquaintances. It causes you to be less magnetic in a personal way, less in the mood for enjoyment, and disposed to magnify and brood over slights, neglects which may not be at all intended, or are caused by circumstances which are beyond their control. Any feeling of jealousy should be avoided and if you feel that your friends are treating you with less consideration than usual, be sure, first of all, that you are not imagining two-thirds of it, and in the next place that your own attitude is not responsible for the remainder, and remember that the harboring of such thoughts is sure to drive away from you the very ones you wish most to hold.

This aspect seldom passes without some sorrow, whether in the form of death of someone dear to you, or the separation from someone you love. New friends made at this time are likely to bring more of sorrow or discipline into the life than pleasure or benefit. This aspect of Saturn to Venus is very unfavorable for social affairs, which do not go rightly, you will be disappointed in things not turning out pleasantly. The people you wish to meet will not be presented to you, or your plans for pleasure will be disappointed. It is an unhappy influence under which to play gaiety, amusement, or anything of the sort, and it is unwise to expect much from a vacation, a social engagement, or a visit, or a meeting between friends, or a love affair, marriage, or anything which concerns the personal happiness under this conditon. Do not marry, become engaged, or arrange for any important social meeting under this aspect. It is particularly bad for artists, actors and musicians as well as poets or all those whose work depends upon art, and at this time their work will not be satisfactory, they will not be magnetic, and their efforts are not likely to be crowned with success. It was owing to the square of Saturn to Augustus Thomas's Venus that he lately has such failures dramatically. It would be the height of folly to plan for a concert entertainment, reading dramatic work, or anything of that nature under this aspect, unless there are very strong contradictory aspects, as for instance, if Saturn were squaring one Venus, Jupiter trining another, and Uranus assisting another, (as there are four), and in all cases, it is very evil for Saturn to be afflicting the radical places, as this leaves more permanent results for evil. In cases where Jupiter were benefitting one, but Saturn afflicting the other, you might expect some good results but some setbacks and owing to Jupiter, the thing might be financially satisfactory, but owing to Saturn it would go off rather dully, and not be altogether a credit, and so of all the others. In the personal way, friends met under this influence are sure to be disappointing in some way and it is an evil omen unless powerfully contradicted.

Saturn to the favorable aspects of Venus—is unimportant, tends to control the affections, regulate the emotions, form associations with older and more serious people, and is a purely negative influence. It does work in the direction of preventing unwise impulsive attachments, and adds to the power to withstand temptation, and set with caution and prudence in matters of the affections.

Saturn afflicting Mars or in conjunction—Is apt to make one feel abused, ill treated and sometimes brings treachery and stirs up jealousy and enmity. One should avoid feeling bitter, revengeful and avoid also cruelty, unfeeling acts, and unkindness, as well as an unforgiving spirit. It is apt to bring very trying experiences, to make one's work difficult or arduous and often brings accidents especially if Mars is afflicted. The accidental condition is very important, and must not be overlooked. People, under this aspect, are apt to feel abusive, very bitter toward the world, and express themselves rather harshly and vindictively.

The good aspect is not important, except as a restraining force and tends to the government and regulating of the impulses.

Saturn in conjunction or evil aspect to Jupiter—This aspect tends toward economy, prudence, caution and circumspection of financial matters, in conjunction. It slows all financial affairs and often brings in a period in which matters of this sort are delayed, hindered and money is scarce, or expenses large. Usually, when anyone is in financial straits, Saturn is afflicting Jupiter. It does not tend so much to loss, as it does to expense. Small returns, delayed payments, etc. This is an unfavorable time for making investments, or for taking chances where money is concerned, and you will be sure to do the wrong thing. Everything at this time tends to lower the bank account. If you own property, it will need repairs, be an anxiety or decrease in value. It is a poor time for considering building or buying real estate. It is a poor time also for reaching for honors, getting involved with the law, and it is best at this time to be diplomatic, settle disputes out of court, and run no risks financially. It lessens one's faith in oneself and the Universe, and destroys confidence. During the period of Saturn's affliction to Jupiter, especially if the place of Jupiter is afflicted, a great deal of financial trouble is likely to result, and it is a good thing to have the two places of Jupiter well separated, so that Saturn cannot get at them at the same time. This aspect is unfavorable for the liver, makes it sluggish, and you should avoid biliousness and torpid liver.

In conjunction where Jupiter is not afflicted, it is good for economy, real estate, matters of land and house property, and all affairs where returns are slow and sure.

The favorable aspect of Saturn to Jupiter favors care, thrift, saving, and caution in financial matters, and is also good for real estate, farms, house and land, mines, etc. This is a good aspect under which to invest in some slow, sure form of investment, and anything of the nature of Saturn.

EDITOR'S NOTE: The author gave no indication of his experience of the transit of Saturn to Uranus or Neptune.

THE TRANSITS OF THE PLANET URANUS

If the transits of Jupiter are the most beneficial and those of Saturn the most unfortunate, those of Uranus are the most important and interesting. Uranus is the developer, the bringer to the surface of the latent possibilities, and he augments the powers of the planets he aspects to the nth power.

If any point in the horoscope awaits development, there is nothing that will bring it out more than the transits of Uranus, and there is nothing that will afford experiences of the unusual type more readily than the conjunction – – – adverse aspects of this planet. The greatest opportunities – – – of life come, as a rule, from the conjunction, trine, and sextile of the Sun, and the periods in which this aspect rules – – – always marked. If the Sun is aspected favorably, – – – becomes very important. At the time of the founding of the – – – Society, Uranus was on H.P.B.'s Sun, and – – – it. She had the Sun opposite to Uranus radically, and – – – crisis in her life. The combined transit of Uranus is most powerful, irresistible, and destructive in evil aspect to the Sun, or other important parts of the horoscope.

This is a very important transit, and first of all, will bring people into the life who will afford the means of developing and utilizing the latent possibilities. It stirs up the ambitions and activities, awakens the latent energies, and supplies the means of enlarging the sphere of influence, and bringing the native in contact with larger affairs than he has here-to-fore met. It often connects one with governmental matters or corporations, and with inventions, untried enterprises, and undertakings of a unique and unusual sort. Anything may come of this aspect, and as it is in the nature of Uranus to bring the unexpected into the life, whatever happens is likely to be not in accord with preconceived plans, and one may expect the unexpected. Opportunities drop from the clouds.

This is a very constructive influence, and a very propitious time for having dealings with people of unusual ability, unique characters, and those whose interests are Universal, and who are concerned in large undertakings. It favors preferment, and the realization of hopes, wishes and ambitions you may have been cherishing for years, and this aspect seldom passes without bringing opportunities of an unusual sort which should not be neglected, as they are likely to lead to large developments. The people with whom you will be thrown at this time will be powerful, well disposed, and especially those you might meet for the first time. Under this transit, people of large calibre always enter the life, and it is for you to utilize them, and let them utilize you. It increases the powers, the ambitions, the nervous energies, and the efficiency, and it is likely to be a most active and interesting time generally.

To a woman, this aspect also presents great opportunities. It usually brings into the life men of power and prominence, and those who are interested in some man of parts. It is highly fortunate for any man who might be in her life at the time, whether the father, husband or otherwise, and indicates success, increased power and opportunity, and the possibility of their advancement and promotion. Under this influence, a woman is more magnetic, has more power over the men in her life, and is in every way more powerful for the time. It is impossible to say just what it will bring, or just what peculiar changes may take place in order to bring about the desired advancement, but it is always favorable and a very active influence. It is a good time for her to seek favors from men of wealth, power and ability, and to further both her own interest and those of any man in her life. Any man coming into the life under this influence is likely to play a very important, helpful and interesting part, and to appeal to the highest and best in her.

The Sun transited by the square, opposition of Uranus, or the conjunction when the Sun is afflicted at birth—This is a very disturbing influence, and first of all leads to nervous diseases and complaints of an obscure type which the average physician finds it hard to diagnose or cure. Next, it arouses and intensifies the ambitions, makes a person restless, dissatisfied with old conditions, conventional ways of doing things, and turns the ambitions in the direction of untried, novel and sometimes impracticable undertakings, mostly connected with inventions, discoveries, corporations, and the government, and usually the ideas one has regarding these things are unsafe, much too sanguine, too ahead of the times, and impracticable. One is likely to be thrown with people who encourage one in these ideas, and who are either misled, fraudulent, or else totally unwise. It is often a cause for a man to be very ill-advised and always he advocates the unpopular cause, the thing that can never be attained, and he feels inclined to force issues, to pit his individual will against the "world-will" which Uranus in a sense represents, and the result is bound to be disastrous. One is led to take unusual and extraordinary points of view, and to antagonize those with whom one works, associates, or his business dealings, and the usual result is the loss of friends, especially the safe and sane ones, and those that are really trustworthy and one is left the victim of the woozy, the dishonest, and the dissatisfied. It is impossible for a man under this aspect to feel satisfied with things, and it is also impossible for things to be· satisfactory. The aspect is, in its nature, confusing, worrying, leading to intense activity, usually misdirected and therefore productive of anxiety, great expenditure of energies, and nothing to show for it. Things seem to promise well to the last minute and then fall through without a moment's warning. Nothing can really be trusted that is not strictly along the lines of the greatest conservatism and nothing of a new, venturesome order ought to be taken up at this time. But that, of course, is just what will be taken up. It causes sudden deaths, separations, and misunderstandings with the family life or the business life, on the male side always. The father may die, the business partner die, or something unexpected and unlooked for usually eventuates at this time—always from the most unexpected quarter. In very well balanced horoscopes, the aspect might pass without much disturbance, but where the Sun is at all afflicted, such will be the case, and it is quite the most radical and extreme of all the transits. The thing to do is not to allow oneself to make important changes under this influence, as it is totally misleading, and any important change made under it is not likely to turn out well at all, but be disastrous.

In the case of a woman, it is very disturbing to the married life, usually bringing about misunderstanding, and sometimes death of the husband, but always complicating things, being evil for the business interests of the husband, and health and affairs of the man in the life generally and usually brings some very strong influence into the life in the way of a man, who is a fascination in some way, a great temptation, and endanger the future interests. Under this aspect, women are led astray, leave their husbands, and do all sorts of foolish things, and if married, the husband at this time is likely to be a severe trial, and things go very wrong. Usually the time a man enters the life, is married, or at least has not "honorable intentions" and to the unmarried, it frequently brings a marriage or an engagement which ends disastrously, and the influence that comes in under this aspect does not last long. As a rule, it enters very suddenly and leaves as suddenly, and usually in some peculiar way, and the first meeting usually is more or less unconventional. It is the worst possible influence under which to become engaged, marry, or enter into relations with a man, and nothing really and permanently good can possibly come of it. The main things for both men and women are the following: Don't take up new schemes, or if you do, don't expect things to turn out as you plan them. Don't play too far ahead, for Fate will overturn all your plans. Expect the unexpected. Don't trust new people. People that approach you in a business way, or with enterprises, are unreliable so watch out for yourself. Don't overdo or you will have a nervous breakdown. Avoid the impossible, the impractical, the new and visionary, and be as sane, safe, conservative and humdrum as possible. Be prepared to accept the inevitable. (This is the aspect that destroyed Teddy Roosevelt.)

Uranus in conjunction, or evil aspect to the Moon—Conjunction with afflicted Moon—This is as disturbing to a man as the Sun is to a woman. It upsets the domestic life, usually causes the ill health of the wife or mother or some woman in the life, and turns the private life upside down and he is lucky if there is not some form of scandal connected with it all. The wife is apt to have some nervous complaint, be ill, or in some way upset the serenity of the home. She may die suddenly. Some death is likely of a woman intimate in the life or home circle. Whatever happens will be unexpected, will come about suddenly, and all domestic plans are likely to be upset at this time. The influence of Uranus here is very disturbing to the personal life, and some woman is likely to come into the life and play a very disturbing part, perhaps cause a lot of trouble, but be very fascinating, and the men under this aspect sometimes have love affairs or sometimes their wives do unusual things. It always brings some woman into the life who has a strong influence, comes suddenly and departs as suddenly. It leads to travel sometimes, and domestic changes, and in all cases, a disordered state. The wife or mother is always a cause of worry or some other woman. It is unfavorable for dealings with the public, and sometimes brings on nervous complaints, as will be indicated by the Moon's sign, and the planets afflicting her.

Women have peculiar experiences through their own sex. Women usually have some strong female influence in their life, which is not for the best, and which is misleading and productive of disturbance and trouble and sometimes ends in sudden misunderstanding, jealousy and separation. It is a great disturbance in the personal and private life.

Uranus in trine, sextile or in conjunction—well aspected to the Moon—Tends to travel, and to interesting experiences, and brings women into the life through whom one gains mentally, gets a wider and more comprehensive viewpoint, and it has the general tendency to broaden the mental and spiritual horizon. This takes place through the help of women as a rule. Some one woman plays a very important and very helpful part in the life at this time, and "initiates" one, as it were, into bigger and better things. In 1901 with Uranus trine Moon, a woman who was herself noninterested, took upon herself to send me all books she could get hold of on Astrological sort, and "mothered" my mental development as best she could. I was so situated that I could not do this for myself at the time. She gave me absolute "carte blanche" and through her, I was able to study and get well under way. This is the sort of thing this aspect does, and always, the influence is very disinterested, very humanitarian, unselfiish, and acting along high and broad lines. It sometimes acts in a very occult manner, and always is for the uplifting, ennobling and expanding of the mind and soul. It is splendid for the wife and mother, and for all women in your life at the time. Women with this transit are apt to become interested in clubs, large movements, and humanitarian interests, sometimes travel, and always expand and enlarge their horizon. It works, as Uranus always does, unexpectedly, in peculiar ways, and does strange things. It is rather a subjective aspect, unless other planets are in the aspect, such as Mars, Jupiter or Venus, and one hardly realizes what is happening at the time. During the period I absorbed the bigger ideas of life, "ate" astrology and laid the real foundation for all my future work, as well as made my "discovery."

Uranus in conjunction to afflicted Mercury, or square or oppo-

sition Mercury—This is a very disturbing influence indeed, leading to nervous complications which arise largely from worried and confused mental conditions and too great excitability, and one's mental affairs are likely at this time to be most active, very disordered, and distracting. One's correspondence is awry, things happening unexpectedly and the tendency is in every way to throw the mind into the greatest activity and confusion. At this time one is apt to feel very much out of harmony with one's usual associates, one's accustomed ideas, and the mind is reaching out for new lines of thought, new experience and knowledge, and one feels restless, nervous, unsettled and cranky. The judgment is not likely to be as conservative or safe as usual, the memory treacherous, and it is a poor time to make important decisions. The subconscious mind is more active, one may have unaccountable moods and sensations and some unusual experience along mental lines, and it will be very hard for one to stick to routine work. It is likely that one will take up with new and peculiar ideas and be led astray by ideas which are impractical and visionary. Avoid being sarcastic and disagreeable, too critical, and you may, by adopting too radical an attitude, and being too extreme in the expression of your opinions, antagonize your associates, and have quarrels and misunderstandings with the people you ordinarily talk and live with, and this may lead to your making unwise changes in regard to your friends and associations. It tends to travel, and some sort of change is sure to arrive. For it means mental expansion, and whatever is necessary to bring this about will take place. It tends to some form of notoriety through mental affairs, such as public speaking, lecturing, writing for the press, advertising, or some form of publicity, and may bring unpleasant criticism, or involve one in some controversy, legal complications, or some form of worry that will be very harassing and annoying. Avoid quarrels, disputes, the law and try and be cautious in what you say and do, as you are most likely to express yourself unconventionally, be misunderstood, misquoted, libelled, and generally talked about for your "crazy notions," etc. Be guarded as to what studies you take up, or what ideas you follow, as you are more than likely to be led astray.

e of the conjunction, a great deal of judgment is required, as is really the case with all conjunctions, and the meaning of the conjunction is, of course, great mental development and it will largely depend upon the aspects as to whether it will be beneficial or not. In any case, new forms of thought and study and new mental experience of the most interesting sort will take place, one will try mental experiments, take up untried ideas, and meet with people who will give one the impetus for branching out. Important transits to Mercury are usually indicative of people coming into the life who associate with one, whether in connection with their business or their social life, on the mental plane, gives one the means of development, stimulates thought, and introduces one to new ideas. With the conjunction of Uranus to Mercury, at the present time, I have been constantly thrown with people who are presenting ideas of various sort to me, and who are talking about matters of occult nature, etc., and my mind is in just the state to take up some new line of thought, as well as the fact that I am doing a certain amount of speaking and getting a little publicity. You with Mercury conjuncting Uranus radically, always have a certain amount of this sort of thing. The tendency is to make the mental life more interesting, to develop the intellect, to afford new experience, to improve the expression and bring the mind to its fullest development. The conjunction favors writing, lecturing, publicity of all sorts and travel. Some dominant influence is likely to be felt at this time, and some one may come who is able to instruct and assist the intellectual life.

Uranus trine and sextile Mercury—This is very favorable, means mental advancement, activity in the intellectual realm, new friends in research, and an added interest in science, ideas out of the common, and all things which tend to develop the mind. It quickens the abilities, causes one to learn and absorb readily, to be open to new ideas, and the advice and counsel of others and one readily adopts new plans and methods for the management of one's affairs, and is more responsive to suggestions than at other times. You are likely to be brought in contact with people of inventive, scientific and progressive turn of mind and profit by association with them. Correspondence, writing and publicity are favored, also legal affairs, the press, scientific and literary matters, and it is a good time to advertise and gain publicity, and one, under this influence, says the right thing, and expresses themselves in the best way. Favorable for thinking up new ideas, inventions, dealings with the government in regard to patents, etc., and the management of anything that requires quick and able mental action. Good for lecturers, reporters, writers, journalists, and all those who use the pen largely in their pursuits. It usually brings some strong influence into the life in the way of a friend or associate who stimulates one's thought, awakens one's mind, and encourages one in broadening and developing. It is a good time in which to take up new studies, and lines of thought, and in the case of people who are not intellectual, they usually adopt new and better methods of running their business, such as installing new systems, or bookkeeping, indexing, etc., so as to make their mental work easier. Or else, they may listen to the suggestions of some scientific person, and improve their way of living or working through some means of an advanced sort. Under this aspect, people are cleverer, more ingenious, active, alert and alive than usual, and the mind works at its best.

Under the sextile of Uranus to Mercury, Uranus being in Sagittarius on the ascendant, I met one of the greatest friends of my life who assisted me in developing my mind, encouraged me in many ways, and by talking things of all works over with me, "fertilized" my intelligence. Uranus in Sagittarius was sextile my Mercury and conj. his Mercury at the time of contact. We met on the deck of an ocean steamer and both recognized the other instantaneously as a kindred mind, and from that moment, for 11 years we were in constant touch. He having the Moon square Saturn, finally, when Uranus left him high and dry, slumped mentally and I went ahead of him so rapidly after a while, that I knew I had to leave him behind. He wouldn't interest me for a moment now, and he would think I was "buggy." But, under the temporary stimulus of Uranus, he was brilliant, fertile, original and daring mentally, and for a time we made it warm for everyone. This was the time when I first woke up mentally, and was one of the means employed. The important transits to Mercury, especially of Jupiter and Uranus usually bring as I have said, important influences into the life which act upon the mind, and cause development. The greatest friendship that can happen will come under a combination where Uranus transits to aspects of Mercury, showing mental contact, while Venus is also transited by Uranus or Jupiter, showing emotional contact or perhaps Jupiter will be transiting Mercury by good aspect or conjunction and Uranus to good aspect of Venus. In other words, Jupiter and Uranus being the great opportunities, the time when they act in concert on Venus and Mercury are always times when you have the most interesting people in your life, and when you are associated with people who understand you, and who enter into your real life. As, for instance, when Uranus trines your Mercury and then proceeds to conjunct Venus, you will have such a friendship (Mercury, Libra and Venus Aquarius) and one of the best and most happy as well as intense of your life. Something to live for, for it will mean mental growth, a great deal of illumination, and since Venus is Aquarian, the stimulation of the aesthetic faculties, and a great deal of pleasure of the best sort. Congratulations!

Under the adverse aspects of Uranus to Mercury—avoid legal matters as you will the plague, and do all possible to keep the nervous system in good order. Avoid sudden changes which are "notional" and be guided by best judgment. Don't trust new ideas, and if you are interested by brilliant people, admire the brilliance, and take it for what it is worth.

Uranus conjunction, trine and sextile Venus—The conjunction well aspected—This is one of the most important of influences socially and personally and makes one very magnetic, disposed to be more conventional than usual in matters of social life, friendship and affection, especially in the case of the conjunction, and attentive to matters of dress, personal attractiveness and culture. The tendency is to develop the social side of the life to its utmost, to broaden the acquaintance, to break away from a narrow or limited environment, and there is a strong desire for companionship, love and sympathy, and a strong personal interest. This usually comes in the form of someone who plays a very fascinating part in the life, and it all depends upon the horoscope as to whether it will be a very conventional "affair" or a friendship or love affair of the very highest type. In a great many cases, this brings in the greatest and most tremendous love of the whole life, and especially if, at the same time, there be powerful aspects to Venus by direction, especially of the Sun, or Mars, so that Uranus in aspecting Venus, also gets the aspect of other planets. It is also very fortunate to have, either radically or at this time the conjunction, trine or sextile of Mercury to Venus, so that both are included in the aspect, when great mental as well as emotional and aesthetic development may be expected, and a great deal of pleasure, happiness and intercourse of the most interesting and profitable sort. The person who comes into the life under this aspect understands and seems to get more in touch with you than is ordinarily the case, and the contact of Uranus with Venus keys up the emotions, the aesthetic sentiments, and the social feelings to the utmost, so that you are more magnetic, more in the mood for pleasure, more able to take advantage of a great friendship, than would ordinarily be the case. In less advanced horoscopes, this will bring unusual experience, great happiness, a very unconventional period of social life, and tend toward experiences and contact with people that is beyond the power of the person to either control, appreciate, or live up to, and as soon as the aspect dies out, they will be left behind. It is the greatest time for forming interesting attachments that may be made to last out a lifetime, but the tendency of Uranus is to bring the unexpected, and the hero or heroine of the occasion is quite likely to arrive suddenly, unexpectedly, and somewhat unconventionally "love at first sight" perhaps, and in any case instant recognition, the feeling that you have known the person before, or some peculiar and marked psychic or intuitive incident in connection with the meeting. They "come to a climax" swiftly as a rule, the friendship progressing by leaps and bounds, and the mutual attraction is intense, but not feverish in the case of the sextile or trine. The conjunction is overpowering and unless Venus is well protected by Jupiter, Saturn, or other favorable aspects, the person is likely to act unwisely, break all the conventions and let their emotional nature play the deuce with them. It is a great period, and worth living for. The transit of Uranus over your

Aquarian Venus will be a splendid example, and you ought to get the very best of experiences, with little to regret out of it, as Venus is so well placed in this sign, and not afflicted. Augular, too. You are lucky. Then Mercury is trine also. That's worth going through years of waiting for, and aeons of boredom. You'll have the time of your life in the nicest of ways, and with the very nicest of persons. You had better begin to prepare for it.

The conjunction, trine and sextile of Uranus—is very fortunate for artistic matters of all sorts, brings great opportunities to artists, musicians, and actors, and all those who make their living through art in any form at all, and means the upmost development of their talent and abilities, and the opportunity to "come out." In horoscopes of people who are artists, this is the transit to look for, and the first aspect by sextile, trine or conjunction to Venus is likely to bring them to the front. The same in regard to literary people, Uranus transiting Mercury. It usually brings favors, gifts, pleasure, increase of social activity, new friends, and all that makes life worth while from this standpoint.

The square, opposition, and conjunction-afflicted of Uranus to Venus—Is also interesting, unconventional, and very powerful in its effect upon the emotional nature, being even more marked than the trine or sextile, and stirring up the affections to a feverish degree, causing the person to break all bonds, conventions, and ordinary limitations, and undergo a period of bohemianism, freedom and oftentimes an "affair" which may bring some notoriety, or provoke Mrs. Grundy to action. It is a time when people should try and be guided by common sense and discretion, not let their feelings get away with them too far and be a little reasonable in the demonstration of their emotions. It brings someone into the life suddenly and unexpectedly, as a rule, who is fascinating, clever, talented and who arouses the love nature to the utmost, and people met under this influence are apt to go out of the life as suddenly as they came in. Under this influence, old friends disappear, die or are separated from one, or else one gets out of patience with their old-fashioned way of doing things, their frowning and solemn respectability and determines to go the pace. Afflicted Venuses behave very giddily, their hair curls up, their complexion blots, and

their costume gets posterized. Old maids take courses in oscula-
tion, exercise the eyes, and walk around the flatiron three times
every windy day. Married ladies weary of the stale wedding cake,
and indulge in Plato, and Eleanor Glyn,—Whoops my dear!

The safest course is not to take seriously anyone who comes
bounding into your aura about this time—they will fascinate but
they will soon disappear, and "leave the wreck behind," and woe
to the maiden whose tendrils have curled around this broken reed,
for the ax of the woodman will sever her twigs. Nothing satisfactory, permanent or in any way productive of lasting happiness
comes out of this aspect, and it is disruptive to the social life of the
individual and all to no purpose. It leaves them with broken
friendships, and old shrines deserted, and all for a passing shadow,
that only irritated and upset them, and gave them no real happiness. People are prone to behave rather foolishly under this aspect,
and it takes a very steady Venus to withstand it. The worst of it is
that it inclines people to do things that bring notoriety, criticism,
and scandal, and they seem to desire to be talked about, and to aid
their idiocy as thoroughly as possible.

Uranus transiting evil aspects or conjunction Mars—This is
dangerous and indicates recklessness, want of caution and prudence, the disposition to run into danger, to take risks, and to act
upon sudden and mad impulses, to do things for love of adventure,
love of actual danger, and regardless of common sense. It causes
people to do things which they would at other times refrain from in
the way of running into experiences of the dangerous sort, taking
their life into their hands, etc., if the horoscope admits of all this,
and under this influence they are likely to do unusual and foolhardy things. It, therefore leads to accidents and mishaps and all
sorts of physical hurts. Under the aspect of Uranus square Mars in
Pisces, I had a nasty accident to my foot. It stirs up the initiative,
the element of adventure, of courage and of physical activity, and
gives love of excitement, and may make the more aggressive, quar-
relsome, positive and cause the temper to be quick, peculiar and
sometimes uncontrollable for the time being, where Mars is
afflicted at birth.

The good aspects to Mars bring out the more constructive side of this influence, giving boldness, the ability to do reckless things without danger, and run into experiences without mishap. Where Mars is prominent and well aspected, it may bring fame or notoriety through courage, war, surgery, acts of bravery or physical recklessness and adventure.

Uranus transiting evil aspects of Jupiter and afflicted conjunction—This is a very treacherous influence financially, leading to risks of all sorts, speculation, games of chance, and consequent losses. At this time, one is approached by schemes and schemers, and it is dangerous to listen to them. Take no chances where money is concerned, or you will surely lose. It brings the most promising schemes and opportunities which may appear quite practical, but are apt to "peter out." It sometimes causes one to make quite large sums of money in some unusual way, and then to have it all swept away so quickly that you hardly know you have had it. Often a bank president and people who have money in trust at these times speculate with money that is not theirs and in the hope of making large winnings but lose and are disgraced. It is an evil time for going to law, changing investments, buying or selling property, reaching out for new honors, and whatever is done in this way under this aspect nearly always turns out unfortunate. The thing to do is to be as conservative as possible in money matters, and take no chances. Uranus stirs up the ambitions and causes one to want to accomplish wonders financially, but his impulses in the bad aspects are misleading and treacherous. He also sometimes stirs up the religious instincts and awakens the more humanitarian feelings, but in these aspects, inclines to fanaticism, unpractical schemes and unreliable feelings.

Uranus in good aspect to Jupiter—This develops the spiritual powers, adds to the wish and the power to do others good, and is an inspiring influence. It broadens the sympathies and causes people to be less selfish in the attitude towards mankind generally, more generous and kind. It is a spiritual aspect and in horoscopes that favor that sort of thing it is quite likely to have marked effect. But in a very subtle way. It is a delicate influence and may bring someone into the life who aids in bringing about some change for the better in the character and this may take place through books, or in some non-personal way.

The transit of Uranus in aspect to Neptune works largely on the imaginative plane and not requiring actual physical manifestation. Whatever does take place is likely to be very personal and perhaps very occult, and the outer world may never know it, but they will be likely to realize that some change has taken place.

Note: The word "parts" is a Nineteenth Century idiom meaning "importance."

THE TRANSITS OF THE PLANET NEPTUNE

Neptune afflicting the Moon is likely to bring some woman into the life who either has an unfavorable influence morally or who leads one into unpractical lines of thought, manages to give one the wrong viewpoint or interests one in matters which afterwards prove misleading. Sometimes the wife or mother is affected peculiarly, and strange experiences come through them, or to them. It encourages psychic phases, such as clairovyance and trance, may give rise to some form of indulgence and is a misleading influence. The good aspects will, as a rule, bring some influence into the life that will prove to be uplifting and expanding and during the transit one should benefit in some rather unusual or peculiar and subtle way, through some woman. *The good aspect* favors higher thought and meditation, a deeper understanding of the more hidden laws of the Universe and may be a means of inspiration and religious experience. All depends upon the horoscope.

Neptune afflicting Mercury leads to false ideas, study along impractical and unprofitable lines, and one is apt to be deceived, led astray and waste a good deal of time and thought to no purpose. It tends to meditation, inactivity, desire for strange ideas and experiences, interest in uncommon books and subjects, and one may be associated with some person of strange mentality who temporarily influences one to take up ideas and lines of thought which afterwards prove useless. It tends to deception, fraud, peculiar experiences through correspondence and is a very woozy aspect. Tends in the direction of indulgence and immorality in such horoscopes, and leads the mind in the direction of dangerous ideas and practices.

The favorable aspect leads to contemplation, meditation, study in higher things, spiritualism, mysticism, etc., and one may, at this time, gain much unusual information and insight.

The adverse aspect to Venus of Neptune leads to deceptive love affairs where one imagines they are in love, and are really not, or where one imagines peculiar circumstances connected with the whole affair. It is a dangerous aspect, and may associate one temporarily with someone who arouses the emotions to a very great degree, and leads to peculiar mysterious and unique experiences. It is an aspect of masquerade, and it does not do to have a love affair that takes place under it. You are to be deceived and most of it will be in the mind. It tends in the direction of romance, sentiment and a most sensuous state, and may lead to, in some cases very unwise action.

The good aspect to Venus tends to friendships and attractions of a very spiritual order, where the bond is psychic and intangible. and gives the highest order of spiritualized affection. Whoever it is that is in the life at this time, is likely to play upon the higher nature and call out the most unselfish and impersonal side of the affections, and there will be a peculiar state of exaltation in regard to it. It brings often a very lofty refining influence.

The transits of Neptune are very subtle, working on the psychic plane, mostly and sometimes with apparently no effect but they must be used with discretion. In horoscopes that are not at all sensitive, Neptune cannot do much; the idea being that amid the vibrations of positive planets like Mars and Jupiter the very evanescent vibrations of Neptune are lost to sight at least and can do no more than add an impervious something to the combination.

Neptune in evil aspect to the Sun—or conjunction afflicted—A peculiar and disintegrating influence, tending to destroy the will power, acting directly upon the psychic and emotional nature and sometimes subjecting people to strange and inexplicable lines of action the motive of which will always be the desire to sacrifice oneself for indulgence to or for others. In totally sensual and self-ish horoscopes, the more the desire for indulgence of a highly exotic and emotional type. In horoscopes where the tendency is shown, they may take to drugs, indulge in fainting trance or coma and undergo symptoms of obscure sort. The best sort of treatment usually is complete change of environment and also complete change of associates—someone may be vampirizing them and it may be the one they are most fond of. It tends to forms of activity which are romantically alluring, dangerous either to the health, real interests, or incompatible with common sense, involving self-sacrifice, obliteration of the personality and the submerging of oneself in some idea and the sort of thing, for example that Father Damion did—going among the lepers. It may bring about a temporary psychic phase and under such cases—anaemia. It may bring temporary bad health so as to result in deviltry, weakness and over-strain. The advice is to avoid the weird, romantic, exotic, erotic and try to cultivate sane thoughts, keep with sane people, and be as normal as you can. This transit is likely to throw you into association with people (men) who are rather queer and don't be influenced by them. Keep the health up to par, avoid any unusual form of indulgence and you will be all right. If depleted, tired or nervous, take a few days change of surroundings, and get right away from people you are habitually related to, even if you don't like to do so. Vampirization is a very common thing under this aspect. Women may have peculiar experiences with men, or their husbands, fathers, fiances, or very good friends. May either suffer from some illness or undergo unusual experiences, or there may be something extraordinary in their relations with them at this time. Whatever it is, it will be largely the work of the imagination and after it is all over they will see that they have been deceived. Neptune is a defrauder.

The favorable aspect to the Sun is entirely to subtle and purely spiritual or psychic to pay much attention to in practical notes of this sort and you will have to watch very closely to detect its effect. It ought to be entirely on the higher altruistic plane, and ought to lead to actions and aims of a very unselfish sort, and for the time, the person may have some spiritual experience, develop some psychic phase, or be actuated by some very unusually lofty sentiment, charitable, and brings unexpected benefits through inventions or untried and novel enterprises and is a propitious time for starting undertakings in which chance plays a part, matters connected with the governments, corporations, and in general where the interests of many people are involved. It sometimes brings money from unusual and unexpected sources and is a good time to invest. It is a period of gain and financial expansion, and when any opportunities of a financial sort should be looked into, and taken advantage of and opportunities which may not at first appear favorable are likely to turn out so later. It is wise to take chances under this aspect, provided there are not very strong and contradictory aspects, and it is by branching out, being unconventional and taking a certain amount of risk that the real benefits of this aspect will appear.

Neptune afflicting Jupiter warns against bubble schemes, dishonesty, fraud, people imposing on your good nature, generosity, getting money from you on false pretense, and you should not allow your sympathies and feelings to sway you in a financial way. Under this aspect, the sympathies the altruism and the higher religious feelings and emotions are called into play, and those who come in contact with you realize that you are so actuated and will be ready to take advantage of you and assist you to part with your property, which you will delight in doing under this influence. You will feel temporarily that it is your duty to be unselfish, help the helpless to be still more helpless, increase the bread line, repopulate the park benches, and put an attractive premium on idleness, and if you live up to the opportunities of the aspect, you will have a mendicant waiting for you on every corner, three pious frauds on the doorstep, several missionaries in the parlor and when you go to church, the usher will welcome you with a fat smile. In the end your finances will have fled and you will realize the text "Seek ye first the kingdom of heaven, and his righteousness, and all these things shall be taken away from you." So the thing to do is to cultivate a stern and austere appearance and when you see the wily tear-extractor heading your way, scowl like Satan, subdue your welling emotions, and close up your bowels of compassion lest they drain you dry. It's a poor policy to buy emotional exaltations from the street vendors, go to a Tristan like a decent body and get a good sound dollar's worth of dole or attend a revival meeting, have a real nice sloppy seance with a neighboring medium, or do anything but be made a bally fool of on the public streets. Take just enough change with you for carfare, one nut sundae, and a package of hair-pins, and put your excess wealth in the porcelain pig on the mantle.

On the other hand, under the favorable aspects of the beautiful Neptune, you may safely open up and allow your feelings leeway, give your temperament an airing and indulge in a spirituality without any fear. This aspect develops the unselfish sentiments without making a darn fool of you and leads to altruism of the sensible sort. You may have some profitable and special benefits which will come your way which are unusual and for which you have done nothing. I can't be certain for I have had Neptune trining Jupiter and I don't think anything remarkable has happened.

TRANSITS

The motion of the Moon is irregular, sometimes less than twelve degrees per day, and sometimes over 15 degrees. At 12 degrees per day we have a method which denotes 1 year of life. Her motion is the same as that of the planet Saturn by transit, or, to make it plainer, say at 10 days after birth, the Moon is in Taurus 10 degrees and at 11 days after birth in Taurus 22 degrees, her motion would then be 12 degrees for the 24 hours, hence the Moon's motion would then be 12 degrees for the 24 hours, which would be 12 degrees per year or the same motion, without a few minutes, as Saturn by transit.

Now in long periods of trouble, grief or losses, you will almost invariably find the place of the Moon by local moton,* either in conjunction, square or opposition to Saturn by transit; that is,

* Progression.

suppose the place of the Moon to be in Taurus you will find that Saturn is by transit either in Taurus, Leo, Scorpio or Aquarius, and so every good direction of the Moon is destroyed by the evil transit or excitement of Saturn and all evil aspects that she may form are excited by Saturn into action, but if the Moon be swift in motion, say 14 or 15 degrees per day, she will pass the transit of Saturn in two or three years, and then the unfortunate time will be over; but where you find the Moon by direction in bad aspect of Saturn by transit and the motion of the Moon about 12 degrees per day, then the man or woman will have a long spell of bad luck, and have a hard fight against fate, and if the directions be heavy or numerous it may bring about the total ruin of the native, but look to the nativity for the intensity, length and extent of the evil will depend upon the disposition of the planets at birth.

Again have regard to the place of Uranus by transit, for when the Moon arrives by local motion to the conjunction or opposition of that place or even the square—the former are most powerful. Then a most unsettled time will occur, when the mind is in constant dread of impending evil, rather supposed evil, restlessness and annoyances.

If the nativity shows it, the native may travel or leave his native land. The motion of Uranus by transit is only about 4 degrees a year and as the Moon's least motion is almost 12 degrees, this evil is not of very long continuance. This point is decided by the working of the directions.

Now the planets Jupiter and Mars in their exciting are very transitory, their motions being very swift at times, however, and they are stationary in certain places which may produce events of longer duration. Of this you must judge for yourself. If both planets are direct, the excitement will soon be past, and the event must soon happen. Hence sudden events both good and bad are caused by the transit of the two planets over or in aspect to the place of direction.

Periods of success may be judged by the position of the Moon and Saturn chiefly.

When Saturn by transit is in sextile or trine to the place of the

Moon by local motion it is good provided the Moon does not run against Uranus. A lull in success will occur and for a certain time the native's affairs will be upside down.

The evil transit of Uranus to the Moon does not cause so much loss of money as it does perpetual worry and excitement. A dread of evil about to happen is present. If the veil is likely to operate on the private affairs, which may be learned from the nativity, the effect will be serious, leading to discord, jealousy, separation, adultery, loss, change of employment. The native will act rashly without thought or reason.

Now respecting the Sun, he is very important in every nativity and rules chiefly the life and honor of a man. His motion is 1 degree per day, sometimes a minute more and sometimes a little less. His average motion per day is about 1 degree, which, in our method of reckoning, would be 1 degree per year. Hence, the transits of all the planets to the place of the solar directions are soon past as no planet moves at less than 2 degrees per year. Notice the periods when Saturn by transit forms the conjunction or other bad aspects of the Sun by local motion and if a bad solar direction happens about the same time, heavy losses, ill health, loss of honor and credit will follow—but Uranus is the chief destroyer of credit. When the Sun and Uranus are in bad aspect, either by direction or transit there being a bad solar direction to some other planet at the same time, much trouble will pour in upon the native affecting his honor and credit. If Saturn afflicts the Moon at the same time, much misfortune will occur and probably result in the ruin of the native.

When the Sun and Moon are both afflicted in a nativity, it is a very dangerous time for the health and welfare of the native. Death frequently occurs at such a time.

If the nativity does not show an accident, do not judge one. Let the directions be what they will, the same with sickness, for if the nativity be a healthy one it will take much stronger directions to produce sickness than if it is unhealthy.

The house in which the transitory planet is placed, for instance, Saturn afflicting the Moon from the ascendant, he predisposes to a grave and melancholy state of mind, grief, and sorrow and denotes damage by the native's own acts, or thru errors in judgment.

If from the 2nd house, it will affect his money, property, or even his liberty, and so on with the other houses, because the excitement comes from a certain house and the evil will arise by or thru something ruled or signified by that house.

As the transits of planets over the places of the planets at birth or the luminaries, they signify nothing except when a direction occurs at the same time. But transits of planets thru different houses in the same nativity are very important. Uranus by transiting the Midheaven and the Moon by direct conjunction, square or opposition, produces worry and trouble in business, perpetual alarm, affliction to native's mother. But if Uranus were in the 11th, evil would come from friends or something ruled by that house, and the same with the other houses.

The Moon as noted moves very fast, and in many cases before she is clear on one aspect or direction she is applying to another. This is why the positions of the planets by transit have such potent effects.

I will here mention that there are what I call unimportant nativities, or such wherein the planets are mostly cadent, and in common signs. In such cases the direction must be very potent to produce any great results, and many small directions will pass without being observed.

The former will be chiefly obscure persons, such as are in the employ of others, but if you find the planets in Cardinal signs and angular, then every direction that is excited to action will tell in a marked degree and produce events prominent and observable and such persons will generally be noted characters or masters and employers of men, etc.

Observe also the Moon when it is slow in motion by direction for this is not good for success and gain. The Moon slow in motion in a nativity is also unfavorable. Swift in motion signifies success, activity and progress in general. Hence when Saturn afflicts the Moon as mentioned, and the Moon is slow in motion, it is very bad, but if the Moon is swift, the evil is not so great. If the relations of the Moon are swift, the evil is not so great. If the relations of the Moon and Saturn are of a benign nature, and she swift in motion it is very good, but if slow, the benefit will not be so great.

Saturn rising in any nativity gives some impediment in the speech, more especially if he be in Aries, Taurus, Cancer, Leo, Scorpio, Capricorn, or Pisces, and Mercury at the time being in evil aspect will cause the native to stammer and he will be of a very nervous, suspicious temperament and can easily be overcome by mesmerism.

By looking steadily at the native he will be unable to speak at all, unless with determined effort, that shakes the whole frame. If Mars should be in aspect to Saturn it will improve the speech and one will stutter less, but will talk fast and lisp badly. It is a curious fact that persons with Saturn rising have very round tongues. That is, the end of the tongue is round and not pointed whereas the Mercurial and Lunar persons have sharp pointed tongues and can articulate very clearly and fluently. If Mercury be in Sagittarius or Pisces, or even Cancer and rising and not in any aspect to Saturn, the native will be a great talker upon whose words not a shadow of dependence can be placed.

Venus and Saturn in conjunction, square or opposition makes persons with a depraved taste and the practice of bad and unnatural habits. They are much attached to places and persons and have very keen feelings. Such persons suffer disappointment in love, sometimes committing suicide, and if Mercury be afflicted by Saturn they will be much given to shed tears and will cry and weep bitterly upon slight provocation.

THE CUSPS

You may hear someone say, "I am born on a cusp." What does that mean?

The expression is used to mean a birth date that is on the line between two signs of the zodiac. In other words, someone born on

April 19 might be considered to be born on a cusp. Was the Sun in Aries or was it in Taurus?

Many wonder why astrological books and other literature do not agree as to what day of the month the Sun leaves one sign and enters another.

There is a good reason for this. It lies in the fact that society has adopted a calendar that is not at all accurate.

One book may give the Sun in Aries on April 19, while another gives the Sun in Taurus on that date. In one year, it may be in Aries, and in another year it may be in Taurus. It varies from year to year. Nor does the Sun enter Taurus exactly at midnight as we leave one day behind and begin another. It can make the change at any time during a 24-hour period.

Perhaps it is in Aries until 11:33 A.M. on April 19 and in Taurus after that. The following year, it will be completely different. If it is in Aries until 11:33 A.M. Greenwich Time, that means 6:33 A.M. New York Time, 5:33 A.M. Chicago Time, 4:33 A.M. Denver Time or 3:33 A.M. Los Angeles Time. There are many factors.

Thus, if you were born on April 19 at 10:00 A.M. in Los Angeles while another person was born at 10:00 A.M. in England, one of you would have the Sun in one sign, the other in another sign. Twins born a half hour apart might have the Sun in different signs.

The zodiac itself is a mathematical figure. It is a circle divided into 12 equal parts. It is divided by 12 mathematical lines. A mathematical line has no width. Consequently, the Sun may be partly in one sign and partly in another; but technically it is the center of the Sun, a mathematical point, that interests us. When does this mathematical point cross this mathematical line? That's what we want to know. It isn't too easy to find out.

The American Ephemeris and Nautical Almanac will supply us with the information down to the second, but even this information is somewhat questionable, because although astronomers claim such preciseness, there is no real way to calculate that accurately. An astronomer can measure through a telescope, but no telescope furnishes us with that kind of accuracy. The Sun is over 90 million miles away. Where is its center? Just where is that mathematical point?

When Russia sent its first space probe to Venus, it was a perfect hit except for one thing. Venus wasn't where the astronomers said it was. It was 22,000 miles away from there, and that's why the Russians missed. The engineers were accurate, but the astronomers were not. Yet the Sun is more than three times farther away than Venus was at that time. If the astronomers can be wrong by 22,000 miles relative to the position of Venus when it is at its closest point to the earth, imagine how wrong they can be about the Sun.

This may explain to you why tables showing the date when the Sun enters a particular sign of the zodiac may appear to be in disagreement. It enters the sign at different times for different places on the earth, on slightly different dates in different years; and on top of that, the most accurate information at our disposal is not too accurate.

Theoretically, the Sun is in one sign or it is in another, because it is that mathematical point in the exact center which counts—not the Sun itself. The mathematical line that separates two signs has no width, and a mathematical point can be on one side of it or on the other. It could be on it theoretically but only for a time element that has no width, and consequently no real existence. Thus, nobody could be born within a time element that has no real existence. *The Sun has to be in one sign or the other.*

If you were born on the cusp, how can you know which sign the Sun was in on the day you were born and at the time of day when you were born?

If you consult an astrologer and have him calculate the position for the time and place of your birth, you are likely to have the right answer. But there might be an occasional case where it is so close that you cannot be sure. In that case, you must study the characteristics of the two signs and decide yourself which "fits" you. In most cases, you will find that one set of characteristics fits while the other set does not. Two adjoining signs are never similar in characteristics. They are definitely different.

Yet there can be confusion for other reasons. Characteristics are not determined by the Sun position alone. All the planets plus the Moon have to be considered, and the zodiacal sign on the eastern horizon, where the ecliptic crosses it, is vitally important. If you are born at or near sunrise, then both the Sun and Ascendant are going to be in the same sign, and you will take on the characteristics of that sign to a much greater degree.

One person might be born at sunrise at a time when most of the planets are in one zodiacal sign, as they were on February 4, 1962. This individual would be a very pronounced type. He would be almost all of one sign. There are other people who are born when the planets are scattered all over the sky, and these people will have many different characteristics from different signs. Some of them will be in complete conflict with themselves. Any psychologist knows there are such people, filled with disturbing elements.

Theoretically, to be a pure type, a person would have to be born at a time when all planets, Sun, Moon and Ascendant were in one sign, and insofar as we know, that has never happened—at least not during recorded history.

If there is doubt in your mind about whether a person was born in one sign or the next, try an experiment we have tried. Take a good writeup of each of the two sign characteristics. Select about five people who know the person well, ask them to read the two interpretations and tell you which one fits best. See if they don't agree. We have found that usually they will all select the *same* interpretation.

Yet, there can be exceptions. One person might have the Sun in Taurus but a number of planets in Aries. In that event there would be both Aries and Taurus characteristics, and this could confuse the observers, with the result that some of them might see more of the Aries, while others would see the Taurus. If the Sun is on the cusp of Taurus, any astrologer can check to see whether there were any planets in Aries on that particular day.

The planets can also get involved with cusps. It would be almost impossible to measure the exact day when Pluto crosses from one sign into another because it is so small and so far away. You can't see it without a powerful telescope. Thus there are cases where it would be very difficult for us to say which sign Pluto might be in, but not many such cases, because it takes Pluto many years to go through one sign.

In the old astronomy, it was assumed that light travels in straight lines, but today we know that the course of light is distorted through space, and things may not be just where they appear to be when we look through a telescope. At the time of an eclipse we can sometimes see stars that we know are behind the Sun. We couldn't see these stars if light traveled in straight lines. Errors of this kind can also knock out of line all the figures by which astronomers have calculated the distance to stars by triangulation.

It is not always easy to be certain about some of these cuspal factors, but because the characteristics of two adjoining signs are quite different in nature, this should not give you too much trouble. A Fire (vital) Sign is always followed by an Earth (physical) Sign. Where the Fire Sign has energy and vitality, the Earth Sign has endurance. A Fire Sign is quick on the trigger, shooting from the hip, while an Earth Sign is slow to get started because of conservatism. An Earth Sign is always followed by an Air Sign. The Air Signs are intellectual. While the consciousness of an Earth Sign is concerned with the physical, that of the Air Sign is concerned with ideas, principles and abstractions. An Air Sign is always followed by a Water (emotional) Sign. The Water Sign always sees everything through its own feelings, and consequently, everything takes on the coloring of the feelings and that which has already been accepted as true by the emotions. The Water Signs are inclined to see what their emotions tell them to see. If one Water Sign could be followed by another Water Sign, it would be more difficult to distinguish between them, but it is not possible.

You will find it very helpful to keep a notebook containing the birthdays of all the people you know born under the different signs. You will soon see that all the Leo people have certain characteristics in common. They are not like the Virgo people. The more you study large numbers of people, the clearer these characteristics will become, and then when there is one Cancer person who appears to be in some way different from other Cancer people, you can quickly detect it. Before you know it, you will be so interested that you will be studying astrology in earnest, looking up planetary positions, calculating aspects and setting up horoscopes for the exact moment and place of birth.

MELVIN POWERS SELF-IMPROVEMENT LIBRARY

ASTROLOGY
____ ASTROLOGY—HOW TO CHART YOUR HOROSCOPE Max Heindel 7.00
____ ASTROLOGY AND SEXUAL ANALYSIS Morris C. Goodman 7.00
____ ASTROLOGY AND YOU Carroll Righter 5.00
____ ASTROLOGY MADE EASY Astarte 7.00
____ ASTROLOGY, ROMANCE, YOU AND THE STARS Anthony Norvell 10.00
____ MY WORLD OF ASTROLOGY Sydney Omarr 10.00
____ THOUGHT DIAL Sydney Omarr 7.00
____ WHAT THE STARS REVEAL ABOUT THE MEN IN YOUR LIFE Thelma White 3.00

BRIDGE
____ BRIDGE BIDDING MADE EASY Edwin B. Kantar 15.00
____ BRIDGE CONVENTIONS Edwin B. Kantar 10.00
____ COMPETITIVE BIDDING IN MODERN BRIDGE Edgar Kaplan 7.00
____ DEFENSIVE BRIDGE PLAY COMPLETE Edwin B Kantar 20.00
____ GAMESMAN BRIDGE—PLAY BETTER WITH KANTAR Edwin B. Kantar 7.00
____ HOW TO IMPROVE YOUR BRIDGE Alfred Sheinwold 7.00
____ IMPROVING YOUR BIDDING SKILLS Edwin B. Kantar 7.00
____ INTRODUCTION TO DECLARER'S PLAY Edwin B. Kantar 7.00
____ INTRODUCTION TO DEFENDER'S PLAY Edwin B. Kantar 7.00
____ KANTAR FOR THE DEFENSE Edwin B. Kantar 7.00
____ KANTAR FOR THE DEFENSE VOLUME 2 Edwin B. Kantar 7.00
____ TEST YOUR BRIDGE PLAY Edwin B. Kantar 10.00
____ VOLUME 2—TEST YOUR BRIDGE PLAY Edwin B. Kantar 10.00
____ WINNING DECLARER PLAY Dorothy Hayden Truscott 10.00

BUSINESS, STUDY & REFERENCE
____ BRAINSTORMING Charles Clark 10.00
____ CONVERSATION MADE EASY Elliot Russell 5.00
____ EXAM SECRET Dennis B. Jackson 5.00
____ FIX-IT BOOK Arthur Symons 2.00
____ HOW TO DEVELOP A BETTER SPEAKING VOICE M. Hellier 5.00
____ HOW TO SAVE 50% ON GAS & CAR EXPENSES Ken Stansbie 5.00
____ HOW TO SELF-PUBLISH YOUR BOOK & MAKE IT A BEST SELLER Melvin Powers . . 20.00
____ INCREASE YOUR LEARNING POWER Geoffrey A. Dudley 5.00
____ PRACTICAL GUIDE TO BETTER CONCENTRATION Melvin Powers 5.00
____ PUBLIC SPEAKING MADE EASY Thomas Montalbo 10.00
____ 7 DAYS TO FASTER READING William S. Schaill 7.00
____ SONGWRITER'S RHYMING DICTIONARY Jane Shaw Whitfield 10.00
____ SPELLING MADE EASY Lester D. Basch & Dr. Milton Finkelstein 3.00
____ STUDENT'S GUIDE TO BETTER GRADES J.A. Rickard 3.00
____ TEST YOURSELF—FIND YOUR HIDDEN TALENT Jack Shafer 3.00
____ YOUR WILL & WHAT TO DO ABOUT IT Attorney Samuel G. King 7.00

CALLIGRAPHY
____ ADVANCED CALLIGRAPHY Katherine Jeffares 7.00
____ CALLIGRAPHY—THE ART OF BEAUTIFUL WRITING Katherine Jeffares 7.00
____ CALLIGRAPHY FOR FUN & PROFIT Anne Leptich & Jacque Evans 7.00
____ CALLIGRAPHY MADE EASY Tina Serafini 7.00

CHESS & CHECKERS
____ BEGINNER'S GUIDE TO WINNING CHESS Fred Reinfeld 7.00
____ CHESS IN TEN EASY LESSONS Larry Evans 10.00
____ CHESS MADE EASY Milton L. Hanauer 5.00
____ CHESS PROBLEMS FOR BEGINNERS Edited by Fred Reinfeld 7.00

____ CHESS TACTICS FOR BEGINNERS   Edited by Fred Reinfeld 7.00
____ HOW TO WIN AT CHECKERS   Fred Reinfeld 5.00
____ 1001 BRILLIANT WAYS TO CHECKMATE   Fred Reinfeld 10.00
____ 1001 WINNING CHESS SACRIFICES & COMBINATIONS   Fred Reinfeld 10.00

COOKERY & HERBS

____ CULPEPER'S HERBAL REMEDIES   Dr. Nicholas Culpeper 5.00
____ FAST GOURMET COOKBOOK   Poppy Cannon 2.50
____ HEALING POWER OF HERBS   May Bethel 5.00
____ HEALING POWER OF NATURAL FOODS   May Bethel 7.00
____ HERBS FOR HEALTH—HOW TO GROW & USE THEM   Louise Evans Doole 7.00
____ HOME GARDEN COOKBOOK—DELICIOUS NATURAL FOOD RECIPES   Ken Kraft 3.00
____ MEATLESS MEAL GUIDE   Tomi Ryan & James H. Ryan, M.D. 4.00
____ VEGETABLE GARDENING FOR BEGINNERS   Hugh Wilberg 2.00
____ VEGETABLES FOR TODAY'S GARDENS   R. Milton Carleton 2.00
____ VEGETARIAN COOKERY   Janet Walker 10.00
____ VEGETARIAN COOKING MADE EASY & DELECTABLE   Veronica Vezza 3.00

GAMBLING & POKER

____ HOW TO WIN AT POKER   Terence Reese & Anthony T. Watkins 7.00
____ SCARNE ON DICE   John Scarne 15.00
____ WINNING AT CRAPS   Dr. Lloyd T. Commins 5.00
____ WINNING AT GIN   Chester Wander & Cy Rice 3.00
____ WINNING AT POKER—AN EXPERT'S GUIDE   John Archer 10.00
____ WINNING AT 21—AN EXPERT'S GUIDE   John Archer 10.00

HEALTH

____ BEE POLLEN   Lynda Lyngheim & Jack Scagnetti 5.00
____ COPING WITH ALZHEIMER'S   Rose Oliver, Ph.D. & Francis Bock, Ph.D. 10.00
____ DR. LINDNER'S POINT SYSTEM FOOD PROGRAM   Peter G Lindner, M.D. 2.00
____ HELP YOURSELF TO BETTER SIGHT   Margaret Darst Corbett 7.00
____ HOW YOU CAN STOP SMOKING PERMANENTLY   Ernest Caldwell 5.00
____ MIND OVER PLATTER   Peter G Lindner, M.D. 5.00
____ NATURE'S WAY TO NUTRITION & VIBRANT HEALTH   Robert J. Scrutton 3.00
____ NEW CARBOHYDRATE DIET COUNTER   Patti Lopez-Pereira 2.00
____ REFLEXOLOGY   Dr. Maybelle Segal 5.00
____ REFLEXOLOGY FOR GOOD HEALTH   Anna Kaye & Don C. Matchan 7.00
____ 30 DAYS TO BEAUTIFUL LEGS   Dr. Marc Selner 3.00
____ WONDER WITHIN   Thomas S. Coyle, M.D. 10.00
____ YOU CAN LEARN TO RELAX   Dr. Samuel Gutwirth 5.00

HOBBIES

____ BEACHCOMBING FOR BEGINNERS   Norman Hickin 2.00
____ BLACKSTONE'S MODERN CARD TRICKS   Harry Blackstone 7.00
____ BLACKSTONE'S SECRETS OF MAGIC   Harry Blackstone 7.00
____ COIN COLLECTING FOR BEGINNERS   Burton Hobson & Fred Reinfeld 7.00
____ ENTERTAINING WITH ESP   Tony 'Doc' Shiels 2.00
____ 400 FASCINATING MAGIC TRICKS YOU CAN DO   Howard Thurston 7.00
____ HOW I TURN JUNK INTO FUN AND PROFIT   Sari 3.00
____ HOW TO WRITE A HIT SONG AND SELL IT   Tommy Boyce 10.00
____ MAGIC FOR ALL AGES   Walter Gibson 7.00
____ STAMP COLLECTING FOR BEGINNERS   Burton Hobson 3.00

HORSE PLAYER'S WINNING GUIDES

____ BETTING HORSES TO WIN   Les Conklin 7.00
____ ELIMINATE THE LOSERS   Bob McKnight 5.00
____ HOW TO PICK WINNING HORSES   Bob McKnight 5.00
____ HOW TO WIN AT THE RACES   Sam (The Genius) Lewin 5.00
____ HOW YOU CAN BEAT THE RACES   Jack Kavanagh 5.00

_____SEXUALLY FULFILLED MAN Dr. Rachel Copelan 5.00
_____STAYING IN LOVE Dr. Norton F. Kristy 7.00

MELVIN POWERS'S MAIL ORDER LIBRARY
_____HOW TO GET RICH IN MAIL ORDER Melvin Powers 20.00
_____HOW TO SELF-PUBLISH YOUR BOOK Melvin Powers 20.00
_____HOW TO WRITE A GOOD ADVERTISEMENT Victor O. Schwab 20.00
_____MAIL ORDER MADE EASY J. Frank Brumbaugh 20.00
_____MAKING MONEY WITH CLASSIFIED ADS Melvin Powers 20.00

METAPHYSICS & OCCULT
_____CONCENTRATION—A GUIDE TO MENTAL MASTERY Mouni Sadhu 7.00
_____EXTRA-TERRESTRIAL INTELLIGENCE—THE FIRST ENCOUNTER 6.00
_____FORTUNE TELLING WITH CARDS P. Foli 5.00
_____HOW TO INTERPRET DREAMS, OMENS & FORTUNE TELLING SIGNS Gettings 5.00
_____HOW TO UNDERSTAND YOUR DREAMS Geoffrey A. Dudley 7.00
_____MAGICIAN—HIS TRAINING AND WORK W.E. Butler 7.00
_____MEDITATION Mouni Sadhu 10.00
_____MODERN NUMEROLOGY Morris C. Goodman 5.00
_____NUMEROLOGY—ITS FACTS AND SECRETS Ariel Yvon Taylor 5.00
_____NUMEROLOGY MADE EASY W. Mykian 5.00
_____PALMISTRY MADE EASY Fred Gettings 5.00
_____PALMISTRY MADE PRACTICAL Elizabeth Daniels Squire 7.00
_____PROPHECY IN OUR TIME Martin Ebon 2.50
_____SUPERSTITION—ARE YOU SUPERSTITIOUS? Eric Maple 2.00
_____TAROT Mouni Sadhu 10.00
_____TAROT OF THE BOHEMIANS Papus 10.00
_____WAYS TO SELF-REALIZATION Mouni Sadhu 7.00
_____WITCHCRAFT, MAGIC & OCCULTISM—A FASCINATING HISTORY W.B. Crow 10.00
_____WITCHCRAFT—THE SIXTH SENSE Justine Glass 7.00

RECOVERY
_____KNIGHT IN RUSTY ARMOR Robert Fisher 5.00
_____KNIGHT IN RUSTY ARMOR (Hard cover edition) Robert Fisher 10.00
_____KNIGHTS WITHOUT ARMOR (Hard cover edition) Aaron R. Kipnis, Ph.D. 10.00
_____PRINCESS WHO BELIEVED IN FAIRY TALES Marcia Grad 10.00

SELF-HELP & INSPIRATIONAL
_____CHARISMA—HOW TO GET "THAT SPECIAL MAGIC" Marcia Grad 10.00
_____DAILY POWER FOR JOYFUL LIVING Dr. Donald Curtis 7.00
_____DYNAMIC THINKING Melvin Powers 5.00
_____GREATEST POWER IN THE UNIVERSE U.S. Andersen 10.00
_____GROW RICH WHILE YOU SLEEP Ben Sweetland 10.00
_____GROW RICH WITH YOUR MILLION DOLLAR MIND Brian Adams 7.00
_____GROWTH THROUGH REASON Albert Ellis, Ph.D. 10.00
_____GUIDE TO PERSONAL HAPPINESS Albert Ellis, Ph.D. & Irving Becker, Ed.D. .. 10.00
_____HANDWRITING ANALYSIS MADE EASY John Marley 10.00
_____HANDWRITING TELLS Nadya Olyanova 7.00
_____HOW TO ATTRACT GOOD LUCK A.H.Z. Carr 7.00
_____HOW TO DEVELOP A WINNING PERSONALITY Martin Panzer 7.00
_____HOW TO DEVELOP AN EXCEPTIONAL MEMORY Young & Gibson 10.00
_____HOW TO LIVE WITH A NEUROTIC Albert Ellis, Ph.D. 10.00
_____HOW TO OVERCOME YOUR FEARS M.P. Leahy, M.D. 3.00
_____HOW TO SUCCEED Brian Adams 7.00
_____HUMAN PROBLEMS & HOW TO SOLVE THEM Dr. Donald Curtis 5.00
_____I CAN Ben Sweetland 10.00
_____I WILL Ben Sweetland 10.00
_____KNIGHT IN RUSTY ARMOR Robert Fisher 5.00
_____KNIGHT IN RUSTY ARMOR (Hard Cover) Robert Fisher 10.00

____LEFT-HANDED PEOPLE Michael Barsley 5.00
____MAGIC IN YOUR MIND U.S. Andersen 10.00
____MAGIC OF THINKING SUCCESS Dr. David J. Schwartz 8.00
____MAGIC POWER OF YOUR MIND Walter M. Germain 10.00
____MENTAL POWER THROUGH SLEEP SUGGESTION Melvin Powers 3.00
____NEVER UNDERESTIMATE THE SELLING POWER OF A WOMAN Dottie Walters 7.00
____NEW GUIDE TO RATIONAL LIVING Albert Ellis, Ph.D. & R. Harper, Ph.D. 10.00
____PRINCESS WHO BELIEVED IN FAIRY TALES Marcia Grad 10.00
____PSYCHO-CYBERNETICS Maxwell Maltz, M.D. 10.00
____PSYCHOLOGY OF HANDWRITING Nadya Olyanova 7.00
____SALES CYBERNETICS Brian Adams 10.00
____SCIENCE OF MIND IN DAILY LIVING Dr. Donald Curtis 7.00
____SECRET OF SECRETS U.S. Andersen 7.00
____SECRET POWER OF THE PYRAMIDS U.S. Andersen 7.00
____SELF-THERAPY FOR THE STUTTERER Malcolm Frazer 3.00
____SUCCESS CYBERNETICS U.S. Andersen 7.00
____10 DAYS TO A GREAT NEW LIFE William E. Edwards 3.00
____THINK AND GROW RICH Napoleon Hill 10.00
____THINK LIKE A WINNER Walter Doyle Staples, Ph.D. 10.00
____THREE MAGIC WORDS U.S. Andersen 10.00
____TREASURY OF COMFORT Edited by Rabbi Sidney Greenberg 10.00
____TREASURY OF THE ART OF LIVING Sidney S. Greenberg 10.00
____WHAT YOUR HANDWRITING REVEALS Albert E. Hughes 4.00
____WONDER WITHIN   Thomas F. Coyle, M.D. 10.00
____YOUR SUBCONSCIOUS POWER Charles M. Simmons 7.00
____YOUR THOUGHTS CAN CHANGE YOUR LIFE Dr. Donald Curtis 7.00

SPORTS

____BILLIARDS—POCKET • CAROM • THREE CUSHION Clive Cottingham, Jr. 7.00
____COMPLETE GUIDE TO FISHING Vlad Evanoff 2.00
____HOW TO IMPROVE YOUR RACQUETBALL Lubarsky, Kaufman & Scagnetti 5.00
____HOW TO WIN AT POCKET BILLIARDS Edward D. Knuchell 10.00
____JOY OF WALKING Jack Scagnetti 3.00
____LEARNING & TEACHING SOCCER SKILLS Eric Worthington 3.00
____RACQUETBALL FOR WOMEN Toni Hudson, Jack Scagnetti & Vince Rondone 3.00
____SECRET OF BOWLING STRIKES Dawson Taylor 5.00
____SOCCER—THE GAME & HOW TO PLAY IT Gary Rosenthal 7.00
____STARTING SOCCER Edward F Dolan, Jr. 5.00

TENNIS LOVER'S LIBRARY

____HOW TO BEAT BETTER TENNIS PLAYERS Loring Fiske 4.00
____PSYCH YOURSELF TO BETTER TENNIS Dr. Walter A. Luszki 2.00
____TENNIS FOR BEGINNERS Dr. H.A. Murray 2.00
____TENNIS MADE EASY Joel Brecheen 5.00
____WEEKEND TENNIS—HOW TO HAVE FUN & WIN AT THE SAME TIME Bill Talbert ... 3.00

WILSHIRE PET LIBRARY

____DOG TRAINING MADE EASY & FUN John W. Kellogg 5.00
____HOW TO BRING UP YOUR PET DOG Kurt Unkelbach 2.00
____HOW TO RAISE & TRAIN YOUR PUPPY Jeff Griffen 5.00

The books listed above can be obtained from your book dealer or directly from Melvin Powers. When ordering, please remit $2.00 postage for the first book and $1.00 for each additional book.

Melvin Powers
12015 Sherman Road, No. Hollywood, California 91605